Macmillan Professional Masters

Contract Law

Macmillan Professional Masters

Titles in the series

Contract Law

Ewan McKendrick
LLB, BCL
Fellow, St. Anne's College, Oxford

Law series editor: Marise Cremona
Principal Lecturer in Law
at the City of London Polytechnic

MACMILLAN

First published 1990 by
THE MACMILLAN PRESS LTD
Houndmills, Basingstoke, Hampshire RG21 2XS
and London
Companies and representatives
throughout the world

ISBN 0–333–46109–6

A catalogue record for this book is available
from the British Library.

Printed in China

10   9   8   7   6   5
00   99   98   97   96   95   94   93   92

Contents

Preface

My aim in writing this book has been to provide a clear and straightforward account of the basic rules of English contract law. I have also sought to introduce the reader to some of the debates about the nature, the scope and the functions of the law of contract and to discuss some of the wider controversies which surround certain basic doctrines of English contract law, such as consideration and privity. In discussing these issues I have attempted to build a bridge between this introductory work and some of the more advanced and detailed writings on the law of contract by making frequent reference throughout the book to both the periodical literature and the standard textbooks on the law of contract (full citations are contained in the bibliography located at the end of the book). My hope is that these references will encourage the reader to pursue the issues raised in this book in greater detail in the writings to which I have made reference.

I have incurred a number of debts in writing this book. My thanks are due to Marise Cremona, the general editor of the series, who invited me to write this book, and to Jane Wightwick at Macmillan for her help throughout the production process. Vanessa Finch and Norman Palmer spared some time from their own busy schedules to read sections of the manuscript and made a number of helpful comments and suggestions. My secretary, Elizabeth Durant, provided invaluable assistance in the preparation of the tables and the bibliography. Finally, I would like to record my gratitude to my family: Jenny, who is two, made her own distinctive and highly original contributions on the word processor; Sarah, who arrived during the writing of this book, slept soundly when required, and, most of all, I would like to thank my wife, Rose, for her encouragement and support throughout the writing process and for her acceptance of the absences from the family home which the writing of this book necessitated.

This book is dedicated to the memory of my Grandad, who died very shortly after the manuscript was submitted to the publishers.

I have endeavoured to state the law on the basis of the materials available to me as at 15 November 1989.

EWAN MCKENDRICK

Table of Cases

Table of Statutes

1 Introduction

1.1 Introduction

'If the "law of contract" were not already entrenched in the traditions of legal education, would anyone organise a course around it, let alone produce books expounding it?' (Wightman, 1989)

The fact that a lawyer can ask such a question would, no doubt, confound laymen. Yet it is true that the scope, the basis, the function and even the very existence of the law of contract are the subject of debate and controversy among academic lawyers.

But such questioning seems absurd. After all, we enter into contracts as a regular part of life and generally we experience no difficulty in so doing. A simple case is the purchase of a morning newspaper or the purchase of a bus ticket when travelling to work. What doubt can there possibly be about the existence of such contracts or their basis? However, behind the apparent simplicity of these transactions there lurks a fierce controversy. In an introductory work of this nature we cannot give full consideration to these great issues of debate. The function of this chapter is simply to identify some of these issues so that the reader can bear them in mind when reading the ensuing chapters and to enable the reader to explore them further in the readings to which I shall make reference.

1.2 The Scope of the Law of Contract

A good starting-point is the scope of the law of contract. Contracts come in different shapes and sizes. Some involve large, others trivial sums of money. Some are of long duration, while others are of short duration. The content of contracts varies enormously and may include contracts of sale, hire purchase, employment and marriage. Nevertheless we shall not be concerned with all such contracts in this book. Contracts of employment, marriage contracts, hire purchase contracts, consumer credit contracts, contracts for the sale of goods, contracts for the sale of land, mortgages and leasehold agreements all lie largely outside the scope of this book. Such contracts have all been the subject of distinct regulation and are dealt with in books on employment law, family law, consumer law, commercial law, land law and landlord and tenant law respectively. At this stage the reader might be forgiven for asking the question: if this book is not about these contracts, what is it about and what is its value?

The answer to the first part of such a question is that this book is concerned with what are called the 'general principles' of the law of contract and these general principles are usually derived from the common law (or judge-made law). Treatises on the general principles of the law of contract are of respectable antiquity in England and can be traced back to Pollock (1875) and Anson (1879). This tradition has been maintained today in works such as Treitel (1987), Anson (1984) and Cheshire, Fifoot and Furmston (1986). One might have expected that these treatises would have gradually disappeared in the light of the publication of books on the contract of employment, the contract of hire purchase and so on, which subject the rules relating to such contracts to close examination. Yet textbooks on the 'general principles' of the law of contract have survived and might even be said to have flourished.

The existence of such general principles has, however been challenged by Professor Atiyah (1986b) who maintains that these 'general' principles

'remain general only by default, only because they are being super-seded by detailed *ad hoc* rules lacking any principle, or by new principles of narrow scope and application.'

Atiyah argues that 'there is no such thing as a typical contract at all.' He maintains (1986a) that it is 'incorrect today to think of contract law as having one central core with clusters of differences around the edges.' He identifies the classical model of contract as being a discrete, two-party, commercial, executory exchange but notes that contracts can be found which depart from each feature of this classical model. Thus some contracts are not discrete but continuing (landlord and tenant relationships), some are not two-party but multiparty (the contract of membership in a club), some are not commercial but domestic (marriage), some are not executory (unperformed) but executed (fully performed) and finally some do not depend upon exchange, as in the case of an enforceable unilateral gratuitous promise. Atiyah concludes by asserting that 'we must extricate ourselves from the tendency to see contract as a monolithic phenomenon'.

Atiyah uses this argument in support of a wider proposition that contract law is 'increasingly merging with tort law into a general law of obligations'. But one does not need to agree with Atiyah's wider proposition to accept the point that the resemblance between different types of contracts may be very remote indeed. A contract of employment is, in many respects, radically different from a contract to purchase a chocolate bar. The considerations applicable to a contract between commercial parties of equal bargaining power may be very different from those applicable to a contract between a consumer and a multinational supplier (see Chapter 17).

This fragmentation of the legal regulation of contracts has reached a critical stage in the development of English contract law. The crucial question which remains to be answered is: do we have a law of contract or a law of contracts? My own view is that we are moving slowly in the direction of a law of contracts as the 'general principles' decline in importance.

Given this fragmentation, what is the value of a book on the general principles of contract law? The principal value is that, because much of the regulatory legislation concerning contracts has been built upon the foundation of the common law principles, it remains important to have an understanding of the general principles before progressing to study the detailed rules which have been applied to particular contracts. The general principles of formation, privity, content, misrepresentation, mistake, illegality, capacity, duress and discharge apply to all contracts, subject to statutory qualification. These principles therefore remain 'general', but only 'by default'.

1.3 The Basis of the Law of Contract

The basis of the law of contract is also a matter of considerable controversy. Atiyah has written (1986e) that 'modern contract law probably works well enough in the great mass of circumstances but its theory is in a mess'. There are many competing theories which seek to explain the basis of the law of contract.

The classical theory is the will theory. Closely associated with *laissez-faire* philosophy, this theory attributes contractual obligations to the will of the parties. The law of contract is perceived as a set of power-conferring rules which enable individuals to enter into agreements of their own choice on their own terms. Freedom of contract and sanctity of contract are the dominant ideologies. Parties should be as free as possible to make agreements on their own terms without the interference of the courts or Parliament and their agreements should be respected, upheld and enforced by the courts. But today the will theory has been largely discredited. It is not possible to attribute many of the doctrines of contract law to the will of the parties. Doctrines such as those of consideration, illegality, frustration and duress cannot be ascribed to the will of the parties, nor can statutes such as the Unfair Contract Terms Act 1977.

However, the will theory has been revived and subjected to elegant refinement by Professor Fried (1981). Fried maintains that the law of contract is based upon the 'promise-principle', by which 'persons may impose on themselves obligations where none existed before'. The source of the contractual obligation is the promise itself. But, at the same time, Fried concedes that doctrines such as mistake and frustration (Chapter 14) cannot be explained on the basis of his promise-principle. Other non-promissory principles must be invoked, such as the 'consideration of fairness' or 'the encouragement of due care'.

But Fried's theory remains closely linked to *laissez-faire* ideology. He maintains that contract law respects individual autonomy and that the will theory is 'a fair implication of liberal individualism'. He rejects the proposition that the law of contract is an appropriate vehicle for engaging in the redistribution of wealth. But his theory is open to attack on two principal grounds.

The first is that it is difficult to explain many modern contractual doctrines in terms of liberal individualism or *laissez-faire* philosophy. The growth of standard form contracts and the aggregation of capital within fewer hands has enabled powerful contracting parties to impose contractual terms upon consumers and other weaker parties. The response of the courts and Parliament has been to place greater limits upon the exercise of contractual power. Legislation has been introduced to regulate employment contracts and consumer credit contracts in an effort to provide a measure of protection for employees and consumers. Such legislation cannot be explained in terms of *laissez-faire* ideology, nor can the expansion of the doctrines of duress and undue influence, or the extensive regulation of exclusion clauses which has been introduced by Parliament (see Chapter 11). Conceptions of fairness seem to underpin many of the rules of contract law (see Chapter 17). Such departures from the principles of liberal individualism have led some commentators to argue that altruism should be recognised as the basis of contract law (Kennedy, 1976), while others have argued that the law of contract should have as an aim the redistribution of wealth (Kronman, 1980). We shall return to this issue in Chapter 17.

A second attack on the promise-principle has been launched on the ground that, in many cases, the courts do not uphold the promise-principle because they do not actually order the promisor to carry out his promise. The promisee must generally content himself with an action for damages. But, as we shall see (in Chapter 20), the expectations engendered by a promise are not fully protected in a damages action. One of the principal reasons for this is the existence of the doctrine of mitigation (see 20.10). Suppose I enter into a contract to sell you 10 apples for £2. I then refuse to perform my side of the bargain. I am in breach of contract. But you must mitigate your loss. So you buy 10 apples for £2 at a nearby market. If you sue me for damages, what is your loss? You have not suffered any and you cannot enforce my promise. So how can it be said that my promise is binding if you cannot enforce it? Your expectation of profit may be protected but, where that profit can be obtained elsewhere at no loss to you, then you have no contractual claim against me. Your expectations have been fulfilled, albeit from another source.

Although you cannot enforce my promise, it is very important to note that in our example you suffered no loss and I gained no benefit. Let us vary the example slightly. Suppose that you had paid me in advance. The additional ingredients here are that you have acted to your detriment in reliance upon my promise and I have gained a benefit. Greater justification now appears for judicial intervention on your behalf. Can it therefore be argued that the source of my obligation to you is not my promise, but your detrimental reliance upon my promise or your conferment of a benefit upon me in reliance upon my promise. Atiyah has written (1986b) that 'wherever benefits are obtained, wherever acts of reasonable reliance take place, obligations may arise, both morally and in law'. This argument is one of enormous significance. It is used by Atiyah (1979) in an effort to establish a law of obligations based upon the 'three basic pillars of the law of obligations, the idea of recompense for benefit, of protection of reasonable reliance, and of the voluntary creation and extinction of rights and liabilities'. The adoption of such an approach would lead to the creation of a law of obligations and, in consequence, contract law would cease to have a distinct identity based upon the promise-principle or the will theory (see further 1.4). This is why this school of thought has been called 'the death of contract' school (see Gilmore, 1974). We shall return to these arguments at various points in this book, especially in Chapters 20 and 21.

My own view is that Fried correctly identifies a strong current of individualism which runs through the law of contract. A promise does engender an expectation in the promisee and, unless a good reason to the contrary appears, the courts will call upon a defaulting promisor to fulfil the expectation so created. But the critics of Fried are also correct in their argument that the commitment to individual autonomy is tempered in its application by considerations of fairness, consumerism and altruism. These conflicting ideologies run through the entire law of contract (for a fuller examination of these ideologies under the titles of 'Market-Individualism' and 'Consumer-Welfarism' see Adams and Brownsword, 1987). The law of contract is not based upon one ideology; both ideologies are present in the case-law and the legislation. Indeed the tension between the two is a feature of the law of contract. Sometimes 'market-individualism' prevails over 'consumer-welfarism', at other times 'consumer welfarism' triumphs over 'market individualism'. At various points in this book we shall have occasion to note these conflicting ideologies and the tensions which they produce within the law.

1.4 Contract, Tort and Restitution

A further difficulty lies in locating the law of contract within the spectrum of the law of civil obligations. Burrows (1983) has helpfully pointed out that the law of obligations largely rests upon three cardinal principles. The first principle is that expectations engendered by a binding promise should be fulfilled. Upon this principle is founded the law of contract. The second principle is that compensation must be granted for the wrongful infliction of harm. This principle is reflected in the law of tort. A tort is a civil wrong, such as negligence or defamation. Let us take an example to illustrate the operation of the law of tort. You drive your car negligently and knock me down. You have committed the tort of negligence. Harm has wrongfully been inflicted upon me and you must compensate me. The aim of the award of compensation is not to fulfil my expectations. It is to restore me to the position which I was in before the accident occurred; to restore the *status quo* or to protect my 'reliance interest'.

The third principle is that unjust enrichments must be reversed. This principle is implemented by the law of restitution. There are three stages to a restitutionary claim. First, the defendant must be enriched by the receipt of a benefit; secondly, that enrichment must be at the expense of the plaintiff; and, finally, it must be unjust for the defendant to retain the benefit without recompensing the plaintiff. The latter stage does not depend upon the unfettered discretion of the judge; there are principles to guide a court in deciding whether, in a particular case, it is unjust that the defendant retain the benefit without recompensing the plaintiff (see Goff and Jones, 1986; Birks, 1985). The classic restitutionary claim arises where I pay you money under a mistake of fact. I have no contractual claim against you because there is no contract between us. Nor have you committed a tort. But I do have a restitutionary claim against you. You are enriched by the receipt of the money, that enrichment is at my expense, and the ground on which I assert that it is unjust that you retain the money is that the money was paid under a mistake of fact.

Contract, tort and restitution therefore divide up most of the law based upon these three principles and they provide a satisfactory division for the exposition of the law of obligations. This analysis separates contract from tort and restitution on the ground that contractual obligations are voluntarily assumed, whereas obligations created by the law of tort and the law of restitution are *imposed* upon the parties by the operation of rules of law. Occasionally, however, these three principles overlap, especially in the context of remedies (Chapter 20). Overlaps will also be discussed in the context of misrepresentation (Chapter 13) and privity (Chapter 7).

Finally, it must be noted that these divisions are not accepted by Professor Atiyah. His recognition of reliance-based and benefit-based liabilities cuts right across the three divisions. The writings of Atiyah deserve careful consideration, but they do not, as yet, represent the current state of English law. Although we shall make frequent reference to the writing of Atiyah, we shall not adopt his analysis of the law of obligations. Instead it will be argued that the foundation of the law of contract lies in the mutual promises of the parties and, being founded upon such voluntary agreement, the law of contract can, in the vast majority of cases, be separated from the law of tort and the law of restitution.

1.5 Contract and Empirical Work

Very little empirical work has been done on the relationship between the rules that make up the law of contract and the practices of the community which the rules seek to serve. The limited work that has been done (see Beale and Dugdale, 1975; Lewis, 1982) suggests that the law of contract may be relied upon in at least two ways. The first is at the planning stage.

The rules which we shall discuss in this book may be very important when drawing up the contract and in planning for the future. For example, care must be taken when drafting an exclusion clause to ensure, as far as possible, that it is not invalidated by the courts (see Chapter 11). Secondly, the law of contract may be used by the parties when their relationship has broken down. Here the rules of contract law have a less significant role to play than at the planning stage. The rules of contract law are often but one factor to be taken into account in the resolution of contractual disputes. Parties may value their good relationship and refuse to spoil it by resort to the law. Litigation is also time-consuming and extremely expensive and so the parties will frequently resort to cheaper and more informal methods of dispute resolution. In the remainder of this book we shall discuss the rules that make up the law of contract, but it must not be forgotten that, in the 'real world', the rules may be no more than chips to be used in the bargaining process on the breakdown of a contractual relationship.

Part 1

The Formation and Scope of a Contract

2 Agreement: Clearing the Ground

To say that contract is based upon the agreement of the parties may be a trite statement but it is also a statement which begs a number of questions. Two of these questions will be dealt with in this chapter. The first is: who decides whether or not the parties have indeed reached agreement? Is it the parties or is it the courts? The second question is: how is it decided that the parties have actually reached agreement?

2.1 Who Decides that an Agreement Has Been Reached?

In considering the standard which is adopted in deciding whether or not a contract has been concluded a useful starting-point, which is quoted in most of the reference works on the law of contract, is the judgment of Blackburn J in *Smith* v. *Hughes* (1871) LR 6 QB 597. He said:

'If, whatever a man's real intention may be, he so conducts himself that a reasonable man would believe that he was assenting to the terms proposed by the other party, and that other party upon that belief enters into the contract with him, the man thus conducting himself would be equally bound as if he had intended to agree to the other party's terms.'

This establishes the important point that the test for the existence of an agreement is objective rather than subjective. A subjective test attempts to ascertain the actual intention of the contracting parties, whereas an objective test examines what the parties said and did and not what they actually intended to say or do (see further 2.3). The commercial justification for the adoption of an objective test is that great uncertainty would be caused if a person who appeared to have agreed to certain terms could escape liability by claiming that he had no 'real' intention to agree to them.

Some confusion has however, been caused by the judgment of Lord Diplock in *The Hannah Blumenthal* [1983] 1 AC 834. Lord Diplock stated that

to create a contract by exchange of promises between two parties where the promise of each party constitutes the consideration for the promise of the other, what is necessary is that the intention of each *as it has been communicated to and understood by the other* (even though that which has been communicated does not represent the actual state of mind of the communicator) should coincide.

In *The Leonidas D* [1985] 1 WLR 925, Robert Goff LJ interpreted Lord Diplock as saying that the 'actual intentions of both parties should in fact coincide', which he took to be a reference to a subjective test. It is, however, highly unlikely that Lord Diplock intended to overturn established principles of contract law in such a way (see Atiyah, 1986f) and, in so far as he intended to state that the test was a subjective one, it is likely that, as was the case with Robert Goff LJ in *The Leonidas D*, his dicta will not be followed.

A good example of the application of the objective test is *Centrovincial Estates plc* v. *Merchant Investors Assurance Company Ltd* [1983] Com LR 158. The plaintiffs let premises to the defendants at a yearly rent of £68 320, subject to review from 25 December 1982. The parties were obliged by their contract to endeavour to reach agreement before 25 December 1982 on the then current market rental value of the property and to certify the amount of the current market rental value. The plaintiffs wrote to the defendants inviting them to agree that the current market rental value should be £65 000. The defendants accepted. When the plaintiffs received the defendants' written acceptance they contacted the defendants to inform them that they had meant to propose £126 000 and not £65 000. The defendants refused to agree to this new figure and insisted that a contract had been concluded at a rental value of £65 000. So the plaintiffs sought a declaration that no legally binding agreement had been entered into between the parties. The Court of Appeal refused to grant such a declaration, holding that the parties had entered into a contract at a rental value of £65 000. Slade LJ said that:

'it is contrary to the well-established principles of contract law to suggest that the offeror under a bilateral contract can withdraw an unambiguous offer, after it has been accepted in the manner contemplated by the offer, merely because he has made a mistake which the offeree neither knew nor could reasonably have known when he accepted it.'

An alternative argument which was relied upon by the plaintiffs in *Centrovincial* was that the objective test of intention was founded upon the principle of estoppel. Estoppel is based upon the proposition that a representor will be prevented from going back on his representation when the representation was intended to be acted upon and is acted upon to his detriment by the representee. The plaintiffs argued that the defendants had not relied upon the plaintiffs' offer to their detriment because the proposed rent of £65 000 was lower than the original rent of £68 320. This argument was rejected by the court on the ground that 'the mutual promises alone will suffice to conclude the contract'.

Professor Atiyah (1986f) has attacked the decision in *Centrovincial* on the ground that he can see no reason why an offeree should be entitled 'to create legal rights for himself by the bare act of acceptance when he has in no way relied upon the offer before being informed it was made as a result of a mistake and did not in reality reflect the intention of the offeror'. He has further argued that the decision of the House of Lords in *The Hannah Blumenthal* (above) lends support to his argument that *Centrovincial* was wrongly decided.

The Hannah Blumenthal concerned an agreement between two parties to settle a dispute by reference to arbitration. There was then a delay of some six years, during which time nothing happened in relation to the arbitration. When the buyers attempted to fix a date for the arbitration the sellers sought an order that the buyers were not entitled to proceed with the arbitration because of the delay which had occurred. One of the grounds relied upon by the sellers was that the parties had, by their silence and inactivity, agreed to abandon the reference to arbitration, the offer being made by the buyers and the acceptance by the sellers. Lord Brandon held that there were two ways in which the parties could agree to abandon a contract to arbitrate. The first was where they actually agreed to do so. The second was where one party created a situation in which he was estopped from asserting that he had not abandoned the contract. In the latter context it was held that the sellers must have 'significantly altered [their] position in reliance' upon their belief that the contract had been abandoned. Lord Diplock also placed emphasis upon the need for detrimental reliance, saying that this was 'an example of a general principle of English law that injurious reliance on what another person did may be a source of legal rights against him'. However it must be remembered that *Hannah Blumenthal* is a rather unusual case in that it was alleged that the parties had entered into a contract to abandon an arbitration by mere inactivity on both sides. In the absence of express communication between the buyers and the sellers, the only way of showing that the sellers had accepted the buyers' offer to abandon the arbitration was to show that they had acted in reliance on the fact that the contract had been abandoned. The function of reliance was therefore to provide *evidence* of the fact that the sellers had accepted the buyers' offer to abandon the agreement to arbitrate; it is not the case that the House of Lords was laying down a rule that such reliance was a prerequisite to the formation of any contract. Thus interpreted, *Hannah Blumenthal* does not cast doubt upon the correctness of *Centrovincial* because in *Centrovincial* the defendants' acceptance was evidenced by the fact that they wrote and accepted the plaintiffs' offer. In such a case, the acceptance concludes the contract without the need for any further act in reliance upon the offer.

2.2 A Residual Role for a Subjective Approach

It should not be assumed, however, that the subjective intentions of the parties are irrelevant to the law of contract. In many cases the subjective intentions of the parties will coincide with the interpretation put upon their intentions by the objective test and to that extent their subjective intentions are protected. Further, as was made clear by Slade LJ in *Centrovincial*, there are two situations in which the objective test is displaced by a subjective test.

The first arises where the offeree knows that the offeror is suffering from a mistake as to the terms of the offer; then the usual objective test is replaced by a subjective test. The operation of this rule can be seen in the case of *Hartog* v. *Colin and Shields* [1939] 3 All ER 566. The defendants entered into a contract to sell 3000 Argentinian hare skins to the plaintiffs. However by mistake they offered them for sale at 10 $\frac{1}{4}$d per pound instead of 10 $\frac{1}{4}$d per piece. When they discovered their mistake, the defendants refused to deliver the skins. The plaintiffs brought an action in respect of the defendants' non-delivery of the skins. It was held that they were not entitled to succeed because the negotiations had proceeded upon the basis that the skins were to be sold at a price per piece and that, as there were three pieces to the pound, the plaintiffs could not reasonably have thought that the defendants' offer matched their true intention. The plaintiffs were thereby prevented from snatching a bargain which they knew was not intended by the defendants.

The second situation in which the subjective intentions of the parties are relevant is where the offeree is at fault in failing to note that the offeror has made a mistake. Such was the case in *Scriven Bros* v. *Hindley* [1913] 3 KB 564. An auctioneer acting for the plaintiffs put up for sale lots of hemp and tow. The auction catalogue was misleading because it implied that the lots were the same when, in fact, the second lot only contained tow. Tow was considerably cheaper than hemp. The defendants bid for the lot thinking that it was hemp when in fact it was tow. The auctioneer did not realise that the defendants had misunderstood what was being auctioned; he merely thought that they had overvalued the tow. When the defendants discovered their mistake they refused to pay the price and so the plaintiffs sued them for it. It was held that no contract for the sale of the tow had been concluded when the tow was knocked down to the defendants because the auctioneer intended to sell tow and the defendants intended to purchase hemp and the defendants' mistake had been induced by the carelessness of the plaintiffs in preparing the auction catalogue. The importance of the misleading nature of the auction catalogue can be seen in the fact that, had it not been misleading, a contract would have been concluded on the plaintiffs' terms because, in the usual case, an auctioneer is entitled to assume that a bidder knows what he is bidding for. Thus in the ordinary case a contract would have been concluded for the sale of tow.

A further situation in which it has been argued (see Spencer, 1974) that the subjective intentions of the parties are relevant arises where the parties are subjectively agreed but that subjective agreement is at variance with the result achieved by applying the objective test. Spencer gives the admittedly rather far-fetched example of two immigrants who have little command of the English language and who enter into a contract under which one is to sell to the other a 'bull'. Both parties intend to use the word 'bull' but they both think that the word 'bull' means cow. The application of the objective test, Spencer argues, leads to the conclusion that a contract has been concluded for the sale of a bull. But, as Spencer points out, this is absurd as the seller does not have a bull to sell and the buyer does not want one. He argues that, while 'it may be acceptable for the law occasionally to force upon *one* of the parties an agreement he did not want . . . surely there is something wrong with a theory which forces upon *both* of the parties an agreement which neither of them wants'. Thus Spencer concludes that the subjective intentions of the parties must prevail. But if both parties in fact wished to contract to sell a cow and a cow was delivered and accepted then the law of contract would not force upon the parties an agreement which neither of them wanted because, in such a case, the objective approach would lead to the conclusion that a contract had been made for the sale of a cow. The actions of the parties, in delivering and accepting delivery of the cow, would displace the inference which had been raised by the words which they had used. There is thus no question of forcing upon the parties an agreement which neither of them wants and no need to invoke any reference to the subjective understandings of the parties.

It is important to understand that the subjective understandings of the parties will not generally prevail over their intention, objectively ascertained. As Lord Normand stated in *Mathieson Gee (Ayrshire) Ltd* v. *Quigley* 1952 SC (HL) 38, 'when the parties to a litigation put forward what they say is a concluded contract and ask the Court to construe it, it is competent for the Court to find that there was in fact no contract and nothing to be construed'. The existence or non-existence of a contract is ultimately a question for the court which will be decided by the application of the objective test and it is only in exceptional situations that resort will be had to a subjective test. We have noted only two such exceptional situations and it may be argued, as a basis for the development of the law, that they illustrate a wider proposition that the objective test must be applied by the court unless there is something unconscionable in the conduct of the party seeking to uphold the application of the objective approach, in which case the court may have regard to the subjective intentions of the parties.

2.3 The Objective Test

So the general rule is that the intention of the parties is to be assessed objectively. Thus far it has been assumed that there is only one objective test which can be applied by the courts but Howarth (1984) has argued that there are, in fact, three different interpretations of the objective test which can be applied by the courts. The first is the standard of detached objectivity. This approach takes as its standpoint the perspective of the detached observer or the 'fly on the wall'. In other words, it asks what interpretation would a person watching the behaviour of the contracting parties place upon their words and actions. The second possible interpretation suggested by Howarth is to interpret the words as they were reasonably understood by the promisee (called 'promisee objectivity' by Howarth). This is the standard which finds the greatest support in the case law (see *Smith* v. *Hughes* (above)). The third and final interpretation is the standard of the reasonable person in the shoes of the person making the offer (called 'promisor objectivity' by Howarth). The approach which is preferred by Howarth is 'detached objectivity', but there is little judicial support for such a test (Vorster, 1987).

However the distinction which Howarth draws between 'promisor' and 'promisee' objectivity has been criticised on the ground that it is misleading because, in a bilateral contract, each party is both a promisor and a promisee (Vorster, 1987, especially pp. 276–8). Thus, for example, in *Scriven Bros* v. *Hindley* (above) the defendant purchaser was a promisor in relation to his promise to pay for the lot and a promisee concerning the auctioneer's promise to sell him the tow. On the other hand, the auctioneer was a promisor in relation to the promise to sell the lot and a promisee concerning the defendant's promise to purchase the lot. It is true that the nomenclature which Howarth employs is rather misleading but it should not blind us to his essential point, which is that there are two parties to a contract and that a court could elect to apply the perspective of one or other contracting party. One could meet the criticism by restyling the classification as 'plaintiff' and 'defendant' objectivity to underline the point that one is simply looking at the contract from the position of one or other contracting party.

Although it is true that, in our terminology, 'defendant' objectivity has the greatest support in the case law, this may be a product of the way in which the cases have come before the courts rather than distinct judicial preference. The case of *Scriven Bros* v. *Hindley* (above) provides a good example of this point. In that case the court considered whether the plaintiffs were entitled to recover the price of the lot which they alleged that the defendants had contracted to buy. The emphasis of the court was upon the defendants' understanding of the offer made by the auctioneer. This was because the defence to the claim was based on the defendants' understanding of the offer and therefore the court was forced to examine that understanding. It is crucial to note that the defendants simply denied liability; they did not take the further step of asking the court to enforce their version of the 'contract'. This had the consequence that the court did not consider whether the defendants would have been able to sue the plaintiffs for breach of a contract to sell hemp. Had the defendants counterclaimed for breach of their version of the 'contract', the roles would have been reversed and the court would have been compelled to consider the plaintiffs' understanding of the bid made by the defendants. The infrequency of such counterclaims by defendants means that 'defendant' objectivity is most commonly considered by the courts, but it does not follow that the courts are averse to applying 'plaintiff' objectivity; it is simply the case that they are not often asked by defendants to apply such a standard.

2.4 Has Agreement Been Reached?

An instructive example of the approach which the courts adopt in deciding whether or not the parties have reached agreement is provided by the case of *Butler* v. *Ex-Cell-O Corporation (England) Ltd* [1979] 1 WLR 401. The sellers, Butler, offered to sell a machine tool to the buyers, the offer being made on Butler's standard terms of business, which included, *inter alia*, a price variation clause. The buyers sent an order for the machine tool which, in turn, was on their own standard terms of business, which made no provision for a price variation clause and stated that the price of the machine tool was to be fixed. The buyers' order form contained a tear-off acknowledgement slip, which stated that 'we [the sellers] accept your order on the terms and conditions stated thereon'. The sellers signed and returned this slip to the buyers, together with a letter stating that they were carrying out the order on the terms of their original offer. After constructing the machine tool, but before delivering it, the sellers sought to invoke the price variation clause contained in their original offer and claimed the additional sum of £2892. The buyers refused to pay this increase in price, claiming that they were not contractually bound to do so. The sellers accordingly sued the buyers for £2892 in damages. The Court of Appeal held that they were not entitled to recover the sum claimed because a contract had been concluded on the buyers' terms which did not include the price variation clause. Although the Court of Appeal was unanimous in holding that a contract had been concluded on the buyers' terms, the court was divided in its reasoning.

The reasoning of the majority, Lawton and Bridge LJJ, proceeded by applying the traditional 'mirror image' rule of contractual formation. According to this rule, the court must be able to find in the documents which passed between the parties a clear and unequivocal offer which is matched or 'mirrored' by an equally clear and unequivocal acceptance. A purported acceptance which does not accept all the terms of the original offer is not in fact a true acceptance at all but is a counter-offer which 'kills off' the original offer and amounts to a new offer which can in turn be accepted by the other party. Applying this, they held that the buyers' order could not be construed as an acceptance of the sellers' offer because it did not mirror exactly the terms of the sellers' offer and therefore amounted to a counter-offer. They held that this counter-offer was accepted by the sellers when they signed the tear-off acknowledgement on the buyers' order form. The letter accompanying the acknowledgement slip was held not to be an attempt to reintroduce the terms of the sellers' original offer and so was not a counter-offer, but was simply a means of identifying the order for the machine tool.

This traditional approach has a number of advantages. The first is that it provides some degree of certainty because legal advisers at least know the principles which the courts will apply in deciding whether or not a contract has been concluded. There is no separation between the formation of the contract and the ascertainment of the terms of the contract because the offer and acceptance must mirror each other exactly before a contract is concluded. Thus it gives the parties a clear standard against which to measure their conduct and sends out a message that a failure to reach agreement on all points may lead a court to hold that a contract has not been concluded. The second advantage of this approach is that it provides a standard which can be applied to every type of contract.

However the traditional approach has also been subjected to considerable criticism. One such criticism is that it is excessively rigid. It produces an 'all or nothing' result, in the sense that it is either the terms of the buyer or the terms of the seller which govern the relationship of the parties; the court cannot pick and choose between the respective sets of terms and conditions or seek to find an acceptable compromise. This is unfortunate in cases involving the 'battle of the forms' (as cases such as *Butler* are commonly called) where both parties may reasonably believe that their terms are the ones which govern their relationship and where a compromise may produce the fairest result on the facts of the case. The traditional approach has also been criticised in its application to battle of the forms cases on the ground that it encourages businessmen to continue to exchange their standard terms of business in the hope of getting the 'last shot' in and it places the party in receipt of the last communication in a very difficult position. If he refuses to accept the goods, it is likely that it will be held that no contract has come into existence, but if he accepts the goods it is likely that he will be held to have accepted them on the sellers' terms.

The strains on the traditional approach have led some judges to reject it in favour of a new approach. In *Butler* Lord Denning, who was in the minority, rejected the traditional mirror image approach to contractual formation, holding it to be 'out-of date' (see too his judgment in the case of *Gibson* v. *Manchester City Council* [1978] 1 WLR 520, 523, when he said that 'to my mind it is a mistake to think that all contracts can be analysed into the form of offer and acceptance'). He held that the

> 'better way is to look at all the documents passing between the parties and glean from them, or from the conduct of the parties, whether they have reached agreement on all material points, even though there may be differences between the forms and conditions printed on the back of them'.

He also held that, even where the terms used by the parties were mutually contradictory, it was possible for a court to 'scrap' the terms and replace them by a 'reasonable implication'. Applying this reasoning, he held that the signing of the tear-off acknowledgement by the sellers was the 'decisive document', which made it clear that the contract was concluded on the buyers' terms.

This approach clearly conflicts with the mirror image approach to contractual formation because it adopts a two-stage approach. At the first stage it must be decided whether a contract has been concluded and at the second stage it must be decided what are the terms of the contract. At the latter stage the court has considerable discretion in filling the gaps. The approach adopted by Lord Denning seeks to construct a more flexible framework for the law of contract which can accommodate inconsistent terms and an apparent lack of consensus within the law of contract.

This approach has in turn been criticised on the ground that it produces uncertainty because it gives too little guidance to the courts, or to legal advisers, in determining whether or not an agreement has been reached. Certainty is a particularly important commodity in the law of contract because businessmen will often want to know the standard which the law applies so that they can plan their affairs accordingly.

Despite the attempt by Lord Denning to introduce this new general approach to the issue of agreement, English law remains wedded to the traditional approach. This was confirmed by Lord Diplock in *Gibson* v. *Manchester City Council* [1979] 1 WLR 294, 297, when he said that, although there may be certain 'exceptional' cases which do not 'fit easily into the normal analysis of a contract as being constituted by offer and acceptance', these cases were very much the exception and they have not displaced the traditional rule. It would be a mistake, however, to think that the traditional rule is always rigidly applied by the judiciary. In *The Eurymedon* [1975] AC 154, 167 Lord Wilberforce stated that 'English law, having committed itself to a rather technical and schematic doctrine of contract, in application takes a practical approach, often at the cost of forcing the facts to fit uneasily into the marked slots of offer, acceptance and consideration.' We shall see, when discussing issues such as the application of the rules of offer and acceptance to transactions in the supermarket (see 3.2), that the courts do have some discretion in identifying the offer and the acceptance and so have some flexibility in applying the rules in a particular factual context.

In the next chapter we shall give consideration to the schematic approach to agreement by examining in greater detail the constituent elements of offer and acceptance. Then, in Chapter 4, we shall give further consideration to the application of the objective test.

Summary

1 The test for the existence of an agreement is objective rather than subjective. The justification for this is the need to promote certainty.

2 The objective test is, however, displaced by a subjective test where the offeree knows that the offeror is suffering from a mistake as to the terms of his offer or where the offeree is at fault in failing to note that the offeror has made a mistake.

3 There are three potential forms of the objective test: detached objectivity, plaintiff (or promisor) objectivity and defendant (or promisee) objectivity. The latter form has the greatest support in the case law but this may be a product of the way in which the cases have come before the courts rather than distinct judicial preference.

4 The courts apply the 'mirror image' rule in deciding whether or not a contract has been concluded. The acceptance must mirror the offer exactly. The general approach to contract formation advocated by Lord Denning has been rejected.

Exercises

1 Do you think that *Centrovincial Estates plc* v *Merchant Investors Assurance Company Ltd* was correctly decided?

2 Andrew, an old man aged 80, agreed to sell his house to David for £6800. Andrew in fact meant to sell it for £68 000. David is now seeking to enforce the agreement. Advise Andrew.

3 Compare and contrast the reasoning of the majority and the minority in *Butler v. Ex-Cell-O Corporation*. Which approach do you prefer and why?

3 Offer and Acceptance

We noted in Chapter 2 that the courts adopt the 'mirror image' rule of contractual formation; that is to say, they must find a clear and unequivocal offer which is matched by an equally clear and unequivocal acceptance. In this chapter we shall give more detailed consideration to the constituent elements of an offer and an acceptance. However, three points should be noted at the outset of our discussion.

The first point is that most of the cases which we shall discuss in this chapter are cases which came to court because one party was alleging that the other had broken the contract between them. This can be seen in *Butler* v. *Ex-Cell-O Corporation* [1979] 1 WLR 401 (see 2.4), where the discussion of the rules of offer and acceptance was crucial because the court had to find the existence of a contract and ascertain its terms before it could decide whether or not the buyers were in breach of contract. Thus the context of most of these cases is an allegation of *breach* of contract.

The second point which should be borne in mind relates to the way in which the courts use the requirements of offer and acceptance in deciding cases. Professor Atiyah has argued (1989) that the courts could either 'reason forwards' or they could 'reason backwards'. By 'reasoning forwards' Professor Atiyah means that the courts reason from the legal concepts of offer and acceptance towards the solution to the dispute. This is the traditional approach which has been adopted by the courts; they 'find' the existence of an offer and an acceptance and only then do they reason towards their conclusion. On the other hand, the courts could 'reason backwards'; that is to say, they could reason from the appropriate solution back to the legal concepts of offer and acceptance. On such a model the court can decide which solution it wishes to adopt and then fit the negotiations within the offer and acceptance framework to *justify* the decision which they have already reached. The distinction which Professor Atiyah is seeking to draw is a difficult one to grasp in the abstract but it is one to which we shall return when discussing some of the cases.

The third point is that, on a number of occasions, we shall note that great difficulty is experienced in accommodating many everyday transactions within the offer and acceptance framework. This point will lead us to conclude by discussing the utility of the offer and acceptance model. With these preliminary points in mind let us examine the detailed rules of law relating to offer and acceptance.

3.1 Offer and Invitation to Treat

An offer is a statement by one party of a willingness to enter into a contract on stated terms, provided that these terms are, in turn, accepted by the party or parties to whom the offer is addressed. There is generally no requirement that the offer be made in any particular form; it may be made orally, in writing or by conduct.

Care must be taken, however, in distinguishing between an offer and an invitation to treat. An invitation to treat is simply an expression of willingness to enter into negotiations which, it is hoped, will lead to the conclusion of a contract at a later date. The distinction between the two is said to be primarily one of intention; that is, did the maker of the statement intend to be bound by an acceptance of his terms without further negotiation or did he only intend his statement to be part of the continuing negotiating process? Although the dichotomy is easy to state at the level of theory, it is not so easy to apply at the level of practice, as can be seen from the case of *Gibson* v. *Manchester City Council* [1978] 1 WLR 520 (CA) and [1979] 1 WLR 294 (HL).

In 1970 the defendant council prepared a brochure explaining how a council tenant could purchase his council house and sent a copy to those tenants who had previously expressed an interest in purchasing their council house. Mr Gibson completed the form contained in the brochure and sent it to the council, together with a request that he be told the purchase price of the house. The treasurer of the council wrote to inform him that the 'council may be prepared to sell the house' to him at a stated price and that if he wished to make a 'formal application' to purchase the house he should complete a further form. Mr Gibson completed the form, but he left the purchase price blank because he wished to know whether the defendants would repair the path to his house or whether he could deduct the cost from the purchase price. The council stated that the price had been fixed according to the condition of the property and so allowance had been made in the price for the condition of the path. Mr Gibson accepted this and asked the council to continue with his application. The council took the house off the list of houses for which they were responsible for maintenance and Mr Gibson carried out maintenance to the house. At this point the Labour Party gained control of the council after the local elections and promptly discontinued the policy of selling off council houses, unless a legally binding contract had already been concluded. The council refused to sell the house to Mr Gibson because they claimed that no contract had been concluded for the sale of the house.

The trial judge and the Court of Appeal held that a contract had been concluded between the parties. Lord Denning, in a broad and sweeping judgment, held that a contract had been concluded because there was agreement between the parties on all material points, even though the precise formalities had not been gone through. The House of Lords took a different view and held that no contract had been concluded. It was held that the letter written by the treasurer, which stated that the council *may* be prepared to sell, was not an offer as it did not finally commit the council to selling the house. It was simply an expression of their willingness to enter into negotiations for the sale of the house and was not an offer which was capable of being accepted. This was further evidenced by the fact that Mr Gibson was invited to make a 'formal application' to purchase the house and not to signify his agreement to the stated terms.

The difficulty in a case such as *Gibson* arises from the fact that it is not easy to ascertain when the preliminary negotiations end and a definite offer is made. The court must examine carefully the correspondence which has passed between the parties and seek to identify from the language used and from the actions of the parties whether, in the opinion of the court, either party intended to make an offer which was capable of acceptance. *Gibson* shows that judges can and do differ in the results which they reach in this interpretative exercise and that each decision must ultimately rest on its own facts (contrast the decision of the Court of Appeal in *Storer* v. *Manchester City Council* [1974] 1 WLR 1403, where the court held that a contract had been concluded where the negotiations had advanced beyond the stage reached in *Gibson* but had not resulted in an exchange of contracts.

In a case such as *Gibson* the court is clearly engaged in trying to ascertain the intention of the parties from the documents which have passed between them (although it should be noted that, even in *Gibson*, the case was seen as a test case for 350 other similarly placed prospective purchasers and these purchasers would be presumed to have the same intention as Mr Gibson). There is, however, another group of cases, which concern certain stereotyped transactions, such as advertisements and shop-window displays, where the courts are less concerned with the intention of the parties and are more concerned to establish clear rules of law to govern the particular transaction. Professor Treitel has stated (1987) that 'it may be that these rules can in some cases be displaced by evidence of contrary intention, but if there is no evidence of intention [these rules of law] will determine the distinction between offer and invitation to treat'. These situations are discussed in sections 3.2–3.6.

3.2 Display of Goods for Sale

As a matter of principle, there are at least three different approaches which could be adopted to the display of goods for sale in a shop or supermarket. The first is to hold that the display of goods is an offer which is accepted when the goods are picked up by the prospective purchaser and put into his shopping basket. However, such a conclusion would have the undesirable consequence that a purchaser would be bound as soon as he picked up the goods; he could not change his mind and return them to the shelves without being in breach of contract. The second approach is to hold that the display of goods is an offer which is accepted when the purchaser takes the goods to the cash desk. This solution avoids the weakness of the first conclusion, but it has been argued that it too is undesirable. Three criticisms have been levelled against this solution. The first is that it has been argued that a shop is a place for bargaining and not for compulsory sales and that to hold that the display of goods is an offer will take away the shopkeeper's freedom to bargain (Winfield, 1939). This argument can be countered by pointing out that, apart from second-hand shops, bargaining is not a reality in the shops of today. Goods are displayed on a 'take it or leave it' basis. If the customer is not prepared to comply with the stated terms he can go elsewhere. Secondly it has been argued that this conclusion is undesirable because it takes away the freedom of the shopkeeper to decide whether or not to deal with a particular customer. It would compel the shopkeeper to trade with his worst enemy. However it is submitted that, in an era when shopping in vast superstores has become commonplace, such an argument can no longer be regarded as conclusive. Thirdly it has been argued that to treat a display of goods as an offer might result in the vendor being bound to a series of contracts which he would be unable to fulfil (see *Partridge* v. *Crittenden* [1968] 1 WLR 1204, discussed at 3.3). This objection can be countered by holding that the shopkeeper's offer is subject to the limitation that it is only capable of acceptance 'while stocks last'.

The third possible conclusion is that the display of goods constitutes an invitation to treat and that the offer is made by the customer when he presents the goods at the cash desk, where the offer may be accepted by the shopkeeper. This conclusion preserves the freedom of the shopkeeper to decide whether or not to deal with a particular customer but it can fail to protect the interests of the customer. For example, a customer who takes the goods to the cash desk may be told that the goods are in fact on sale at a higher price than the display price and there would be no way that the customer could compel the shopkeeper to sell the goods at the display price. It is true that the seller may be subject to criminal sanctions under the Trade Descriptions Act 1968 where he gives a misleading indication as to the price at which the goods or services are available for sale, but that does not assist the purchaser with his civil action. He is still left without a civil remedy.

In this simple everyday situation the rules of offer and acceptance simply do not demand that a particular conclusion be reached. Nor can the intention of the parties provide a useful guideline because, in truth, the parties often have no discernible intention one way or the other. The general rule which the courts have, in fact, adopted is that the display of goods in a shop window is an invitation to treat rather than an offer (*Fisher* v. *Bell* [1961] 1 QB 394). The application of this rule can be seen in the case of *Pharmaceutical Society of GB* v. *Boots Cash Chemists* [1953] 1 QB 401 (*see* Montrose, 1954). The defendants organised their shop on a self-service basis. They were charged with a breach of the

Pharmacy and Poisons Act 1933, which required that a sale of drugs take place under the supervision of a registered pharmacist. There was no pharmacist present close to the shelves, but a pharmacist was present at the cash desk. It was held that the sale took place at the cash desk and not when the goods were taken from the shelves; the display of the goods was simply an invitation to treat and therefore there had been no breach of the Act.

However a rigid application of the rule established in *Boots* could lead to injustice in certain cases. An instructive example of a factual situation in which the application of the *Boots* test may lead to injustice is provided by the American case of *Lefkowitz* v. *Great Minneapolis Surplus Stores* 251 Minn 188 (1957). The defendants placed an advertisement in a newspaper which stated 'Saturday 9 am sharp; 3 Brand new fur coats, worth to $100; First come first served, $1 each.' On two occasions the plaintiff was the first person in the store on a Saturday morning, but in both cases the defendants refused to sell him the fur coat for $1. The conclusion reached by the Supreme Court of Minnesota was that the advertisement was an offer and not an invitation to treat. But would such a conclusion be reached in this country? Some authority can be adduced for treating a display of goods as an offer; in *Chapleton* v. *Barry UDC* [1940] 1 KB 532, it was held that the display of deck chairs for hire on a beach was an offer which was accepted by a customer taking a chair from the stack (*see too Carlill* v. *Carbolic Smoke Ball Co* [1893] 1 QB 256, discussed at 3.3). But if a court was to rely on the authority of *Chapleton* would it not be because the court thought that it was unfair to leave the plaintiff without a remedy? Would this not be an example of what Professor Atiyah calls 'reasoning backwards'; that the court feels that the plaintiff ought to have a remedy and it justifies that conclusion by treating the advertisement as an offer rather than an invitation to treat?

3.3 Advertisements

The general rule is that a newspaper advertisement is an invitation to treat rather than an offer. In *Partridge* v. *Crittenden* [1968] 1 WLR 1204, the appellant advertised "Bramblefinch cocks and hens" for sale at a stated price. He was charged with the offence of 'offering for sale' wild live birds contrary to the Protection of Birds Act 1954. It was held that the advertisement was an invitation to treat and not an offer and so the appellant was acquitted. Lord Parker CJ stated that there was 'business sense' in treating such advertisements as invitations to treat because if they were treated as offers the advertiser might find himself contractually obliged to sell more goods than he in fact owned. However, as we have seen, this argument is not conclusive because it could be implied that the offer is only capable of acceptance 'while stocks last'.

Nevertheless there are certain cases where an advertisement may be interpreted as an offer rather than an invitation to treat. The classic example is the case of *Carlill* v. *Carbolic Smoke Ball Co* (see above). The defendants, who were the manufacturers of the carbolic smoke ball, issued an advertisement in which they offered to pay £100 to any person who caught influenza after having used one of their smoke balls in the specified manner, and they deposited £1000 in the bank to show their good faith. The plaintiff caught influenza after using the smoke ball in the specified manner. She sued for the £100. It was held that the advertisement was not an invitation to treat but was an offer to the whole world and that a contract was made with those persons who performed the condition which was stipulated in the advertisement. The plaintiff was therefore entitled to recover £100.

3.4 Auction Sales

The general rule is that an auctioneer, by inviting bids to be made, makes an invitation to treat. The offer is made by the bidder which, in turn, is accepted when the auctioneer strikes the table with his hammer (*British Car Auctions Ltd* v. *Wright* [1972] 1 WLR 1519). The advertisement of an auction sale is generally only an invitation to treat (*Harris* v. *Nickerson* (1873) LR 8 QB 286), but it is unclear what is the effect of the addition of the words 'without reserve', that is, that the auction is to take place without a reserve price. In *Warlow* v. *Harrison* (1859) 1 E & E 309, Martin B stated *obiter* that in such a case the auctioneer makes an offer that the sale will be without reserve and that that offer is accepted by the highest bidder at the auction. It should be noted that the offer is made by the *auctioneer* and not the owner of the goods, so that there is no concluded contract of sale. Such an analysis is not without its problems (see the debate between Slade, 1952, 1953 and Gower, 1952). The contract is presumably made with the highest bidder, but how can it be shown who is the highest bidder if the auctioneer does not bring down his hammer?

An alternative analysis put forward by Professor Gower (1952) is to the effect that the advertisement of the auction as being without reserve constitutes an offer to the whole world by the auctioneer that the sale will be without reserve and that offer is accepted by anyone who, in reliance upon the advertisement, attends and bids at the auction. The consequence of this analysis is that a contract is made with all those who attend the auction and bid in reliance upon the advertisement and that a withdrawal of the goods after bidding has begun constitutes a breach of contract with every such person at the auction. However Professor Gower argues that the only person who suffers damage as a result of the breach is the person who is the highest bidder and that breach is therefore the only one worth suing on.

But this analysis also has its problems. The problem of identifying the highest bidder remains because, until the hammer is brought down, there is always the possibility of a last minute bid being made. It also has the consequence that liability can be avoided by refusing to hold the auction at all because acceptance only takes place by attending *and bidding* at the auction. Despite these difficulties, it must be conceded that the intimation that an auction is to be held without reserve raises an expectation in those attending the auction that the goods will be sold to the highest bidder and that *Warlow* provides protection for these expectations and prevents an auctioneer ignoring a condition of the sale which he himself has set. *Warlow* may be another example of the courts reasoning backwards, in that they decide that in such a case the bidder ought to have a remedy and they then accommodate that conclusion within the offer and acceptance framework, even though the fit is somewhat uneasy.

3.5 Tenders

Where a person invites tenders for a particular project the general rule is that the invitation to tender is simply an invitation to treat. The offer is made by the person who submits the tender and the acceptance is made when the person inviting the tenders accepts one of them. However in an appropriate case a court may hold that the invitation to tender was an offer. Such was the case in *Harvela Investments Ltd* v. *Royal Trust Co of Canada* [1986] AC 207. The first defendants decided to sell their shares by sealed competitive tender. They invited each of the two parties most likely to be interested in the shares to submit a single sealed offer for their shares and stated that they would accept the highest 'offer' received by them which complied with the terms of their invitation. The plaintiffs tendered a fixed bid of \$2 175 000. The second defendant tendered a 'referential' bid of '\$2 100 000 or . . . \$101 000 in excess of any other offer . . . whichever is the higher'. The first defendants accepted the second defendant's bid, treating it as a bid of \$2 276 000. But the House of Lords held that the first defendants were bound to accept the plaintiffs' bid. It was held that the invitation to tender was an offer of a unilateral contract to sell the shares to the highest bidder, despite the fact that the invitation asked the plaintiffs and the second defendant to submit an 'offer'. The bid submitted by the second defendant was held to be invalid because the object of the vendors' invitation was to ascertain the highest amount which each party was prepared to pay and this purpose would be frustrated by a referential bid.

3.6 Timetables and Vending Machines

It is remarkable how difficult it is to distinguish between an offer and an invitation to treat in many everyday transactions. A simple example is boarding a bus. One could say that the bus timetable and the running of the bus are an offer by the bus company which is accepted by boarding the bus (although it should be noted that most timetables contain express disclaimers of any obligation to provide the services contained in the timetable). Such was the view of Lord Greene in *Wilkie* v. *London*

Transport Board [1947] 1 All ER 258, when he stated that the offer was made by the bus company and that it was accepted when a passenger 'puts himself either on the platform or inside the bus'. Alternatively, it could be said that the acceptance takes place when the passenger asks for a ticket and pays the fare. A further possibility is to say that the bus timetable is an invitation to treat, the offer is made by the passenger in boarding the bus and the acceptance takes place when the bus conductor accepts the money and issues a ticket. Finally it could be said that the bus conductor makes the offer when he issues the ticket and this offer is accepted by paying the fare and retaining the ticket.

In many ways the issue may seem to be an academic one, devoid of any practical consequence. But this is not the case. It has serious consequences if there is an exclusion clause contained on the back of the ticket (see further Chapter 11). If the first analysis is adopted then the exclusion clause is not part of the contract because the contract is concluded before the ticket is handed over. On the other hand if the final alternative is adopted then the exclusion clause is part of the contract because it is contained in the offer made by the conductor. A court might adopt the first of these alternatives in our exclusion clause example in order to protect the passenger, but would it also apply it where the same passenger boards the bus by mistake and wishes to get off the bus before it moves from the stop without paying for his fare? As Professor Treitel has stated (1987), the cases 'yield no single rule' and all that can be said is that 'the exact time of contracting depends in each case on the wording of the relevant document and on the circumstances in which it was issued'.

Other everyday examples could be provided which defy simple classification. What is the status of a menu outside a restaurant? What about a vending machine selling tea and coffee? The former is probably an invitation to treat but, in *Thornton* v. *Shoe Lane Parking Ltd* [1971] 2 QB 163, Lord Denning stated that an automatic machine which issued tickets outside a car park made a standing offer which was accepted by a motorist driving so far into the car park that the machine issued him with a ticket.

3.7 Acceptance

An acceptance is an unqualified expression of assent to the terms proposed by the offeror. There is no rule that acceptance must be made by words; it can be made by conduct, as was the case in *Carlill* v. *Carbolic Smoke Ball Co* (see above).

A purported acceptance which does not accept all the terms and conditions proposed by the offeror but which in fact introduces new terms is not an acceptance but a counter-offer, which is then treated as a new offer which is capable of acceptance or rejection. The effect of a counter-offer is to 'kill off' the original offer so that it cannot subsequently be accepted by the offeree. This rule can be seen in operation in the case of *Hyde* v. *Wrench* (1840) 3 Beav 334. The defendant offered to sell some land to the plaintiff for £1000 and the plaintiff replied by offering to purchase the land for £950. The defendant refused to sell for £950. So the plaintiff subsequently wrote to the defendant agreeing to pay the £1000; but the defendant still refused to sell. It was held that there was no contract between the parties. The plaintiff's offer of £950 was a counter-offer which killed off the defendant's original offer so as to render it incapable of subsequent acceptance. It is this rule that acceptance must be unqualified which has given rise to difficulties in the battle of the forms cases, such as *Butler* v. *Ex-Cell-O Corp* (see above 2.4).

3.8 Communication of the Acceptance

The general rule is that an acceptance must be communicated to the offeror. The acceptance is generally only validly communicated when it is actually brought to the attention of the offeror. The operation of this rule was illustrated by Denning LJ in *Entores* v. *Miles Far East Corporation* [1955] 2 QB 327. He said that, if an oral acceptance is drowned out by an overflying aircraft, such that the offeror cannot hear the acceptance, then there is no contract unless the acceptor repeats his acceptance once the aircraft has passed over. Similarly, where two people make a contract by telephone and the line goes 'dead' so that the acceptance is incomplete, then the acceptor must telephone the offeror to make sure that he has heard the acceptance. Where the acceptance is made clearly and audibly, but the offeror does not hear what is said, a contract is nevertheless concluded unless the offeror makes clear to the acceptor that he has not heard what was said. In the case of instantaneous communication, such as telephone and telex, the acceptance takes place at the moment the acceptance is received by the offeror and at the place at which the offeror happens to be (see *Brinkibon Ltd* v. *Stahag Stahl* [1983] 2 AC 34).

3.9 Acceptance in Ignorance of the Offer

An offer is effective when it is communicated to the offeree. This requirement generally does not give rise to problems, but difficulty does arise in the following type of case. X offers £100 for the safe return of his missing dog. Y returns the dog but is unaware of X's offer. Is Y entitled to the money? A good argument can be made out to the effect that Y should be entitled to the money. X has got what he wanted and there seems no reason in justice why he should not be required to pay what he has publicly promised to pay. At the same time Y has performed a socially useful act in returning the dog and he should be rewarded for so doing. On the other hand, in the case of a bilateral contract which imposes mutual obligations upon the parties, the effect of such a rule would be to subject the 'accepting' party to obligations of which he was unaware. For example, if X offered to sell the dog for £50 to the first person who returned it to him, Y, who returns the dog, unaware of the offer, should not thereby be held to have accepted an offer to purchase the dog for £50. In the light of these considerations it has been argued that the best approach to adopt is to hold that knowledge of the offer is not necessary in the reward type of case but that knowledge should be required in the case of bilateral contracts (Hudson, 1968).

However the rule which has been adopted in England is that a person who, in ignorance of the offer, performs the act or acts requested by the offeror is not entitled to sue as on a contract. The case of *Gibbons* v. *Proctor* (1891) 64 LT 594, which was thought to stand for the contrary proposition, appears on closer examination of the facts to be a case where the person claiming the reward knew of the offer at the time when the information was given to the police (Treitel, 1987). It is here that we see the importance of the schematic approach to agreement because it is not sufficient that the parties were, at some moment in time, in agreement; there must be a definite offer which is mirrored by a definite acceptance. For the same reason cross-offers which are identical do not create a contract unless or until they are accepted (*Tinn* v. *Hoffman & Co* (1873) 29 LT 271). These cases reinforce the points made in Chapter 2 that contract law adopts an objective rather than a subjective approach to agreement and therefore the fact that the parties are subjectively agreed is not conclusive evidence that a contract exists (contrast the view of Spencer discussed at 2.2).

Once it is shown that the offer has been communicated to the other party, a person who knows of the offer may do the act required for acceptance with some motive other than that of accepting the offer (*Williams* v. *Carwardine* (1833) 4 B & Ad 621). But the offer must have been present to his mind when he did the act which constituted the acceptance. Thus in *R* v. *Clarke* (1927) 40 CLR 227, where the party claiming the reward had forgotten about the offer of a reward at the time he gave the information, it was held that he was not entitled to the reward.

3.10 Prescribed Method of Acceptance

Where the offeror prescribes a specific method of acceptance, the general rule is that the offeror is not bound unless the terms of his offer are complied with. However the offeror who wishes to state that he will be bound *only* if the offer is accepted in a particular way must use clear words to achieve this purpose. Where the offeror has not used sufficiently clear words a court will hold the offeror bound by an acceptance which is made in a form which is no less advantageous to him than the form which he prescribed. This can be seen in the case of *Manchester Diocesan Council for Education* v. *Commercial and General Investments Ltd* [1969] 3 All ER 1593. The plaintiff decided to sell some property by tender and inserted a clause in the tender stating that the person whose bid was accepted would be informed by means of a letter sent to the address given in the tender. The plaintiff sent the letter of acceptance to the defendant's surveyor and not to the address on the tender. It was held that communication to the address in the tender was not the sole permitted means of communication of acceptance and that therefore a valid contract had been concluded. The object of the stipulation relating to the address was simply to ensure that the plaintiff knew where an acceptance could validly be sent.

3.11 Acceptance by Silence

The general rule is that acceptance of an offer will not be implied from mere silence on the part of the offeree and that an offeror cannot impose a contractual obligation upon the offeree by stating that, unless the latter expressly rejects the offer, he will be held to have accepted it. The rationale behind this rule is that it is thought to be unfair to put an offeree to time and expense to avoid the imposition of unwanted contractual arrangements. The principal English authority on this point is *Felthouse* v. *Bindley* (1862) 11 CB (NS) 869. The plaintiff and his nephew were negotiating for the sale of a horse. The plaintiff stated that, if he heard nothing further from his nephew, then he considered that the horse was his at a price of £30 15s. The nephew did not respond to this offer but he decided to accept it and told the auctioneer not to sell the horse because it had already been sold. Nevertheless the auctioneer mistakenly sold the horse and the plaintiff sued the auctioneer. The auctioneer argued that the plaintiff had no title to sue because his offer to buy the horse had not been accepted by his nephew and this argument was accepted by the court on the ground that the nephew's silence did not amount to an acceptance of the offer. The application of the general rule to the facts of *Felthouse* has been the subject of criticism on the ground that the uncle had waived the need for communication of the acceptance and the nephew had manifested his acceptance by informing the auctioneer that the horse had been sold (see Miller, 1972).

But the rule itself has not emerged unscathed from the line of cases represented by *The Hannah Blumenthal* (see 2.1), where the House of Lords held that a contract to abandon a reference to arbitration could be concluded by the silence of both parties. As Bingham J noted in *Cie Française d'Importation et de Distribution SA* v. *Deutsche Continental Handelsgesellschaft* [1985] 2 Lloyds Rep 592, 599, this line of authority does 'some violence . . . to familiar rules of contract such as the requirement that acceptance of an offer should be communicated to the offeror unless the requirement of communication is expressly or impliedly waived'. However it is submitted that these cases do not apply outside the rather rarefied atmosphere of contracts to abandon a reference to arbitration and in none of these cases was *Felthouse* v. *Bindley* overruled.

Instead it is submitted that these arbitration cases remind us that the rule that silence does not amount to an acceptance is not an absolute one and that it does admit of exceptions. For example, a course of dealing between the parties may give rise to the inference that silence amounts to acceptance. It is also unclear whether the general rule will apply where the offeree assumes that his silence has been effective to conclude a contract and then acts in reliance upon that belief. It is suggested that, in such a case, the general rule should give way and a court should hold that a contract has been concluded between the parties (see Miller, 1972). As we have noted, the purpose behind the general rule is to protect the offeree and therefore it should not apply where its application would cause him hardship. However, where the offeree only mentally assents to the offer but does not act in reliance upon it, it is suggested that the general rule should apply because otherwise the offeree would be able to speculate against the offeror, by stating that he had accepted the offer when the contract was a good one for him and by stating that he had not accepted it when the contract turned out to be a bad one. Therefore it is submitted that action in reliance is necessary to provide evidence that the offeree had in fact accepted the offer.

3.12 Exceptions to the Rule requiring Communication of Acceptance

The rule that acceptance must be communicated to the offeror is not an absolute one. For example, the terms of the offer may demonstrate that the offeror does not insist that the acceptance be communicated to him (*Carlill* v. *Carbolic Smoke Ball Co* (see above)). The offeror may be prevented by his conduct from arguing that the acceptance was communicated to him (*Entores* v. *Miles Far East Corporation*, see above 3.8). But the major and most controversial exception relates to acceptances sent through the post.

As a matter of theory any one of a number of possible solutions could be used to ascertain when an acceptance sent by post takes effect. It could be when the letter is posted, when it reaches the address of the offeror, when it is read by the offeror, or when, in the ordinary course of the post, it would reach the offeror. The general rule which English law has adopted can be traced back to *Adams* v. *Lindsell* (1818) 1 B & Ald 681, which is now understood to stand for the proposition that acceptance takes place when the letter of acceptance is posted by the offeree.

However the justifications put forward in support of this rule are, to say the least, rather tenuous (see Evans, 1966). The first justification is that the Post Office is the agent of the offeror and so receipt of the letter by the agent is equivalent to receipt by the offeror. This justification is open to the criticism that it cannot be said in any meaningful sense that the Post Office is the agent of the offeror because the Post Office has no power to contract on behalf of the offeror. The second justification is that the offeror has chosen to start negotiations through the post and so the risk of delay or loss in the post should be imposed upon him. However it is not necessarily the offeror who has started the negotiations through the post. It could be the case that the offeree initiated negotiations through the post by asking the offeror for the terms on which he was prepared to do business. Nevertheless it must be conceded that this justification has some element of validity because, in *Henthorn* v. *Fraser* [1892] 2 Ch 27, it was held that the postal rule only applies where it is reasonable to use the post. However it is reasonable to use the post where the parties live at a distance from each other; it is not necessary for the offeror to have commenced the negotiations by post. So it is not entirely true to say that the offeror has accepted the risk of delay in the post. A more promising justification is that the offeree should not be prejudiced once he has dispatched his acceptance and he should be able to rely on the efficacy of his acceptance. This argument is a strong one but it could be met by providing that, once the acceptance has been posted, the offeror can no longer revoke his offer; it does not demand that the acceptance be treated as taking effect when it is dispatched.

Not only are the justifications for the general rule weak, but the operation of the rule can give rise to manifest injustice. Take the following example. X makes an offer to Y and states that it will be open for acceptance until 5 pm on Friday. Applying the general rule, Y may validly 'accept' that offer by posting his acceptance at 4.45 on Friday afternoon, even though it will not reach X until Monday or Tuesday. It is true that X could avoid such hardships by stating in his offer that the acceptance must *reach* him by 5 pm on Friday (see below) but the fact that the parties can contract out of the general rule is no justification for the general rule itself.

In addition to creating injustice, the general rule gives rise to practical difficulties. Two such difficulties will be dealt with here. The first arises where the letter of acceptance is lost in the post. A logical application of the general rule leads to the result that a contract has been concluded because the acceptance takes effect when it is posted and not when it reaches the offeror. This was held to be the case in England in *Household Fire Insurance* v. *Grant* (1879) 4 Ex D 217. But in Scotland this view was rejected by Lord Shand in *Mason* v. *Benhar Coal Co* (1882) 9 R 883. He stated that, in his opinion, no contract came into existence when the acceptance was posted but never reached the offeror. It is suggested that the latter rule is the preferable one because it is the offeree who has sent the acceptance and so he is in the best position to know when his acceptance is likely to reach the offeror and to take steps to check that it does so reach the offeror. Nevertheless English law is presently committed to the view that a contract is concluded on the posting of the letter of acceptance, even where it gets lost in the post, although Professor Treitel has argued (1987) that, where the reason for the loss of the letter is that it has been incorrectly addressed by the offeree, then the acceptance should not take place on posting because, while the offeror may take the risk of delay or loss in the post, he does not take the further risk of carelessness by the offeree.

The second practical difficulty arises where the offeree posts his acceptance and then sends a rejection by a quicker method so that the rejection reaches the offeror before the acceptance. Once again a logical application of the general rule leads to the result that the contract was concluded when the letter of acceptance was posted and so the subsequent communication is not a revocation of the offer but a breach of contract, which may be accepted or rejected by the offeror. But it can be argued that it would be absurd to hold that a contract has been concluded when both parties have relied on the fact that there was no contract. On the other hand it can be argued that to hold that the contract was not concluded when the letter of acceptance was posted allows the offeree to speculate at the offeror's expense by sending a rejection by a faster means where the contract turns out to be a bad one for him. It is unclear which of these approaches will be adopted in English law (for contrasting views see the Scottish case *Countess of Dunmore* v. *Alexander* (1830) 9 S 190, and the South African case *A to Z Bazaars (Pty) Ltd* v. *Minister of Agriculture* 1974 (4) SA 392).

Given these practical difficulties to which the general rule gives rise it is no surprise to find that the postal rule is subject to some limitations. In the first place, as we have seen, it must have been reasonable for the offeree to use the post (see *Henthorn* v. *Fraser* (above)). Secondly, the offeror can avoid the operation of the rule by stating that the acceptance will only be effective when it actually reaches him. Thirdly, it is interesting to note that the rule has not been adopted in many other cases where the parties are not dealing face to face. Thus in *Entores* v. *Miles Far East Corp* (above) it was held that the postal rule did not apply to telexes and that it was confined to non-instantaneous forms of communication. Therefore a distinction has been drawn between instantaneous and non-instantaneous forms of communication, only the latter being caught by the postal rule. This distinction is likely to pose difficulties in its application to new forms of technology, but it is suggested that, in the case of communication via computers, communication is virtually instantaneous and therefore is unlikely to be governed by the postal rule. The widest exception to the general rule was recognised in *Holwell Securities Ltd* v. *Hughes* [1974] 1 WLR 155, where it was suggested that the postal rule ought not to apply 'where it would lead to manifest inconvenience and absurdity'.

The width of the latter exception illustrates the lack of justification behind the general rule and that, rather than recognise this point, the English courts have proceeded to widen the scope of the exceptions to the general rule. It is submitted that the better approach would be to abolish the general rule and replace it with the normal rule that acceptance takes place when the acceptance is received by the offeror, subject to the qualification that the offeror cannot revoke the offer once the acceptance has been posted.

3.13 Acceptance in Unilateral Contracts

A unilateral contract is a contract whereby one party promises to pay to the other a sum of money or to do some other act if that other party will do or refrain from doing something without making a promise to that effect. Classic examples are the reward cases or *Carlill* v. *Carbolic Smoke Ball Co* (see above). The effect of classifying a contract as unilateral rather than bilateral is that acceptance can be made by fully performing the requested act; there is no need to give advance notification of acceptance. The principal difficulty lies in determining when the offer can be withdrawn, which, in turn, depends upon when the offer has been 'accepted'. For example, X offers Y £10 000 if Y will walk from London to Newcastle. Does Y accept the offer when he expresses an intention to accept the offer, when he reaches York, or only when he gets to Newcastle? The general rule which English law has adopted was described by Goff LJ in *Daulia Ltd* v. *Four Millbank Nominees Ltd* [1978] Ch 231, in the following terms:

'Whilst I think the true view of a unilateral contract must in general be that the offeror is entitled to require full performance of the condition which he has imposed and short of that he is not bound, that must be subject to one important qualification, which stems from the fact that there must be an implied obligation on the part of the offeror not to prevent the condition becoming satisfied, which obligation it seems to me must arise as soon as the offeree starts to perform.'

The willingness of the courts to imply an obligation not to 'prevent the condition becoming satisfied' can be seen by contrasting the following two cases. The first is *Errington* v. *Errington* [1952] 1 KB 290. A father bought a house for £750 and took out a mortgage for £500. His son and daughter-in-law moved into the house and the father stated that, if they paid off the mortgage, the house was theirs. The couple moved into the house and began to pay off the mortgage, without promising to continue with the payments. The father died and the father's personal representatives sought to revoke the arrangements. The Court of Appeal held that they could not do so because the 'father's promise was a unilateral contract', which could not be revoked once the couple had embarked upon performance provided that they did not leave performance 'incomplete and unperformed'.

On the other hand, a different result was reached in the case of *Luxor (Eastbourne) Ltd* v. *Cooper* [1941] AC 108. The plaintiff agreed with the defendants that, if he introduced a purchaser who would buy the defendants' two cinemas for at least £185 000 each, he would be paid a commission. The plaintiff succeeded in introducing to the defendants a purchaser who was ready and willing to complete the purchase, but the defendants refused to proceed with the sale. It was held that the plaintiff was not entitled to the commission because it was only payable on completion of the sale. The House of Lords refused to imply a term that the defendants would do nothing to prevent the plaintiff from earning his commission because it was contrary to the common understanding of the parties, which was that the plaintiff took 'the risk in the hope of a substantial remuneration for a comparatively small exertion'.

3.14 Termination of the Offer

There are five principal methods by which an offer may be terminated. The first is that the offer may be withdrawn. An offer can be withdrawn by the offeror at any time before it has been accepted. However to withdraw an offer the notice of withdrawal must actually be brought to the attention of the offeree. There is no requirement that the offeror himself must be the one to bring the withdrawal to the attention of the offeree. Thus in *Dickinson* v. *Dodds* (1876) 2 Ch D 463, the defendant offered to sell a house to the plaintiff for £800, the offer to be left open until Friday. On Thursday the defendant sold the house to a third party and the plaintiff was informed of this by another third party. Nevertheless the plaintiff sent the defendant his letter of acceptance on the Friday. It was held that no contract had been concluded between the parties because the offer had been withdrawn before it was accepted.

The rule that the withdrawal must be brought to the attention of the offeree has odd effects in relation to offers sent through the post. This can be seen in the case of *Byrne* v. *Van Tienhoven* (1880) 5 CPD 344. The defendants sent the plaintiffs an offer on 1 October. This offer was received by the plaintiffs on 11 October and they sent off an immediate acceptance. However, in the meantime, the defendants had sent, on 8 October, a letter revoking their offer, which reached the plaintiffs on 20 October. It was held that a contract was concluded between the parties on 11 October. To be effective the withdrawal must be drawn to the attention of the other party and, for this purpose, the postal rule does not apply, so that the revocation only takes effect when it actually reaches the other party. So the purported withdrawal could not take effect until 20 October but, by that time, a contract had already been concluded and the withdrawal was therefore too late. This case is a good example of the objective approach which the courts adopt to the issue of agreement because at no time were the parties actually subjectively agreed; by the time the plaintiffs accepted the offer on 11 October, the defendants had already dispatched their 'withdrawal' of the offer.

Although it is clear that the revocation must be brought to the attention of the offeree it is not entirely clear when the revocation is treated as being brought to his attention. It could be when the letter reaches his business or it could be when he actually reads it. There is no clear English authority on this point, although in *The Brimnes* [1975] QB 929, the Court of Appeal held that, in the case of a revocation sent by telex during ordinary business hours, the revocation was effective when it was received on the telex machine. There was no requirement that it actually be read by any particular person within the organisation.

Secondly, an offer can be terminated by a rejection by the offeree. We have already seen how a rejection or counter-offer has the effect of 'killing off' the original offer (*Hyde* v. *Wrench* (above)). Thirdly, an offer may be terminated by lapse of time. An offer which is expressly stated to last only for a specific period of time cannot be accepted after that date. An offer which specifies no time limit is deemed to last for a reasonable period of time.

Fourthly, an offer which is stated to come to an end if a certain event occurs cannot be accepted after that event has actually taken place. Finally, an offer may be terminated by the death of the offeror, although the law is not entirely clear on this point. On one view it could be said that death always terminates an offer because the parties cannot enter into an agreement once one of the parties is dead. However it seems to be the case that an offeree cannot accept an offer once he knows that the offeror has died but that his acceptance may be valid if it is made in ignorance of the fact that the offeror has died, provided that the contract is not one for the performance of personal services. There is no authority on the position where it is the offeree who dies. The generally accepted view is that, on the offeree's death, the offer comes to an end by operation of law.

3.15 The Limits of Offer and Acceptance

We have noted at various points in this chapter how difficult it is to fit many everyday transactions within the offer and acceptance framework. Simple examples which give rise to difficulty are boarding a bus, buying goods in a supermarket and making a contract through the post. Battle of the forms poses difficulties for the businessman. These difficulties have led some commentators to doubt the utility of the offer and acceptance model. It is true that there are difficulties with this model but these problems are often experienced because of the tension between the court's wish to give effect to the intention of the parties, their desire to achieve a just result on the facts of the case and the need to establish a clear rule which can be applied to all such cases in the future.

Some commentators argue that there is too much uncertainty within the present law. Certainty is an extremely important commodity in the law of contract. Greater degree of certainty could be provided by adopting legislative formulae to prescribe solutions for difficult and uncertain areas, such as the battle of the forms. An example of this approach is Article 19 of the United Nations Convention on Contracts for the International Sale of Goods which provides that:

'(1) A reply to an offer which purports to be an acceptance but contains additions, limitations or other modifications is a rejection of the offer and constitutes a counter-offer.

(2) However, a reply to an offer which purports to be an acceptance but contains additional or different terms which do not materially alter the terms of the offer constitutes an acceptance, unless the offeror, without undue delay, objects orally to the discrepancy or dispatches a notice to that effect. If he does not so object, the terms of the contract are the terms of the offer with the modifications contained in the acceptance.

(3) Additional or different terms relating, among other things, to the price, payment, quality and quantity of the goods, place of delivery, extent of one party's liability to the other or the settlement of disputes are considered to alter the terms of the offer materially.'

This type of approach seeks to achieve a solution which is practical, without being excessively rigid, and which is easy to apply. Yet Article 19 in turn has been criticised for being uncertain (see Vergne, 1985). For example, is any alteration proposed by the offeree an 'addition, limitation or other modification' or does some form of *de minimis* rule apply? Secondly, although the definition of materiality in paragraph (3) is helpful, it is clearly not exhaustive, but it is unclear how much further it goes. It is important to note that none of the many legislative solutions proposed for battle of the forms cases has escaped criticism (see McKendrick, 1988). The variety of battle of the forms cases is such that no single formula can provide an acceptable solution to all possible cases. Absolute certainty of this type is unattainable because of the infinite variety of intentions held by contracting parties. It is submitted that English law is unlikely to be improved by the adoption of such formulations, which will still give rise to uncertainty and yet impose an unacceptable level of rigidity.

Other commentators argue that the present rules can give rise to injustice in certain cases. This could be ameliorated by the adoption of Lord Denning's general approach in *Butler* v. *Ex-Cell-O Corporation* but, as we have noted (see 2.4), the general approach has its own problems because it gives rise to so much uncertainty.

It is submitted that the present law strikes a reasonable balance between the need for certainty and the desire to achieve a just result which is consistent with the intention of the parties. The offer and acceptance model has a core of well-established rules which are understood by lawyers and which are capable of being understood by the business community. At the same time the model is applied with some degree of flexibility by the courts so that a conclusion can be reached which is consistent with the intention of the parties. The present state of the law cannot be said to be entirely satisfactory but it is better than a system which imposes an unacceptable level of rigidity or a system which imposes an unacceptable level of uncertainty.

Summary

1 An offer is a statement by one party of a willingness to enter into a contract on stated terms, provided that these terms are, in turn, accepted by the party to whom the offer is addressed.

2 An offer must be distinguished from an invitation to treat. A display of goods in a shop and advertisements are, subject to cases such as *Carlill* v. *Carbolic Smoke Ball Co,* regarded as invitations to treat. An auctioneer, by inviting bids to be made, makes an invitation to treat (except, perhaps, where the auction is to take place without a reserve price) and an invitation to parties to submit a tender is generally an invitation to treat.

3 An acceptance is an unqualified expression of assent to the terms proposed by the offeror. An acceptance must generally be communicated to the offeror.

4 A purported acceptance which does not mirror the terms of the offer is not an acceptance but a counter-offer which kills off the original offer.

5 An offer cannot be accepted by someone who is ignorant of the existence of the offer or by someone who does not have the offer in his mind when he does the act which he alleges constitutes the acceptance.

6 Where the offeror prescribes a specific method of acceptance, the general rule is that the offeror is not bound unless the terms of his offer are complied with.

7 The general rule is that acceptance of an offer will not be implied from mere silence on the part of the offeree.

8 A letter of acceptance takes effect whenever it is posted, provided that it was reasonable for the offeree to have used the post. This rule applies even where the letter gets lost in the post and never reaches the offeror. It is unclear what is the legal position where the offeree posts his acceptance and then sends a rejection by a quicker method so that the rejection reaches the offeror before the acceptance.

9 In the case of a unilateral contract the offeror is only bound by full performance of the requested act but, in certain cases, the court will imply an obligation on the part of the offeror not to prevent completion of performance, which obligation arises as soon as the offeree starts to perform.

10 An offer may be terminated by revocation, rejection by the offeree, lapse of time, the occurrence of a stipulated event and, possibly, the death of one or other of the parties. In the case of revocation the general rule is that the revocation must actually be brought to the attention of the offeree.

Exercises

1 Distinguish between an offer and an invitation to treat. Give examples to illustrate the distinction.

2 Do you think that *Lefkowitz* v. *Great Minneapolis Surplus Stores* would be followed in this country? Give reasons for your answer.

3 In offer and acceptance cases do the courts 'reason forwards' or 'reason backwards' ?

4 What is the 'postal rule'? Do you think it is a good rule?

5 Do you think Article 19 of the United Nations Convention on Contracts for the International Sale of Goods is an improvement upon the principles established in *Butler* v. *Ex-Cell-O Corp?*

6 Billy wishes to know whether or not he can refuse to carry out the following arrangements without finding himself in breach of contract. Advise him.

(a) Billy offered to sell his car to Jimmy for £5000 and stated that he would assume that Jimmy had accepted his offer unless he informed Billy to the contrary. Jimmy has not been in contact with Billy but he has contacted his bank manager and agreed a loan to purchase the car.

(b) Billy offered to sell a consignment of bricks to Jimmy, subject to his terms and conditions which stated that Jimmy would be responsible for collecting the bricks. Jimmy accepted the offer, subject to his terms and conditions which stated that Billy would be responsible for delivery of the bricks. Billy still possesses the bricks.

(c) Billy offered to sell his golf clubs to Jimmy. Jimmy immediately replied by letter accepting Billy's offer but, owing to his carelessness in wrongly addressing the letter, the acceptance never reached Billy.

4 Certainty and Agreement Mistakes

In Chapter 2 we noted that the test for the existence of an agreement is objective rather than subjective. In this chapter we shall consider the application of the objective test in two areas, namely certainty and mistake.

4.1 Certainty

In order to create a binding contract, the parties must express their agreement in a form which is sufficiently certain for the courts to enforce. The traditional reason for this is that it is for the parties, and not the courts, to make the contract. The function of the court is limited to the interpretation of the contract which the parties have made and it does not extend to making contracts on their behalf (Fridman, 1962). This sentiment was classically expressed by Viscount Maugham in *Scammell and Nephew Ltd* v. *Ouston* [1941] AC 251, when he said that

'in order to constitute a valid contract the parties must so express themselves that their meaning can be determined with a reasonable degree of certainty. It is plain that unless this can be done . . . *consensus ad idem* would be a matter of mere conjecture.'

The traditional stance has to be tempered, however, in its application to commercial contracts where businessmen wish to avoid rigid agreements which give them no room to manoeuvre in a fluctuating economy. It is not uncommon for building and civil engineering contracts to contain terms which permit the contractor to vary the work which he is required to do, or which make provision for a variation of the time for performance or for the price to be recalculated in the light of events occurring during the agreement. The courts are also reluctant to find that no contract has been concluded where the parties have acted on the assumption that a contract has been entered into.

Thus this area of law is characterised by a tension between the traditional refusal of the courts to make a contract for the parties and the desire of the courts to put into effect what they believe to be the intention of the parties. The dominant judicial philosophy may be said to be one which leans in favour of upholding an agreement and treating it as a valid contract. Thus in *Hillas* v. *Arcos* (1932) 147 LT 503, Lord Wright said:

'Business men often record the most important agreements in crude and summary fashion . . . It is . . . the duty of the court to construe such documents fairly and broadly, without being too astute or subtle in finding defects.'

However there are limits to the benevolence of the courts. Lord Wright himself recognised that such a liberal approach did not mean that 'the court is to make a contract for the parties'. In comparing these two statements of Lord Wright we can see that he is making a contrast between 'construing' (or interpreting) a contract and 'making' a contract; the former being legitimate, the latter being illegitimate. Some academic commentators have accepted the existence of such a distinction (Fridman, 1962) but others have subjected it to heavy criticism (Samek, 1970; Ellinghaus, 1971). In application the distinction is by no means obvious. This is so for two reasons. The first is that the test for the existence of an agreement is objective and, as we have seen in cases such as *Gibson* v. *Manchester City Council* [1979] 1 WLR 294 (see 3.1), the courts can and do differ in the application of this test. Secondly, as is clear from the judgment of Viscount Maugham in *Scammell* v. *Ouston* (quoted above), the courts do not insist upon absolute certainty: 'a reasonable degree of certainty' will suffice. There is no hard and fast line between what is certain and what is uncertain. What is sufficiently certain to one judge may be uncertain to another. Thus the distinction between 'construing' a contract and 'making' a contract is one of degree and not one of kind.

The consequence of this is that the approach which has been adopted by the courts is not wholly consistent, with some judges being more willing than others to find the existence of a contract. This conflict can be seen by contrasting the following two decisions of the House of Lords. In *May and Butcher* v. *R* [1934] 2 KB 17, the parties entered into a written agreement under which the British government was to sell tentage to the plaintiff and the agreement provided that the price and date of payment 'shall be agreed upon from time to time'. It was held that, the parties not having reached agreement on these matters, no contract had been concluded because, according to Lord Buckmaster, 'an agreement between two parties to enter into an agreement in which some critical part of the contract matter is left undetermined is no contract at all'. On the other hand, a different approach was adopted in the case of *Hillas* v. *Arcos* (see above). In 1930 the parties entered into a contract under which the plaintiffs bought from the defendants 22 000 standards of 'softwood goods of fair specification'. The 1930 contract also contained a provision which stated that the plaintiffs had an option 'of entering into a contract with sellers for the purchase of 100 000 standards for delivery during 1931'. When the plaintiffs sought to exercise this option the defendants argued that the clause was too uncertain to be enforced. This argument was rejected by the House of Lords, who held that the words could be given a reasonable meaning and that therefore the option was binding. Lord Tomlin said that, before the conclusion that no contract has been completed is reached, 'it is necessary to exclude as impossible all reasonable meanings which would give certainty to the words'. But it should be noted that in *Hillas* there was a prior contract between the parties which assisted the court in giving a meaning to the option clause.

It can be seen that the approach adopted by the House of Lords in these two cases seems to differ. The House in *Hillas* was more willing than the House in *May and Butcher* to uphold the agreement entered into by the parties. It is the more liberal approach in *Hillas* which has been followed with the greatest regularity in later cases (see, for example, *Foley* v. *Classique Coaches* [1934] 2 KB 1). Judges generally do not want to 'incur the reproach of being the destroyer of bargains' (per Lord Tomlin in *Hillas* v. *Arcos*) and therefore they tend to gravitate towards the upholding and enforcement of agreements. Nevertheless it must be borne in mind that the distinction between 'construing' a contract and 'making' a contract is one of degree and that judges will continue to differ in their approach, with some preferring to adopt a more restrictive approach, as in *May and Butcher* v. *R.*

4.2 Vagueness

The uncertainty may arise from one of a number of different sources. The terms of the agreement may be too vague for the courts to enforce. Such was the case in *Scammell and Nephew Ltd* v. *Ouston* (above), where the parties entered into an agreement to buy goods on 'hire purchase'. It was held that this agreement was too vague to be enforced because there were many different types of hire purchase agreements in use, these agreements varied widely in their content and it was not clear what type of hire purchase agreement was envisaged.

However, as we have noted, the courts are reluctant to find that an agreement is so vague that it cannot be enforced. There are a number of devices available to a court in such circumstances. The court may be able to ascertain the meaning of the phrase by reference to the custom of the trade in which the parties are contracting (*Shamrock SS Co* v. *Storey and Co* (1899) 81 LT 413), or it may be able to enforce the agreement by severing a clause which is meaningless (*Nicolene Ltd* v. *Simmonds* [1953] 1 QB 543), or, finally, the court may be able to interpret the vague phrase in the light of what is reasonable (*Hillas* v. *Arcos* (above)).

4.3 Incompleteness

Alternatively, the agreement may be incomplete because the parties have failed to reach agreement upon a particular issue. It is at this point that cases such as *May and Butcher* and *Hillas* become relevant. Once again, however, a number of devices are available to a court which wishes to avoid the conclusion that the agreement is incomplete and therefore cannot be enforced. The first is to invoke section 8(2) of the Sale of Goods Act 1979, which provides that, where the price of goods in a contract of sale is not 'determined' by the contract (on which see section 8(1) of the Act), 'the buyer must pay a reasonable price' (see also section 15(1) of the Supply of Goods and Services Act 1982). This section only comes into play where the contract is silent as to the price; where, as in *May and Butcher*, provision is made for calculating the price but the provision is not implemented then the section is inapplicable. Secondly, where, as in *Hillas* v. *Arcos*, the parties have agreed criteria by which an incomplete matter can be resolved it is much easier for the court to uphold the agreement.

Thirdly, the contract itself may provide for machinery to resolve the dispute between the parties. However difficulties emerge where the machinery has, for some reason, failed to come into effect. It was once thought that such a failure was fatal to the existence of an enforceable contract because the court would not substitute its own, different, machinery for that agreed by the parties.

However, this view was rejected by the House of Lords in *Sudbrook Estates Ltd* v. *Eggleton* [1983] 1 AC 444. A lease gave to tenants (the lessees) an option to purchase the premises at a price to be agreed upon by two valuers, one to be nominated by the lessors and the other by the lessees and, in default of agreement, by an umpire to be appointed by the valuers. When the lessees sought to exercise the option the lessors refused to appoint a valuer and claimed that the option clause was void for uncertainty. It was held by the House of Lords that the crucial question in each case was whether the machinery agreed upon by the parties was an essential factor in determining the price to be paid or whether it was simply a means of ensuring that a fair price was paid. It was only where the machinery was essential and had not been implemented that the agreement would be held to be incomplete and not binding. An example of machinery which may be held to be essential is the appointment of a particular valuer because of his special skill or his special knowledge. On the facts, it was held, Lord Russell dissenting, that the reference to the valuers was an indication that the price was to be a reasonable and fair one and that the machinery for appointing the valuers was subsiduary to the main purpose of ascertaining a fair and reasonable price. Therefore, given that the machinery was not essential, the House of Lords was able to substitute its own machinery for ascertaining the price to be paid and an inquiry was ordered into what was the fair value of the premises.

4.4 A General Rule?

The general impression which is left by a study of the English case law on uncertainty is that the courts have adopted a rather piecemeal approach, which has resulted in a degree of inconsistency in the case law. The courts have not laid down a general rule which could provide a unifying basis for the law in this area. Such a general rule has been adopted in America in section 2-204 of the Uniform Commercial Code which states that 'even though one or more terms are left open a contract for sale does not fail for indefiniteness if the parties have intended to make a contract and there is a reasonably certain basis for giving an appropriate remedy'. It is a matter for consideration whether such a general rule would constitute an improvement upon the present state of English law. It would provide a basis for a coherent development of the law, but it would also bring its own problems of interpretation. For example, how would the courts decide whether the parties had an intention to contract, and what meaning would be given to the phrase a 'reasonably certain basis for giving an appropriate remedy'? Although these problems of interpretation would remain, it is suggested that the adoption of such a rule would improve the present state of the law.

4.5 A Restitutionary Approach?

It should not be assumed, however, that the law of contract, and the law of contract alone, can resolve the problems raised by agreements which appear to lack certainty. A role may be found for the law of restitution, as can be seen from the case of *British Steel Corporation* v. *Cleveland Bridge and Engineering Co Ltd* [1984] 1 All ER 504. The parties entered into negotiations for the manufacture by the plaintiffs of steel nodes for the defendants. The defendants sent the plaintiffs a letter of intent which stated their intention to place an order for the steel nodes and proposed that the contract be on the defendants' standard terms. The plaintiffs refused to contract on these terms. Detailed negotiations then took place over the specifications of the steel nodes, but no agreement was reached on matters such as progress payments and liability for loss arising from late delivery, and no formal contract was ever concluded. After the final node had been delivered the defendants refused to pay for them. The plaintiffs brought an action against the defendants, who counterclaimed for damages for late delivery or delivery of the nodes out of sequence. Robert Goff J discussed three possible analyses of the plaintiffs' claim.

The first was to hold that an executory contract had come into existence after the letter of intent had been sent. But he rejected this solution on the ground that, since the parties were still negotiating and had not reached agreement, it was impossible to say what were the material terms of the contract. The second solution was to hold that there was a unilateral contract or a standing offer made by the defendants which, if acted upon before it was lawfully withdrawn, would result in a contract. But, because of the disagreement between the parties, Robert Goff J held that it could not be assumed from the fact that the plaintiffs had commenced the work that a contract had thereby been created on the terms of the defendants' standing offer. The third solution, and the one which Robert Goff J adopted, was to allow the plaintiffs to recover in a restitutionary action for the reasonable value of the work which they had done. He held that, because the defendants had requested the plaintiffs to deliver the nodes, they had received a benefit at the expense of the plaintiffs and that it was unjust that they retain that benefit without recompensing the plaintiffs for the reasonable value of the nodes. The conclusion which was reached in the case was not altogether satisfactory because, no contract having been concluded, the defendants' counter-claim for damages for breach of contract was held to be without foundation. Thus the defendants were given no protection for their expectations (see Ball, 1983; but for a refutation of this criticism see McKendrick, 1988). So, instead of liberalising the rules relating to certainty (or possibly in addition to such liberalisation), an alternative approach would be to hold that no contract was concluded and to look to the emerging law of restitution for a solution.

4.6 Mistake Negativing Consent

This is an extremely difficult area of law. It is important to distinguish at the outset between two different types of mistake. The first is called common mistake and arises where both parties enter into the contract sharing the same mistake which nullifies their contract (see further 14.2–14.7). The second type of mistake, and the type with which we shall be concerned here, is called unilateral mistake, which negatives consent and prevents a contract coming into existence because one party is labouring under a mistake or the parties are at cross-purposes. Professor Goodhart has written (1941) that 'there is no branch of the law of contract which is more uncertain and difficult than that which is concerned with the effect of mistake on the formation of a contract'.

Despite this uncertainty, it is at least clear that the mere fact that one party to the contract is mistaken in his 'innermost mind' is not sufficient, of itself, automatically to render a contract void. This is because, as we have seen, the courts have adopted an objective rather than a subjective test of agreement (see 2.1). The objective test of agreement considerably reduces the scope of the doctrine of mistake and this restriction is traditionally justified on the ground that it promotes certainty in com-mercial transactions. Despite these restrictions, mistake can operate to negative consent in the following cases.

The first case arises where the terms of the offer and acceptance suffer from such latent ambiguity that it is impossible reasonably to impute any agreement between the parties. The classic, if confusing, case in this category is *Raffles* v. *Wichelhaus* (1864) 2 H & C 906. The defendants agreed to buy from the plaintiffs a cargo of cotton to arrive 'ex Peerless from Bombay'. There were, unknown to the parties, two ships called 'Peerless' and both sailed from Bombay. The defendants meant the *Peerless* which sailed in October, whereas the plaintiffs meant the *Peerless* which sailed in December. When the cotton eventually arrived, the defendants refused to accept delivery because they argued that the plaintiffs were obliged to deliver the cotton on the *Peerless* which sailed in October, not the *Peerless* which sailed in December. The plaintiffs therefore sued for the price of the cotton. Judgment was given for the defendants but, as no reasoned judgment was given in the case, it is not clear whether judgment was given for the defendants because there was no contract or because there was a contract to deliver the cotton on the October *Peerless*, which the plaintiffs had breached. Despite the obscurity of the case *Raffles* has generally been understood by contract lawyers to stand for the proposition that latent ambiguity in the terms of an offer and acceptance can operate to negative consent in an appropriate case.

The second case is where one contracting party is under a mistake as to the terms of the contract, and that mistake is known to the other contracting party. Here the normal rule of objective interpretation is replaced by a subjective test (see *Hartog* v. *Colin and Shields* [1939] 3 All ER 566, discussed at 2.2). In *Smith* v. *Hughes* (1871) LR 6 QB 597 a buyer purchased from a seller a quantity of oats in the belief that they were old oats when, in fact, they were new oats and therefore unsuitable for the buyer's proposed use. When he discovered his mistake the buyer refused to accept the oats and the seller sued for the price. The jury found in favour of the buyer but the Court of Queen's Bench ordered a new trial because of a misdirection given to the jury by the trial judge. The Court of Queen's Bench held that a distinction must be drawn between two different types of case. The first is where the buyer correctly understands that the seller's offer is an offer to sell oats but the buyer mistakenly believes these oats to be old oats, and this mistake is known to the seller. In such a case the seller is not under an obligation to inform the buyer that he has made a mistake. The responsibility lies with the buyer to ensure that the oats are as he believed them to be; he cannot escape from what is a bad bargain for him by arguing that it is the responsibility of the seller to inform him of his error (see further Brownsword, 1987). In the second class of case the seller knows that the buyer is mistaken, but this time the buyer is mistaken as to the *terms* of the seller's *offer*. The buyer mistakenly believes that the seller's offer is an offer to sell old oats and the seller knows that the buyer has thus misunderstood his offer. In such a case there is an offer and acceptance mistake and the seller is under an obligation to inform the buyer of the true nature of his offer.

The third case is where there is a mistake as to the identity of the other contracting party. The identity of the person with whom one is contracting or proposing to contract is often immaterial. However a mistake is sufficiently material to negative consent if one party is mistaken as to the *identity* of the other contracting party. Where the mistake is simply one as to the *attributes* of the other contracting party the mistake is not sufficiently fundamental to render the contract void. The distinction between identity and attributes can best be understood by contrasting the following two cases.

In *Cundy* v. *Lindsay* (1878) 3 App Cas 459, a dishonest person called Blenkarn, who gave his address as 37, Wood Street, Cheapside, ordered handkerchiefs from the plaintiffs. Blenkarn signed his name to make it look like Blenkiron & Co, a respectable firm who carried on business at 123 Wood Street and who were known by reputation to the plaintiffs. The plaintiffs duly sent the handkerchiefs to 'Blenkiron & Co, 37 Wood St' where Blenkarn received them. He did not pay for the goods, but rather sold them to the defendants. When they discovered their mistake, the plaintiffs sought to recover the goods from the defendants. The question whether the contract between the plaintiffs and Blenkarn was void for mistake was crucial to the defendants' rights. A contract which is void is set aside for all purposes. So, if the contract was void, Blenkarn could not have obtained title to the goods and was therefore incapable of giving title to the defendants. But a contract which is voidable remains a good contract until it is set aside by the innocent party. Therefore, if the contract was merely voidable on the ground of fraud then, provided Blenkarn sold the goods to the defendants before the contract between the plaintiffs and Blenkarn was set aside by the plaintiffs, the defendants would have obtained good title. However it was held that the contract was void because the plaintiffs did not intend to deal with Blenkarn but with Blenkiron & Co, a firm which they knew; thus they had made a mistake as to identity.

On the other hand, a different result was reached in the case of *King's Norton Metal Co* v. *Edridge Merrett & Co Ltd* (1897) 14 TLR 98. The plaintiffs sent goods on credit to Hallam and Co, which purported to be a large firm in Sheffield, but was in fact an impecunious rogue called Wallis. Wallis failed to pay for the goods and sold them to the defendants. The plaintiffs, when they discovered their mistake, sought to recover the goods from the defendants. But it was held that the plaintiffs had not made a mistake as to the identity of Wallis. They intended to contract with the writer of the letters; they had simply made a mistake as to one of his attributes, namely his creditworthiness, and so the defendants got good title to the goods. The distinction between the two cases is that the mistake in *Cundy* was a mistake as to identity because the plaintiffs intended to deal with an indentifiable third party (Blenkiron & Co, a company which they knew), whereas in *King's Norton* the plaintiffs had not heard of Hallam and Co and simply intended to contract with the writer of the letters.

This distinction between a mistake as to identity and a mistake as to attributes has led to acute difficulties where the contracting parties meet face to face. The difficulties begin with the case of *Phillips* v. *Brooks* [1919] 2 KB 243. A man called North entered the plaintiff's shop and asked to see some pearls and rings. He selected a ring and produced a cheque book to pay for it, saying that he was Sir George Bullough (a wealthy man known by reputation to the plaintiff) and gave Sir George's address. The plaintiff checked the address in a directory and let North take the ring away for a cheque, which was later dishonoured. North sold the ring to the defendant, from whom the plaintiff sought to recover it. It was held that he could not do so because the contract between the plaintiff and North was not void, no mistake as to identity having been made. The plaintiff intended to contract, and did contract, with the person in his shop.

However, a different approach was adopted in the case of *Lake* v. *Simmonds* [1927] AC 487. The plaintiff, a jeweller, was insured against loss of his stock by theft, with the exception of jewellery entrusted to a customer. A woman called Ellison, who pretended to be the wife of a wealthy customer, took two pearl necklaces 'on approval' for her supposed husband and never returned them. The plaintiff sought to recover for his loss under the insurance policy. The House of Lords held that the plaintiff was entitled to recover as he had not entrusted the jewellery to Ellison, because he did not in fact consent to her obtaining possession of the jewellery. Such a conclusion appears to be inconsistent with *Phillips* but Lord Haldane sought to reconcile the instant case with *Phillips* on the ground that in *Phillips* the sale was concluded before any mention was made of Sir George Bullough, so the mistake did not induce the contract. However it is not clear that this finding is consistent with the facts as found by the trial judge in *Phillips*.

The issue was reconsidered by the Court of Appeal in *Ingram* v. *Little* [1961] 1 QB 31. The plaintiffs, who were two sisters, were visited by a rogue who called himself Hutchinson and who wished to buy their car. He produced a cheque to pay for it, but one of the plaintiffs said that they would not accept a cheque. The rogue then said that he was a certain P. G. M. Hutchinson of Stanstead House, Caterham. Neither of the plaintiffs had heard of this person, but one of them went to the Post Office, checked in the telephone directory and confirmed that there was such a person. Believing the rogue to be P. G. M. Hutchinson they allowed him to take the car on handing over the cheque, which later proved to be worthless. The rogue then sold the car to the defendants. When the plaintiffs discovered their mistake they sought recovery of the car from the defendants. The Court of Appeal held that the contract between the plaintiffs and the rogue was void because of a mistake as to identity. They held that there was a prima facie presumption that a party contracts with the person in front of him, but held that the presumption was displaced on the facts of the case. The decisive factor appears to be that the plaintiffs refused to accept the rogue's offer to enter into a contract on terms that he paid by cheque until they had checked his identity in the telephone directory, which showed that his identity was crucial to the creation of a contract.

The final case on this point is the decision of the Court of Appeal in *Lewis* v. *Avery* [1972] 1 QB 198. A rogue, claiming to be the actor Richard Greene, offered to buy the plaintiff's car. He signed a cheque, but the plaintiff did not want him to take the car away until the cheque had been cleared. In order to persuade the plaintiff to allow him to take the car away immediately, the rogue produced an admission pass to

Pinewood Studios, bearing the name Richard A. Greene, his address, his photograph and an official stamp. The plaintiff then let the rogue take the car in return for a cheque, which proved to be worthless. The rogue then sold the car to the defendant, from whom the plaintiff sought recovery when he discovered his mistake. In giving judgment for the defendant the Court of Appeal held that there was nothing to displace the prima facie presumption that the plaintiff intended to deal with the party in front of him and they confined *Ingram* to its 'special facts'. The 'special facts' would appear to be that in *Ingram* no contract was concluded until the plaintiffs had ascertained the rogue's identity; thus the mistake was as to identity, whereas in *Lewis* a contract had been concluded and the identity of the rogue was only crucial to the method of payment; thus the mistake was one as to his attributes, namely his creditworthiness.

It can be seen from this brief discussion of the leading cases that the distinction between a mistake as to identity and a mistake as to attributes is a very fine one. The fineness of the distinction was recognised by Devlin LJ in an important dissenting judgment in *Ingram*. He suggested that the more appropriate solution was to divide the loss between the parties in such proportion as is just in all the circumstances. Such a solution would avoid the apparent harshness of cases such as *Ingram* and *Lewis* where the plaintiff either gets everything or he gets nothing and there are few distinguishing facts between the cases. However it is unlikely that such a reform will be introduced in the foreseeable future because the common law has traditionally set its face against such loss-splitting devices, preferring to use an all or nothing solution.

Instead the courts are likely in future to follow *Lewis* in preference to *Ingram*. This is so for three reasons. The first is the effect of the presumption that a contracting party intends to contract with the person in front of him and that presumption will only be displaced upon 'special facts'. The second is that the courts have sought to protect third party rights and such a policy would be frustrated by holding that the contract was void on the ground of mistake. The third and final reason is the strength of the objective approach which, as we have seen in this chapter, is applied by the courts in determining whether or not a contract has been concluded.

Summary

1 An agreement must be expressed with sufficient certainty before it will be enforced by the courts.

2 The principal causes of uncertainty are vagueness and incompleteness.

3 There are, however, a number of devices available to a court which wishes to avoid the conclusion that an agreement is too uncertain to be enforced.

4 It should not be forgotten that a remedy may be found in the law of restitution where it is held that the agreement is too uncertain to constitute a contract.

5 A mistake may negative consent and prevent a contract coming into existence where one party is labouring under a mistake or the parties are at cross-purposes.

6 Mistake operates within very narrow confines. Mistake has been held to negative consent where the terms of the offer and acceptance suffer from such latent ambiguity that it is impossible reasonably to impute any agreement between the parties, where one party was under a mistake as to the terms of the contract and that mistake was known to the other party and where there was a mistake as to the identity (not attributes) of the other contracting party.

7 Where the parties are dealing face to face there is a prima facie presumption that a party contracts with the person in front of him but, as in *Ingram* v. *Little*, that presumption can be displaced by 'special facts'.

Exercises

1 Compare and contrast the decisions of the House of Lords in *May and Butcher* v. *R.* and *Hillas* v *Arcos*.

2 List the devices which are available to a court which wishes to avoid the conclusion that an agreement is too uncertain to be enforced.

3 Would there be any advantages in introducing into English law a provision equivalent to section 2-204 of the American Uniform Commercial Code?

4 Distinguish between common mistake and unilateral mistake. Give some examples of the distinction.

5 What is the difference between a contract which has been held to be void and one which has been held to be voidable?

6 Compare and contrast the decisions of the Court of Appeal in *Ingram* v. *Little* and *Lewis* v. *Avery*.

5 Consideration and Form

It is clear that no legal system treats all agreements as enforceable contracts. In every legal system there exist rules which identify the types of agreement that are to be treated as enforceable contracts. The function of these rules is to give what we shall call the 'badge of enforceability' to certain agreements. In English law that function is performed principally by the doctrine of consideration and, to a lesser extent, by a doctrine of formalities. Of course, it could be argued that the rules relating to duress, misrepresentation and illegality play a role in identifying those agreements which are to be treated as enforceable contracts (see Atiyah, 1986c) and, to some extent, this is true. But English law has, historically, viewed the requirements of consideration and form as being separate and distinct from doctrines such as duress and this is the approach which we shall adopt in this chapter.

5.1 Requirements of Form

A legal system may grant the 'badge of enforceability' only to those agreements which are entered into in a certain form. Historically, English law has placed considerable reliance upon requirements of form. The Statute of Frauds 1677 required that certain classes of contracts be evidenced in writing, but most of its provisions were repealed in 1954. Requirements of form are therefore no longer a significant feature of English contract law, except in a residual category of contracts. For example, a lease for more than three years must be under seal (Law of Property Act 1925 ss. 52, 54(2)) and a unilateral gratuitous promise is only enforceable if it is made under seal. Compliance with this requirement is relatively straightforward; a document bearing the word 'seal' or some other indication that it is intended to take effect as a deed under seal must be signed and 'delivered'. However it must be noted that section 1(1)(b) of the Law of Property (Miscellaneous Provisions) Act 1989, which at the time of writing is not yet in force, abolishes sealing as a requirement for the valid execution of an instrument as a deed by an individual, replacing it with a simpler procedure which requires only the signature of the individual, the attestation of that signature and delivery of the deed (ss.1(2), (3)).

Bills of exchange (Bills of Exchange Act 1882 s.3(1)), bills of sale (Bills of Sale Act 1878 (Amendment) Act 1882) and contracts for the sale or other disposition of an interest in land (Law of Property (Miscellaneous

Provisions) Act 1989 s.2, applying to contracts made on or after 27 September 1989) must be made in writing. Contracts of guarantee (Statute of Frauds Act 1677 s.4) must be *evidenced* in writing. However it is vital to note that, apart from the case of contracts entered into under seal, such formal requirements do not replace consideration; they are an additional requirement.

Professor Atiyah has argued that 'insistence on form is widely thought by lawyers to be characteristic of primitive and less well-developed legal systems' (1989, p.172). Yet many major legal systems in the world continue to place heavy reliance upon formal requirements. Many provinces in Canada (see Fridman, 1986) and states in Australia (see Greig and Davis, 1987) are still governed by the Statute of Frauds, either in its original or a modified form. Scotland, which does not have a doctrine of consideration, places great emphasis upon formal requirements. In Scotland many contracts can be constituted in any form and be proved by any form. But certain contracts (*obligationes literis*), of which the principal example is contracts relating to heritage (land and buildings), must be entered into or constituted in writing. Other contracts, such as a contract of loan of a sum of money in excess of £8.33, innominate and unusual contracts and gratuitous obligations, can be created informally but must be proved by the writ or oath of the party alleged to be bound (see McBryde, 1987).

What are the functions of such formal requirements? Professor Fuller (1941) has identified three functions. The first is the evidentiary function; in cases of dispute a formal requirement, such as writing, provides evidence of the existence and content of the contract. For this reason businessmen frequently reduce their contracts to writing, even though it is not mandatory to do so. Secondly, formalities have a cautionary function, 'by acting as a check against inconsiderate action'. A requirement that a contract be under seal impresses upon the parties the importance of the agreement into which they are about to enter. This cautionary function has recently been recognised by Parliament in sections 60 and 61 of the Consumer Credit Act 1974, which provide that a regulated consumer credit agreement is not 'properly executed' unless it complies with certain formal requirements which are designed to ensure, as far as possible, that the consumer is fully informed of the nature and consequences of the agreement before entering into it. Such formal, statutory paternalistic requirements may become an increasingly common feature of English contract law. The third function of formalities is the channelling function, that is to say, formalities provide a simple and external test of enforceability.

On the other hand, requirements of form are attended by considerable disadvantages. In the first place formalities tend to be cumbersome and time-consuming. It would be ridiculous and impractical to insist that every contract be reduced to writing, so that every time I bought my morning newspaper I had to sign a written contract. This leads to a second difficulty which is that, given that it is impractical to apply formal requirements to all contracts, which contracts should be governed by requirements of form? For example, in England contracts of guarantee must be evidenced in writing, but no such requirement applies to contracts of indemnity. Yet the two contracts are very similar and the cases have 'raised many hair-splitting distinctions of exactly that kind which bring the law into hatred, ridicule and contempt by the public' (*Yeoman Credit Ltd* v. *Latter* [1961] 1 WLR 828, 835). Scotland has the anachronistic rule that contracts of loan of over £8.33 must be proved by the writ or oath of the party alleged to be bound. It is extremely difficult, if not impossible, to identify any rational theory which explains why certain contracts are subjected to requirements of form while others are not. It is equally difficult to explain why some contracts must actually be in writing, while others need only be evidenced in writing. Other difficult questions arise. What type of writing is required? Must the contract be signed? What constitutes a signature? These issues have all been the subject of extensive litigation under the Statute of Frauds 1677 (see Treitel, 1987, pp.139–43) and are an inevitable concomitant of a system based upon requirements of form.

A final difficulty created by requirements of form arises where an 'innocent' party has acted to his detriment upon a 'contract' which did not comply with the relevant formalities. A good illustration of the difficulties which can arise is provided by cases relating to s.40(1) of the Law of Property Act 1925 (now repealed by s.2 of the Law of Property (Miscellaneous Provisions) Act 1989, which, interestingly, retains a role for constructive trusts, which will probably play the role developed by the doctrine of part performance in relation to s.40(1) of the 1925 Act). In *Wakeham* v. *Mackenzie* [1968] 1 WLR 1175, the deceased orally promised the plaintiff that he would leave his house to her if she moved into his house and looked after him until his death. She complied with his request but he failed to leave the house to her on his death. Could the plaintiff enforce the oral contract despite the fact that it did not comply with the formal requirements of s.40(1) of the Law of Property Act 1925 (which, it must be remembered, re-enacted part of s.4 of the Statute of Frauds 1677)? At common law the answer was 'no' because the defect in form rendered the contract unenforceable (but not void). But it was held that the contract was enforceable in equity under the doctrine of part performance. The doctrine of part performance was developed by equity in response to the hardships created by a strict application of the Statute of Frauds. The doctrine came into play where the acts of the plaintiff were referable to the alleged contract, it was a fraud for the defendant to rely on the Statute, the contract was specifically enforceable and there was proper evidence of the agreement. All these requirements were satisfied on the facts of *Wakeham*. It was not easy to reconcile the existence of the doctrine of part performance with the Statute of Frauds; in truth, it was incompatible with the Statute but it mitigated the hardships which would otherwise have been caused by its rigorous application.

There is no doubt that there are genuine difficulties experienced by legal systems which place heavy reliance upon requirements of form. But, as we have seen, formalities do perform useful evidentiary and cautionary functions. Although it is highly unlikely that Parliament will ever re-enact the Statute of Frauds, Parliament can usefully continue its practice of imposing requirements of form where it is satisfied that such requirements will 'provide a check against inconsiderate action' (as in the case of ss.60 and 61 of the Consumer Credit Act 1974 (above)). When it does so it can also devise a solution which will protect those who are in need of protection, while ensuring that the formalities do not become a trap for the unwary (see s.127 of the Consumer Credit Act 1974 which, as against the debtor, places severe restrictions upon the enforceability of regulated consumer credit agreements which are not 'properly executed' but otherwise gives the court considerable discretion to reach an appropriate solution).

5.2 Consideration Defined

Having largely rejected formal requirements, English law has developed a doctrine of consideration to play the principal role in selecting those agreements to be given the 'badge of enforceability'. However the basis of the doctrine of consideration has been a battleground for leading contract scholars in recent years. The orthodox interpretation of consideration is that it is based upon the idea of 'reciprocity'; that a promisee should not be able to enforce a promise unless he has given or promised to give something in exchange for the promise or unless the promisor has obtained (or been promised) something in return. The classic definition was expressed in *Currie* v. *Misa* (1875) LR 10 Ex 153, in the following terms:

> 'a valuable consideration, in the sense of the law, may consist either in some right, interest, profit or benefit accruing to the one party, or some forbearance, detriment, loss or responsibility given, suffered or undertaken by the other'.

However, this orthodox interpretation has been subjected to a powerful challenge by Professor Atiyah (1986c). Atiyah argues that there is no coherent doctrine of consideration based upon reciprocity. He states that

> 'the truth is that the courts have never set out to create a doctrine of consideration. They have been concerned with the much more practical problem of deciding in the course of litigation whether a particular promise in a particular case should be enforced . . . When the courts found a sufficient reason for enforcing a promise they enforced it; and when they found that for one reason or another it was undesirable to enforce a promise, they did not enforce it. It seems highly probable that when the courts first used the word "consideration" they meant no

more than there was a "reason" for the enforcement of a promise. If the consideration was "good", this meant that the court found sufficient reason for enforcing the promise.'

Professor Treitel has, in turn, launched a vigorous counter-attack on Atiyah's thesis. Treitel argues (1987) that English law does, in fact, recognise the existence of a 'complex and multifarious body of rules known as the "doctrine of consideration" '. He rejects the argument that consideration means a reason for the enforcement of a promise and maintains (1976) that such a proposition is a 'negation of the existence of any applicable rules of law' because it does not tell us the circumstances in which the courts will find the existence of such a 'good reason'.

Yet even Treitel has to admit (1976) that in some cases the courts have 'invented' consideration, that is to say the courts 'have treated some act of forbearance as consideration quite irrespective of the question whether *the parties* have so regarded it'. This concession is necessary if the cases are to be reconciled with the traditional theory. Atiyah argues (1986c) that 'Professor Treitel has himself invented the concept of an invented consideration because he finds it the only way in which he is able to reconcile many decisions with what he takes to be the "true" or "real" doctrine'. Although Atiyah challenges the orthodox interpretation of consideration, he does recognise that the presence of 'benefit or detriment is normally a good reason for enforcing a promise'. But, he argues, '[it] does not in the least follow that the presence of benefit or detriment is always a sufficient reason for enforcing a promise; nor does it follow that there may not be other very good reasons for enforcing a promise'.

The difference between the two schools of thought is that Treitel adheres to the benefit/detriment analysis (suitably expanded to encompass cases of 'invented consideration') while Atiyah maintains that there are other 'good reasons' for the enforcement of a promise. In the remaining sections of this chapter we shall consider whether the cases can be accommodated within a 'benefit/detriment' analysis or whether there are, as Atiyah argues, other reasons which support the enforcement of promises.

5.3   Consideration and Motive

Before we enter into a discussion of the substance of the doctrine of consideration, one further preliminary point must be made. That point relates to the distinction between consideration and motive. In *Thomas* v. *Thomas* (1842) 2 QB 851, a testator, shortly before he died, expressed the desire that his widow should have the house for the rest of her life. After his death, his executors promised to carry out the testator's desire provided that the widow paid £1 per annum towards the ground rent and kept the house in repair. Now, although the testator's desire was the motive for the transaction, that desire was not the consideration; rather, the consideration was the widow's promise to pay £1 and to keep the house in good repair. It was only the latter which was of value in the eyes of the law.

5.4 The Scope of the Doctrine

The rules which make up the doctrine of consideration may be divided into three categoories. The first is that consideration must be sufficient but it need not be adequate (see 5.5–5.12), the second is that past consideration is not good consideration (5.14) and the third is that consideration must move from the promisee (5.15). Once we have ascertained the scope of the doctrine of consideration, we shall consider the extent to which the law of contract protects those who rely to their detriment upon promises which are not supported by consideration (5.16–5.24).

5.5 Consideration Must Be Sufficient But It Need Not Be Adequate

The first rule of the doctrine of consideration is that consideration must be sufficient but it need not be adequate. That is to say, the courts will not enforce a promise unless something which the law regards as being of value is given in return for the promise. This is what is meant by saying that consideration must be 'sufficient'. On the other hand, the courts do not, in general, ask whether adequate value has been given in return for the promise or whether the agreement is harsh or one-sided (although here a significant role is played by the doctrines of duress and undue influence, on which see Chapter 17). This is what is meant by saying that consideration need not be 'adequate'. So if a house worth £160 000 is sold for £1 that is sufficient consideration, even though it is manifestly inadequate. In the following sections (5.6–5.14) we shall discuss in greater detail the scope of the rule that consideration must be sufficient but that it need not be adequate.

5.6 Trivial Acts

The maxim that consideration must be sufficient but need not be adequate has resulted in very trivial acts being held to constitute consideration. The classic illustration is *Chappel & Co* v. *Nestle* [1960] AC 87. Nestle offered for sale gramophone records in return for 1/6d and three wrappers from their chocolate bars. The House of Lords held that the wrappers themselves, although of very trivial economic value, were nevertheless part of the consideration. This was so even though Nestle threw away the wrappers. As Lord Somervell said:

> 'a contracting party can stipulate for what consideration he chooses. A peppercorn does not cease to be good consideration if it is established that the promisee does not like pepper and will throw away the corn'.

Atiyah has argued (1986c) that this case does not fit within the 'benefit/detriment' analysis because it would be 'ridiculous to assert that the sending or the receipt of the wrappers necessarily involved an actual detriment to the sender or a benefit to the defendants'. He argues that the receipt of the wrappers was not a benefit but was the motive which inspired the promise and that therefore this was a case in which a court would have enforced a promise despite the lack of benefit to the promisee. Treitel has replied (1976) by asserting that Atiyah has failed to take account of the principle that the courts will not investigate the adequacy of the consideration and that, once it is realised that consideration need only be of *some* value, 'there is no doctrinal difficulty in holding that a piece of paper or some act of forbearance of a very small value can constitute consideration'.

The crucial question which must now be asked is: what does the law of contract recognise as 'value'? Professor Treitel has stated (1987) that consideration must have 'some economic value', even though that value cannot be 'precisely quantified'. But, as we shall see, the courts have not adopted a consistent approach to the identification of 'value' or 'benefit'. In some cases (such as *Stilk* v. *Myrick*, below, 5.10), they have ignored a factual benefit obtained by the promisor and held that no consideration was provided. In other cases (such as *Cook* v. *Wright*, below 5.8), the courts have found the existence of consideration despite the apparent lack of either benefit to the promisor or detriment to the promisee. Some cases have adopted an extremely subjective interpretation of benefit (see, for example, *Bainbridge* v. *Firmstone* (1838) 8 A & E 743), but in other cases the courts have adopted an objective interpretation (see, for example, *White* v. *Bluett*, below 5.7). One of the most difficult tasks in analysing the doctrine of consideration is to stabilise the concept of value or benefit (see further 5.13).

5.7 Intangible Returns

It is clear that 'natural affection of itself is not a sufficient consideration' (*Bret* v. *JS* (1600) Cro Eliz 756). Thus, in *White* v. *Bluett* (1853) 23 LJ Ex 36, a son's promise not to bore his father with complaints about the father's distribution of his property among his children was held not to be good consideration for the father's promise not to sue the son on a debt owed by the son to the father. Pollock CB said that the son had 'no right to complain' because it was for the father to decide how he wanted to distribute his property. But, on the other hand, the son was doing nothing wrong in complaining to his father, so in that sense he did have a 'right' to complain.

White should be contrasted, however, with the American case of *Hamer* v. *Sidway* (1891) 27 NE 256. An uncle promised to pay his nephew $5000 if the nephew refrained from 'drinking liquor, using tobacco, swearing and playing cards or billiards for money' until he (the nephew) was 21. This promise was held to be enforceable because the nephew had a legal right to engage in such activities and, in giving up his rights, he had provided consideration for the promise. Professor Atiyah has argued (1986c) that *Hamer* is a case which does not fit within the 'benefit/detriment' analysis because there was no benefit to the uncle (apart from the fact that he wanted his nephew to abstain from such practices, but that is a matter of motive, not benefit), nor was there a detriment to the nephew (on the ground that giving up smoking is a benefit rather than a detriment). Rather, Atiyah argues, this is a case in which the nephew was induced to act on the promise and the court thought it just to enforce the promise. But the court did not perceive matters in this way. It was of the opinion that the nephew had incurred a detriment because he had 'restricted' his lawful freedom of action within certain prescribed limits upon the faith of the uncle's agreement (see too Treitel, 1976).

Although *Hamer* is an American case it is generally assumed that it represents English law (see Beale, Bishop and Furmston, 1985), but it is not easy to reconcile with *White*. It may be that the promise of the son in *White* was too uncertain to constitute consideration for the father's promise (Anson, 1984, p.90) or it may be the case that the activities of the son in *White* were thought to be less socially valuable and therefore less deserving of protection than the conduct of the nephew in *Hamer*. Whatever the precise ground of distinction, a limitation upon the principle in *Hamer* is that, if the nephew had never intended to drink, smoke, swear or gamble because, for example, he had a religious objection to engaging in such practices, then he could not have enforced his uncle's promise. This is because 'it is not consideration to refrain from a course of conduct which it was never intended to pursue' (*Arrale* v. *Costain Civil Engineering Ltd* [1976] 1 Lloyds Rep 98, 106).

5.8 Compromise and Forbearance to Sue

A promise not to enforce a valid claim is good consideration for a promise given in return, as is a promise not to enforce a claim which is doubtful in law. On the other hand, it is clear that a promise not to enforce a claim which is known to be invalid is not good consideration for a promise given in return (*Wade* v. *Simeon* (1846) 2 CB 548). The difficulty lies in the case where the claim is clearly bad in law but is believed by the promisee to be good. In *Cook* v. *Wright* (1861) 1 B & S 559, the plaintiffs honestly believed that the defendant was under a statutory obligation to reimburse them in respect of certain expenditure which they had incurred in work on a street adjoining the house in which the defendant was residing. The defendant denied that he was under such an obligation, but he eventually promised to pay a reduced sum after he was threatened with litigation if he did not pay. When the defendant discovered that he was not in fact under a statutory obligation to pay, he refused to honour his promise. He maintained that his promise was not supported by consideration because the plaintiffs had given nothing in return for it. But the court held that the promise was supported by consideration and that he was liable to pay the sum promised. Nevertheless it is difficult to find the consideration supplied by the plaintiffs. They had given up an invalid claim and in so doing they had suffered no detriment and the defendant was not benefited in any way by their promise to accept the reduced sum in full satisfaction of their invalid claim. It could be argued that the plaintiffs' honest belief in the validity of their claim provided the consideration. But consideration must actually be of value in the eyes of the law and not merely something believed to be of value by the parties. Alternatively, it could be argued that the defendant benefited because he escaped the vexation which is inherent in litigation. Such a rationale proves too much because it would apply equally where the claim was known to be bad, and yet we know from *Wade* v. *Simeon* (above) that a promise not to enforce a claim which is known to be bad is not good consideration for a promise given in return (unless it is possible to confine *Wade* v. *Simeon* on public policy grounds, namely that proceedings should not be instituted where the claim is known to be a bad one). *Cook* is therefore a case which is very difficult to accommodate within the 'benefit/detriment' analysis (although it should be noted that Treitel (1976) includes the case within his category of 'invented' consideration).

5.9 Performance of a Duty Imposed by Law

The general rule is that performance of a duty imposed by law is not good consideration for a promise given in return (*Collins* v. *Godefroy* (1831) 1 B & Ad 950). The general rule can be supported on the ground that it prevents public officials extorting money in return for the performance of their existing legal duties. But in other cases the rule can give rise to hardship because it ignores real benefits obtained by the promisor or real detriments incurred by the promisee.

In *Ward* v. *Byham* [1956] 1 WLR 496, the father of an illegitimate child promised to pay the mother of the child £1 per week provided that the child was well looked after and happy. The mother was under a legal duty to look after the child. The mother sued the father when he stopped making payments. The father argued that the mother had not provided any consideration for his promise because, by looking after the child, she was simply carrying out her existing legal duty. Denning LJ rejected this argument and launched a direct assault on the general rule. He held that the mother provided consideration by performing her legal duty to support the child. He stated that the father was benefited by the mother's promise to look after the child, just as he would have been benefited if a neighbour had promised to look after the child for reward. Lord Denning returned to this theme in *Williams* v. *Williams* [1957] 1 WLR 148, when he said:

'a promise to perform an existing duty is, I think, sufficient consideration to support a promise, so long as there is nothing in the transaction which is contrary to the public interest.'

Although this statement of principle has much to commend it, the majority of the Court of Appeal in *Ward* did not agree with it. Rather, they affirmed that performance of an existing legal duty does not constitute consideration, but they found consideration in the fact that the mother had promised to do more than her legal duty by promising to keep the child 'happy'. There is no doubt that a promise to do more than one is legally obliged to do is good consideration (*Glasbrook Ltd* v. *Glamorgan CC* [1925] AC 270). But there must be some doubt about the application of this rule to the facts of *Ward* because it could only be said that the mother did more than she was legally obliged to do by promising to keep the child 'happy'. Yet we have already noted that natural affection of itself is not a sufficient consideration (*Bret* v. *JS*, discussed at 5.7). Despite these doubts about the majority judgment in *Ward*, it must be conceded that the general rule remains that performance of an existing legal duty does not constitute consideration.

5.10 Performance of a Contractual Duty Owed to the Promisor

The general rule is that the performance of an existing contractual duty owed to the promisor is no consideration for a fresh promise given by the promisor. This rule can be illustrated by reference to the case of *Stilk* v. *Myrick* (1809) 2 Camp 317 and 6 Esp 129. Stilk was a seaman who agreed with the defendants to sail to the Baltic and back at a rate of pay of £5 per month. Originally, there were 11 men in the crew, but two men deserted during the voyage. The master was unable to find replacements for the deserters and so he agreed with the remainder of the crew that he would share the wages of the two deserters between them if they would work the ship back to London. The crew members agreed. When they returned to London, Stilk demanded his share of the money, but the master refused to pay. Stilk sued for the money. He was unsuccessful in his claim. The case was reported twice and, unfortunately, the two reports differ as to the reason for the failure of Stilk's claim.

In the Espinasse report Stilk was unsuccessful on grounds of policy; the policy ground being that a successful claim would open up the prospect of sailors on the high seas making unreasonable and extortionate demands upon their masters as the price for performing their contractual duty to bring the ship back to the home port. In Campbell's report Stilk's claim failed, not on grounds of policy, but because he had provided no consideration for the master's promise as he had only done what he was already contractually obliged to do. The difference between these two reports is crucial. If the former report is correct, it is possible to confine the rule to cases where there is a possibility of duress being exercised. Where such fear is absent, there is no objection to the enforcement of the promise. However Espinasse is not highly regarded as a law reporter and it is the second, wider rule derived from Campbell's report which has been accepted into English law (see *North Ocean Shipping Co* v. *Hyundai Construction Co* [1979] QB 705).

Professor Atiyah argues that cases such as *Stilk and Ward* v. *Byham* (above, 5.9) cannot be accommodated within the 'benefit/detriment' analysis because this time, as a matter of fact, there is a benefit to the promisor and a detriment to the promisee, but nevertheless there is no consideration. In *Stilk* there is no doubt that, as a matter of fact, the master of the ship was benefited by Stilk's promise to work the ship back home, yet the court concluded that no consideration had been provided. Those who adopt the orthodox interpretation of consideration attempt to meet this argument by asserting that it is legal benefit or legal detriment which is important and not factual benefit or factual detriment (see Treitel, 1987). But, as Corbin has pointed out (1963), this does not explain *why* the courts have resorted to the concepts of legal benefit and detriment.

Whatever the answer to Corbin's question, it is clear that the rule in *Stilk* as described in Campbell's report does not apply in two situations. The first is where the promisee has done, or has promised to do, more than he was obliged to do under his contract. In *Hanson* v. *Royden* (1867) LR 3 CP 47, the plaintiff was promoted from able seaman to second mate and it was held that, in carrying out the job of second mate, he had done more than he was obliged to do under his contract and so had provided consideration for the promise of extra pay. The second situation arises where, before the new promise was made, circumstances had arisen which entitled the promisee to refuse to carry out his obligations under his contract. In *Hartley* v. *Ponsonby* (1857) 7 E & B 872, 17 of a crew of 36 deserted and only four or five of the remaining crew were able seamen. The desertion of such a large proportion of the crew rendered it unsafe to continue the voyage and would have entitled the remaining seamen to abandon the voyage. The seamen agreed to continue the voyage on being promised extra pay on its completion. The master refused to fulfil his promise on their return to the home port but it was held that the seamen were entitled to enforce the master's promise because, in agreeing to continue with the voyage when they were not obliged by the terms of their contract to do so, they had provided consideration.

5.11 Part Payment of a Debt

A close relation of the rule that performance of an existing contractual duty owed to the promisor does not constitute consideration is the rule that a promise to accept part payment of a debt in discharge of the entire debt is not supported by consideration. The debtor is already contractually obliged to repay the entire debt and so provides no consideration for the creditor's promise to accept part payment (unless, for example, the debtor agrees to repay the debt at an earlier date, in which case he does provide coonsideratiion). This rule can be traced back to *Pinnel's case* (1602) 5 Co Rep 117a, and was upheld by the House of Lords in *Foakes* v. *Beer* (1884) 9 App Cas 605. In *Foakes* a creditor promised to abandon her claim to interest on the debt but it was held that her promise to forbear was unsupported by consideration. Although such an agreement is not supported by consideration, in many cases a creditor will, as a matter of fact, be benefited by receipt of part payment because, in the words of Corbin (1963), 'a bird in the hand is worth much more than a bird in the bush'. This is another example of a court concluding that a promise is unsupported by consideration, despite the presence of a factual benefit to the promisor (this rule is the subject of numerous common law limitations; see Treitel, 1987, pp.97–100 and for the equitable evasions of this rule see 5.21).

5.12 Performance of a Duty Imposed by Contract with a Third Party

Despite the rule that performance of an existing contractual duty owed to a promisor is not good consideration, performance of a contractual duty owed to a third party does constitute good consideration. In *Shadwell* v. *Shadwell* (1860) 9 CB (NS) 159, the plaintiff, who was engaged to EN, received a letter from his uncle, in which the uncle promised to pay the plaintiff £150 per year after he was married. The plaintiff sued to enforce the promise and it was held that he could do so because he had provided consideration for his uncle's promise by marrying EN (the nephew was at the time contractually bound to marry EN). The proposition that performance of a contractual duty owed to a third party can constitute consideration has recently been affirmed by the House of Lords in *The Eurymedon* [1975] AC 154 (see 7.6 for a full discussion of this case).

In *Jones* v. *Waite* (1839) 5 Bing NC 341 it was held that a promise to perform (as opposed to actual performance of) a contractual duty owed to a third party did not constitute consideration. But in Scotson *v.* Pegg (1861) 6 H & N 295 and *Pao On* v. *Lau Yiu Long* [1980] AC 614 it was held that such a promise could constitute consideration and the latter view is the one which is accepted by most scholars. There does not seem to be any rational theory which is capable of explaining why performance of an existing contractual duty owed to a third party can constitute consideration when performance of an existing contractual duty owed to a promisor does not constitute consideration (although it should be noted that both *Shadwell* v. *Shadwell* and *Scotson* v. *Pegg* are treated by Treitel (1976) as examples of 'invented' consideration).

5.13 Conceptions of Value

It can readily be seen from the cases which we have discussed that the courts adopt an inconsistent approach to the identification of a benefit or detriment. In *Stilk* v. *Myrick* the court ignored an obvious factual benefit to the promisor. Yet in *Cook* v. *Wright*, *Shadwell* v. *Shadwell* and *Scotson* v. *Pegg* the court found the existence of consideration upon the flimsiest of evidence. It will not do to say, as does Professor Treitel, that in some cases the courts have 'invented' consideration because that does not tell us why they have invented consideration, nor does it tell us when they are likely to invent it again in the future. Nevertheless it must be conceded that the courts do tend to employ the language of 'benefit' and 'detriment'. But their use of 'benefit' and 'detriment' is inconsistent, which suggests that, on occasions, the courts do, as Atiyah argues, enforce a promise because there was a 'good reason' so to do. The conclusion must be that the English courts have built a theory of consideration upon the foundations of benefit and detriment without subjecting to stringent analysis the coherency of their conceptions of benefit and detriment (see further Atiyah, 1986c).

5.14 Past Consideration

If I promise to reward you for acts which you have already performed prior to my promise, the general rule is that you cannot enforce my promise because the consideration which you have provided is past. By 'past consideration' lawyers mean that your consideration was already completed before I made my promise, so that you have not given anything new in return for my promise. The rule that past consideration is not good consideration is closely linked to the bargain theory of consideration. The fatal objection is that there is no reciprocity; the promisee does not give anything in return for the promise of the promisor.

It follows from this that, as a general rule, if two parties have already made a binding contract and one of them subsequently promises to confer an additional benefit on the other party to the contract, that promise is not binding because the promisee's consideration, which is his entry into the original contract, is past. In *Roscorla* v. *Thomas* (1842) 3 QB 234, the defendant agreed to sell a horse to the plaintiff. Shortly afterwards the defendant added a promise that he would give a warranty as to the soundness of the horse. It was held that the defendant's promise was unenforceable because the only consideration which the plaintiff had provided was his entry into the original contract of sale and that consideration was past. However, the courts do have some degree of latitude in applying this rule and do not always take a strictly chronological view of the sequence of events. If the court is satisfied that the new promise and the act of the promisee which is alleged to be the past consideration are, in fact, part of the same overall transaction, the exact order in which the events occurred will not be decisive (*Thornton* v. *Jenkyns* (1840) 1 Man & G 166). In identifying whether consideration is actually past or not, the courts look, not to the wording of the contract, but to the actual sequence of events. Thus in *Re McArdle* [1951] Ch 669, a promise made 'in consideration of your carrying out' certain work was held to be unenforceable as the consideration for it was past. Although the wording of the contract suggested that the work was to be done at some future time it had, as a matter of fact, been done prior to the making of the contract and was therefore past.

The rule as to past consideration is a harsh one. In *Eastwood* v. *Kenyon* (1840) 11 A & E 438, the guardian of a young girl raised a loan to educate the girl and to improve her marriage prospects. After her marriage, her husband promised to pay off the loan. It was held that the guardian was unable to enforce this promise because the consideration which he had provided, which was bringing up and financing the girl, was past. The court conceded that the husband might have been under a moral obligation to pay, but that moral obligation could not be converted into a legal obligation because of the absence of consideration.

The harshness of the past consideration rule has been mitigated to some extent by the doctrine of implied assumpsit. Where the act of the promisee was performed at the request of the promisor and, subsequent to the performance of the act by the promisee, the promisor promises to pay for it, then such a promise may be enforceable. An early example is *Lampleigh* v. *Brathwait* (1615) Hob 105. The defendant, who was under sentence of death, requested the plaintiff to ride to Newark to obtain a pardon from King James I. The plaintiff did so. The defendant then promised to pay the plaintiff £1000. It was held that the plaintiff could enforce the contract. But the doctrine of implied assumpsit operates within narrow confines. The Privy Council, in *Pao On* v. *Lau Yiu Long* [1980] AC 614, held that three conditions must be satisfied by a promisee who wishes to invoke the doctrine. The first is that he must have performed the original act at the *request* of the promisor. The second is that it must have been clearly understood or implied between the parties when the act was originally requested that the promisee would be rewarded for doing the act. The third is that the eventual promise of payment after the act was completed must be one which, had it been made prior to or at the time of the act, would have been enforceable.

Parliament has also intervened to mitigate the hardships caused by the past consideration rule by providing that an antecedent debt or liability is good consideration for a bill of exchange (Bills of Exchange Act 1882 s.27(1)(b)) and by providing that a written acknowledgement of a debt by a debtor shall be deemed to have accrued on and not before the date of acknowledgement (Limitation Act 1980 s.27(5)).

5.15 Consideration Must Move from the Promisee

A person to whom a promise is made can only enforce the promise if he himself provides consideration for the promise. If the consideration is provided by a third party, the promisee cannot enforce the promise (*Tweddle* v. *Atkinson* (1861) 1 B & S 393, discussed further at 7.1).

5.16 Reliance Upon Non-bargain Promises

A plaintiff who is able to establish the existence of consideration can, absent any other vitiating factors, bring an action on the contract to enforce the defendant's promise. But what of the plaintiff who relies to his detriment upon a promise of the defendant which is not supported by consideration? Can he enforce that promise or recover compensation for the extent to which he has detrimentally relied upon it? Once again the debate between Treitel and Atiyah assumes enormous significance. If Treitel is correct, and consideration is built upon reciprocity, then such a promise cannot be enforced because of the lack of consideration (although more limited effect may be given to the promise). But, if Atiyah is correct and consideration means a reason for the enforcement of a promise, then such a promise may be enforceable where the court can find a 'good reason' for its enforcement.

A factual situation which will provide a useful background to our discussion of these issues is provided by the American case of *Ricketts* v. *Scothorn* 57 Neb 51 (1898). Scothorn was at work when her grandfather gave her a promissory note under which he promised to pay her $2000 at 6 per cent per annum. On giving her the promissory note he told her that none of his other grandchildren worked and now 'you don't have to'. Scothorn gave up work in reliance upon his promise but, when her grandfather died, his executors refused to honour his promise. Could she enforce the promise? Her claim does appear to be a just one because she acted to her detriment in reliance upon the promise. But how do we reconcile such a claim with the doctrine of consideration which, as we have seen, requires that something of value be given in return for the promise? Two possible arguments suggest themselves. The first is that Scothorn did, in fact, provide consideration by giving up her work. The second is to challenge the rule that a promise is unenforceable if it is unsupported by consideration. It may seem rather odd to canvass the first argument when purporting to discuss reliance upon promises which are unsupported by consideration. But plaintiffs do, as a matter of practice, attempt to bring themselves within the fold of the doctrine of consideration before embarking upon the more hazardous task of seeking to persuade a court to enforce a promise which is unsupported by consideration. The issues are also related because the wider the scope of the doctrine of consideration, the less need there is to find a substitute for consideration.

5.17 The Role of Consideration

We have already seen that consideration is a rather elastic doctrine and that the courts have scope to 'invent' consideration. Could a court not find or invent consideration in a case such as *Ricketts*? The difficulty is that the grandfather did not request Scothorn to give up her work and so there does not appear to be any bargain under which she promised to give up work in return for the promised sum of money. But could we not imply such a bargain? After all, the grandfather must have known that Scothorn would be likely to give up work as a result of his promise. Should a court not imply that, where it is foreseeable to a promisor that a promisee will act to her detriment in reliance upon his promise, the reliance of the promisee is at the request of the promisor and so constitutes consideration?

Such an approach was, however, rejected by the English Court of Appeal in *Combe* v. *Combe* [1951] 2 KB 215. A husband promised to pay his wife £100 per annum on their separation. The husband did not make any of the payments and six years later the wife brought an action to recover the arrears. She argued that she had supplied consideration for her husband's promise because she had refrained from applying to court for a permanent maintenance order. But the Court of Appeal held that there was no request, express or implied, by the husband that the wife should refrain from applying to the court for maintenance. Therefore no consideration was provided for the husband's promise and it was unenforceable.

But there were facts in *Combe* upon which the court could have implied a request by the husband that the wife forbear from applying for maintenance (see Goodhart, 1951 and 1953, but contrast the alternative explanation of the case put forward by Denning, 1952, p.2). Indeed, cases can be found in which a court has been prepared to make such an implication. For example, in *Alliance Bank* v. *Broom* (1864) 2 Dr & Sm 289, the defendant owed £22 000 to the plaintiff bank. The bank demanded some security for the loan and this was promised by the defendant. The defendant failed to honour his promise and, when the bank sought to enforce it, he argued that his promise was not supported by consideration and was therefore unenforceable. The court held that the promise was enforceable because, as a result of the defendant's promise, the plaintiffs had refrained from suing him to recover the debt and the defendant had therefore received 'the benefit of some degree of forbearance' (contrast *Miles* v. *New Zealand Alford Estate Co* (1886) 32 Ch D 267). Although the defendant had not expressly requested the plaintiff to forbear, the court felt able to imply such a request. But why did the court imply a request on the facts of *Allied Bank* but not in *Combe*? The answer to that question is unclear. It could be argued that the bank in *Allied Bank* was much more likely to institute proceedings than was the wife in *Combe* and therefore it was easier for the court to imply such a request. Alternatively, it could be argued that the reason for the court's refusal to imply a request on the facts of *Combe* was that the 'justice of the case [did] not require that it should be' implied because the wife had an income in excess of that of her husband and she had delayed for six years in bringing her action (see Atiyah, 1986c). Whatever the precise ground of distinction between the two cases, it is clear that the courts do have considerable discretion in implying such a request. The readier they are to find a request, the wider will be the scope of the doctrine of consideration and hence the need to find a substitute for consideration will be radically diminished.

5.18 Estoppel

Where, as in *Ricketts* and *Combe*, the court is unable to find the existence of consideration, can the promise be enforced despite the absence of consideration? The orthodox answer is that such a promise will not be enforced. But limited effects may be given to the promise under the doctrine of estoppel. The essential ingredients of estoppel were defined by Lord Birkenhead in *Maclaine* v. *Gatty* [1921] 1 AC 376, 386, in the following terms:

> 'where A has by his words or conduct justified B in believing that a certain state of facts exists, and B has acted upon such belief to his prejudice, A is not permitted to affirm against B that a different state of facts existed at the same time'.

But the picture is in fact more complicated than this quotation from the judgment of Lord Birkenhead would suggest. In the first place Lord Birkenhead was referring to estoppel by representation but, under the umbrella of 'estoppel', there are, in fact, many distinct doctrines: estoppel by representation, promissory estoppel, proprietary estoppel, estoppel by convention and related doctrines such as waiver and variation. It is not easy to identify the relationship between these different types of estoppel. The second difficulty lies in ascertaining whether there is a single unifying principle which unites them (see Jackson, 1982). The final difficulty lies in discerning the relationship between estoppel and the doctrine of consideration.

The latter point needs some amplification before we embark upon an analysis of the leading cases. If the courts were to hold that a promise was enforceable simply because a promisee had acted upon it to his detriment, then a great hole would be blown in the doctrine of consideration. But, as Denning LJ stated in *Combe* v. *Combe* (above), 'the doctrine of consideration is too firmly fixed to be overthrown by a side-wind'. So estoppel must be reconciled with consideration. The reconciliation achieved by the courts is a rather uneasy one and is summed up in the well-worn maxim that estoppel can be used as a 'shield but not as a sword'. This means that estoppel cannot be used to create a new cause of action. The estoppel must relate to the existing legal rights of the promisor; that is to say, there must be a pre-existing legal relationship between the parties under which the promisor promises to give up some of his rights under that relationship. The effect of the estoppel is to prevent the promisor going back on his promise where the promisee has acted upon it to his detriment. But where there is no pre-existing legal relationship between the parties, as in *Combe* v. *Combe*, then the promisee cannot invoke estoppel because such an estoppel would create a completely new cause of action. To permit an estoppel to create a new cause of action would, on traditional analysis, undermine the doctrine of consideration. In the remaining sections of this chapter we shall consider the orthodox cases in which estoppel is used as a 'shield'. We shall then discuss some cases in which it has been sought to use estoppel as a 'sword', and conclude by analysing the relationship between these cases and the doctrine of consideration.

5.19 Estoppel by Representation

Estoppel clearly acts as a shield in the case of estoppel by representation. The basic principle is that a person who makes a representation of existing fact which induces the other party to act to his detriment in reliance on the representation will not be permitted subsequently to act inconsistently with that representation. It is a rule of evidence which *permanently* prevents a representor from averring or proving facts which are contrary to his own representation (see *Avon County Council* v. *Howlett* [1983] 1 WLR 603, 622, per Slade LJ). There are two particular features of this estoppel. First, the representation must be one of fact. This limitation was initially established at common law, but was extended to its equitable counterpart in the controversial decision of the House of Lords in *Jorden* v. *Money* (1854) 5 HL Cas 185. Therefore the doctrine does not apply to representations of law or intention. Although the courts have shown some inclination to construe a representation of fact from what appears to be a statement of intention (see Thompson, 1983), a promise is clearly beyond the scope of the doctrine. The second feature of this type of estoppel is that it operates as a defence; it does not create a cause of action. In *Avon County Council* v. *Howlett* (above) the defendant was overpaid by his employers, the plaintiffs. They sought to recover the money as paid under a mistake of fact. The defendant argued that the plaintiffs were estopped from pursuing their claim because they had made a representation of fact to him that he was entitled to the money and he had spent money in reliance upon their representation. The Court of Appeal upheld the defendant's argument. The effect of the estoppel was to act as a 'shield' and to defeat a claim which would otherwise have succeeded.

5.20 Waiver and Variation

The role of estoppel as a shield can also be seen in cases where contracting parties agree to modify or abandon an existing contract. A preliminary point must be made here, which is that consideration applies to the discharge or variation of a contract as well as to its formation. Where the discharge or variation is capable of benefiting either contracting party then the variation or discharge is supported by consideration and is enforceable (*WJ Alan & Co Ltd* v. *El Nasr Export and Import Co* [1972] 2 QB 189). But where the variation or discharge can confer a legal benefit upon only one contracting party then the agreement is not supported by consideration. The classic example is the creditor who agrees to accept part payment of a debt in discharge of the entire debt (5.11). In such a case the variation can only operate to the benefit of the debtor and so is unsupported by consideration.

A variation which is unsupported by consideration has no contractual effect. But effect may be given to a promise to forgo rights under the doctrine of waiver. A variety of meanings have been attributed to the word 'waiver' (see Dugdale and Yates, 1976) and the present scope of the doctrine is a matter of some uncertainty. Part of that uncertainty is due to the fact that waiver appears to have been subsumed within the larger doctrine of equitable or promissory estoppel (see, for example, *Prosper Homes* v. *Hambro's Bank Executor & Trustee Co* (1979) 39 P & CR 395, 401). So we shall consider the elements of waiver within our discussion of promissory estoppel. Here it is sufficient to give one example of the operation of the doctrine of waiver.

In *Hickman* v. *Haynes* (1875) LR 10 CP 598, the parties entered into a contract for the sale of goods. The buyer subsequently requested the seller to delay the delivery of the goods. The seller agreed and tendered delivery on the later date, but the buyer refused to accept delivery. The seller brought an action for damages against the buyer, who argued that the seller could not succeed because he was in breach of contract in failing to deliver on time. The court held that the buyer had waived his right to demand delivery on time and that he could not subsequently reassert it without the giving of reasonable notice (see on the giving of reasonable notice *Charles Rickard Ltd* v. *Oppenhaim* [1950] 1 KB 616). It should be noted that, in contrast to *Avon County Council* v. *Howlett* (above), the estoppel in *Hickman* was invoked by the *plaintiff* and the effect of the waiver was to enable a claim to succeed which otherwise would have failed. But the estoppel did not create a new cause of action; the parties were in a pre-existing contractual relationship and the effect of the estoppel was simply to prevent the buyer from going back upon his representation.

5.21 Promissory Estoppel

As we have already noted, there is a very close relationship between the doctrines of waiver and promissory (or equitable) estoppel. The leading case on promissory estoppel is *Hughes* v. *Metropolitan Railway Co* (1877) 2 App Cas 439. A landlord gave six months' notice to a tenant, requiring him to carry out certain repairs. The tenant responded by inquiring whether the landlord wished to purchase his interest in the premises for £3000. The landlord entered into negotiations for the purchase of the lease but, when these negotiations broke down, he sought to forfeit the lease because the tenant had not carried out the repairs within six months of his original notice. The House of Lords held that the tenant was entitled to equitable relief against forfeiture of the lease on the ground that the running of the six month period was suspended during the negotiations to purchase the lease and did not recommence until the negotiations broke down.

Hughes lay in obscurity for many years until it was resurrected by Denning J in the famous case of *Central London Property Trust Ltd* v. *High Trees House Ltd* [1947] KB 130. In 1937 the plaintiffs let a block of flats in London to the defendants on a 99-year lease at an annual rent of £2500. In 1940 the defendants discovered that, as a result of the outbreak of war and the evacuation of people from London, they were unable to let many of the flats. So the plaintiffs agreed to reduce the rent to £1250. This promise to accept a reduced rent was unsupported by consideration. At the end of the war in 1945 the property market had returned to normal and the flats were fully let. The plaintiffs demanded that the defendants resume payment of the entire rent from 1945, but the defendants refused to pay. Denning J held that the plaintiffs were entitled to demand the entire rent from the date of their notice in 1945. The interest of this case lies in his broad statement of the scope of promissory estoppel:

> 'where, by words or conduct, a person makes an unambiguous representation as to his future conduct, intending the representation to be relied on and to affect the legal relations between the parties, and the representee alters his position in reliance on it, the representor will be unable to act inconsistently with the representation if by so doing the representee would be prejudiced'.

This definition of promissory estoppel can be divided into five elements.

The first is that there must be a promise or a representation as to future conduct which is intended to affect the legal relations between the parties and which indicates that the promisor will not insist on his strict legal rights against the promisee. The promise or representation must be clear and unequivocal so that the promisor does not lose his rights simply because he has failed throughout to insist upon strict performance of the contract by the promisee. Although this requirement originated in estoppel by representation, it has since been extended to cases of promissory estoppel and waiver.

The second element is that the promise or representation must have been relied upon by the promisee. There are dicta which suggest that the promisee must have acted to his 'detriment' in reliance upon the promise but the better view is that it is sufficient to show that the promisee committed himself to a course of action which he would not otherwise have adopted. The third requirement is that it must be 'inequitable' for the promisor to go back upon his promise. This will usually be satisfied by demonstrating that the promisee has acted in reliance upon the promise (however, see *The Post Chaser* [1981] 2 Lloyds Rep 693, where the promisee acted in reliance upon the promise but could not show that it was 'inequitable' for the promisor to go back upon his promise).

The fourth element is that the effect of promissory estoppel is generally suspensory; it does not extinguish the promisor's rights. In *Hughes* v. *Metropolitan Railway Co* (above) the landlord's right to enforce the repairing covenant was not extinguished. It was suspended and could be resurrected by his giving reasonable notice. But in *High Trees* the estoppel had permanent effects because Denning J held that the lessors were not entitled to demand the rent waived between 1940 and 1945. Such a proposition is difficult to reconcile with *Foakes* v. *Beer* (see

5.11) and has been criticised (see Treitel, 1987). But the better view is that, in cases of post-breach representations or where it is not possible or practicable to return the parties to their original position, then promissory estoppel may have permanent effects (see Dugdale and Yates, 1976 and Thompson, 1983).

The final point is that promissory estoppel cannot act as a cause of action; it acts as a shield but not as a sword (see *Combe* v. *Combe* (above)).

5.22 Estoppel by Convention

So far we have been dealing with cases in which estoppel acted as a shield and did not create a new cause of action. But the effect of estoppel by convention may be to create a cause of action. The leading authority is *Amalgamated Investment and Property Co Ltd* v. *Texas Commerce International Bank Ltd* [1982] QB 84, where estoppel by convention was defined in the following terms:

> 'when the parties have acted in their transaction upon the agreed assumption that a given state of facts is to be accepted between them as true, then as regards that transaction each will be estopped against the other from questioning the truth of the statement of facts so assumed'.

In the *Texas Bank* case the common assumption of the parties was that they had entered into a contract of guarantee under which the plaintiffs had promised to guarantee loans made by a subsidiary of the defendants to a subsidiary of the plaintiffs. In fact, the wording of the guarantee covered loans made by the defendants, but not loans made by the defendants' subsidiary. When the plaintiffs went into liquidation the defendants applied money which they owed to the plaintiffs in discharge of the plaintiffs' alleged ability under the guarantee. The plaintiffs sought a declaration that the defendants were not entitled to apply the money in such a way because the guarantee was not effective to cover the loans made by the subsidiary. But the court held that the parties had entered into the guarantee under the shared assumption that the guarantee did cover such loans and the effect of the estoppel was to prevent the plaintiffs from denying the efficacy of the guarantee. So the defendants used the estoppel as a shield to the plaintiffs' claim for a declaration. But could they have sued on the guarantee to recover the sums which they alleged were due? The majority (Brandon LJ and Lord Denning) held that they could have done so, but Brandon LJ held that, in such a case, it would be the contract and not the estoppel which created the cause of action. This point is difficult to understand. The contract of guarantee was not enforceable. Only the estoppel could validate the contract and thereby render the guarantee enforceable. Thus stated, is it not the estoppel which creates the cause of action?

5.23 Proprietary Estoppel

Whatever doubts we may harbour about the ability of estoppel by convention to create a cause of action, there can be no doubt that proprietary estoppel can be used to found a cause of action. Cases of proprietary estoppel can be divided into two broad categories. The first group of cases relate to the situation in which a landowner 'stands by' while another person improves his land in the mistaken belief that he is the owner of the land. In the second group of cases the promisee relies to his detriment upon the landowner's promise that he has or will be given an interest in the land. (For a useful summary of the ingredients of proprietary estoppel see the judgment of Nourse LJ in *Brinnand* v. *Ewens* (1987) 19 HLR 415.)

The operation of proprietary estoppel can be illustrated by reference to the case of *Pascoe* v. *Turner* [1979] 1 WLR 431. The plaintiff and the defendant lived together for a number of years. The plaintiff left the defendant and went to live with another woman, but he told the defendant that the house and everything in it was hers. In reliance upon this assurance, the defendant spent some £230 in repairs upon the house. The plaintiff subsequently decided that he wanted the house and he sued for possession. The defendant counterclaimed for a declaration that the house and everything in it was hers and her counterclaim succeeded in the Court of Appeal. Although she had not provided any consideration for the plaintiff's promise, the defendant had acted to her detriment in reliance upon his promise. This created an equity in her favour and that equity could only be satisfied by an order that the plaintiff convey to her the fee simple in the house. The effect of the estoppel in *Pascoe* was clearly to create a new cause of action. There was no pre-existing legal relationship between the parties and yet the promise of the plaintiff was enforced, despite the absence of consideration.

According to orthodox analysis, proprietary estoppel may be triggered by detrimental reliance by a promisee upon a promise, express or implied, that he will acquire rights in or over the promisor's land (*Dillwyn* v. *Llewelyn* (1862) D, F & G 517, Inwards v. Baker [1965] 2 QB 29). It should not, however, be thought that the courts will in all cases order the promisor to convey the fee simple to the promisee. More limited forms of relief may be granted (see *Inwards* v. *Baker* (above). The remedy granted depends upon all the circumstances of the case and it is difficult to discern any principled basis upon which the courts decide what is the most appropriate remedy (but see the useful analysis by Moriarty, 1984).

Thus far, proprietary estoppel has been confined to cases in which a promisee has been induced to believe that he will acquire an interest in the promisor's land, although Megaw LJ recognised in *Western Fish Products* v. *Penwith DC* [1981] 2 All ER 204, 218, that it may extend to the case where the promisee is induced to believe that he will acquire an interest in other forms of property. There is, as yet, no clear authority which suggests that proprietary estoppel extends beyond such cases (but see *Pacol Ltd* v. *Trade Lines Ltd* [1982] 1 Lloyds Rep 456).

However there are some dicta which suggest a more expansive role for proprietary estoppel. In *Crabb* v. *Arun DC* [1976] Ch 179, Scarman LJ said that he did not find the distinction between 'promissory and proprietary estoppel' helpful and in *Amalgamated Investment and Property Co Ltd* v. *Texas Commerce International Bank Ltd* (above) Robert Goff J called proprietary estoppel an 'amalgam of doubtful utility'. Oliver J identified a much broader base for proprietary estoppel in *Taylor Fashions Ltd* v. *Liverpool Victoria Trustees Co Ltd* [1982] QB 133. The focus of his inquiry was upon

'whether, in particular individual circumstances, it would be unconscionable for a party to be permitted to deny that which, knowingly or unknowingly, he was allowed or encouraged another to assume to his detriment [rather than to inquire] whether the circumstances can be fitted within the confines of some preconceived formula serving as a universal yardstick for every form of unconscionable behaviour'.

This type of approach has been labelled 'unhelpful' by Treitel (1987) on the ground that it provides 'no basis on which a legal doctrine capable of yielding predictable results can be developed'. On the other hand, the present restriction upon the scope of proprietary estoppel cannot be justified. Why is it that detrimental reliance upon a promise to create an interest in property can create a cause of action, but that detrimental reliance upon any other promise cannot create a cause of action? No answer has been provided to this question. The only possible objection is that such a wide-ranging jurisdiction of the type advocated by Oliver J would be irreconcilable with the doctrine of consideration. And that is the issue which we must now consider.

5.24 Conclusion

The relationship between estoppel and consideration has recently been exhaustively analysed by the High Court of Australia in *Walton Stores (Interstate) Ltd* v. *Maher* (1988) 164 CLR 387. The parties were involved in the negotiation of a major leasing and construction project. The plaintiff was the owner of the land which he hoped to lease to the defendants. It was also intended that the plaintiff would demolish the existing building on the site and erect a new building to the defendants' specifications. The negotiations reached an advanced stage and solicitors were instructed to prepare the formal documents. The plaintiff signed the requisite documents and they were forwarded to the defendants' solicitors for execution and exchange. He was informed by his solicitors that the contracts had been sent to the defendants and he believed that they would shortly exchange and complete. Because of this belief and because the project was one of extreme urgency, the plaintiff began to demolish the building on his land. Meanwhile, the defendants were beginning to have second thoughts about the deal and they instructed their solicitors to 'go slow', even though they knew that the plaintiff had commenced work on the site. After the plaintiff had completed a substantial amount of the work, the defendants informed him that they had decided to withdraw from the project. The plaintiff sought a declaration that a binding agreement existed between the parties, and consequential relief. His difficulty was that no exchange had ever taken place. However he argued that the defendants were estopped from withdrawing from their implied promise to complete the contract.

The defendants argued that the plaintiff could not use estoppel to create a cause of action. There was no pre-existing legal relationship between the parties and therefore nothing to which an estoppel could apply. The defendants' argument was rejected by the High Court who, by a majority, held that promissory estoppel could, in an appropriate case, create a cause of action; it could act as a sword as well as a shield. They held that such a proposition was not irreconcilable with the doctrine of consideration because the function of the estoppel was not 'to make a promise binding' or to make good the expectations engendered by a promise, but to 'avoid the detriment' which the promisee would suffer as a result of the unconscionable conduct of the promisor in departing from the terms of his promise (the differences between a contract and an equity created by an estoppel are fully set out in the judgment of Brennan J). Nor was it necessary to establish a pre-existing legal relationship between the parties before estoppel could be invoked. As *Walton Stores* amply demonstrates, the action of the promisor in going back upon his promise can be as unconscionable where there is no pre-existing legal relationship between the parties as when there is such a relationship.

The difficulty which remains lies in ascertaining when it is unconscionable for a promisor to go back upon his promise where there is no pre-existing legal relationship between the parties. As was pointed out by Mason CJ and Wilson J, a failure to fulfil a promise does not of itself amount to unconscionable conduct. It therefore follows that mere reliance upon a promise will not suffice to bring promissory estoppel into play; something more must be established. That 'something more' they held, could be

> 'found, if at all, in the creation or encouragement by the party estopped in the other party of an assumption that a contract will come into existence or a promise will be performed and that the other party relied on that assumption to his detriment to the knowledge of the first party'.

These factors were all present on the facts of *Walton Stores*. It may be that there are other factors which will be found to be relevant but these can be worked out over time. The judgments of the majority are of immense importance in their demonstration that such an approach does not undermine consideration and in their establishment of a principled foundation for the resolution of future disputes. This first, crucial step having been taken by the High Court of Australia, all that remains is for a bold House of Lords to sweep aside *Combe* v. *Combe* and follow in its footsteps.

Summary

1 English contract law does not generally insist upon requirements of form.

2 The classical definition of consideration is that a promisee should not be able to enforce a promise unless he has given or promised to give something in exchange for the promise or unless the promisor has obtained (or been promised) something in return.

3 Consideration must be sufficient but it need not be adequate and it must be something which the law regards as being of value.

4 Natural love and affection, performance of an existing legal duty, performance of an existing contractual duty owed to the promisor and part payment of a debt do not constitute good consideration.

5 Performance of a contractual duty owed to a third party does constitute good consideration.

6 Past consideration is not good consideration. The harshness of this rule is mitigated by the doctrine of implied assumpsit.

7 Consideration must move from the promisee.

8 Where the act of the promisee can be shown to be at the request, express or implied, of the promisor then the act of the promisee will constitute good consideration.

9 Estoppel can act as a shield but not as a sword. There must be a pre-existing legal relationship between the parties under which the promisor promises to give up some of his rights under that relationship. The effect of the estoppel is to prevent the promisor going back on his promise where the promisee has acted in reliance upon it.

10 The maxim that estoppel acts as a shield but not as a sword operates in the case of estoppel by representation, waiver and promissory estoppel, but not in the case of proprietary estoppel (the position is unclear in relation to estoppel by convention).

11 It is a matter for debate whether the English courts should follow the High Court of Australia and conclude that, in an appropriate case, promissory estoppel can create a cause of action.

Exercises

1 What is meant by the maxim 'consideration must be sufficient but it need not be adequate'? Give examples to illustrate your answer.

2 Can performance of an existing duty ever constitute consideration? Should it ever constitute consideration?

3 What is past consideration? Do you think that the decision of the court in *Eastwood* v. *Kenyon* is (a) correct as a matter of principle and (b) fair?

4 What is implied assumpsit?

5 What is 'estoppel'? How many different types of estoppel are there and what is the relationship between them?

6 Describe the fact situation in the following two cases and explain their legal significance:

(a) *Combe* v. *Combe* [1951] 2 KB 215

(b) *Central London Property Trust Ltd* v. *High Trees House Ltd* [1947] KB 130.

7 What is meant by the phrase 'estoppel can act as a shield but not as a sword'? Can estoppel ever act as a sword?

6 Intention to Create Legal Relations

6.1 Introduction

The fact that the parties have reached agreement does not necessarily mean that they have concluded a legally enforceable contract, even where the agreement is supported by consideration. The following fact situation will demonstrate the point. I promise to pay my wife £50 if she will type the manuscript of this chapter of the book. My wife agrees. Does this agreement create a legally enforceable contract? On the face of it there appears to be no reason why it should not. We have reached agreement and the agreement is supported by consideration. But it is likely that an English court would conclude that we had not entered into a legally binding contract because we lacked an 'intention to create legal relations', which has been held to be an essential element in any contract. Before examining the relevant case law, we must stop and contemplate the juristic basis of this doctrine of intention to create legal relations.

It could be said that the doctrine is based on the intention of the parties, objectively interpreted; that is to say, my wife and I did not intend that our agreement would have any legal consequences. But my wife certainly expected to receive the £50 if she typed the manuscript, although it is unlikely that either of us intended that she would have to go to court to get her money. However to say that we did not intend that she would have to go to court to get her money is not the same thing as saying that, if the case did come to court, we thought her action would fail.

Alternatively, it could be said that the doctrine is based upon public policy; that is to say that, as a matter of policy, the law of contract ought not to intervene in domestic situations because the courts would then be swamped by trifling domestic disputes. Thus the Scottish Law Commission has stated (1977) that 'it is, in general, right that courts should not enforce entirely social engagements, such as arrangements to play squash or to come to dinner, even though the parties themselves may intend to be legally bound thereby'. In such a case it is for the court to decide, as a matter of policy, whether the agreement is 'entirely social' and hence not legally enforceable.

6.2 Balfour v. Balfour

The approach which has been adopted in the English courts is best illustrated by reference to the case of *Balfour* v. *Balfour* [1919] 2 KB 571.

A wife sought to enforce a promise by her husband to pay her £30 per month while he worked abroad. The action failed because the wife had not provided any consideration for the promise of her husband and because it was held that the parties did not intend their agreement to 'be attended by legal consequences'. Atkin LJ said that 'agreements such as these are outside the realm of contracts altogether. The common law does not regulate the form of agreements between spouses . . . The consideration that really obtains for them is that natural love and affection which counts for so little in these cold Courts.'

But how did Atkin LJ know that the parties did not intend to create legal relations? Did he inquire into the intention of the parties or did he lay down this rule as a matter of policy? It appears from his judgment that he was more concerned with policy than with ascertaining the intention of the parties because he said that

'it would be of the worst possible example to hold that agreements such as this resulted in legal obligations which could be enforced in the Courts . . . The small Courts of this country would have to be multiplied one hundredfold if these arrangements were held to result in legal obligations.'

It was the need to prevent what was, in the opinion of the court, unnecessary litigation and the desire of the court to keep the law out of the marriage relationship ('each house is a domain into which the King's writ does not seek to run') which were the predominant factors behind the finding that there was no intention to create legal relations.

However it does not necessarily follow from the fact that the judgment of Atkin LJ is based primarily upon considerations of policy that the intention of the parties is thereby completely irrelevant. The rule laid down in *Balfour* has been interpreted subsequently as a *presumption* that parties to a domestic agreement do not intend to create legal relations. Cases concerning intention to create legal relations are thus commonly divided into two categories: the first, concerning domestic and social agreements, where the presumption is that the parties did not intend to create legal relations, and the second, concerning commercial agreements, where the presumption is that the parties did intend to create legal relations. Both presumptions may be rebutted by evidence of contrary intention. But the fact that the initial presumption may be rebutted by evidence of contrary intention does not mean that the presumption itself is based upon the intention of the parties. Rather, as the judgment of Atkin LJ in *Balfour* makes clear, the initial presumption is a matter of policy. The policy which underpins these presumptions is one of 'keeping contract in its place; to keep it in the commercial sphere and out of domestic cases, except where the judges think it has a useful role to play' (Hedley, 1985).

6.3 Rebutting the Presumption

Although we have noted that evidence of intention is relevant to the rebuttal of the presumption, even here the role of intention is, at best, marginal. This is so for two reasons. The first is that in the case of many domestic and social agreements the parties have no discernible intention one way or the other. The second reason is that it is a very difficult task to rebut a presumption because of the strength of the initial presumption. In domestic agreements 'clear' evidence is required of an intention to create legal relations, whereas in commercial cases the presumption of legal relations is a 'heavy one' which is not discharged easily (*Edwards* v. *Skyways* [1964] 1 WLR 349). The marginal role of intention will be demonstrated by examining the scope of the two presumptions and then the factors which have been held to be relevant to the rebuttal of these presumptions.

6.4 Domestic and Social Agreements

As we have seen, an agreement between a husband and a wife is presumed not to be legally enforceable (*Balfour* v. *Balfour* (above)). Similarly, agreements between parents and children are presumed not to be legally binding. In *Jones* v. *Padavatton* [1969] 1 WLR 328, a mother persuaded her daughter, who was a secretary in Washington DC, to give up her work and read for the English Bar by promising to pay her $200 maintenance per month. After the daughter had begun to read for the Bar, the agreement was varied. The mother bought a house in London so that the daughter could live there rent free and the rent from letting out the other rooms to tenants would provide the daughter with her maintenance. Eventually, after the daughter had had more than one unsuccessful attempt at passing the Bar examinations, the mother and daughter fell out. The mother came to England and sought to gain possession of the house. The daughter relied upon their agreement as a defence to her mother's action. The Court of Appeal held that the agreement was not intended to be legally binding and that the mother was entitled to possession (see too *Hardwick* v. *Johnson* [1978] 1 WLR 683).

Social arrangements are also presumed not to give rise to legal relations. In *Lens* v. *Devonshire Social Club The Times* 4 December 1914, it was held that the winner of a competition held by a golf club could not sue for his prize because no-one involved in the competition intended that legal consequences should flow from entry into the competition.

The presumption may, of course, be rebutted by evidence of contrary intention, but a mere subjective intention to create legal relations will not suffice. There must be some objective evidence of a contrary intent. Although a complete list cannot be drawn up of the factors to which the court will have regard in considering whether or not the presumption has been rebutted, in practice the following three factors are among the most important.

The first is the context in which the agreement is made. If an agreement is entered into by family members in what the courts perceive to be a 'business context' the court will be readier to infer that the presumption has been rebutted. In *Snelling* v. *John G Snelling Ltd* [1973] QB 87, it was held that legal relations were created when three brothers, who were directors of a family company, entered into an agreement relating to the running of the company. Similarly where a husband and a wife are about to separate or have separated the presumption does not operate because in such a case the parties 'bargain keenly' and do not rely on 'honourable understandings' (*Meritt* v. *Meritt* [1970] 1 WLR 1121, 1123 per Lord Denning).

Secondly, the court will have regard to any reliance which has been placed upon the agreement. Where one party has acted to his detriment on the faith of the agreement a court may be more willing to conclude that the agreement was intended to have legal consequences. Such was the case in *Parker* v. *Clark* [1960] 1 WLR 286. The defendants, who were an elderly couple, suggested that the plaintiffs, who were their friends, come to live with them. The plaintiffs were agreeable to the proposal but pointed out that, if they were to live with the defendants, they would have to sell their own house. The defendants replied stating that the problem could be resolved by the defendants leaving to the plaintiffs a share of their house in their will. The plaintiffs accepted this offer, sold their house, lent the balance of the money to their daughter to enable her to purchase a flat and moved in with the defendants. However the parties soon began to disagree over certain matters and the result was that the defendants asked the plaintiffs to leave. The plaintiffs left the house to avoid being evicted and brought an action against the defendants for breach of contract. The defendants argued that there was no contract between them because of a lack of intention to create legal relations. It was held that the parties had intended to create legal relations. Devlin J stated that

'I cannot believe . . . that the defendant really thought that the law would leave him at liberty, if he so chose, to tell the [plaintiffs] when they arrived that he had changed his mind, that they could take their furniture away, and that he was indifferent whether they found anywhere else to live or not.'

Similarly, there is some authority for the proposition that an agreement between workmates under which one is to provide the other with a lift to work in return for a contribution towards the petrol does not create legal relations with regard to journeys to be undertaken in the future (see Upjohn LJ in *Coward* v. *Motor Insurers' Bureau* [1963] 2 QB 259, 271) but that it does create legal relations with regard to journeys which have already been undertaken (see Lord Cross in *Albert* v. *Motor Insurers'*

Bureau [1972] AC 301, 340). In these cases the determining factor appears to be the fact that the parties have acted in reliance upon the agreement. The courts are reluctant to allow the parties to go back on their agreement once it has been acted upon.

Finally, the court will consider the certainty of the agreement which has been entered into by the parties. In *Vaughan* v. *Vaughan* [1953] 1 QB 762, it was held that a promise by a husband to allow his deserted wife to stay in the matrimonial home did not have contractual force because its vagueness evidenced that it was neither intended to have, nor was understood as having, contractual force. The husband did not state how long she could live there, nor did he indicate the terms on which she could stay. Similarly, the uncertainty of the agreement in *Jones* v. *Padavatton* (above) was a factor which persuaded the court to hold that there was no intention to create legal relations, despite the fact that the daughter had detrimentally relied upon the agreement. The daughter had been in London for six years and this was held to be long enough to complete her Bar exams. The mother's promise of support could not be treated as lasting indefinitely.

6.5 Commercial Agreements

The presumption is that parties to commercial agreements do intend to create legal relations, and the presumption is a heavy one. The operation of the presumption can be seen in the case of *Esso Petroleum Ltd* v. *Commissioners of Custom and Excise* [1976] 1 WLR 1. Esso supplied garages with World Cup Coins in 1970, instructing the garages to give away one coin with every four gallons of petrol sold. It was sought to subject these coins to a purchase tax on the ground that they had been sold. On the facts it was held that the coins were not supplied under a contract of sale. But the House of Lords divided on the issue of whether or not there was an intention to create legal relations. The majority, Lord Simon, Lord Wilberforce and Lord Fraser, held that there was an intention to create legal relations. They placed heavy reliance on the onus of proof in commercial transactions and on the fact that Esso envisaged a bargain of some description between the garage owner and the customer. But the minority, Lord Russell and Viscount Dilhorne, relying upon the language of the advertising posters which said that the coins were 'going free' and the minimal value of the coins, held that there was no intention to create legal relations (see too *J Evans & Son (Portsmouth) Ltd* v. *Andrea Merzario Ltd* [1976] 1 WLR 1078).

The presumption may be rebutted by an express term of the contract which states that the parties do not intend to create legal relations. The parties must, however, make their intention clear. Thus agreements for the sale of land are usually made 'subject to contract' and, on that ground, do not create legal relations. At common law a collective agreement entered into between trade unions and an employer was held not to give rise to legal relations (*Ford Motor Co Ltd* v. *AEF* [1969]

1 WLR 339). This common law rule has been reinforced by a statutory presumption to the effect that a collective agreement is conclusively presumed not to have been intended by the parties to be a legally enforceable contract unless it is in writing and expressly provides to the contrary (see s.18, Trade Union and Labour Relations Act 1974).

The most interesting example in this category is, however, what is known as an honour clause. In *Rose and Frank Co* v. *J R Crompton and Bros Ltd* [1925] AC 445, an agreement stated: 'this arrangement is not entered into as a formal or legal agreement, and shall not be subject to legal jurisdiction in the Law Courts but is only a definite expression and record of the purpose and intention of the parties concerned to which they each honourably pledge themselves'. The court held that this agreement was not a legally binding contract because it was not intended that it would have such an effect. The courts interpret such clauses restrictively and clear words must be used to create such an honour clause (see *Home Insurance Co* v. *Administratia Asiguraliror* [1983] 2 Lloyds Rep 674, 677).

Summary

1 An intention to create legal relations is an essential element in any contract.
2 In cases of domestic and social agreements the presumption is that the parties did not intend to create legal relations. The presumption may be rebutted by 'clear' evidence to the contrary.
3 Factors which may persuade a court to hold that the presumption has been rebutted include the context in which the agreement was made (that is, was it a business context?) and any reliance which has been placed upon the agreement.
4 In cases involving commercial agreements the presumption is that the parties did intend to create legal relations. This presumption is also a 'heavy' one.
5 Clear evidence is required to rebut the presumption. The presumption has been rebutted in cases of agreements to sell land 'subject to contract', collective agreements and 'honour clauses'.

Exercises

1 Is the doctrine of intention to create legal relations based on considerations of policy or does the court genuinely seek to discover the intention of the parties?
2 Reagan Ltd are considering inserting an 'honour clause' in their contract with their major supplier, Jones Ltd. Advise them as to the advantages and disadvantages of such a course of action.
3 John offers £50 to anyone who will remove rubbish from his garden. The following people comply with the terms of his offer:

(a) his wife, Beatrice;
(b) his ex-wife, Brenda;
(c) his mistress, Belinda;
(d) his son, Billy;

(e) his nephew, Brian, whom he had never seen before;
(f) his god-child, Bernard; and
(g) his next-door neighbour, Benedict.

Advise John whether or not, in these circumstances, any legally enforceable contracts have been concluded.

7 Privity

7.1 Introduction

The doctrine of privity of contract consists of two distinct general rules. The first is that a third party cannot be subjected to a burden by a contract to which he is not a party. The second is that a person who is not a party to a contract cannot claim the benefit of it, even though the contract was entered into with the object of benefiting that third party.

English law has not always adopted this view. Some old authorities can be found in the books in which a third party has been held to be entitled to sue upon a contract (see further Flannigan, 1987). But the doctrine as we know it today was established in two principal cases. The first is *Tweddle* v. *Atkinson* (1861) 1 B & S 393. In this case John Tweddle and William Guy entered into an agreement under which each promised to pay a sum of money to William Tweddle on the occasion of William Tweddle's marriage to William Guy's daughter. However William Guy failed to pay the promised sum and, on his death, William Tweddle sued the executor of William Guy for the promised amount. It was held that he could not maintain such a cause of action. Now there was one obvious reason why he could not sue; he had provided no consideration for William Guy's promise. The consideration had been provided by John Tweddle. Indeed, Wightman, Crompton and Blackburn JJ all appeared to base their judgments on the rule that a stranger to the consideration cannot enforce the promise. There is therefore no need to explain the result in *Tweddle* on the basis of an independent doctrine of privity.

The second leading case is *Dunlop Pneumatic Tyre Company Ltd* v. *Selfridge* [1915] AC 847. In this case the plaintiffs attempted to operate a price-fixing ring. For this purpose they extracted a promise from dealers called Dew & Co that they in turn would obtain a written undertaking from any third party to whom they sold Dunlop products that the third party would not sell at a price below Dunlop's price list. The defendants, Selfridge, bought Dunlop products from Dew and gave the required undertaking to Dew but nevertheless sold Dunlop products at less than the list price. In these circumstances Dunlop brought an action for an injunction and damages against Selfridge. The action failed. The majority held that the action failed because Dunlop had provided no consideration for the promise of Selfridge; the consideration had been provided by Dew. But Viscount Haldane, in a judgment which has since assumed considerable significance, held that, independently of the need for consideration, it was a fundamental principle of English law that 'only a person who is a party to a contract can sue on it' and that, because Dunlop were not a party to the contract between Dew and Selfridge, they could not sue on it.

Tweddle and *Dunlop* both demonstrate that there is a very close relationship between the doctrines of privity and consideration. Indeed, on one view, there is no difference between the doctrine of privity and the rule that consideration must move from the promisee (see Furmston, 1960). Privity then becomes swallowed up in the larger rule that consideration must move from the promisee. *Tweddle* and *Dunlop* are both consistent with this view because the majority view in each case was that the plaintiff could not sue because he had not provided consideration for the defendant's promise. Despite the strength of this argument, the more widely accepted view, and the one subsequently adopted by the House of Lords in the cases of *Scruttons Ltd* v. *Midland Silicones Ltd* [1962] AC 446, and *Beswick* v. *Beswick* [1968] AC 58, is that expressed by Viscount Haldane in *Dunlop*, namely that the doctrine of privity is separate and distinct from the rule that consideration must move from the promisee. The following example is often used to illustrate the point. X makes a promise to Y and Z to pay £100 to Z in exchange for consideration provided by Y. In such a case Z is privy to the contract but cannot maintain an action against X unless he has provided consideration for X's promise. In such a case privity and consideration constitute two hurdles for Z to surmount and not one.

However, even those who maintain that privity and the rule that consideration must move from the promisee are two separate rules, nevertheless concede that there is a very strong relationship between privity and consideration and that the one cannot be reformed without the other. For example, in *Tweddle* and *Dunlop* there would be little point in abolishing the doctrine of privity if the plaintiffs were then to be met by the argument that they still could not sue because they had not provided any consideration.

7.2　The Development of Privity and the Challenge of Lord Denning

Although *Dunlop* appeared to root privity firmly into English law, a serious attempt was subsequently made by Lord Denning to uproot it. His clearest attack was launched in the case of *Smith and Snipes Hall Farm Ltd* v. *River Douglas Catchment Board* [1949] 2 KB 500, when he said that a promise deliberately made was enforceable

'not only at the suit of the party who gave the consideration, but also at the suit of one who was not a party to the contract, provided that it was made for his benefit and that he has a sufficient interest to entitle him to enforce it, subject always, of course, to any defences which may be open to him on the merits'.

This judgment is one of enormous significance. It recognises that the doctrine of privity is, in many cases, commercially inconvenient and that it also produces results which are fundamentally unjust. The result in *Dunlop* may be said to be fundamentally unjust because, in the words of Lord Dunedin, it made it possible

'for a person to snap his fingers at a bargain deliberately made, a bargain not itself unfair, and which the person seeking to enforce it has a legitimate interest to enforce'.

Yet, despite recognising the inconvenience to which the doctrine gives rise and its potential for unfairness, the House of Lords chose to reject the views of Lord Denning and to re-establish the doctrine of privity in the case of *Scruttons Ltd* v. *Midland Silicones Ltd* (above). Lord Reid stated that

'although I may regret it, I find it impossible to deny the existence of the general rule that a stranger to a contract cannot in a question with either of the contracting parties take advantage of provisions of the contract, even where it is clear from the contract that some provision in it was intended to benefit him.'

Despite this decision Lord Denning continued his attack upon the doctrine of privity. He launched a further assault in the Court of Appeal in the case of *Beswick* v. *Beswick* [1966] 3 WLR 396, but once again his views were overruled by the House of Lords ([1968] AC 58). *Beswick* concerned a contract under which Peter Beswick sold his coal round and the goodwill of his business to his nephew John Beswick in return for a promise to pay £6 10/- a week to Peter Beswick for the rest of his life and thereafter £5 a week to Peter Beswick's widow for the rest of her life. The nephew ceased making payments to the widow shortly after Peter Beswick's death. The widow brought an action to compel the nephew to continue making the payments and the House of Lords held that she was entitled to such an order. The crucial point to note is that the widow did not succeed in her action in her own name because she was not privy to the contract between Peter Beswick and John Beswick. She only succeeded in her capacity as administratrix of her husband's estate (when a person dies the administrator or administratrix of the estate, broadly speaking, acquires the rights of the deceased). So, in the final analysis, no exception was created to the doctrine of privity because it was as if Peter Beswick himself was suing and, of course, he was privy to the original agreement.

While all the judgments delivered in the House of Lords in *Beswick* affirmed the existence of the doctrine of privity, the doctrine did not escape judicial criticism. Lord Reid referred to the report of the Law Revision Committee (Cmnd. 5449) which had reported in 1937 and which had recommended that English law adopt the rule that 'where a contract by its express terms purports to confer a benefit directly on a third party it shall be enforceable by the third party in his own name'. After noting that the Committee's recommendation had not been implemented, he continued:

> 'if one had to contemplate a further long period of Parliamentary procrastination, this House might find it necessary to deal with this matter.'

Some 12 years later, after still further Parliamentary procrastination, Lord Scarman expressed similar sentiments in the case of *Woodar Investment Development Ltd* v. *Wimpey Construction U.K. Ltd* [1980] 1 WLR 227, when he said:

> 'I hope the House will reconsider *Tweddle* v. *Atkinson* and the other cases which stand guard over this unjust [privity] rule.'

Parliament has still not found time to legislate on this matter and, indeed, it is unlikely to do so unless it is persuaded that the commercial inconvenience of the doctrine of privity is such that England is losing substantial trade as a result of the doctrine. Therefore reform, if it is to come at all, is most likely to come from the judiciary. In my opinion, it is highly unlikely that the judges will pick up the gauntlet thrown down by Lord Reid and Lord Scarman. Far from using Parliamentary procrastination as a justification for judicial abolition or reform of the doctrine of privity, such procrastination is likely to be used as a justification for the preservation of the *status quo*. It would be a bold court which abolished a doctrine which has been accepted as part of English law since 1861.

In fact, one of the most striking features of the development of the doctrine of privity is that, while the judges in cases such as *Midland Silicones* and *Woodar* have expressed regret at the present state of the law, they have, Lord Denning apart, been remarkably orthodox in their interpretation and application of the doctrine. Indeed the decision of the House of Lords in *Midland Silicones* constituted a much-criticised extension of the doctrine of privity (see 7.6) and in *Woodar* the House of Lords rejected a device which would have enabled the courts to avoid some of the unfair consequences produced by the application of the privity doctrine (see 7.4). Other such evasive devices have been similarly rejected by the courts (see 7.9). Although occasional instances can be found in which the courts have been prepared to evade privity (see the judgments of Dunn LJ in *Northern Regional Health Authority* v. *Derek Crouch Construction Co Ltd* [1984] 2 All ER 175, and May LJ in *Norwich City Council* v. *Harvey* [1989] 1 All ER 1180), these remain isolated examples and there is little prospect of radical reform of the doctrine of privity on the horizon (contrast the Australian case of *Trident General Insurance Co Ltd* v. *McNiece Bros Pty Ltd* (1988) 165 CLR 107, noted by Reynolds, 1989). The most that can be expected is a gradual widening of the exceptions to the general rule (see 7.7).

7.3 The Scope of the Doctrine of Privity

Thus far we have been discussing cases in which a third party has sought to enforce a contract to which he was not a party. Before discussing the various exceptions to this rule, it is necessary to consider three other issues relating to the scope of the doctrine of privity. The first relates to the contractual remedies which are available to the promisee against the promisor and whether such remedies can be of any benefit to the third party (7.4), the second is the extent to which a contract between two parties can impose obligations upon a third party (7.5) and the third is the question whether a third party can rely upon an exclusion clause contained in a contract between the plaintiff and another party as a *defence* to the plaintiff's action against him in tort (7.6). Once we have considered these three issues we will discuss the situations in which English law does in fact recognise the existence of enforceable third party rights.

7.4 Action by the Contracting Party

If A and B enter into a contract under which, in return for some act to be performed by B, A agrees to pay £50 to C, a failure by A to pay the £50 to C will constitute a breach of contract between A and B. Although the doctrine of privity precludes C from bringing an action against A, it does not prevent B from suing A. In such a case what remedies does B have against A and can these remedies be of any use to C? There are at least four actions which B could bring against A.

The first possibility is to bring an action for damages for breach of contract. The difficulty here is that B does not appear to have suffered any loss as a result of A's breach and so his damages are likely to be nominal (although if the £50 was to be paid to discharge a debt owed by B to C then B might be entitled to more than nominal damages; see Windeyer J in *Coulls* v. *Bagot's Executor* (1967) 119 CLR 460, 501–2). But even if B could recover substantial damages this would be of no avail to C because the damages recovered by B would be held on his own behalf and not on behalf of C. So B would not be under any obligation to give any portion of the damages recovered to C (although in the case of a debt owed by B to C, B would remain liable to repay the debt).

Secondly, B could seek to recover damages on behalf of C. Some authority for such a proposition was provided by Lord Denning in the case of *Jackson* v. *Horizon Holidays* [1975] 1 WLR 1468. In this case the plaintiff entered into a contract with the defendants under which the defendants promised to provide the plaintiff and his family with a holiday of a certain standard. The holiday did not comply with the promised standard and the defendants admitted that they were in breach of contract. The plaintiff was awarded damages of £1 100, which included £500 for 'mental distress'. The defendants appealed, alleging that the damages awarded were excessive. The majority of the Court of Appeal upheld the award of damages to the plaintiff on entirely orthodox grounds. They held that the plaintiff had simply been compensated for his own loss, albeit that his loss had been increased as a result of his witnessing the distress and disappointment suffered by the other members of his family. However Lord Denning took a different view. He held that £500 was excessive if it was regarded solely as compensation for the plaintiff's own loss. But he nevertheless upheld the award on the ground that the plaintiff could recover, not only in respect of his own loss, but also in respect of the losses suffered by the rest of his family; the latter compensation being held by the plaintiff on trust for the rest of his family. Lord Denning instanced other examples where such a principle would operate: a vicar making a contract for a coach trip for the church choir, a host making a contract with a restaurant for dinner for himself and his friends. In all such cases Lord Denning thought that the contracting party could, in the event of breach, recover damages on behalf of himself and the other members of the group.

However the view of Lord Denning was disapproved by the House of Lords in *Woodar Investment Development Ltd* v. *Wimpey Construction U.K. Ltd* [1980] 1 WLR 227. Purchasers of land agreed to pay £850 000 to the vendors and £150 000 to a third party on completion of the contract. One question which arose was whether, if the purchasers were in breach of contract, the vendors could recover damages in respect of the £150 000 payable to the third party. In considering this issue, the House of Lords took the opportunity to disapprove of the judgment of Lord Denning in *Jackson*. They did not disapprove of the result of the case; that was justified on the ground that the damages awarded did in fact represent the loss which the plaintiff himself had suffered. But Lord Wilberforce did not shut the door completely on Lord Denning's proposition; he left the door slightly ajar by saying that *Jackson* could possibly be supported as

'an example of a type of contract, examples of which are persons contracting for family holidays, ordering meals in restaurants for a party, hiring a taxi for a group, calling for special treatment'.

This 'special treatment' would be that the contracting party could recover damages on behalf of the group. However no appellate court has yet applied this 'special treatment'. So, these special cases apart, it is clear that a promisee cannot recover damages on behalf of a third party and so, in our example, B would not be able to recover damages on behalf of C.

Thirdly, B could seek an order of specific performance against A (that is an order of the court that the promisor carry out his promise). This was of course what happened in *Beswick* v. *Beswick* (above). Such a remedy would be of supreme significance to C because it would ensure that he obtained the £50 promised to him by A. However it must be noted that specific performance is a discretionary remedy which, as a general rule, is only available where damages are inadequate and, while it was available on the facts of *Beswick*, it should not be assumed that it is widely available (see further 21.9). It should also be noted that there does not appear to be any procedure by which C could compel B to sue A, so that B could refuse to sue A and thereby leave C without a remedy. If the promise which B sought to enforce was a negative one then B could, in an appropriate case, be entitled to an injunction to restrain the threatened breach of contract by A (see further 21.10).

Finally, if the promise made by A to B had been a promise not to sue C, and A nevertheless, in breach of contract with B, had commenced an action against C, B could ask the court, in its discretion, to stay the proceedings against C (*Snelling* v. *John G Snelling* [1973] QB 87; but contrast *Gore* v. *Van Der Lann* [1967] 2 QB 31).

7.5 Interference with Contractual Rights

As we noted at the beginning of this chapter, the general rule is that a third party cannot be subjected to a burden by a contract to which he is not a party. However a contract between two parties may nevertheless impose certain obligations upon a third party. The first such obligation is that a third party must not seek to persuade one contracting party to break his contract with the other. Thus, it is a tort for a third party, without lawful justification, to interfere intentionally or recklessly with a contract between A and B, either by persuading A to break his contract with B or by preventing A from performing his contract with B by the use of some direct or indirect unlawful means. The case of *Lumley* v. *Gye* (1853) 2 El & Bl 216, provides a useful illustration of the operation of this tort. The plaintiff was a theatre owner who entered into a contract with a famous opera singer, Miss Wagner, under which she was to sing only at his theatre for a period of time. The defendant, who was the owner of a rival theatre, procured Miss Wagner to break her contract with the plaintiff by promising to pay her more than she was receiving from the plaintiff. When Miss Wagner, in breach of contract, refused to continue to perform at the plaintiff's theatre, the plaintiff brought an action against the defendant alleging that the defendant had induced Miss Wagner to break her contract with him and that this had caused him loss. It was held that the defendant had indeed committed a tort and the plaintiff was therefore entitled to claim damages from the defendant to compensate him for his loss.

It has also been argued that a third party who acquires property in the knowledge that that property is affected by a contract between two other parties is bound by the terms of that contract and may be restrained from acting inconsistently with the terms of the contract. This indeed occurred in the case of *Tulk* v. *Moxhay* (1848) 2 Ph 774. The plaintiff sold land subject to a restrictive covenant that the land must not be built upon but must be preserved in its existing condition. After a number of conveyances the land was eventually conveyed to the defendant, who had notice of the covenant but nevertheless sought to build on the land. It was held that the plaintiff was entitled to an injunction to restrain the proposed building. The defendant was therefore bound by an agreement to which he was not a party, simply because he had notice of the covenant. The question which arises is whether this principle applies only within the rather rarified atmosphere of land law and restrictive covenants or whether it is of general application. The answer is that it is a matter of land law and, even within the confines of land law, the scope of the principle has been narrowed; for example, the plaintiff must now show that he has retained ownership of other land in the immediate vicinity which is capable of being benefited by the covenant.

However the prospect of extending the scope of *Tulk* v. *Moxhay* beyond the province of restrictive covenants was held out by the Privy Council in *Lord Strathcona Steamship Co* v. *Dominion Coal Co Ltd* [1926] AC 108. The owner of a ship chartered her to the plaintiffs for a number of summer seasons. The owner sold the ship during the winter season. After a series of sales the ship was bought by the defendants who, although aware of the charterparty at the date of purchase, nevertheless refused to deliver the ship to the plaintiffs for the summer season. The Privy Council held that the defendants were bound by the terms of the charterparty and granted the plaintiffs an injunction to restrain the defendants from using the ship in any way inconsistent with the terms of the charterparty.

The result of the case does not seem to be entirely unfair. A person who buys property subject to the rights of third parties will generally pay a lower price for the property and, if he could then take advantage of the rules of privity to disregard those rights, he would thereby free the property and be able to sell it at a considerable profit. Nevertheless it is difficult to reconcile *Strathcona* with the rule that a contract of hire only creates personal and not proprietary rights and that therefore the purchaser should be free to ignore the contract of hire. *Strathcona* is therefore an extremely controversial case (see Gardner, 1982 and Tettenborn, 1982) and, indeed, in the case of *Port Line Ltd* v. *Ben Line Steamers Ltd* [1958] 2 QB 146, Diplock J said that he thought the case was wrongly decided and refused to follow it (contrast *Swiss Bank Corporation* v. *Lloyds Bank Ltd* [1979] Ch 548, where Browne-Wilkinson J followed *Strathcona* on the ground that it was the equitable counterpart of the tort of knowing interference with contractual rights). The present standing of *Strathcona* is therefore unclear. The case may be confined to its own facts. But, if it is to be followed, it can only apply where the purchaser has actual knowledge of the contract at the time of the purchase and the only remedy available is an injunction restraining the purchaser from acting inconsistently with the contract. The plaintiff cannot obtain a specific performance order requiring the purchaser to carry out the terms of the contract (*Port Line Ltd* v. *Ben Line Steamers* (above)).

7.6 Exclusion Clauses and Third Parties

In some cases defendants have sought to rely on an exclusion clause contained in a contract between the plaintiff and another party as a defence to the plaintiff's action in tort. In such cases, in the absence of an implied contract between the plaintiff and the defendant, defendants have sought to invoke the doctrine of 'vicarious immunity', that is to say, they have argued that, as employees or agents of a contracting party (the contracting party being the party with whom the plaintiff has contracted), they are entitled to the benefit of any exclusion clause negotiated by that contracting party. Some authority for the existence of such a doctrine can be found in the case of *Elder Dempster* v. *Paterson, Zochonis and Co* [1924] AC 522 (for the different interpretations of this confusing case see Treitel, 1987, pp. 477–8).

But this authority was decisively rejected by the House of Lords in *Scruttons Ltd* v. *Midland Silicones Ltd* (above). The plaintiffs, who were the owners of a drum of chemicals, entered into a contract with a firm of carriers for the transportation of the drum. Under the contract the carriers limited their liability to the plaintiffs to $500. Stevedores, who were employed by the carriers to discharge the drum, negligently dropped it and the plaintiffs brought an action in tort against them in respect of the resulting damage. The stevedores sought to rely on the limitation clause contained in the contract between the plaintiffs and the carriers but it was held that they could not do so because they were not privy to that contract. The House of Lords held that English law knew of no doctrine of vicarious immunity and that, in any case, the limitation clause only referred to the carriers and so was incapable of providing protection for the stevedores. This conclusion gave rise to considerable commercial inconvenience because it made it extremely difficult for an employer to give his employees and agents the benefit of an exclusion clause negotiated by the employer, even where the exclusion clause was a valid and legitimate method of allocating the risks under the contract between the employer and the plaintiff.

So it is not surprising that attempts have been made to mitigate the rigours of *Midland Silicones*. Furmston has argued (1960) that, in an appropriate case, the exclusion clause in the contract between the plaintiff and the carrier should enable the defendant to invoke the defence of *volenti non fit injuria* where it can be shown from the exclusion clause that the plaintiff willingly accepted the risk of injury as a result of the negligence of the third party. Alternatively, it could be argued that the effect of the exclusion clause is, in an appropriate case, to demonstrate that the plaintiff has assented to the risk of damage by the third party and that the effect of the exclusion clause is therefore to negative or limit the duty of care which would otherwise be owed by the third party to the plaintiff (see Lord Roskill in *Junior Books Ltd* v. *Veitchi Ltd* [1983] 1 AC 520, 546, and see also *Norwich City Council* v. *Harvey* [1989] 1 All ER 1180)). These possibilities have not yet been developed in the courts. Rather the courts have sought to find the existence of a contract between the plaintiff and the third party, under which the third party can enjoy the same immunity as that given to his principal under the contract.

The origins of this approach can be found in the judgment of Lord Reid in *Midland Silicones*. Lord Reid thought that stevedores might be able to claim the protection of an exclusion clause

> 'if (first) the bill of lading makes it clear that the stevedore is intended to be protected by the provisions in it which limit liability, (secondly) the bill of lading makes it clear that the carrier, in addition to contracting for these provisions on his own behalf, is also contracting as agent for the stevedore that these provisions should apply to the stevedore, (thirdly) the carrier has authority from the stevedore to do that, or perhaps later ratification by the stevedore would suffice, and (fourthly) that any difficulties about consideration moving from the stevedore were overcome'.

Lord Reid therefore envisaged that, at the moment the carrier signed the contract, two contracts would come into existence; the first between the owner and the carrier and the second between the owner and the stevedore. But, at that moment in time, it is extremely difficult to find any consideration supplied by the stevedore; indeed, at the moment of signing the contract, it might not be known which firm of stevedores is to unload the goods. Lord Reid's solution was therefore not entirely satisfactory.

The issue was considered by the Privy Council in *New Zealand Shipping Co Ltd* v. *A. M. Satterthwaite & Co Ltd (The Eurymedon)* [1975] AC 154, in which the stevedores were held to be entitled to the benefit of the exclusion clause contained in the contract between the consignors and the carriers. The fact situation was similar to *Midland Silicones*, except that the bill of lading was much more complex and clearly sought to give the stevedores the benefit of the exclusion clause. The first three of Lord Reid's four conditions were satisfied. The bill of lading expressly extended the benefit of the exclusion clause to any servants, agents and independent contractors employed by the carriers. The carriers had also contracted as the agents of the stevedores and they were authorised by the stevedores so to act. The principal problem lay in locating the consideration provided by the stevedores for the consignor's offer of immunity and in accommodating the solution within the offer and acceptance framework. The solution adopted by the Privy Council proceeded in the following stages. First, they held that when the consignors signed the bill of lading they made a unilateral offer to all the world that anyone who unloaded their goods at the port of discharge would be entitled to the benefit of the exclusion clause. Secondly, they held that this offer was accepted by the stevedores unloading the goods at the port of discharge and at that moment a binding contract came into existence. The consideration supplied by the stevedores was the performance of their contractual duty owed to the carriers and, as we noted at 5.12, performance of a contractual duty owed to a third party is good consideration for a promise given by the plaintiff.

Although this analysis is an improvement upon the solution advocated by Lord Reid in *Midland Silicones*, it gives rise to three further problems. The first problem is that a court may decide that the main contract cannot be interpreted as an offer of immunity to the sub-contractor and, equally, the sub-contractor may find it difficult to persuade the court that the main contractor was acting as his agent when he entered into the main contract (*Southern Water Authority* v. *Carey* [1985] 2 All ER 1077). The second difficulty is that, as we have already noted (3.9), an 'acceptance' is not generally valid if it was made in ignorance of the existence of the offer. In most of these cases, when the stevedores unloaded the goods, they did so in pursuance of a contract with the carriers and were unlikely to be aware of the owner's offer. Does this mean that the stevedores cannot claim the benefit of the exclusion clause? The Privy Council, in *The New York Star* [1981] 1 WLR 138, brushed aside such technicalities and deprecated the use of such 'fine distinctions' in an effort to diminish the applicability of the principles established in *The Eurymedon*. So it would appear that there is no requirement that the stevedores must be aware of the offer at the time of their acceptance (see too *Celthene Pty Ltd* v. *WKJ Hauliers Pty Ltd* [1981] 1 NSWLR 606).

The third problem is that the *Eurymedon* solution cannot be invoked by the stevedore who damages the goods before he starts to unload them because the acceptance of the owner's offer only takes place when the stevedore begins to unload the goods (see *Raymond Burke Motors Ltd* v. *Mersey Docks & Harbour Co* [1986] 1 Lloyds Rep 155). Despite this last difficulty, the approach adopted by the majority in *The Eurymedon* displays a welcome, if rather isolated, willingness to evade the undesirable consequences of the doctrine of privity, even although it is at the cost of a rather cavalier approach to the rules of offer, acceptance and consideration.

7.7 Evading the Rule

As we noted above (7.2), the courts are unlikely to abolish the doctrine of privity. Instead, the most likely development is for the courts and Parliament to widen the scope of the exceptional situations in which a third party can sue to enforce a contract. The importance of these exceptions should not be underestimated; they are examples of cases in which English law does recognise the existence of enforceable third party rights.

It should be noted that there is some disagreement as to what exactly constitutes an exception to the rule. For example, in the case of collateral contracts (7.8) and agency (7.9) the plaintiff or principal is regarded as being privy to the contract and so it could be argued that they are not true exceptions to the rule. But they are treated as exceptions here because in effect, if not in theory, they undermine the privity rule. With this point in mind let us give further consideration to these exceptions.

7.8 Collateral Contracts

One useful device which may be available to a court which wishes to evade the clutches of the doctrine of privity is to find the existence of a collateral contract between the promisor and the third party. A good illustration of the utility of the collateral contract device is the case of *Shanklin Pier* v. *Detel Products Ltd* [1951] 2 KB 854. Contractors employed by the plaintiffs to paint the plaintiffs' pier were instructed by the plaintiffs to use paint manufactured by the defendants. The contract to purchase the paint was actually made between the contractors and the defendants but a representation was made by the defendants to the plaintiffs that the paint would last for seven years. The paint only lasted three months. It was held that the plaintiffs were entitled to bring an action for breach of contract against the defendants on the ground that there was a collateral contract between them to the effect that the paint would last for seven years, the consideration for which was the instruction given by the plaintiffs to their contractors to order the paint from the defendants.

The collateral contract device has also been usefully employed in cases of hire-purchase. In many cases consumers are unaware of the exact legal technicalities of a hire-purchase agreement. These technicalities are that the dealer will sell the goods to the finance house who in turn will lease the goods to the consumer on hire-purchase terms. Thus the contracts are between the dealer and the finance house and between the finance house and the consumer; there is no contract between the dealer and the consumer. But in *Andrews* v. *Hopkinson* [1957] 1 QB 229, it was held that the dealers' false warranty as to the roadworthiness of a car gave rise to a collateral contract between the dealer and the consumer, thereby enabling the consumer to bring an action for breach of contract.

The limitation of the collateral contract device, however, is that the court must be able to find evidence upon which to imply such a contract and that consideration must be found to support the collateral contract. The latter requirement can give rise to some difficulty, as is illustrated by the case of *Charnock* v. *Liverpool Corporation* [1968] 1 WLR 1498. The plaintiff's car was damaged in an accident and he left his car to be repaired by the defendant garage, the defendants having promised to do the repairs reasonably quickly. The car was repaired under a contract between the plaintiff's insurance company and the defendants, but it was held that the plaintiff could nevertheless bring an action in respect of the defendants' failure to carry out the repair reasonably quickly. It was held that there was consideration to support the collateral contract because, although there was no detriment to the plaintiff, the defendants were benefited by virtue of the opportunity given to them to enter into a contract with the insurance company for the repair of the car (note that Treitel, 1976, treats this as a case of 'invented' consideration, and Atiyah, 1986c, p.223 argues that this is a case of 'fictitious consideration' because the 'real' consideration was supplied by the insurers and not by the plaintiff).

7.9 Agency

It would cause great commercial hardship if a businessman who appointed an agent to enter into a contract on his behalf was prevented by the doctrine of privity from suing upon that contract himself. So the doctrine of agency exists to give the businessman such a right of action. An agency relationship arises where one party, the agent, is authorised by another, the principal, to negotiate and to enter into contracts on behalf of the principal. Once an agency relationship is created the agent is thereby authorised to commit the principal to contractual relationships with third parties. Agency is now a specialised area of law and we will not deal with it in this book, except to give a very brief account of the relationship between agency and privity (for fuller consideration of the doctrine of agency see Treitel, 1987, ch. 17).

When the agent discloses to the third party that he is acting as an agent of a principal and he concludes the contract within the scope of his authority, the general rule is that the contract is made between the principal and the third party and the agent cannot sue or be sued on the contract. Such a transaction is not generally regarded as an exception to the doctrine of privity because the function of the agent is to negotiate the contract on behalf of his principal and, once he has done that, he 'drops out of the picture', leaving his principal as the true party to the contract.

However there are certain aspects of the law of agency which appear to flout the doctrine of privity. One such aspect is the rule that a principal may, in certain limited circumstances, sue upon the contract even though the agent has not disclosed to the third party that he is acting as an agent for the principal (see Treitel, 1987, pp.549–51). In these situations the third party can find himself in a contractual relationship with a person of whose existence he was blissfully unaware at the time that he entered into the contract. The ability of a principal to ratify the unauthorised act of his agent is also said to be an exception to the doctrine of privity (see Treitel, 1987, pp.544–8).

Privity also appears to be flouted by the controversial case of *Watteau* v. *Fenwick* [1893] 1 QB 346. In this case the agent, who was the manager of a public house, was prohibited by his principal (the owner of the public house) from purchasing cigars on credit for the purpose of the business. Despite this prohibition, the agent purchased cigars in his own name on credit from the plaintiffs, who were unaware of the existence of the principal and therefore unaware of the prohibition placed upon the agent. It was held that the principal was nevertheless bound by the contract and was liable to the plaintiffs. The rationale of the case appears to be that the principal, by employing the agent as his manager, was regarded as having given the agent the authority which was usually given to managers of a public house, which included the authority to purchase cigars. Further, the agreement between the principal and agent, under which the agent's authority was restricted, was not binding on a third party who was unaware of that restriction. So the principal was bound. But *Watteau* demonstrates that agency and privity are strange bedfellows. It is highly anomalous that the existence of an agency relationship should enable a plaintiff to sue a defendant who expressly disavows any intention to benefit the plaintiff third party, whereas privity, in cases such as *Tweddle* v. *Atkinson* (see 7.1), prevents a plaintiff third party from suing a defendant who has expressly declared an intention to benefit the plaintiff.

7.10 The Trust Concept

We have already noted that, if A and B enter into a contract under which, in return for some act to be performed by B, A agrees to pay £50 to C, a failure by A to pay the £50 to C will constitute a breach of contract between A and B. There is no doubt that, in such a case, B has a right to sue A for breach of contract. A further question which may be asked is: in what capacity does B hold his contractual right to sue A for breach of contract? The answer to this question would appear to be an obvious one, namely that he holds it in his own capacity and for his own benefit. An alternative answer, however, is that he holds his contractual right to sue A on trust for the benefit of C. A trust is an equitable obligation to hold property on behalf of another. In this case the subject matter of the trust is A's promise to pay C and that promise can be held by B on trust for C. The property right created by the trust enables the beneficiary, C, to enforce the trust in his own name, although he was not a party to the agreement.

Such an analysis was adopted by the House of Lords in *Les Affréteurs Réunis* v. *Walford* [1919] AC 801. A term of a charterparty between a shipowner and a charterer stated that the shipowner would pay a commission to the broker who had negotiated the contract but was not party to the contract. It was held that the broker was a beneficiary of the trust, the subject matter of the trust being the promise by the shipowner to pay the broker, and that, as the beneficiary, he could enforce the promise. On the facts of *Walford*, the finding of an intention to create a trust of the promise appears to be no more than a fiction designed to do justice on the facts of the case by enabling the broker to sue the shipowner. The device may have been inelegant and artificial, but it effectively evaded the doctrine of privity. Indeed, Corbin argued (1930) that this was a device by which privity might be discarded in its entirety when a third party could show that he was the intended beneficiary of a promise.

However, since *Walford* was decided, the courts have had a change of heart and this device is now practically defunct. The courts have undermined it by insisting upon strict proof of an intention to create a trust of the promise (*Re Schebsman* [1944] Ch 83), instead of treating the requirement of intention as a fiction which simply enabled the court to invoke the doctrine. To establish the existence of a trust of the promise it must now be shown that the promisee intended the benefit of the contract to be enjoyed by the third party (*Vandepitte* v. *Preferred Accident Corp. of New York* [1933] AC 70) and the promise to benefit the third party must generally be intended to be irrevocable. By a rigorous insistence upon compliance with these requirements, the courts have rendered this device practically insignificant.

7.11 The Role of the Law of Tort

Instead of bringing a contractual action, a third party may elect to bring an action against the promisor in the tort of negligence. Two cases illustrate this process. The first is *Ross* v. *Caunters* [1980] Ch 297. The defendant, who was a solicitor, failed to inform a testator that attestation of a will by the spouse of a beneficiary would invalidate any gift to that beneficiary. The plaintiff, whose husband had signed the will, sued the defendant in negligence for the loss of her gift under the will. It was held that the plaintiff was entitled to recover from the defendant because the defendant had been negligent and there was a close relationship of proximity between the defendant and the plaintiff since the defendant could foresee that the plaintiff, as an individual, would suffer damage as a result of his negligence. Now the point to note here is that the plaintiff was not privy to the contract between the solicitor and the testator, nor had she provided any consideration, but the *effect* of granting a remedy in tort was to put the plaintiff in the position which she would have been in had the contract between the defendant and the testator been performed by the defendant with reasonable care. Rules of privity and consideration were circumvented by framing the action in tort (for criticism see Jaffey, 1985).

The second and more infamous case is *Junior Books Ltd* v. *The Veitchi Co Ltd* [1983] 1 AC 520. The defendants were contractors who specialised in laying floors. The plaintiffs had entered into a contract with the main contractors for the construction of a factory but they nominated the defendants to lay the factory floor. So the main contractors sub-contracted the laying of the floor to the defendants. The plaintiffs argued that the floor had been laid defectively by the defendants and claimed damages from them, including the cost of replacing the factory floor. Thus they were seeking to be put in the position in which they would have been if the sub-contractors had laid the floor in accordance with their contract with the main contractors. Once again it should be noted that there was no contract between the defendants and the plaintiffs. The contracts were between the defendants and the main contractors and between the main contractors and the plaintiffs. Nevertheless the House of Lords held that the plaintiffs were entitled to succeed in an action in tort against the defendants because of the extremely close relationship between the parties. The crucial elements in this relationship appear to be, firstly, the fact that the plaintiffs relied upon the skill of the defendants in laying the floor, as indicated by the fact that they nominated the defendants to do the work and, secondly, the fact that the defendants assumed an obligation towards the plaintiffs. It is not easy to see in what respects the defendants did assume an obligation towards the plaintiffs because the contractual relationships between the parties were structured in such a way that the defendants did *not* assume any direct responsibility towards the plaintiffs. In later cases courts have held that the assumption of a contractual responsibility by a sub-contractor to a main contractor makes it very difficult to establish that the sub-contractor has assumed an additional obligation in tort to the plaintiff (see *Simaan General Contracting Co* v. *Pilkington Glass Ltd (No 2)* [1988] QB 758).

In any event *Junior Books* is a highly anomalous case. The damaged floor was not the cause of personal injury, nor did it damage any other property of the plaintiffs. It was simply the case that the floor was less valuable than it would have been had the contracts been performed according to their terms. To allow the plaintiffs to recover in respect of such damage in a tort action conflicts with the general rule that, where the defect simply renders the product less valuable, the plaintiff's remedy, if any, lies in contract (see *D & F Estates Ltd* v. *Church Commissioners for England* [1989] AC 177).

The tort action therefore provides only a limited exception to the doctrine of privity. The most obvious limitation is that the promisor must have been negligent; it would not avail the plaintiff in *Tweddle* v. *Atkinson* where the defendant was not negligent but simply refused to carry out his promise. The second limitation is that there must be an extremely close relationship between the plaintiff and the defendant in order to justify the imposition of a duty of care upon the defendant.

7.12 Assignment

We have already seen that, if A and B enter into a contract under which, in return for some act to be performed by B, A agrees to pay £50 to C, C will be prevented by the doctrine of privity from suing to enforce the contract. However if B validly assigned to C his contractual rights against A then, provided the assignment has been validly made, C may sue A for the money. It is highly anomalous that English law allows for the assignation of rights which have already been created, but prevents A and B from conferring enforceable rights upon C from the very outset of their agreement.

Although at common law it was not possible to assign rights, rights can be assigned in equity or under s.136(1) of the Law of Property Act 1925 (for the detailed requirements of each method of assignment see Treitel, 1987, ch. 16). The principal disadvantage of assignment from the perspective of the assignee is that any defence which would have succeeded against the assignor will also succeed against the assignee; the assignee takes 'subject to equities'.

7.13 Negotiable Instruments

A negotiable instrument is a type of written promise under which the right to enforce that promise may be transferred either by delivery or by delivery and indorsement of the person to whom the debt was payable. The principal categories of negotiable instruments are bills of exchange, cheques and promissory notes. For example, a cheque is a written order by a person ('the drawer') to his bank ('the drawee') to pay on demand a stated sum of money to a named person. Now that person can transfer the cheque to another party and that third party can demand payment from the bank, even though he was not privy to any contract with the bank and has not himself furnished the bank with any consideration. The advantage of a negotiable instrument as compared with an assignment is that a bona fide holder for value who is without notice of any defect in the title of the transferor obtains a good title and is able to demand payment and therefore does not take 'subject to equities'.

7.14 Statutory Exceptions

There are a number of statutory exceptions to the doctrine of privity. These exceptions have no coherent rationale but are largely responses to the exigencies of the moment. The importance of these statutory exceptions should not be underestimated. One commentator has remarked that, 'but for the statutory exceptions, the doctrine of privity would undoubtedly have been abolished long ago upon it having become widely appreciated that, for example, third parties had no right to the proceeds of life insurance policies taken out for their benefit' (Flannigan, 1987). Thus section 11 of the Married Women's Property Act 1882 states that, where a man has insured his life for the benefit of his wife and children, the policy shall create a trust in favour of the objects therein named. Third parties have been allowed, in certain circumstances, to sue on fire or marine insurance policies (Marine Insurance Act 1906 s.14(2)) and an injured third party may recover compensation from the insured's insurance company once he has obtained judgment against the insured (Road Traffic Act 1972 s.148(4)). Section 56 of the Law of Property Act 1925 provides that 'a person may take an immediate or other interest in land or other property, or the benefit of any condition, right of entry, covenant or agreement over or respecting land or other property, although he may not be named as a party to the conveyance or other instrument'. Finally, under section 1 of the Bills of Lading Act 1855, a buyer of a cargo at sea who takes the transfer of a bill of lading can enforce the contract of carriage as if he had been a party to it from the outset.

7.15 The Need for Reform?

Although English law recognises the existence of a number of exceptions to the doctrine of privity, it cannot be claimed that the present state of the law is satisfactory. Some of the evasive devices used are artificial, as in the case of the trust of the promise device and the collateral contract device. The contorted reasoning of the Privy Council in *The Eurymedon* (see above 7.6) demonstrates the unnecessary complexities which can arise in seeking to give effect to the intention of the contracting parties in extending the benefit of an exclusion clause to a third party. Would it not be simpler and more elegant to recognise the existence of enforceable third party rights as advocated by Lord Denning in *Smith and Snipes Hall Farm Ltd* v. *River Douglas Catchment Board* (see above, 7.2)?

In my opinion English law should take the step of abolishing the doctrine of privity. The exceptions undermine the rule, they are artificial and inelegant, and the limitations of the exceptions are such that they cannot ensure that injustice will not arise. But it should not be assumed that the introduction of a doctrine of third party enforceable rights will bring an end to all our difficulties. The doctrine of consideration will have to be reconsidered if effective third party rights are to be introduced. Difficult problems will arise in deciding the appropriate *scope* of the third party right. For example, at what point in time will the third party acquire his right: when the two parties conclude the contract for his benefit, when he is told of the existence of the contract or when he acts to his detriment in the belief that he has acquired a right under the contract? When will the third party have a sufficient interest to enforce the agreement? What defences will the promisor enjoy in any action by the third party? Will it be possible to circumvent any limitation placed upon the scope of the third party-enforceable right by an action in tort? (see, for example, *Junior Books*; this was a Scottish case, and Scots law recognises the existence of enforceable third party rights, yet the plaintiffs still had to have resort to the law of tort to secure a remedy.) It is only by facing up to these difficult questions that English contract lawyers can hope to rid themselves of a doctrine of privity which is commercially inconvenient, fundamentally unjust and a blot on English contract law.

Summary

1 The doctrine of privity consists of two distinct rules.

2 The first is that a third party cannot be subjected to a burden by a contract to which he is not a party.

3 The second is that a person who is not a party to a contract cannot claim the benefit of it, even though the contract was entered into with the object of benefiting that third party.

4 Although the two rules are generally thought to be distinct, there is a very close relationship between the doctrine of privity and the rule that consideration must move from the promisee.

5 Where, in breach of contract with a promisee, a promisor has failed to confer a benefit on a third party, the promisee may bring an action for breach of contract against the promisor. The promisee may be able to obtain damages, specific performance or a stay of proceedings, but the general rule is that a promisee cannot recover damages on behalf of a third party.

6 A third party who seeks to procure a contracting party to break his contract without lawful justification commits a tort.

7 A third party cannot generally claim the protection of an exclusion clause contained in a contract between the plaintiff and another party as a defence to the plaintiff's action in tort. However, if the case falls within the scope of *The Eurymedon*, then the third party may be able to enjoy such protection.

8 There are a number of exceptional cases in which English law does recognise the existence of enforceable third party rights.

9 In limited circumstances a court may be prepared to find the existence of a contract between the promisor and the third party which is collateral to the contract between the promisor and the promisee.

10 An agent may bring into existence a contract between his principal and a third party. An agency relationship arises where one party, the agent, is authorised by another, the principal, to negotiate and to enter into contracts on behalf of the principal.

11 Where an intention to create a trust can be shown to exist, a promisee may hold his right to sue the promisor on trust for the third party beneficiary, who can therefore sue to enforce the promise.

12 In limited circumstances a third party may be able to bring an action in the tort of negligence against a negligent promisor.

13 There are a large number of statutory exceptions to the doctrine of privity.

14 Provided that the relevant formalities are complied with a promisee may assign his right to sue the promisor to a third party.

Exercises

1 Explain the relationship between the doctrine of privity and the rule that consideration must move from the promisee.

2 John and Sarah go out for a meal at Freddy's restaurant. Sarah pays for the meal. John's meal is inedible. What remedies are available to Sarah? If Sarah refuses to sue, could John sue? (See *Lockett* v. *AM Charles Ltd* [1938] 4 All ER 170.)

3 In what circumstances can a defendant claim the protection of an exclusion clause contained in a contract to which he was not a party?

4 List the exceptional cases in which English law does recognise the existence of enforceable third party rights. Do these exceptions undermine the rule?

5 Do you think that English law should adopt the proposal of Lord Denning in Smith and Snipes Hall Farm Ltd *v.* River Douglas Catchment Board (see 7.2) that English law should recognise the existence of a doctrine of third party-enforceable rights? What restrictions does Lord Denning place upon the scope of such a third party right? Are these restrictions desirable?

Part II

The Content of a Contract

8 What is a Term?

Having considered what the law recognises as a valid, enforceable contract and who is bound by that contract, we shall now consider the contents of a contract. This part is divided into four chapters. In this chapter we shall consider what constitutes a term of the contract; in Chapter 9 we shall discuss the sources of contractual terms; in Chapter 10 we shall consider the classification of contractual terms; and in Chapter 11 we shall analyse a particular type of contractual term, the exclusion or limitation clause.

8.1 What is a Term?

A contract consists of a number of terms. However not everything that is said or written during the course of negotiations constitutes a term of the contract. An example will illustrate the point. Suppose that I agree to sell my word processor to my neighbour. During the course of negotiations he may ask me many things about it; its age, how often it has been used, whether it does footnotes, the speed of the printer and so on. But the conclusion of the contract may consist simply of my statement, 'I will sell you the word processor for £500' and his statement, 'I accept'. It is, however, highly unlikely that the contract will consist simply of this single term. It is equally unlikely that all my answers to my neighbour's questions will be regarded as terms of the contract. My answers could, in fact, be classified in one of three ways.

The first is that some answers could be treated as mere statements of opinion or 'mere puffs' and will have no legal effect (for example, a statement that the printer 'goes like a bomb'; see further, 13.3). The principal distinction, however, is between the second and the third categories; that is, between a term and a mere representation (note that in some cases the distinction is drawn between 'warranties' and 'mere representations', but this terminology will not be used here because it leads to confusion when, in Chapter 10, we seek to distinguish between a condition and a warranty (both of which are terms of a contract)). The distinction between a term and a mere representation is important because, if a statement is held to be a term of the contract, a failure to comply with it will be a breach of contract, entitling the innocent party to a remedy for breach of contract. On the other hand, if the statement is held to be a mere representation, the innocent party cannot claim that there has been a breach of contract because the statement was not a term of the contract. His remedy, if any, is to seek to have the contract set aside or claim damages for misrepresentation (see further, Chapter 13).

Whether a statement is a contractual term or a mere representation depends, ultimately, on the intention with which the statement is made. In considering the intention with which a particular statement is made, the courts have, once again, adopted an objective approach to intention. The cases have established some principles (see 8.2–8.4) to guide the court in deciding whether a statement is a term or a mere representation. None of these principles is decisive; in each case the court must assess their relative importance (see Lord Moulton in Heilbut, *Symons & Co* v. *Buckleton* [1913] AC 30, 50–51).

8.2 Verification

A statement is unlikely to be a term of the contract if the maker of the statement asks the other party to verify its truth. In *Ecay* v. *Godfrey* (1947) 80 Ll LR 286, a seller of a boat stated that the boat was sound, but advised the buyer to have it surveyed. His statement was held to be a mere representation. On the other hand, in *Schawel* v. *Reade* [1913] 2 IR 64, the plaintiff, while examining a horse with a view to buying it for stud purposes, was told by the defendant: 'You need not look for anything; the horse is perfectly sound. If there was anything the matter with this horse I should tell you.' In reliance upon this statement the plaintiff bought the horse without examining it. It was subsequently discovered that the horse was totally unfit for stud purposes and it was held that the defendant's statement was a term of the contract (contrast *Hopkins* v. *Tanqueray* (1854) 15 CB 130).

8.3 Importance

A statement is likely to be a term of the contract where it is of such importance to the person to whom it is made that, had it not been made, he would not have entered into the contract. In *Couchman* v. *Hill* [1947] KB 554, a heifer was put up for sale at an auction but no warranty was given as to its condition. The plaintiff asked the defendant whether the heifer was in calf and stated that he was not interested in purchasing it if it was. He was told that it was not in calf. Approximately seven weeks after the purchase the heifer suffered a miscarriage and died. The plaintiff brought an action for breach of contract. The statement that the heifer was not in calf was held to be a term of the contract because of the importance attached to it by the plaintiff (contrast *Oscar Chess Ltd* v. *Williams* [1957] 1 WLR 370, discussed at 8.4).

8.4 Special Knowledge

If the maker of a statement has some special knowledge or skill compared to the other party, the statement may be held to be a contractual term. On the other hand if the parties' degrees of knowledge are equal or if the person to whom the statement is made has the greater knowledge, the statement may be held to be a mere representation. These propositions can be illustrated by reference to the following two cases.

The first is *Oscar Chess Ltd* v. *Williams* (above), in which the defendant sold a car to the plaintiffs for £290. The car was described as a 1948 Morris 10; in fact it was a 1939 model (which was worth only £175). The defendant had obtained the information that the car was a 1948 model in good faith from the car log book, but the log book was subsequently discovered to be a forgery. It was held that the defendant's statement as to the age of the car was not a term of the contract but a mere representation. The plaintiffs, who were car dealers, were in at least as good a position as the defendant to know the true age of the car. On the other hand, in *Dick Bentley Productions Ltd* v. *Harold Smith (Motors) Ltd* [1965] 1 WLR 623, the plaintiff asked the defendants, who were car dealers, to find him a 'well vetted' Bentley car. The defendants found a car which they sold to the plaintiff and which they stated had done only 20 000 miles since a replacement engine had been fitted. It had in fact done 100 000 miles. It was held that the defendants' statement as to the car mileage was a term of the contract; the defendants, being car dealers, were in a better position than the plaintiff to know whether their statement was true.

8.5 The Consequences of the Distinction between a Term and a Mere Representation

Although the distinction between a term and a mere representation is important, it is not quite as fundamental as it used to be. At the beginning of this century it was important because damages were only available for misrepresentation in a very narrow range of circumstances. But now, both at common law and under the Misrepresentation Act 1967, damages are available for misrepresentation in a much wider range of circumstances (see 13.9). The distinction is now primarily relevant to the *amount* of damages recoverable rather than to whether damages are recoverable at all (although there do remain cases in which damages are not recoverable for misrepresentation: see 13.9). If the statement is held to be a term, breach will generally entitle the innocent party to damages which will have the effect of putting him in the position which he would have been in had the contract been performed (called his 'expectation interest'), whereas if it is a representation, damages will generally be assessed on the basis of the extent to which the representee has incurred loss through reliance on the misrepresentation (the 'reliance interest') (see further Chapter 20).

8.6 Can a Representation be Incorporated into a Contract as a Term?

This may seem a strange question to ask, given that we have spent a chapter arguing that the two are separate and distinct. The issue can be illustrated by reference to the case of *Pennsylvania Shipping Co* v. *Compagnie Nationale de Navigation* [1936] 2 All ER 1167. A tanker was chartered from the defendants by the plaintiffs. Prior to the conclusion of the contract, the defendants provided the plaintiffs with incorrect information about the heating of the ship. This information was subsequently incorporated into the contract. When the plaintiffs discovered the true position, they sought, *inter alia*, to have the contract set aside on the ground of misrepresentation. Branson J held that the representation became 'merged in the higher contractual right' and that there was therefore no need to set aside the contract on the ground of misrepresentation; the plaintiffs' claim was for breach of contract (contrast *Compagnie Française des Chemins de Fer Paris–Orleans* v. *Leeston Shipping Co* (1919) 1 Ll LR 235). However section 1(a) of the Misrepresentation Act 1967 now provides that a representee who has entered into a contract after a misrepresentation has been made to him may rescind the contract for misrepresentation, even though the misrepresentation is subsequently incorporated into the contract, provided that he would otherwise be entitled to rescind the contract. This may be of very great significance where the representee is unable to rescind the contract for breach because, for example, the term which has been broken is a warranty (see further, 10.3). In such a case, provided the relevant conditions for rescission for misrepresentation are satisfied (on which see 13.8), he may nevertheless be entitled to rescind for misrepresentation.

Summary

1 A contract consists of a number of terms.

2 A term must be distinguished from a statement of opinion or 'mere puff' (which has no legal effect) and a mere representation (which generates an action in misrepresentation).

3 Whether a statement is a term or a mere representation depends upon the intention with which the statement was made. Factors to which the courts will have regard in deciding this issue include whether the maker of the statement advised the other party to verify the truth of his statement, the importance of the statement and the respective states of knowledge of the parties.

4 In certain circumstances the term/representation dichotomy may be crucial to the recoverability of damages, but it is more likely that it will be relevant to the amount of damages recoverable. Where a term of the contract has been broken damages will generally protect the promisee's expectation interest, but in the case of a misrepresentation damages will only protect the misrepresentee's reliance interest.

5 A representee who has entered into a contract after a misrepresentation has been made to him may rescind the contract for misrepresentation, even though the misrepresentation is subsequently incorporated into the contract, provided that he would otherwise be entitled to rescind for misrepresentation.

Exercises

1 Why do lawyers distinguish between a term and a mere representation?

2 Distinguish between a term and a mere representation. What are the consequences of this distinction?

3 John, a specialist racehorse trainer, wished to buy a horse from Fred, who was a farmer who had little knowledge of horses. John believed that the horse was a potential champion and, during the course of negotiations, he asked Fred if he could inspect it. Fred said that there was really no need as his stable-boy had assured him that the horse would make a 'brilliant racehorse'. In reliance on Fred's statement, John bought the horse. When the horse was delivered to John, he found it had a serious leg injury which made it useless as a racehorse. John wishes to know whether his remedy lies for breach of contract or for misrepresentation. Advise him.

4 What is the effect of s.1(a) of the Misrepresentation Act 1967?

9 The Sources of Contractual Terms

9.1 Introduction

There are two principal sources of contractual terms: express terms and implied terms. Express terms are the terms which are agreed specifically by the contracting parties and implied terms are those terms which are not specifically agreed by the contracting parties but which are implied into the contract by the courts or by Parliament. We shall deal with implied terms at 9.8. Here we shall focus our attention on express terms.

Express terms may be agreed orally or in writing. Where the contract is made orally the ascertainment of the contractual terms may involve difficult questions of fact, but the task of a judge is simply to decide exactly what was said by each of the parties. More particular difficulties arise in the case of written contracts. Three such difficulties will be dealt with here. The first and fundamental issue is whether the court can go beyond the written agreement in an attempt to discover the existence of additional terms to the contract (9.2). The second is whether a person is necessarily bound by the terms of a contract which he has signed (9.3). The third and final issue is whether written terms can be incorporated into a contract, either by notice (9.4) or by a course of dealing (9.5). Once we have discussed these issues we shall consider the approach which the courts adopt towards the interpretation of contracts (9.6).

9.2 The Parol Evidence Rule

Once the contracting parties have elected to enshrine their contract in a written document, the courts have held that, as a general rule, the parties cannot adduce extrinsic evidence to add to, vary or contradict the written document; the document is the sole repository of the terms of the contract (*Jacobs* v. *Batavia & General Plantations Trust Ltd* [1924] 1 Ch 287). This rule has been called the 'parol evidence rule'. The purpose behind this rule is said to be the promotion of certainty; that is to say, once the parties have gone to the trouble of drawing up a written document, one party should not be able to allege with impunity that there were, in fact, other terms which were, for some reason, not incorporated into the final written document.

If this rule were to be applied rigidly to all cases there is no doubt that it would produce considerable injustice. For example, the written document may have been procured by fraud and so one party would wish to lead extrinsic evidence to prove that fraud. So it is no surprise to find that the parol evidence rule is not an absolute rule, but is the subject of numerous exceptions. We will now consider the scope of these exceptions and then consider their implications for the status of the rule.

The first exception is that the rule does not apply where the written document was not intended to contain the whole of the agreement (*Allen v. Pink* (1838) 4 M & W 140). As Wedderburn has remarked (1959) this exception reduces the rule to 'no more than a self-evident tautology . . . when the writing is the whole contract, the parties are bound by it and parol evidence is excluded; when it is not, evidence of the other terms must be admitted'. The Law Commission in its recent report (No 154 Cmnd 9700 (1986)) has agreed with this observation, adding that the parol evidence rule is 'no more than a circular statement'. On this view the parol evidence rule does not give rise to injustice because it will never prevent a party from leading evidence of terms which were intended to be part of the contract. On the other hand it must be remembered that the courts will presume that a document which looks like the contract is the whole contract. However this presumption is rebuttable and the presumption operates with less strength today than in former times and it is therefore highly unlikely that the parol evidence rule will preclude a party from leading evidence of terms which were intended to be part of the contract.

Parol evidence is also admissible to prove terms which must be implied into the agreement (*Gillespie Bros & Co v. Cheney, Eggar & Co* [1896] 2 QB 59); to prove a custom which must be implied into the contract (*Hutton v. Warren* (1836) 1 M & W 466); to show that the contract is invalid on the ground of misrepresentation, mistake, fraud or *non est factum* (on which see 9.3 and *Campbell Discount Co v. Gall* [1961] 1 QB 431); to show that the document should be rectified; to show that the contract has not yet come into operation or that it has ceased to operate (*Pym v. Campbell* (1856) 6 E & B 370) and to prove the existence of a collateral agreement (*Mann v. Nunn* (1874) 30 LT 526). The latter exception is of particular significance because in one case extrinsic evidence was actually used to *contradict* the terms of the written agreement. In *City and Westminster Properties (1934) Ltd v. Mudd* [1959] Ch 129, a lease entered into by the parties contained a covenant which stated that the tenant could use the premises for business purposes only. The tenant had been induced to sign the lease by an oral assurance given by the lessors' agent that the lessors would not raise any objection to the tenant continuing his practice of residing in the premises. In an action by the lessors to forfeit the lease on the ground that the tenant was using the premises for residential purposes, it was held that evidence of the assurance given by the lessors' agent was admissible to prove the existence of a collateral agreement, despite the fact that it contradicted the express terms of the written lease. This case had been subjected to some criticism and it does appear to be inconsistent with earlier cases such as *Angell* v. *Duke* (1875) 32 LT 320 and *Henderson* v. *Arthur* [1907] 1 KB 10. However, if the collateral agreement is truly a separate agreement, then there is no reason why it should not be contrary to the terms of the written agreement. That said, it must be conceded that the effect of the decision is largely to undermine the parol evidence rule.

The parol evidence rule has been subjected to considerable criticism. The exceptions are so wide that they subvert the purpose of the rule in promoting certainty. Indeed, the width of the exceptions is such that it must now be doubted whether there is a 'rule' in English law that parol evidence is not admissible to add to, vary or contradict the written document. In the light of these criticisms the Law Commission provisionally recommend in 1976 (Working Paper No 76) that the parol evidence rule be abolished but, in its more recent report (No 154 Cmnd 9700), it concluded that no legislative action need be taken, for two reasons. The first was that the rule did not preclude the courts from having recourse to extrinsic evidence where such a course was consistent with the intention of the parties. The second reason was that any legislative change would be more likely to confuse than clarify the law. Therefore the 'rule' remains in existence but it must be remembered that it is a rule which, because of the width of the exceptions, is unlikely to have significant effects in practice.

9.3 Bound by Your Signature?

Despite the existence of numerous exceptions to the parol evidence rule, English law does attach some importance to the sanctity of written documents and this can be seen in the general rule that a person is bound by a document which he signs, whether he reads it or not. This proposition can be derived from the case of *L'Estrange* v. *F Graucob Ltd* [1934] 2 KB 394. The plaintiff bought an automatic slot machine from the defendants. She signed an order form which contained a clause which excluded liability for all express and implied warranties. When the plaintiff discovered that the machine did not work she brought an action against the defendants for breach of an implied warranty that the machine was fit for the purpose for which it was sold. Judgment was given for the defendants on the ground that they had excluded their liability by virtue of the exclusion clause which was incorporated into the contract by the plaintiff's signature, even though the exclusion clause was in 'regrettably small print' and had not been read by the plaintiff. Given the widespread use of contracts which rely heavily upon the use of small print, such a rule appears singularly unfortunate. However, the rule is subject to exceptions where the signature has been procured by fraud, misrepresentation or the defence of *non est factum* is made out. Fraud and misrepresentation will be dealt with in Chapter 13. Here we shall discuss the defence of *non est factum*.

The defence of *non est factum* is a defence of respectable antiquity in English law. It was originally applied to the case where an illiterate person signed a deed which had been read to him incorrectly by another person. In such a case the illiterate person was not bound by the deed; to put it in technical terms, he could plead *non est factum*, which means 'this is not my deed'. The effect of *non est factum* is to render the deed void so that a third party cannot obtain good title under it (see further on the issue of third party rights the discussion at 4.6). As the doctrine has developed, it has had to grapple with the problem that it is seeking to reconcile two competing policies. These policies are, firstly, the injustice of holding a person to a bargain to which he has not brought a consenting mind and the second is the necessity of holding a person to a document which he has signed, especially where innocent third parties rely to their detriment upon the validity of the signature.

These two competing policies can be seen at work in the important decision of the House of Lords in *Saunders* v. *Anglia Building Society* (also referred to as *Gallie* v. *Lee*) [1971] AC 1004. A widow of 78 made a will in which she left her house to her nephew. However the nephew wished to raise money immediately on the security of the home. The widow was prepared to help her nephew to raise the money provided that she was permitted to live in her home for the rest of her life rent free. The difficulty for the nephew was that he did not want to raise the loan in his own name because he was afraid that his wife would get her hands on the money. So he arranged that a friend of his should raise the money on the security of the house. The nephew arranged for the preparation of a document assigning the house to the friend for £3000. The widow did not read the document because her glasses were broken, but she signed it after the friend told her that it was a deed of gift to the nephew. The friend raised money on a mortgage with the respondent building society but he made no payment either to the building society, the nephew or the widow. The building society sought to recover possession of the property from the widow, who invoked the defence of *non est factum*. Here we have the clash of the competing policies which we noted above. On the one hand there is the injustice of holding the widow to an agreement to which she had not brought a consenting mind, but on the other hand there is the need to protect the building society which had innocently relied to its detriment upon the widow's signature. The House of Lords gave greater weight to the second policy than the first and held that the defence of *non est factum* was not made out on the facts of the case. They established that the defence was only available within narrow confines; its scope can best be considered by asking ourselves three questions.

The first question is: to whom is the plea available? As originally conceived, the doctrine only applied to those who were unable to read. However in *Saunders* it was held that the doctrine was not confined to those who are blind or illiterate. It extends to those 'who are permanently or temporarily unable through no fault of their own to have without explanation any real understanding or purport of a particular document, whether that be from defective education, illness or innate incapacity'. Their Lordships did not say that the defence could never be available to a person of full capacity, but it would only be available to him in the most exceptional of cases and would not be available simply because he was too busy or too lazy to read the document.

The second question is: for what type of mistake is the defence available? Initially it was held that the defence was available if the mistake went to the heart of the transaction (*Foster* v. *MacKinnon* (1869) LR 4 CP 704). But in *Howatson* v. *Webb* [1907] 1 Ch 537 Warrington J drew a distinction between a mistake as to the 'character' of the document and a mistake as to its 'content', only the former being sufficient to support a plea of *non est factum*. However this distinction was rejected by the House of Lords in *Saunders* on the ground that it was 'arbitrary'. Instead it was held that the difference between the document as it was and as it was believed to be must be radical or substantial or fundamental. This test was not satisfied on the facts of *Saunders* because the widow wished to benefit her nephew by enabling him to raise money on the security of the house and the document which she signed was in fact intended to do this, although it was designed to do it by a different route, namely by assignation to the friend instead of by gift to the nephew.

The third and final question is: in what circumstances is a person precluded from relying on the defence? The principal defence here is carelessness on the part of the person who signs the document. In *United Dominions Trust Ltd* v. *Western* [1976] QB 513, the defendant signed a loan agreement with the plaintiff company in connection with the purchase of a car and he left it to the garage owner to fill in the details, including the price. The garage owner increased the price of the car and the plaintiff company paid over the money to the garage owner in good faith. The court held that the onus was on the defendant to show that, in allowing the form to be filled in by the garage owner, he had acted carefully. It was held that he had wholly failed to discharge that onus and therefore could not invoke the defence of *non est factum*.

It is clear that English law has given considerable weight to the idea that a person should be able to rely on the signature of a contracting party. Such protection would be undermined by a wide defence of *non est factum* because it would render agreements void and thus detrimentally affect third party rights. However it should not be assumed that, where the defence of *non est factum* fails, the person who signs the document will therefore be left without a remedy. He may have a remedy in misrepresentation, fraud or undue influence (see *Avon Finance Co* v. *Bridger* [1985] 2 All ER 281). But the important point to note is that misrepresentation, fraud and undue influence only render the contract voidable and so greater protection is thereby afforded to third party rights.

9.4 Incorporation of Written Terms

Contracting parties may agree to incorporate a set of written terms into their contract. Three hurdles must be overcome before such terms can be incorporated. The first is that notice of the terms must be given at or before the time of concluding the contract. It is therefore crucial to determine the *precise* moment at which the contract was concluded. In *Olley* v. *Marlborough Court Ltd* [1949] 1 KB 532, a notice in the bedroom of a hotel, which purported to exempt the hotel proprietors from any liability for articles lost or stolen from the hotel, was held not to be incorporated into a contract with a guest, whose furs were stolen from her bedroom, because the notice was not seen by the guest until after the contract had been concluded at the hotel reception desk.

Secondly, the terms must be contained or referred to in a document which was intended to have contractual effect. It is a question of fact whether or not a document was intended to have contractual effect and the issue must be decided by reference to current commercial or consumer practices. In *Chapleton* v. *Barry UDC* [1940] 1 KB 532, the plaintiff hired a deck-chair from the defendants. On paying his money he was given a ticket, which, unknown to him, contained a number of conditions, including an exclusion clause. The plaintiff was injured when he sat in the deck chair and it gave way beneath him. He sued the defendants, who relied by way of defence on the exclusion clause contained in the ticket. It was held that they could not rely on the exclusion clause because it was contained in a mere receipt which was not intended to havee contractual effect.

Thirdly, and finally, reasonable steps must be taken to bring the terms to the attention of the other party. In *Parker* v. *South Eastern Railway* (1877) 2 CPD 416, it was established that the test is whether the defendant took reasonable steps to bring the notice to the attention of the plaintiff, not whether the plaintiff actually read the notice. Thus, in *Thompson* v. *London, Midland and Scottish Railway Co Ltd* [1930] 1 KB 41, an exclusion clause contained in a railway timetable was held to be validly incorporated, despite the fact that the plaintiff was illiterate and therefore unable to read the clause. The result may be different, however, where the party seeking to rely on the exclusion clause knows of the disability of the other party (*Richardson, Spence and Co Ltd* v. *Rowntree* [1894] AC 217).

What amounts to reasonable notice is a question which depends upon the facts and circumstances of the individual case. In *Thompson* the defendants were held to have taken reasonable steps to bring the exclusion clause to the attention of the plaintiff, even though it was contained on page 552 of the timetable and the timetable cost one-fifth of the price of the railway ticket. It is doubtful whether such a liberal view would be taken today. If the clause is not referred to on the front of the ticket (*Henderson* v. *Stevenson* (1875) LR 2 Sc & Div 470) or if the reference to the clause is obliterated (*Sugar* v. *London, Midland and Scottish Railway Co* [1941] 1 All ER 172) the clause is less likely to be incorporated into the contract. Similarly, the more unusual or unreasonable the exclusion clause, the greater the degree of the notice required by the courts. In *J Spurling Ltd* v. *Bradshaw* [1956] 1 WLR 461, Denning LJ said that some clauses would need to be printed in red ink on the face of the document with a red hand pointing to it before the notice could be held to be sufficient.

All of the 'incorporation' cases which we have considered so far are concerned with attempts to incorporate exclusion clauses into a contract. They generally evince a restrictive approach to incorporation, particularly in cases such as *Spurling* v. *Bradshaw* (above) where Lord Denning enunciated his 'red hand rule'. It could be argued that such a restrictive approach is confined to exclusion clauses and, indeed, that, since the enactment of the Unfair Contract Terms Act 1977, which gives the courts considerable power to control exclusion clauses (see 11.9), there is little need for such a restrictive approach, even in the case of exclusion clauses. But a recent case shows that the restrictive approach is very much alive and, further, that it is not confined to exclusion clauses.

The recent case is *Interfoto Picture Library Ltd* v. *Stiletto Visual Programmes Ltd* [1988] 2 WLR 615 (see further Macdonald, 1988a). The defendants ordered photographic transparencies from the plaintiffs, not having dealt with them before. The plaintiffs duly sent them 47 transparencies, together with a delivery note which contained a number of conditions. Condition 2 stated that a holding fee of £5 per day was payable for every day the transparencies were kept in excess of fourteen days. The defendants failed to return them on time and were sent an invoice for £3783.50, which they refused to pay. In an action by the plaintiffs to recover the £3783.50, the Court of Appeal held that condition 2 was not incorporated into the contract because insufficient notice had been given to the defendants of its terms and that the plaintiffs were only entitled to a restitutionary award of £3.50 per transparency per week. It was held that a party who seeks to incorporate into a contract a term which is particularly onerous *or* unusual must prove that the term has been fairly and reasonably drawn to the attention of the other party. Bingham LJ argued that cases on sufficiency of notice are concerned with the question 'whether it would in all the circumstances be fair (or reasonable) to hold a party bound by any conditions . . . of an unusual and stringent nature'. The utility of this general principle must surely be debatable and its application to the present facts even more so. The defendants were businessmen and were surely capable of reading the conditions on the delivery note. If they did not do so, they must be deemed to have accepted the risk that the terms might prove to be unacceptable to them. The objection that the terms were particularly onerous could have been dealt with by arguing that condition 2 was a penalty clause (an argument which Bingham LJ suggested could have succeeded). There is no need to apply different standards on the issue of incorporation according to the severity of the term sought to be incorporated; the same test should be applied to all terms, regardless of their severity. Any unfairness in the terms sought to be incorporated should be dealt with by doctrines such as duress (see 17.1) and the penalty clause rule (see 21.5) and not by distorting the rules relating to the incorporation of terms into a contract.

9.5 Incorporation by a Course of Dealing

Terms may also be incorporated into a contract by a course of dealing. The courts have never defined course of dealing with any degree of precision, but some useful guidance was given by the House of Lords in *McCutcheon* v. *David MacBrayne Ltd* [1964] 1 WLR 125. There it was held that the course of dealing must be both regular and consistent. What constitutes a 'regular' course of dealing depends upon the facts of the particular case. Thus, in *Henry Kendall Ltd* v. *William Lillico Ltd* [1969] 2 AC 31, the House of Lords held that 100 similar contracts over a period of three years constituted a course of dealing. But in *Hollier* v. *Rambler Motors (AMC) Ltd* [1972] 2 QB 71, three or four contracts over a period of five years was held not to be a course of dealing between a consumer and a garage. The position may be different, however, where the contracting parties are commercial parties of equal bargaining power. In *British Crane Hire Corporation Ltd* v. *Ipswich Plant Hire Ltd* [1975] QB 303, a clause was incorporated into the contract on the basis of two previous transactions and the custom of the trade. The court placed emphasis on the fact that the parties were of equal bargaining power; they were both in the trade and such conditions were habitually incorporated into these contracts.

The course of dealing must not only be regular, it must also be consistent. In *McCutcheon* v. *David MacBrayne Ltd* (above) a ferry belonging to the defendants sank and the plaintiff's car was lost. In the resulting action by the plaintiff, the defendants sought to rely on an exclusion clause contained in a risk note which, contrary to their usual practice, they had not asked the plaintiff's brother-in-law (who made the arrangement for the shipping of the plaintiff's car) to sign. The defendants' argument failed in the House of Lords because it was held that there was no consistent course of dealing on the basis of which the exclusion clause could be incorporated into the contract. Lord Pearce said that there was no consistent course of dealing because the previous transactions had always been in writing (that is, by the signing of the risk note) and in the present case the transaction was entirely oral. But this is surely to take the requirement of consistency too far, because the only reason for the defendants' reliance upon the course of dealing argument was that they had forgotten to ensure that the risk note was signed. If that forgetfulness, of itself, also had the effect of precluding them from relying upon the course of dealing argument, cases of incorporation by a course of dealing will be very rare (see further, Macdonald, 1988b). It is suggested that the better view of the case is that the evidence failed to establish a consistent course of dealing because, although on some occasions the brother-in-law had been asked to sign the risk note, there were other occasions when he had not been asked to sign. On this basis there was clearly no consistent course of dealing.

From the regularity and consistency of the course of dealing will be inferred knowledge of the conditions. In *McCutcheon* Lord Devlin said that previous dealings were only relevant if they proved actual knowledge of the terms and assent to them, but this view was not shared by other judges in the case and appears to have been rejected by the House of Lords in *Henry Kendall Ltd* v. *William Lillico Ltd* (above). However, where it can be shown that one party knows that the other has forgotten to include his usual exclusion clause and seeks to take advantage of it, he will not be allowed to do so and the exclusion clause will be incorporated, even in the absence of a regular and consistent course of dealing.

9.6 Interpretation

Once the terms of the contract have been ascertained, the terms must be interpreted to establish their 'true' meaning. Many contractual disputes arise out of disagreements over the proper interpretation of a particular phrase in a contract. What approach do the courts adopt towards the interpretation of a contract?

The starting-point is that it is for the courts, not the parties, to decide what is the proper interpretation of the contract. The guiding principle which the courts apply is that, in interpreting (or, as lawyers usually say, 'construing') the contract, the court must seek to ascertain and give effect to the intention of the parties. However in many cases the process of imputing an intention to the parties is an extremely artificial one, which is sharply influenced by the court's view of the 'desirability' of the contract term which it is called upon to interpret. There is no better illustration of this than the approach which the courts have adopted to the interpretation of exclusion clauses, where rules of interpretation have been used with particular venom in order to place difficult obstacles in the way of those who seek to exclude their liability towards others (see further 11.5–11.7). That this is indeed the case was recognised by Lord Diplock when he said that 'the reports are full of cases in which what would appear to be very strained constructions have been placed upon exclusion clauses' (*Photo Production Ltd* v. *Securicor Ltd* [1980] AC 827).

With this point in mind let us examine the way in which the courts seek to ascertain the intention of the parties. The general rule is that the intention of the parties must be ascertained from the document in which they have elected to enshrine their agreement (*Lovell & Christmas Ltd* v. *Wall* (1911) 104 LT 85). It is only in very limited circumstances that the courts can go outside the four corners of the document. Therefore the actual words used in the document are of crucial significance. In *Lovell & Christmas Ltd* v. *Wall* (above) Cozens-Hardy MR stated that 'it is the duty of the court . . . to construe the document according to the ordinary grammatical meaning of the words used therein'. But it should not be thought that English courts are 'left behind in some island of literal interpretation' (per Lord Wilberforce in *Prenn* v. *Simmonds* [1971] 1 WLR 1381). In the latter case Lord Wilberforce stated that 'the time has long passed when agreements . . . were isolated from the matrix of facts in which they were set and interpreted purely on internal linguistic considerations'. He said that the court 'must enquire beyond the language and see what the circumstances were with reference to which the words were used, and the object, appearing from those circumstances, which the person using them had in view'.

However the following types of evidence are not generally admissible. Evidence of pre-contractual negotiations is generally inadmissible because, during the negotiating process, the parties' positions are constantly changing and it is only the final document which actually records their agreement. Where there is an ambiguity in the final written document, evidence of pre-contractual negotiations may be admissible to show that the parties had attached a particular meaning to that phrase (*The Karen Oltman* [1976] 2 Lloyds Rep 708). Evidence of conduct subsequent to the making of the contract is also inadmissible because, were it otherwise, the contract could mean one thing on the day on which it was signed but mean something completely different one month after it was signed by virtue of the conduct of the parties after the making of the contract (*Schuler AG* v. *Wickman Machine Tool Sales Ltd* [1974] AC 235). However evidence of conduct subsequent to the making of the contract may be relevant to a plea of estoppel (*James Miller & Partners Ltd* v. *Whitworth Street Estates (Manchester) Ltd* [1970] AC 583). Finally, evidence of the parties' subjective intentions is not admissible (*Prenn* v. *Simmonds* (above)). Although the ascertainment of the intention of the parties is the guiding principle which underpins the process of interpretation, the intention of the parties is to be ascertained from an *objective* assessment of the wording of the contract and of the surrounding circumstances.

9.7 Rectification

Once the contract has been interpreted, one of the parties may argue that the written agreement, as interpreted, fails to reflect the agreement which the parties actually reached. In such a case the court may be asked to rectify the document so that it accurately reflects the agreement which the parties did reach. Such was the case in *Lovell & Christmas Ltd* v. *Wall* (above) where the plaintiff asked the court to adopt a particular interpretation of the contract and, when that argument failed, sought to have the contractual document rectified. However it should be noted that there is a distinction between interpretation and rectification, although in many cases the line between the two is a fine one. Interpretation is the process of ascribing a meaning to a term which is uncertain. Rectification, on the other hand, is a process whereby a document, the meaning of which has already been ascertained, is rectified so that it gives effect to the intention of the parties. Nevertheless it must be conceded that there are cases in which the courts have corrected minor errors in the expression of a document by a process of construction rather than by rectification. Thus in *Nittan (UK) Ltd* v. *Solent Steel Fabrication Ltd* [1981] 1 All ER 633, the Court of Appeal read 'Sargrove Electronic Controls Ltd' as if it read 'Sargrove Automation' and thereby avoided the need to rectify the document. However this process of construction will only be used to correct very minor errors.

Rectification is a remedy which is concerned with defects not in the making, but in the recording, of a contract. This distinction can be illustrated by reference to the case of *Frederick E Rose (London) Ltd* v. *William H Pim Jnr & Co Ltd* [1953] 2 QB 450. The plaintiffs were asked to supply certain buyers of theirs with a quantity of 'Moroccan horsebeans known here as feveroles'. The plaintiffs did not know what feveroles were and so they asked the defendants, who replied that they were simply horsebeans. So the parties entered into a contract for the supply by the defendants to the plaintiffs of 'horsebeans'. At the time of making the contract both parties believed that 'horsebeans' were 'feveroles'. It later transpired that 'feveroles' were a more expensive variety of horsebean than the type which had been supplied to the plaintiffs under the contract. When the plaintiffs' buyers claimed damages from the plaintiffs on the ground that the horsebeans which had been supplied to them were not 'feveroles', the plaintiffs sought to have the contract with the defendants rectified by the insertion of the word 'feveroles'. The Court of Appeal refused to rectify the contract. This was not a case in which the document failed to record the intention of the parties. The document did reflect their prior agreement; it was simply the case that the parties were under a shared misapprehension that 'horsebeans' were 'feveroles'.

Rectification is an equitable discretionary remedy. As such, it is only available in the discretion of the court. Originally the courts were reluctant to exercise this discretion but gradually they have become more willing to do so. In deciding whether to rectify a document a court will have regard to the following considerations.

The first is that a court will only rectify a document where 'convincing proof' is provided that the document fails to record the intention of the parties (*Joscelyne* v. *Nissen* [1970] 2 QB 86). A high degree of proof is needed so that certainty is not undermined (*The Olympic Pride* [1980] 2 Lloyds Rep 67, 73). The second is that the document must fail to record the intention of *both* parties. Unilateral mistake is insufficient of itself to base a claim to rectification (*Riverlate Properties* v. *Paul* [1975] Ch 133). But where one party mistakenly believes that the document correctly expresses the parties' common intention, and the other party is aware of that mistake, rectification may be available (*A Roberts and Co Ltd* v. *Leicestershire County Council* [1961] Ch 555). Thirdly, the document must have been preceded by a concluded contract or by a 'continuing common intention'. It is no longer the case that a prior contract is a prerequisite to rectification. In *Joscelyne* v. *Nissen* (above) a father and daughter agreed that the daughter would purchase the father's business and would, in return, pay all the expenses of the father's home, including the gas, electricity and coal bills. The formal contract signed by the parties made no mention of the fact that the daughter had agreed to pay these bills. There was no prior contract to which the court could have regard, but it was held that there was sufficient evidence of a continuing common intention that the daughter pay the gas, electricity and coal bills to enable the court to rectify the agreement to give effect to their common intention. Finally, rectification will not be granted in favour of a plaintiff who has been guilty of excessive delay in seeking rectification, nor will it be granted against a bona fide purchaser for value without notice.

9.8 Implied Terms

In addition to the terms which the parties have expressly agreed a court may be prepared to hold that other terms must be implied into the contract. Such terms may be implied from one of three sources.

The first is statute. Parliament has, in numerous instances, seen fit to imply terms into contracts. It is clear that these statutorily implied terms are not based upon the intention of the parties but on rules of law or public policy. As an illustration of statutorily implied terms we shall give very brief consideration to sections 12–15 of the Sale of Goods Act 1979. Thus it is an implied condition of a contract for the sale of goods that the seller has the right to sell the goods (s.12(1)) and there is an implied warranty that the goods are free from charges or incumbrances in favour of third parties (s.12(2)). There is also an implied condition that goods sold by description shall correspond with the description (s.13(1)) and that goods sold by sample shall correspond with the sample (s.15). In the case of a seller who sells goods in the course of a business, there is an implied condition that the goods supplied under the contract are of merchantable quality, except in relation to defects drawn to the buyer's attention before the contract was concluded or, in the case where the buyer examines the goods, as regards defects which that examination ought to reveal (s.14(2)). Finally, where the seller sells goods in the course of a business and the buyer makes known to the seller any particular purpose for which the goods are being bought, there is an implied condition that the goods supplied under the contract are reasonably fit for that purpose (s.14(3)). The function of these implied terms is not to give effect to the intention of the parties but to provide some protection for the expectations of purchasers, particularly consumers. This element of 'consumer protection' is further evidenced by the fact that the Unfair Contract Terms Act 1977 places severe restrictions upon the ability of sellers to exclude the operation of these implied terms and, indeed, as against a consumer, they cannot be excluded (see further 11.9).

The second source of implied terms is terms implied by custom. A contract may be deemed to incorporate any relevant custom of the market, trade or locality in which the contract is made (*Hutton* v. *Warren* (1836) 1 M & W 466), unless the custom is inconsistent with the express terms of the contract or its nature (*Palgrave, Brown & Son Ltd* v. *SS Turid (Owners)* [1922] 1 AC 397). A custom will generally be implied into a contract where it can be shown that the custom was generally accepted by those doing business in the particular trade in the particular place and was such that an outsider making inquiries could not fail to discover it (*Kum* v. *Wah Tat Bank Ltd* [1971] 1 Lloyds Rep 439). A custom which satisfies these requirements binds both parties, whether they knew of it or not.

The third source of implied terms is terms implied at common law. There are, broadly speaking, two types of terms which are implied at common law. The first type are sometimes called terms 'implied in fact'. This nomenclature seeks to convey the idea that the term is being implied as a matter of fact to give effect to what the court perceives to be the unexpressed intention of the parties. The test which must be satisfied before such a term will be implied into a contract is a stringent one. The test which is frequently employed by the courts is the 'officious bystander' test, the origin of which lies in the following statement:

'Prima facie that which in any contract is left to be implied and need not be expressed is something so obvious that it goes without saying; so that, if while the parties were making their bargain an officious bystander were to suggest some express provision for it in the agreement, they would testily suppress him with a common 'Oh, of course.' (MacKinnon LJ in *Shirlaw* v. *Southern Foundries Ltd* [1939] 2 KB 206)

To put it another way: the implication must be 'necessary to give the transaction such business efficacy as the parties must have intended' (*The Moorcock* (1889) 14 PD 64). The court does not have power to imply such a term into a contract simply because it is reasonable to do so. Although Lord Denning has advocated such an approach (*Liverpool CC* v. *Irwin* [1976] QB 319) it has been rejected by the House of Lords, who insisted that the term must be a necessary one before it will be implied (*Liverpool CC* v *Irwin* [1977] AC 239). The necessity test at least allows the court to base its reasoning on the intention of the parties and it avoids the court being seen overtly to be 'making' the contract for the parties (on which see 4.1).

So a high standard must be satisfied before such a term will be implied into a contract. Attempts to imply such terms have therefore failed where the alleged term was inconsistent with the express terms of the contract (*Duke of Westminster* v. *Guild* [1985] QB 688), where one of the parties did not know of the term which it was alleged must be implied (*Spring* v. *NASDS* [1956] 1 WLR 585) and where it was not clear that both parties would in fact have agreed to the alleged term (*Luxor (Eastbourne) Ltd* v. *Cooper* [1941] AC 108).

Secondly terms, known as terms 'implied in law', may be implied into all contracts of a particular type. Thus terms are frequently implied into contracts of employment and into contracts between landlords and tenants, not on the basis of the relationship between the particular parties, but as a general incidence of the relationship of employer and employee or landlord and tenant. To take the employment relationship as our example, there is an implied term that an employee will serve his employer faithfully and that he will indemnify his employer for liabilities incurred as a result of his wrongful acts in the course of his employment (*Lister* v. *Romford Ice & Cold Storage Co Ltd* [1957] AC 555). Equally it has been held that there is an implied term to the effect that the employer must not 'without reasonable and proper cause conduct [himself] in a manner calculated or likely to destroy or seriously damage the relationship of confidence and trust between the parties' (*Courtaulds Northern Textiles Ltd* v. *Andrew* [1979] IRLR 84). In these cases and the many other cases in which the courts have implied terms into contracts of employment it seems clear that the implication is not based on the 'officious bystander' test, but on some less stringent test which reflects the court's perception of the nature of the relationship between an employer and an employee and whether such an implied term is suitable or 'reasonable' for incorporation in all such contracts (for an example in the context of a landlord and tenant relationship see *Liverpool CC* v *Irwin* (above)).

Summary

1 Once the contracting parties have elected to enshrine their contract in a written document, the courts have held that, as a general rule, the parties cannot adduce extrinsic evidence to add to, vary or contradict the written document.

2 This 'rule' is called the parol evidence rule, but it is the subject of so many exceptions that it is unlikely to have significant effects in practice.

3 As a general rule a person is bound by a document which he signs, whether he reads it or not, except where his signature has been procured by fraud or misrepresentation, or the defence of *non est factum* is made out.

4 *Non est factum* means 'this is not my deed'. It is a defence which is available to those who are permanently or temporarily unable through no fault of their own to have without explanation any real understanding of a particular document. The difference between the document as it was and as it was believed to be must be radical or substantial or fundamental. A person who signs the document carelessly, without bothering to read it properly, cannot invoke the defence.

5 Contracting parties may agree to incorporate a set of written terms into their contract. In order to do so notice must be given at or before the time of contracting, be contained in a document which was intended to have contractual effect, and reasonable steps must be taken to bring the terms to the attention of the other party.

6 Terms may also be incorporated into a contract by a course of dealing. The course of dealing must be both regular and consistent.

7 When interpreting a contract the court must seek to ascertain and give effect to the intention of the parties. The intention of the parties must generally be derived from the document in which they have expressed their agreement.

8 Evidence of pre-contractual negotiations, of conduct subsequent to the making of the contract and of the parties' subjective intentions is generally inadmissible.

9 Rectification is a remedy which is concerned with defects not in the making, but in the recording, of a contract. It is an equitable discretionary remedy.

10 A court will only rectify a document where 'convincing proof' is provided that the document fails to record the intention of the parties, where the document fails to record the intention of both parties (unless one party knows that the other is mistaken) and the document must have been preceded by a concluded contract or by a 'continuing common intention'.

11 Terms may be implied into a contract by statute, by custom or by the common law. In the case of 'terms implied in fact' a court cannot imply a term simply because it would be reasonable to do so; it must be necessary to imply such a term (in other words it must pass the 'officious bystander' test).

Exercises

1 What is the 'parol evidence rule'? List the principal exceptions to the rule.

2 What is *non est factum*? In what circumstances is the defence available to an adult of full capacity?

3 Is it correct to say that the cases on sufficiency of notice are concerned with the question 'whether it would in all the circumstances be fair (or reasonable) to hold a party bound by any conditions . . . of an unusual and stringent nature'?

4 When is a course of dealing 'regular and consistent'?

5 What types of evidence are inadmissible when a court seeks to interpret a written contract?

6 What is rectification? When is it available?

7 In what circumstances may a term be implied into a contract? Do courts ever imply terms into a contract on the basis that it was 'just and reasonable' so to do?

10 The Classification of Contractual Terms

10.1 The Classification of Terms

Not all contract terms are of equal significance; some are more important than others. For example, if I were to enter into a contract to buy a new car, the make of the car, its roadworthiness and the price would be much more important to me than its colour. This fact has long been reflected in contract law in the distinction which has traditionally been drawn between a condition and a warranty.

A condition is an essential term of the contract which goes to the root or the heart of the contract. Thus, in the example of my purchase of a new car, the terms as to the make of the car, its roadworthiness and the price would all be conditions. A warranty, on the other hand, is a lesser, subsidiary term of the contract, such as the term relating to the colour of the car (unless it was part of the description of the car, in which case it would be treated as a condition under s.13(1) of the Sale of Goods Act 1979; see 9.8). The distinction between a condition and a warranty is vital in the event of a breach of contract. A breach of a condition enables the party who is not in breach of contract ('the innocent party') *either* to terminate performance of the contract and obtain damages for any loss suffered as a result of the breach *or* to affirm the contract and recover damages for the breach. A breach of a warranty only enables the innocent party to claim damages, that is to say he cannot terminate performance of the contract and must therefore continue to perform his obligations under the contract. So if, in our example, I wished to terminate the contract to purchase the car and return the car to the sellers it would be essential for me to show that the sellers had broken a condition of the contract because, if the sellers had only broken a warranty, I would be confined to a remedy in damages.

It may seem odd to discuss the classification of contractual terms at this stage in the book if the primary significance of the classification relates to breach of contract. However the justification for doing so lies in the fact that the distinction is an important one in contract law and we shall encounter it on a number of occasions before we reach the chapter on breach of contract (Chapter 19).

10.2 What is a 'Condition'?

Before embarking upon a more detailed discussion of the distinction between a condition and a warranty, it is necessary to deal with a preliminary point relating to the meaning of the word 'condition'. The word 'condition' can be used in a number of different senses, and it is important to have a clear grasp of the meanings which contract lawyers ascribe to it. In the first place it could mean some event upon which the existence of the contract hinges. Such conditions are commonly called contingent conditions. These conditions may be of two types; conditions precedent and conditions subsequent. A condition precedent provides that the contract shall not become binding until the occurrence of a specified event (*Pym* v. *Campbell* (1856) 6 E & B 370). For example, I enter into a contract to buy a car but the contract provides that the contract shall not become binding until the car passes a road test; if the car fails the road test no contract comes into existence. A condition subsequent provides that a previously binding contract shall come to an end on the occurrence of a stipulated event. So if I enter into a binding contract, supported by consideration, under which I promise to pay £50 a month to my daughter Jenny until she gets married, the occurrence of her marriage will determine the contract between us. In both cases the effect of the occurrence of the condition is to terminate the contract without either party being in breach of contract because, in the case of the condition precedent, neither party promised that the condition would be fulfilled and, in the case of the condition subsequent, neither party promised that the condition would not occur.

However we are not concerned here with such contingent conditions; we are concerned with promissory conditions. A promissory condition is a term of a contract under which one party promises to do a particular thing and a failure on his part to perform the promised act constitutes a breach of contract.

10.3 Distinguishing Between a Condition and a Warranty

Having established that we are discussing promissory conditions, it is now necessary to explain how it is decided whether a term is a condition or a warranty. We shall approach this issue by examining the situations in which a term has been held to be a condition. A term may be held to be a condition in one of three ways: by statutory classification, by judicial classification or by the classification of the parties.

Firstly, a term may be classified as a condition by statute. We have already noted (see 9.8) that sections 12–15 of the Sale of Goods Act 1979 imply certain terms into contracts for the sale of goods. These sections also classify these implied terms; thus the implied terms as to merchantable quality, fitness for purpose and compliance with description and sample are declared to be conditions, whereas the implied term that the goods are free from charges and incumbrances in favour of third parties is stated to be a warranty.

Secondly, a term may be classified as a condition by the courts. There are two grounds, apart from the stipulation of the parties, on which courts may decide that a term is a condition. The first is where performance of the term goes to the root of the contract so that, by necessary implication, the parties must have intended that the term would be treated as a condition, breach of which would entitle the other party to treat himself as discharged (see *Couchman* v. *Hill* [1947] KB 554, discussed at 8.3)). Although the term must go to the root of the contract, it need not be the case that every breach of the term should deprive the innocent party of substantially the whole benefit which it was intended that he should obtain from the contract (*Bunge Corporation* v. *Tradax Export SA* [1981] 1 WLR 711).

The second ground on which a court may decide that a term is a condition is that binding authority requires the court to hold that the term is a condition. In some industries parties trade on standard terms and a decision that a particular standard term is a condition will affect, not only that contract, but also all subsequent contracts of that type. Thus a stipulation in a voyage charterparty relating to the time at which the vessel is expected ready to load is generally treated as a condition (*The Mihalis Angelos* [1971] 1 QB 164). The governing factor here is the need for certainty. But certainty carries with it a price. That price is that, in certain cases, a term has been classified as a condition, even though the breach has caused little or no hardship to the innocent party. The most infamous example, is, perhaps, *Arcos Ltd* v. *E A Ronaasen & Son* [1933] AC 470. Timber, described in the contract as half an inch thick, was bought to be used in making cement barrels. The timber, as delivered, was $\frac{9}{16}$ inch thick, but this did not impair its utility for making cement barrels. Nevertheless the buyers were held to be entitled to reject the timber, even though their motive in rejecting the timber may well have been that the market price for timber had fallen.

The third method of classification is the parties' own classification of the contractual term. Thus, if a contract states that a particular term is a condition, the term will generally be regarded as a condition; similarly where the contract expressly states that breach of the term will entitle the other party to terminate performance of the contract. This ability to classify a term as a condition gives an extremely powerful weapon to contracting parties, as can be seen from the case of *Lombard North Central plc* v *Butterworth* [1987] QB 527. A contract for the hire of computers stated in clause 2 of the agreement that it was of the essence of the contract that the hirer should pay each instalment promptly. The hirer failed to pay certain instalments promptly, whereupon the owners retook possession of the computers and sued the hirer for damages. The Court of Appeal held that making punctual payment of the essence of the contract was sufficient to turn the failure to pay a single instalment into a repudiation of the contract, thus entitling the plaintiff owners to terminate the contract and recover, not only in respect of arrears as at the date of termination, but also the loss of future instalments (subject to a discount for accelerated receipt of the future rentals). The court held that there was no restriction upon the right of the parties to classify the relative importance of the terms of their contract. It has been objected that such a principle 'does not always lead to a desirable result' (Bojczuk, 1987) but Mustill LJ refused to subject such terms to the control of the penalty clause jurisdiction (see 21.5) on the ground that to do so would be 'to reverse the current of more than 100 years' doctrine, which permits the parties to treat as a condition something which would not otherwise be so'.

However the court must be satisfied that the parties intended to use the word 'condition' in its technical sense. In *Schuler AG* v. *Wickman Machine Tool Sales Ltd* [1974] AC 235, clause 7(b) of a four-year distributorship agreement stated that 'it shall be a condition of this agreement that [Wickman] shall send its representatives to visit [six named UK manufacturers] at least once in every week for the purpose of soliciting orders'. Wickman failed to make some visits to the named manufacturers. Schuler claimed that they were therefore entitled to terminate the agreement because Wickman had broken a 'condition' of the agreement. This argument was rejected by the House of Lords. Lord Reid held that the use of the word 'condition' was an 'indication', perhaps even a 'strong indication', that the parties intended the term to be a condition in the technical sense, but it was by no means 'conclusive' evidence. He held that the more unreasonable the consequences of treating a term as a condition in its technical sense, the less likely it was that the parties intended to use the word 'condition' in such a way. On the facts, the consequence that a 'failure to make even one visit' would entitle Schuler to terminate the contract 'however blameless Wickman might be' was so unreasonable that it compelled Lord Reid to interpret 'condition' in clause 7(b) in its non-technical sense.

10.4 The Need for Change?

It can be seen that the primary emphasis in these cases has been upon the importance of the *term* which has been broken rather than upon the importance of the consequences of the *breach* of that term. The result has been that, in cases such as *Arcos* v. *Ronaasen* (above), a term has been classified as a condition even though the consequences of breach were insignificant. The justification for this approach is, firstly, that the parties must be free to classify the relative importance of their own contractual terms (see *Lombard North Central plc* v. *Butterworth* (above)) and, secondly, the need for certainty in commercial transactions. Certainty can be most effectively achieved by deciding whether or not a term is a condition according to the nature of the term broken, not by requiring the parties to wait and examine the consequences of the breach before deciding whether or not they are sufficiently serious to justify the classification of the term as a condition. The cause of certainty is further advanced by the fact that, once a term is classified as a condition, the innocent party is, unless barred by estoppel or by his election to affirm the contract, automatically entitled to terminate performance of the contract. The parties know where they stand.

But the cost of this emphasis on the need to promote certainty is an element of injustice, in cases such as *Arcos* v. *Ronaasen* (above), where the motive for terminating the contract may well have been that the contract had turned out to be a bad deal for the innocent party. Such injustice could be largely avoided if the critical factor in deciding whether a term was a condition and whether the innocent party was entitled to terminate performance of the contract was to become the consequences of the breach. Then the innocent party would only be entitled to terminate performance of the contract where the consequences of the breach to him were sufficiently serious (indeed there was authority for such a proposition in the early case of *Boone* v. *Eyre* (1777) 1 H Bl 273, before the emphasis switched to the importance of the term which had been broken in cases such as *Behn* v. *Burness* (1863) 3 B & S 751 and *Bettini* v. *Gye* (1876) 1 QBD 183). Yet the cost of such a shift in emphasis would be the sacrifice of a degree of certainty.

Here the interests of 'certainty' and 'justice' or 'fairness' conflict. 'Certainty' requires the focus to be upon the nature of the term broken and demands a high degree of remedial rigidity. 'Justice', on the other hand, requires the focus to be on the consequences of the breach and demands a high degree of remedial flexibility. The generally accepted view was that, in cases such as *Arcos* v. *Ronaasen*, the pendulum had swung too far in favour of the promotion of certainty and that it was time to redress the balance.

In seeking to redress the balance, two approaches have been adopted. The first is to seek to limit the number of terms which are classified as conditions. Thus, in *Reardon Smith Line Ltd* v. *Hansen Tangen* [1976] 1 WLR 989, Lord Wilberforce stated that some of the authorities which we have discussed were 'excessively technical and due for fresh examination' by the House of Lords. But these cases still await such 'fresh examination' and it is unlikely that this line of approach will be further developed. The second approach has been to focus more attention on the consequences of the breach and to give the courts greater remedial flexibility. This has been achieved through the recognition of the fact that the distinction between a condition and a warranty is not an exhaustive one.

10.5 Innominate Terms

A third classification has now been recognised in English law: the intermediate or the innominate term. The origin of this development can be found in the judgment of Diplock LJ in *Hong Kong Fir Shipping Co Ltd* v. *Kawasaki Kisen Kaisha Ltd* [1962] 2 QB 26, 70, when he said.

> 'There are many . . . contractual undertakings . . . which cannot be categorised as being 'conditions' or 'warranties' . . . Of such undertakings all that can be predicated is that some breaches will and others will not give rise to an event which will deprive the party not in default of substantially the whole benefit which it was intended that he should obtain.'

An innominate term can be distinguished from a condition on the ground that breach of an innominate term does not automatically give rise to a right to terminate performance of the contract and it can be distinguished from a warranty on the ground that the innocent party is not confined to a remedy in damages. Thus the court is given a greater degree of remedial flexibility and it can focus attention on the consequences of the breach by allowing a party to terminate performance of the contract only where the breach of the innominate term has had serious consequences for him.

The creation of this new category of innominate terms leaves us with the difficulty of distinguishing between an innominate term, a condition and a warranty. In practice judicial classification of a term as a warranty is rare, so the important issue is likely to be whether the term is a condition or an innominate term. If the contract states that the term is a condition then, subject to *Schuler* v. *Wickman*, it will be treated as a condition. A term will also be regarded as a condition where it is classified as such by statute. Where the term has been previously classified by the judiciary as a condition, then, cases such as *Arcos* v. *Ronaasen* apart, it is likely that the term will continue to be regarded as a condition. The principal difficulty is likely to arise in connection with previously unclassified terms.

At this point we return to the conflict which we have already noted between the interests of 'certainty' and 'justice'. If primary attention is given to considerations of fairness, this will favour classification of terms as innominate terms because the remedy can be tailored to the facts of the case. On the other hand, an approach which gives primary attention to considerations of certainty will favour classification as a condition because the remedial consequences will then be clear. Some indication of the likely resolution of this conflict can be gleaned from the case of *Bunge* v. *Tradax* (above). The House of Lords held that a term which related to the time of performance in a commercial contract was a condition and not an innominate term, on the ground that time was generally of the essence in such contracts. However Lord Wilberforce said that 'the courts should not be too ready to interpret contractual clauses as conditions'. This suggests that, apart from terms which are commercially vital where the need for certainty is greatest, greater consideration will be given to the interests of 'justice' by classifying contract terms as innominate terms in order to give the courts flexibility in granting the appropriate relief. The injustice of cases such as *Arcos* v. *Ronaasen* need no longer occur.

Summary

1 Contract terms can be classified either as conditions, warranties or innominate terms.

2 A condition is an essential term of the contract which goes to the root or the heart of the contract. This is a promissory condition which must be distinguished from a contingent condition, which is some event upon which the existence of the contract hinges. A contingent condition may be either a condition precedent or a condition subsequent.

3 A term may be classified as a promissory condition by statute, by judicial classification or by the classification of the parties. In the latter category the court must be satisfied that the parties intended to use the word 'condition' in its technical sense.

4 Breach of a promissory condition entitles the innocent party either to terminate performance of the contract and claim damages or to affirm the contract and claim damages.

5 A warranty is a lesser, subsidiary term of the contract. Breach of a warranty only gives a remedy in damages.

6 The category of innominate terms was recognised by Diplock LJ in the *Hong Kong Fir* case.

7 An innominate term can be distinguished from a condition on the ground that breach of an innominate term does not automatically give rise to a right to terminate performance of the contract and it can be distinguished from a warranty on the ground that the innocent party's remedy is not confined to damages. Classification as an innominate term therefore gives the court an important degree of remedial flexibility.

Exercises

1 Distinguish between a promissory condition and a contingent condition.
2 When will a term be classified as a promissory condition?
3 What are the remedial consequences of classifying a term as:

    (a) a condition;
    (b) a warranty; and
    (c) an innominate term?

11 Exclusion Clauses

An exclusion clause may be defined as a 'clause in a contract or a term in a notice which appears to exclude or restrict a liability or a legal duty which would otherwise arise' (Yates, 1982, p.1). Exclusion clauses are a common feature of contracts today and may take a number of different forms. The most frequently encountered types of exclusion clauses are those which seek to exclude liability for breach of contract or for negligence or which seek to limit liability to a specified sum. Another type of exclusion clause commonly encountered is an indemnity clause, under which one contracting party promises to indemnify the other for any liability incurred by him in the performance of the contract (for a description of other types of exclusion clauses see Yates, 1982, pp.33–41).

11.1 Exclusion Clauses: Defence or Definition?

Despite the common occurrence of exclusion clauses in contracts, different views remain as to their essential nature. Let us take an example to illustrate the point. John, who at present lives in Colchester, wishes to have his furniture transported to his new house in Preston and for this purpose he contracts with Peter. Peter, who is self-employed, offers a price which is substantially lower than any other removal firm because he offers no insurance cover for the goods while they are in transit; instead he relies on the owner of the goods either to use his existing insurance policy (if it is applicable) or to take out his own special insurance policy. In order to give effect to his pricing policy Peter inserts a clause into his contracts to the following effect: 'no liability is accepted for any damage, howsoever caused, to any goods during the course of transit'. Two views may be adopted as to the function of such a clause.

One view holds that this clause simply defines the obligations which the contracting parties have chosen to accept. Peter has only accepted a limited obligation to transmit the goods and has never accepted any liability for damage to the goods during the course of transit. On this view the function of the exclusion clause is to assist in *defining* the obligations of the parties. This view is not, however, the one which the courts have traditionally adopted. Courts have traditionally seen exclusion clauses as performing a defensive function. On this view a failure by

Peter to deliver the goods safely to Preston constitutes a breach of contract and the role of the exclusion clause is to provide Peter with a *defence* to John's action for breach of contract.

Yet a closer examination of this traditional view reveals a serious difficulty. The difficulty is that Peter has not accepted an absolute obligation to deliver John's goods; such a conclusion could only be reached by ignoring the exclusion clause when defining Peter's obligations. But why should the exclusion clause be ignored in defining Peter's obligations, since it is via the exclusion clause that Peter has sought to define the extent of his obligations, and it is only by this means that he can offer a service at a price lower than that of his competitors? If this view of exclusion clauses is adopted then exclusion clauses resemble any other term of the contract which defines the obligations of the parties and should be treated accordingly (this theory was adopted by Coote, 1964, and is also supported by Yates, 1982).

The argument that exclusion clauses define the obligations of the parties has recently been attacked by Adams and Brownsword (1988a) on the ground that it is 'elegantly formalistic' and that it ignores 'both the historical development of the problem, and the realities of the situation'. The 'historical development' is that the growth in the use of standard form contracts has been accompanied by a growth in the use of exclusion clauses and the 'realities' of the situation are that such terms are offered on a 'take it or leave it basis'. In short, these standard form contracts, which so often include sweeping exclusion clauses, are imposed on the weaker party to the transaction. They take away the rights of the weaker party and nullify his expectations, rather than define the obligations of the parties. But it is only by looking outside the contract for the initial existence of these 'rights' or 'expectations' that exclusion clauses can be said to 'take away' the 'rights' of the weaker party or nullify his 'expectations'. These 'rights' and 'expectations' must exist outside the contract because the contract as a whole certainly did not confer them upon the weaker party. How then are we to ascertain the scope of these 'rights' or 'expectations'? Are they to be found in some conception of 'public policy'? Proponents of the 'defensive' view of exclusion clauses do not tell us. Surely the evil which we are seeking to eradicate is not the existence of exclusion clauses or even simply the existence of 'unreasonable exclusion clauses' but the existence of 'unfair' terms in a contract. If this is so, then the correct approach must be to deal with exclusion clauses as part of a general doctrine of duress, inequality of bargaining power or 'unconscionability' (see further Chapter 17) and not by the artificial and misleading process of subjecting exclusion clauses to distinct regulation on the basis that they are a defence to a breach of an obligation (see Yates, 1982, ch. 7). Notwithstanding the force of this criticism, the courts and Parliament have generally treated exclusion clauses as a defence to a breach of an obligation, although, as we shall see, this view has given rise to considerable difficulties.

11.2 The Functions of Exclusion Clauses

Before embarking upon an analysis of the detailed rules of law, we must identify the different functions of exclusion clauses. Exclusion clauses perform a number of useful functions. First, they help in the allocation of risks under the contract. In our example involving Peter and John the risk of damage to the goods is clearly allocated to John and there is no need for Peter to take out insurance cover; double insurance is thereby avoided. Secondly, exclusion clauses can help reduce litigation costs by making clear the responsibilities which each party bears. Thirdly, exclusion clauses are often used in standard form contracts which, by enabling people, such as Peter, to mass-produce their contracts, helps reduce the cost of negotiations and of making contracts.

On the other hand, exclusion clauses can perform a function which is socially harmful in that, as we have already seen, they can be used by the powerful in society to exclude liability towards the weaker party, thereby leaving the weak without a remedy. It is this socially undesirable function of exclusion clauses which has provided significant impetus for reform of this area of law and which explains the restrictive approach which the courts have adopted in their treatment of exclusion clauses.

11.3 An Outline of the Law

A contracting party who wishes to include an exclusion clause in a contract must overcome three hurdles before he can do so. First, it must be shown that the exclusion clause is properly incorporated into the contract (11.4). Secondly, it must be shown that, properly interpreted, the exclusion clause covers the loss which has arisen (11.5–11.7). Thirdly, there must be no other rule of law which would invalidate the exclusion clause (11.8–11.9).

Historically, it was the first two of these three stages which were important. The principal explanation for this is that, although at common law the court has power to strike down contract terms which are 'contrary to public policy' (see Chapter 15), it did not have the power to hold exclusion clauses invalid because they were unreasonable (despite arguments to the contrary by Lord Denning in cases such as *Levison* v. *Patent Steam Carpet Cleaning Co Ltd* [1978] QB 68). Deprived of the ability to strike down unreasonable exclusion clauses by such direct means, the courts sought to achieve such a goal by the indirect means of adopting a restrictive approach towards the incorporation (9.4 and 11.4) and the interpretation (11.5–11.7) of exclusion clauses. Lord Denning recognised this in *Gillespie Bros* v. *Roy Bowles Ltd* [1973] 1 QB 400, when he said that 'judges departed from the ordinary meaning, under the guise of construing the clause so as to reduce it to reasonable proportions'.

But now, since courts have been given statutory power under the Unfair Contract Terms Act 1977 (UCTA) to control exclusion clauses, there is less need for them to use the first two stages to control unreasonable exclusion clauses and hence it can be expected that the focus of attention will switch to the third stage (although contrast the restrictive approach which was adopted towards incorporation in the case of *Interfoto Picture Library Ltd* v. *Stiletto Visual Programmes Ltd* [1988] 2 WLR 615 (discussed at 9.4), which, although not an exclusion clause case, shows that the restrictive approach to incorporation is still very much alive).

11.4 Incorporation

At the first stage it must be shown that the exclusion clause was validly incorporated into the contract. Here the reader should refer to the discussion of incorporation at 9.4.

11.5 Construction of Exclusion Clauses

At the second stage it must be shown that the exclusion clause, properly interpreted or properly construed, covered the damage which was caused. It is here that the defensive approach to exclusion clauses becomes important because exclusion clauses are not interpreted in the same way as other terms of the contract, which they would be if a definitional approach were to be adopted towards exclusion clauses.

The general approach which the courts have adopted to the interpretation of exclusion clauses is a restrictive one, under which the exclusion clause is interpreted strictly against the party seeking to rely on it. This rule is called the '*contra proferentem*' rule. The effect of the rule is that any ambiguity in the exclusion clause will be resolved against the party seeking to rely on the exclusion clause. Although the *contra proferentem* rule is applicable to any ambiguous term in a contract, it has been applied particularly stringently to exclusion clauses. The 'proferens' is simply the person seeking to rely on the exclusion clause; it does not imply that the person seeking to rely on the exclusion clause has 'imposed' it on the other party (*Scottish Special Housing Association* v. *Wimpey Construction UK Ltd* 1986 SLT 173).

The consequence of the application of the *contra proferentem* rule has been a game of 'cat and mouse' between contract draftsmen and the courts, as draftsmen have sought to evade the restrictive interpretations adopted by the courts. This can be illustrated by reference to the following two cases. In *Wallis, Son and Wells* v. *Pratt and Haynes* [1911] AC 394, a contract for the sale of seeds contained a clause which stated that the sellers gave 'no warranty express or implied' as to the description of the seeds. The seeds did not correspond with the description, so the buyers brought an action for damages against the sellers, who sought to rely on the exclusion clause. It was held that they could not do so because it only covered breach of a 'warranty' and, in failing to provide seeds which corresponded with the description, they had broken a condition. The impact of this ruling can be seen in *Andrews Bros (Bournemouth) Ltd* v. *Singer and Co Ltd* [1934] 1 KB 17. This time the exclusion clause stated that 'all conditions, warranties and liabilities *implied* by statute, common law or otherwise are excluded'. The plaintiffs contracted with the defendants to buy some 'new Singer cars'. One of the cars delivered by the defendants was a used car. The plaintiffs sued for damages and the defendants sought, unsuccessfully, to rely on the exclusion clause. Greer LJ said that the defendants were probably trying to escape the effect of *Wallis* but the only problem was that, although they had included the word condition, they had omitted the word 'express' and this was fatal because the court held that the defendants had broken an express term of the contract.

However, this strict approach may now be undergoing some reconsideration. In *Ailsa Craig Fishing Co Ltd* v. *Malvern Fishing Co Ltd* [1983] 1 WLR 964, the House of Lords held that, in the case of limitation clauses, the *contra proferentem* rule did not apply with the same rigour as it applied to exclusion clauses. Lord Fraser and Lord Wilberforce said that limitation clauses were not viewed with the same hostility as exclusion clauses because of their role in risk allocation and because it was more likely that the other party would agree to a limitation clause than to an exclusion clause. This approach is open to the objection that it ignores the risk-allocation function of exclusion clauses and it is by no means certain that the other party would be more willing to agree to a limitation clause, especially where the limit is derisory (see Palmer, 1982). Instead of differentiating between exclusion clauses and limitation clauses, one would have expected uniform rules of construction to be applied to all contract terms, but *Ailsa Craig* has since been followed by the House of Lords in *George Mitchell (Chesterhall) Ltd* v. *Finney Lock Seeds Ltd* [1983] 2 AC 803. However the High Court of Australia, in *Darlington Futures Ltd* v. *Delco Australia Pty Ltd* (1987) 61 ALJR 76, has refused to differentiate between exclusion clauses and limitation clauses in this manner. Instead the court held that

> 'the interpretation of an exclusion clause is to be determined by construing the clause according to its natural and ordinary meaning, read in the light of the contract as a whole, thereby giving due weight to the context in which the clause appears including the nature and the object of the contract and, where appropriate, construing the clause *contra proferentem* in case of ambiguity'.

This approach is to be welcomed in so far as it adopts a more natural interpretation of exclusion clauses. Some support for a more natural interpretation of exclusion clauses can also be found in some English cases. As we have already noted (9.6), in *Photo Production Ltd* v. *Securicor Ltd* [1980] AC 827, Lord Diplock said that 'the reports are full of cases in which what would appear to be very strained constructions have been placed upon exclusion clauses'. He noted that many of these cases involved consumer contracts and continued, 'any need for this kind of judicial distortion of the English language has been banished by Parliament's having made these kinds of contract subject to the Unfair Contract Terms Act 1977'. It should be noted that in neither *Photo Production* nor *Darlington Futures* was the *contra proferentem* rule doubted; all that the court was saying was that in future exclusion clauses should be given a more natural construction.

It is to be hoped that, in future cases, courts will continue to apply a more natural interpretation to exclusion clauses. However there remain at least two situations in which particular rules of construction have been adopted by the courts. These rules apply where one party seeks to exclude liability for his own negligence (11.6) and where he seeks to exclude liability for a 'fundamental breach' (11.7). We shall now discuss these two special rules of construction.

11.6 Negligence Liability

The first relates to the situation where a contracting party seeks to exclude liability for his own negligence (note that UCTA contains severe restrictions on the ability of a contracting party to exclude liability for his own negligence; see 11.9). The courts regard it as inherently unlikely that one party will agree to allow the other contracting party to exclude liability for his own negligence. To give effect to this, the courts have evolved three specific rules of construction which find their origin in the speech of Lord Morton of Henryton in *Canada Steamship Lines Ltd* v. *The King* [1952] AC 192.

The first rule is that if a clause contains language which expressly exempts the party relying on the exclusion clause from the consequences of his own negligence then effect must be given to the clause. This test may be fulfilled by using a word which is a synonym for negligence (*Smith* v. *UBM Chrysler (Scotland) Ltd* 1978 SC (HL) 1). The safest course, however, is to use the word 'negligence' expressly.

If the first test is not satisfied the court must consider whether the words are wide enough, in their ordinary meaning, to cover negligence on the part of the party relying on the exclusion clause. If a doubt arises as to whether the words are wide enough, the doubt must be resolved against the party relying on the exclusion clause. Exclusion clauses which have been held wide enough to satisfy this test include clauses which exclude liability for 'any act or omission' or 'any damage whatsoever'.

Once the second test has been satisfied the court must consider whether the exclusion clause may cover some kind of damage other than negligence. In our example involving Peter and John (see 11.1), Peter may wish the exclusion clause to cover not only negligence on his part, but also any liability which he may incur for late delivery of the furniture through no fault of his own (for example, his van may break down and John may incur expenses living in a hotel in Preston while waiting for the furniture to arrive). It was once thought that *Canada Steamship* stood as authority for the proposition that the mere existence of a possible alternative source of liability meant that the clause could not cover negligence, but the point has been reconsidered by the Court of Appeal in *The Raphael* [1982] 2 Lloyds Rep 42 (see Palmer, 1983). In the latter case it was held that the rules laid down in *Canada Steamship* were merely aids to be used by the courts in identifying the intention of the parties and it was emphasised that, where the alternative source of liability was 'fanciful or remote', it would not prevent the exclusion clause covering liability in negligence. But what if the alternative source of liability was sufficiently realistic for the parties to intend the clause to apply to that other source of liability? Does such an alternative source of liability mean that the clause cannot apply to negligence? Stephenson LJ thought so. On the other hand Lord Donaldson and May LJ held that the point was ultimately one of construction; but even they said that in such a case the clause would generally be interpreted as not excluding liability for negligence.

However, there is no valid justification for the continued existence of these artificial rules of construction. In the case of Peter and John, the parties may agree that the exclusion clause is to cover both negligently caused damage and delay brought about through no fault of Peter. The courts should be free to give effect to the intention of the parties. It would be better if these rules were abandoned and the issue were left as one of construction, with the courts simply having to decide, as a matter of construction, whether or not the exclusion clause covered negligently caused damage. Such was the approach of the House of Lords in *Scottish Special Housing Association* v. *Wimpey Construction UK Ltd* [1986] 2 All ER 957 (to similar effect see *The Golden Leader* [1980] 2 Lloyds Rep 573). An exclusion clause was held, on its proper construction, to exclude liability for negligence, even though the word 'negligence' was not used in the clause. Nowhere in the brief judgment handed down were the rules in *Canada Steamship* mentioned. Instead, the House simply sought to interpret the clause. In so far as this case represents a movement away from artificial rules of construction, it is to be welcomed and – one hopes – developed in the future.

11.7 Fundamental Breach

The second situation in which the courts have evolved specific rules of interpretation is where the breach of contract by the party relying on the exclusion clause is of a fundamental nature. Two distinct approaches have been adopted here and it is vital to understand the difference between the two. The first approach may be called the rule of law approach, under which it was not possible by a clause (however widely drafted) to exclude liability for certain breaches of contract which were deemed to be fundamental. This approach grew under the guiding hand of Lord Denning as a means of control over exclusion clauses which were thought to be unreasonable. The second approach may be called the rule of construction approach. According to this approach the question whether an exclusion clause covered a fundamental breach was a question of construction, under which the clause was interpreted against the party seeking to rely on it.

In *Suisse Atlantique Société d'Armament Maritime SA* v. *NV Rotterdamsche Kolen Centrale* [1967] 1 AC 361, the House of Lords held that the latter approach was the correct one but, unfortunately, their Lordships' judgments were not a model of clarity and their ambiguities were seized upon in cases such as *Harbutt's Plasticine Ltd* v. *Wayne Tank Pump Co Ltd* [1970] 1 QB 477, to resurrect the rule of law approach. However, the rule of law approach was finally laid to rest by the House of Lords in *Photo Production Ltd* v. *Securicor Ltd* [1980] AC 827. The plaintiffs, who were factory owners, entered into a contract with the defendants, under which the defendants contracted to provide periodic visits to the plaintiffs' factory during the night for the purpose of checking that the factory was secure. During one of these visits an employee of the defendants started a fire, apparently to keep himself warm, but which got out of control and burnt down the factory.

The plaintiffs sought to recover damages of £648 000 from the defendants, but the defendants relied on an exclusion clause which stated that 'under no circumstances' were they 'to be responsible for any injurious act or default by any employee . . . unless such act or default could have been foreseen and avoided by the exercise of due diligence on the part of [the defendants]'. The House of Lords held that it was a question of construction whether or not the exclusion clause covered a fundamental breach and that, on the facts, the defendants were not liable because the exclusion clause did, in fact, cover the damage which had arisen.

It is undoubtedly the case that much mystique surrounds the doctrine of fundamental breach. This is largely owing to the difficulties and confusion created by the rule of law approach. Now that the rule of law approach has been laid to rest, the 'doctrine' simply exists as a rule of construction, according to which the more serious the breach, or the consequences of the breach, the less likely it is that the court will interpret the exclusion clause as applying to the breach. Therefore, if a contracting party wishes to exclude liability for breach of a fundamental term of the contract (that is a term which goes to the root of the contract or forms the essential character of the contract, see *Karsales (Harrow) Ltd* v. *Wallis* [1956] 1 WLR 936), a deliberate refusal to perform his obligations under the contract (*Sze Hai Tong Bank Ltd* v. *Rambler Cycle Co Ltd* [1959] AC 576) or a breach which will have particularly serious consequences for the other party, then he must use clear words to such an effect if he is to achieve his purpose. Yet even here, as we have already noted, the House of Lords in *Photo Production* stated that a strained construction should not be put upon words in an exclusion clause which are clearly and fairly susceptible of only one meaning.

11.8   Other Common Law Controls upon Exclusion Clauses

There are certain additional controls over exclusion clauses which exist at common law. The common law limitations are of much less significance since the intervention of Parliament (see 11.9). A party cannot rely on an exclusion clause, the effect of which he has misrepresented to the other party (*Curtis* v. *Chemical Cleaning and Dyeing Co Ltd* [1951] 1 KB 805). Similarly, an exclusion clause which is contained in a written document can be overridden by an express inconsistent undertaking given at or before the time of contracting (*Couchman* v. *Hill* [1947] KB 554). A defendant may also be prevented by the doctrine of privity from taking the benefit of an exclusion clause contained in a contract to which he was not a party (see 7.6). Finally, it must be remembered that the courts had no power at common law to strike down an exclusion clause simply because it was unreasonable (see 11.3).

11.9   The Unfair Contract Terms Act 1977

The major source of the control of exclusion clauses can now be found in the Unfair Contract Terms Act 1977 (UCTA). The Act is a complex and technical piece of legislation. It is important to bear in mind that here we are dealing with an Act of Parliament and the *exact* words used by the Act must be studied and applied.

The first issue which the Act deals with are attempts to exclude or restrict liability for negligence. Section 2 provides that:

'(1) A person cannot by reference to any contract term or a notice given to persons generally or to particular persons exclude or restrict his liability for death or personal injury resulting from negligence.

(2) In the case of other loss or damage, a person cannot so exclude or restrict his liability for negligence except in so far as the term or notice satisfies the requirement of reasonableness.

(3) Where a contract term or notice purports to exclude or restrict liability for negligence a person's agreement to or awareness of it is not of itself to be taken as indicating his voluntary acceptance of any risk.'

A number of points should be noted about this section. The first is that it only applies to 'negligence', so that it does not apply to attempts to exclude or restrict liability which is strict. 'Negligence' is defined in s.1(1) as the *breach*

'(a) of any obligation, arising from the express or implied terms of a contract, to take reasonable care or exercise reasonable skill in the performance of the contract;

(b) of any common law duty to take reasonable care or exercise reasonable skill (but not any stricter duty);

(c) of the common duty of care imposed by the Occupiers' Liability Act 1957 or the Occupiers' Liability Act (Northern Ireland) 1957.'

An act is not prevented from being an act of negligence on the ground that the breach of duty was intentional rather than inadvertent, or because liability for it arose vicariously rather than directly (s.1(4)). It should be noted that this section is drafted in defensive terms, that is to say, it assumes that there has been a *breach* of duty. Section 2 also refers to a party attempting to 'exclude or restrict his liability' for negligence and therefore the section does not appear to extend to clauses which define the obligations of the parties. So how would a court respond to the argument that the exclusion clause simply defined the obligations of the parties and therefore fell outside the scope of section 2?

Such an argument was put to the Court of Appeal in *Phillips Products Ltd* v. *Hyland and Hamstead Plant Hire Co Ltd* [1987] 2 All ER 620. The defendants 'hired' a JCB excavator and driver to the plaintiffs. Condition 8 of the contract stated that the driver was to be regarded as the employee of the plaintiffs and that the plaintiffs alone should be responsible for all claims arising in connection with the driver's operation of the excavator. Owing to the negligence of the driver, the JCB excavator crashed into the plaintiffs' factory wall. The plaintiffs sued for damages and the defendants sought to rely upon condition 8. The plaintiffs argued that condition 8 was caught by s.2(2) of UCTA and that it failed to satisfy the requirement of reasonableness. The defendants argued that condition 8 was not caught by s.2(2), on the ground that there was no negligence within the meaning of s.1(1)(b) because there had been no breach of their obligations as they had never accepted any liability for the acts of the driver. This argument was rejected by the Court of Appeal. Slade LJ asserted that, in considering whether there has been a breach of duty under s.1(1), the court must leave out of account the clause which is relied on by the defendants to defeat the plaintiffs' claim. But why should such a clause be left out of account when it is via the exclusion clause that the defendant has sought to define his obligations? Slade LJ claimed to find support for his interpretation in the words of s.13(1):

'To the extent that this Part of this Act prevents the exclusion of restriction of any liability it also prevents –

(a)   making the liability or its enforcement subject to restrictive or onerous conditions;

(b)   excluding or restricting any right or remedy in respect of the liability, or subjecting a person to any prejudice in consequence of his pursuing any such right or remedy;

(c)   excluding or restricting rules of evidence or procedure; and (to that extent) sections 2 and 5 to 7 also prevent excluding or restricting liability by reference to terms and notices *which exclude or restrict the relevant obligation or duty.*' (emphasis added).

In the last nine words of this subsection, Slade LJ found authority for applying the Act to clauses which exclude or restrict the relevant duty.

So it is clear that s.13(1) does apply to some duty-defining clauses; the difficulty lies in ascertaining the extent to which UCTA applies to duty-defining clauses. Section 13(1) does not give us any criteria by reference to which we can decide which duty-defining clauses are caught by the Act and which are not. The scope of s.13 was recently discussed by the House of Lords in *Smith* v. *Eric S Bush* [1989] 2 WLR 790. Lord Templeman stated that the Act subjected to regulation 'all exclusion notices which would in common law provide a defence to an action for negligence'. Lord Griffiths interpreted s.13 as 'introducing a "but for" test in relation to the notice excluding liability'; that is to say, a court must decide whether a duty of care would exist 'but for' the exclusion clause. Lord Jauncey of Tullichettle stated that the wording of section 13 was 'entirely appropriate to cover a disclaimer which prevents a duty coming into existence'. But surely the Act does not catch all duty-defining clauses? Ridiculous conclusions would be reached if the Act did so (for some examples see Palmer and Yates, 1981; and Palmer, 1986). One example will suffice to illustrate the point: 'an overworked accountant says to a potential investor "this is all I can remember about Company X but I may be wrong so don't rely on me" ' (Palmer, 1986). Is such a statement caught by the Act? The answer is not clear. But, if it is, how can a person qualify his obligations without being caught by the Act? This lack of clarity is almost certain to result in confusion in the courts. Although the courts must share some responsibility for the creation of this confusion, the confusion lies, ultimately, at the heart of UCTA in its misconception of the function of exclusion clauses (see 11.1) and, until that issue is resolved, the courts will continue to experience considerable difficulty in the interpretation of s.13(1) of the Act.

Further difficulties will arise in distinguishing between clauses which 'exclude or restrict' liability, which are caught by the Act, and clauses which 'transfer' liability, which are not caught by the Act. The difficulty can be seen by contrasting *Phillips* v. *Hyland* with the factually similar case of *Thompson* v. *T Lohan* (Plant Hire) Ltd [1987] 2 All ER 631. Once again the case concerned the hiring of an employee and a JCB excavator and a claim arising out of the negligence of the driver. The contract term which was the subject of the dispute was a new version of condition 8 (the variation is of no significance for present purposes). But this time it was held that condition 8 was not caught by section 2 of UCTA. In *Thompson* the driver's negligence led to the death of Mr Thompson. Mr Thompson's widow recovered damages from the general employers and they sought to recover an indemnity from the hiring employers under condition 8. The hiring employers argued that condition 8 was caught by s.2(1) of UCTA and was therefore ineffective. However it was held that condition 8 was not caught by s.2(1) and therefore was effective to transfer liability to the hiring employer. The vital issue which divides these two cases is whether or not it is sought to exclude liability towards the *victim* of the negligent act. In *Thompson* condition 8 did not attempt to exclude liability towards the victim of the driver's negligence (Mr Thompson) because he had recovered from the general employers and the issue was whether that liability could be *transferred* from the general employers to the hiring employers. On the other hand condition 8 in the *Phillips* case was relied upon in an effort to exclude liability towards the *victim* of the driver's negligence (the plaintiffs) and therefore was caught by s.2(2) of UCTA (see further Adams and Brownsword, 1988b). On this reasoning the result in *Phillips* would have been different if the driver had damaged property belonging to someone other than the plaintiffs because, in that event, the effect of condition 8 would have been to transfer liability to the plaintiffs and not exclude liability towards the victim. But should it not be the case that, whether the property which is damaged belongs to the plaintiffs or not, the result in each case should be the same? Either the risk has been fairly allocated to the plaintiffs or it has not. Distinctions of the type drawn in *Phillips* and *Thompson* are incoherent in policy terms and reflect the insecure foundations upon which UCTA is built.

The second point to note about section 2 is that it applies only to attempts to exclude or restrict business liability. Business liability is defined in s.1(3) as liability for breach of obligations or duties arising

'(a) from things done or to be done by a person in the course of a business (whether his own business or another's) or
 (b) from the occupation of premises used for business purposes of the occupier'.

'Business' is defined in s.14 as including a profession and the activities of any government or local or public authority.

The last point to note about section 2 is that it adopts two methods of control. The first, contained in s.2(1), is that any contract term or notice which attempts to exclude or restrict liability for negligence causing death or personal injury is void. Personal injury is defined in section 14 as including any disease and any impairment of physical or mental condition. The second method of control, contained in s.2(2), is that attempts to exclude or restrict liability for negligence causing loss or damage other than death or personal injury are valid only if they satisfy the statutory requirement of reasonableness.

Section 11(1) provides that

'in relation to a contract term, the requirement of reasonableness . . . is that the term shall have been a fair and reasonable one to be included having regard to the circumstances which were, or ought reasonably to have been known to or in the contemplation of the parties when the contract was made.'

It is important to note that reasonableness is to be assessed at the date of making the contract, not the date of breach. The onus lies on the party relying on the exclusion clause to show that it is reasonable (s.11(5)). The courts have taken into account a number of factors in deciding whether an exclusion clause is reasonable: the respective bargaining power of the parties, whether the exclusion clause was freely negotiated, the extent to which the parties were legally advised, the availability of insurance, the availability of an alternative source of supply to the innocent party and the extent to which the party seeking to rely on the exclusion clause sought to explain its effect to the other party (for a review of some of the cases see Lawson, 1981). Thus in *Phillips* v. *Hyland* (above) it was held that condition 8 failed the reasonableness test because the plaintiffs did not generally hire JCB excavators and their drivers, the hire was for a very short period of time, there was little opportunity for the plaintiffs to arrange any insurance cover and the plaintiffs had no control over the choice of driver. All these factors combined to suggest that condition 8 was not reasonable. The question of the reasonableness of a particular clause is a highly discretionary question and it is clear that the courts have not been wholly consistent in the exercise of their discretion, with some judges being more interventionist than others (see Adams and Brownsword, 1988a). The consequence of this is an element of unpredictability and inconsistency in the case law. Appellate courts have largely abdicated their role as the guardians of predictability and consistency by holding that an appellate court must treat the trial judge's finding on the issue of reasonableness with the utmost respect and refrain from interference unless satisfied that the lower court proceeded on some 'erroneous principle or was plainly and obviously wrong' (*George Mitchell (Chesterhall) Ltd* v. *Finney Lock Seeds Ltd* [1983] 2 AC 803). It is likely therefore that inconsistency will continue to be a feature of cases decided under the reasonableness test of UCTA and, to that extent, the interest in preserving commercial certainty has been sacrificed.

Section 3 of the Act controls attempts to exclude or restrict liability for breach of contract. However, by virtue of s.3(1), this section of the Act applies only to two types of contract. The first is where one party 'deals as a consumer', which is defined in s.12 in the following terms:

(1) A party to a contract "deals as a consumer" in relation to another party if –

(a) he neither makes the contract in the course of a business nor holds himself out as doing so; and

(b) the other party does make the contract in the course of a business; and

(c) in the case of a contract governed by the law of sale of goods or hire-purchase, or by section 7 of this Act, the goods passing under or in pursuance of the contract are of a type ordinarily supplied for private use or consumption.

(2) But on a sale by auction or by competitive tender the buyer is not to be regarded as dealing as a consumer.

(3) Subject to this, it is for those claiming that a party does not deal as a consumer to show that he does not.

The second type of contract to which s.3 applies is where one party 'deals . . . on the other's written standard terms of business'. No definition is provided of this phrase. Does the requirement that the terms be 'written' exclude a contract which is partly written and partly oral? How much of a variation is needed before the terms applied cease to be 'standard'? These questions remain to be answered by the courts, but it is submitted that the courts are likely to take a wide view of this subsection, because otherwise the exclusion clause will fall outside the control of the statutory regime.

As against the party who deals as a consumer or deals on the other's written standard terms of business, the other party cannot by reference to any contract term 'when himself in breach of contract, exclude or restrict any liability of his in respect of the breach' except in so far as the contract term satisfies the requirement of reasonableness (s.3(2)(a)). Note that here liability once again means business liability and that the section is also cast in defensive terms, that is to say it assumes the existence of a breach of contract. This time, however, s.13(1) is not available to apply to duty-defining clauses because it states that it only applies to sections 2 and 5–7 of the Act.

Duty-defining terms may, however, be caught by s.3(2)(b) which states that the other party cannot by reference to any contract term claim to be entitled

'(i) to render a contractual performance substantially different from that which was reasonably expected of him, or

(ii) in respect of the whole or any part of his contractual obligation, to render no performance at all,
except in so far as . . . the contract term satisfies the requirement of reasonableness'.

This subsection must apply to situations other than a breach of contract because, if there was a breach of contract, it would be caught by s.3(2)(a). The type of situation the draftsman would appear to have in mind arises where a holiday company reserves the right to change the destination of the holiday or the hotel booked (without breaking the contract) and the alternative which it provides is less than the other contracting party reasonably expected. But how can a court identify the other party's 'reasonable expectations'? Presumably the exclusion clause will be ignored in identifying his reasonable expectations, but how many other terms will be disregarded in so doing? This question remains to be answered by the courts.

The Act also applies to other types of exclusion clauses, but these will only be dealt with in outline here. Section 4(1) states that any person dealing as a consumer cannot be required, as a term of the contract, to indemnify another in respect of liability that may be incurred by that other for negligence or breach of contract, except to the extent that the term satisfies the requirement of reasonableness. This section only applies where the party required to give the indemnity deals as a consumer (see s.12).

In contracts for the sale or hire-purchase of goods the implied terms as to title cannot be excluded or restricted by reference to any contract term (s.6(1)); and the seller's implied undertakings as to the conformity of goods with the description or sample, or as to their quality or fitness for a particular purpose cannot be excluded or restricted by reference to any contract term as against a person dealing as a consumer, although as against a party dealing otherwise than as a consumer the latter liabilities can be excluded or restricted by reference to a contract term only in so far as the term satisfies the requirement of reasonableness (s.6(2), (3)). Two additional points should be noted here. The first is that all attempts to exclude or restrict these implied terms are caught by UCTA, not simply those which seek to exclude or restrict a business liability under s.1(3) (s.6(4)). It should be remembered, however, that the implied terms relating to quality and fitness for purpose apply only where the seller sells the goods in the course of a business (see 9.8). The second is that the Act directs the courts to have regard to specific matters in considering whether such a term is reasonable (s.11(3) and Schedule 2).

A term excluding or restricting liability, which is contained in a separate contract rather than in the contract giving rise to the liability, is ineffective in so far as it attempts to take away a right to enforce a liability which under the Act cannot be excluded or restricted (s.10). Lastly it should be noted that the Act does not apply to certain contracts, such as contracts of insurance, contracts which concern the transfer of an interest in land and contracts for the supply of international goods (s.1. (2) and s.26).

11.10 Conclusion

The Unfair Contract Terms Act 1977 represents a major attempt to regulate the use of exclusion clauses in Britain. It cannot claim to be a wholly satisfactory piece of legislation. The main difficulty still lies in identifying the essential nature of an exclusion clause: does it define the nature of the contractual obligation or is it a defence to a breach of an obligation? The courts have traditionally seen exclusion clauses in defensive terms and, although UCTA is cast primarily in defensive terms, s.13(1) and s.3(2)(b) appear to extend the Act to duty-defining clauses. But, once it is conceded that the Act does apply to duty-defining clauses, on what basis can it be decided which duty-defining terms are caught by the Act and which fall outside the Act? This may become a question of some importance as contract draftsmen seek to evade the clutches of the Act. Yet it is a question to which those who support the defensive view of exclusion clauses have provided no answer. It is suggested that the only solution, however unpalatable it may be, lies in a reconsideration of the whole basis of the Act, in recognising that exclusion clauses perform duty-defining functions and treating them like any other term of the contract, only intervening to control them where they are shown to be 'unfair' or 'unconscionable' (on which see Chapter 17).

Summary

1 Exclusion clauses may be seen either as defining the obligations of the parties or as a defence to a breach of an obligation. The latter is the view which the courts have primarily adopted.
2 Exclusion clauses must be validly incorporated into the contract. Incorporation may take place either by the party who is not relying on the exclusion clause signing the contract containing the exclusion clause, by giving reasonable notice of the exclusion clause or by a course of dealing.
3 The exclusion clause, properly interpreted, must cover the damage which has arisen. The general rule of construction is that the exclusion clause will be interpreted *contra proferentem* (that is, against the party seeking to rely on the exclusion clause).
4 In relation to an attempt by a contracting party to exclude liability for his own negligence three specific rules have been devised by Lord Morton in *Canada Steamship Lines Ltd* v. *The King*. However, these rules are only aids to be used by the court in identifying the intention of the parties.
5 The doctrine of 'fundamental breach' is a rule of construction, according to which the more serious the breach, or the consequences of the breach, the less likely it is that the court will interpret the exclusion clause as covering the breach.
6 The Unfair Contract Terms Act 1977 is now the major source of control of exclusion clauses.
7 Attempts by reference to a contract term or notice, to exclude or restrict liability for negligence causing death or personal injury are void. In relation to other loss or damage caused by negligence, such attempts are only valid if they are held to be reasonable.
8 Where one party deals as a consumer or on the other's written standard terms of business, the other party cannot exclude or restrict liability for his own breach or claim to be entitled to render a contractual performance substantially different from that which was reasonably expected of him or render no

performance at all, except in so far as the contract term satisfies the requirement of reasonableness.

9 Reasonableness is to be assessed as at the date of making the contract and the onus is upon the party relying on the exclusion clause to show that it is reasonable.

10 The court has a wide discretion in deciding whether or not an exclusion clause is reasonable and will consider a number of different factors in reaching its conclusion.

Exercises

Consider the example involving Peter and John set out at 11.1 on the assumption that it includes the following exclusion clause: 'no liability is accepted for any damage, howsoever caused, to goods during the course of transit'.

1 What is the function of such a clause?

2 Peter wishes to know how he can incorporate such a clause into his contracts. How would you advise him?

3 Does the exclusion clause cover the damage done in the following cases?

   (i) Some of John's furniture is damaged as it it loaded into Peter's van;
   (ii) John's furniture is damaged when Peter's van crashes because of Peter's negligent driving;
   (iii) John's furniture is totally destroyed when Peter's van is destroyed by fire;
   (iv) Peter sells John's furniture before he gets to Preston.

4 How does the Unfair Contract Terms Act 1977 affect the exclusion clause in the situations described in question 3(i)–(iv)?

Part III

Policing the Contract

12 A Duty to Disclose Material Facts?

In this part of the book we shall consider various ways in which the law of contract regulates the agreement concluded by the parties and allocates the risk of unforeseen events between the parties. In Chapters 12 and 13 we shall discuss the obligations which are imposed upon contracting parties during the process of contractual negotiation. In Chapter 14 we shall analyse the methods by which the courts allocate the risk between contracting parties when they enter into a contract under a common fundamental mistake or an unforeseen event occurs after they have entered into the contract which destroys the basis on which they entered into the contract. In Chapters 15 and 16 we shall consider the limitations which are placed upon the enforceability of contracts by the doctrine of illegality and by the rules relating to capacity to enter into contracts. Finally, in Chapter 17 we shall discuss the doctrines of duress, undue influence and inequality of bargaining power and conclude this part by discussing the extent to which the law of contract is concerned with the fairness of the bargain reached by the parties.

12.1 Introduction

In terms of disclosing information during the process of contractual negotiation, there are essentially two types of obligation which could be imposed by the courts upon contracting parties. The first is a duty to disclose all known material facts to the other contracting party. The second is a duty to refrain from making active misrepresentations: that is to say, a contracting party is not compelled to disclose information, but, once he does disclose, he must do so truthfully. English law has adopted the latter approach and does not recognise the existence of a general duty to disclose material facts known to one contracting party but not to the other (*Keates* v. *Cadogan* (1851) 10 CB 591).

A number of reasons can be identified for this refusal to countenance the existence of a general duty of disclosure. An instructive example provided by Professor Fried (1981, p.79) will help us to appreciate these reasons:

'An oil company has made extensive geological surveys seeking to identify possible oil and gas reserves. These surveys are extremely expensive. Having identified one promising site, the oil company (acting through a broker) buys a large tract of land from its prosperous farmer owner, revealing nothing about its survey, its purposes or even its identity. The price paid is the going price for farmland of that quality in that region.'

An English court would undoubtedly uphold the validity of such a contract and would not require the buyer to disclose his information to the seller prior to the making of the contract. A number of justifications can be provided for such a rule. The first is the simple proposition that the information acquired by the buyer has a financial value and to expect him to disclose it to the seller without compensation is to deprive him unfairly of his valuable information, to provide a disincentive to the acquisition of such information and to unjustly enrich the seller. The second is that contractual obligations are generally voluntarily assumed by parties who deal 'at arm's length', seeking to make the best bargain they can. In such a context contracting parties are not expected to share information with each other. The third justification is that, if such a duty were to be recognised, the questions would have to be resolved as to when would it arise and what would be its content. This justification may be called the floodgates argument. These are compelling justifications for the refusal of the law to recognise the existence of a *general* duty of disclosure.

But strong arguments can be adduced to support the recognition of a duty of disclosure in certain *particular* cases. For example, few would support a rule which enabled a car dealer to sell a car which he knew to be dangerous without revealing that fact to the purchaser. Thus we find that, in certain exceptional cases, a particular duty of disclosure is held to exist. We shall now consider these exceptions and conclude by considering whether they have any coherent rationale.

12.2 Snatching at a Bargain

The first example of a limited duty of disclosure arises from the rule, which we have already noted (see *Hartog* v. *Colin and Shields* [1939] 3 All ER 566, discussed at 2.2), that a plaintiff will be prevented from snatching at a bargain which he knew was not intended by the defendant. Thus, in *Smith* v. *Hughes* (1871) LR 6 QB 597, the principle was established that a seller who knows that the buyer has misunderstood the terms of his offer is under an obligation to inform the buyer of the true nature of his offer. In other words, he is under a duty to disclose the existence of the mistake. But, where the buyer makes a mistake and that mistake does not relate to the terms of the seller's offer, then the seller, even if he is aware of the buyer's mistake, is not under an obligation to disclose the mistake to the buyer. It is the responsibility of the buyer to discover his mistake and he cannot escape from his bad bargain by arguing that it was the responsibility of the seller to inform him of his mistake (see further, Kronman, 1978a and Brownsword, 1987).

12.3 Representation by Conduct

The second group of exceptions all concern liability for misrepresentation (12.3–12.5). A misrepresentation consists of a false statement of fact (see 13.3) but the courts have, in limited circumstances, been flexible in their identification of a 'statement' of fact so that, in effect, they have imposed a limited duty of disclosure by the back door. For example, a contracting party does not have to open his mouth to make a statement; he can make it by his conduct (see Gleeson and McKendrick, 1987). In *Walters* v. *Morgan* (1861) 3 D F & J 718 Campbell LC said that, while simple reticence does not amount to a legal fraud, 'a nod or a wink, or a shake of the head, or a smile from the purchaser intended to induce the vendor to believe the existence of a non-existing fact, which might influence the price of the subject to be sold' would be a sufficient ground for refusing to enforce a contract.

The refusal to draw a rigid distinction between statements and conduct seems eminently sensible in the examples given by Campbell LC in *Walters*. Conduct can be as misleading as words. An apparently straightforward example of the imposition of liability on the basis of the conduct of the defendant is provided by *Gordon* v. *Selico* (1986) 11 HLR 219. An independent contractor, employed by the defendants, was asked to bring a flat which was infected with dry rot up to a very good standard for the purpose of selling it. The independent contractor simply covered up the dry rot and made no attempt to eradicate it. The plaintiffs purchased the flat and later discovered the presence of the dry rot. It was held that, in concealing the dry rot, the independent contractor had knowingly made a false representation to the plaintiffs that the flat did not suffer from dry rot and that he and the vendors were therefore liable to the plaintiffs in damages.

But, once it is recognised that a representation may be made by conduct, difficulties arise in identifying the meaning to be ascribed to the conduct and in ascertaining the situations in which the defendant is under an obligation to correct the meaning conveyed by his conduct. For example, in a case such as *Gordon* v. *Selico*, what would have been the position if the independent contractor had papered the dining-room prior to selling the house, partly because it needed redecorating anyway and partly to hide the defective state of the plaster? What is the meaning to be attributed to such conduct and is such a vendor under a duty to disclose the reasons why he has papered the room? In the High Court in *Gordon* v. *Selico* (1985) 275 EG 899, 903, Goulding J said that

'the law must be careful not to run ahead of popular morality by stigmatising as fraudulent every trivial act designed to make buildings or goods more readily saleable even if a highly scrupulous person might consider it dishonest'.

The vagueness of such a principle highlights the fact that, in the absence of a general duty of disclosure, it is extremely difficult to mark out the limits of any particular duty of disclosure.

12.4 Representation Falsified by Later Events

A person may also be guilty of misrepresentation where he fails to correct a representation which, when made was true, but which subsequently, to his knowledge, has become false or which, at the time of making it he believed to be true, but which he has subsequently discovered to be false. In *With* v. *O'Flanagan* [1936] Ch 575, negotiations for the sale of a medical practice began at a time when the practice was valued at £2000. But when the contract of sale was concluded the practice had become worthless because of the ill-health of the vendor in the intervening period. It was held that the vendor was under an obligation to disclose the change of circumstances to the buyer. The justification for this rule appears to be that a representation, once made, is deemed to be a continuing representation so that, once it becomes false to the knowledge of the representor and he fails to correct it, it becomes a misrepresentation (*Shankland & Co* v. *Robinson and Co* 1920 SC (HL) 103, per Lord Dunedin). However, where the representation relates to a statement of intention and the contracting party changes his intention before the conclusion of the contract, then there is no obligation to communicate that change of intention (*Wales* v. *Wadham* [1977] 1 WLR 199).

12.5 Statement Literally True but Misleading

A further situation in which liability in misrepresentation may be incurred arises where the statement is literally true but is nevertheless misleading because the maker of the statement has failed to disclose all the relevant information. In *Notts Patent Brick and Tile Co* v. *Butler* (1866) 16 QBD 778, a purchaser of land asked the vendor's solicitors whether the land was subject to restrictive covenants. The solicitor replied that he was not aware of any, but he did not say that the reason for his ignorance was that he had not bothered to check. It was held that, although the solicitor's statement was literally true, it nevertheless amounted to a misrepresentation.

12.6 Contracts Uberrimae Fidei

There are a group of contracts which are known as contracts 'uberrimae fidei' or contracts of the utmost good faith. Insurance contracts are contracts 'uberrimae fidei'; in such contracts the insured is under a duty to disclose all facts which a reasonable or prudent insurer would regard as material. The insured is in the best position to know the relevant facts and therefore a duty of disclosure is placed upon him.

12.7 Fiduciary Relationships

There is also a limited class of fiduciary relationships in which the party in whom the trust is reposed is placed under an obligation to disclose information to the person who has placed his trust in him (a good example is the cases in which the presumption of undue influence is held to arise, see 17.3). Where such a fiduciary relationship exists the parties do not bargain 'at arm's length' and the objection to the imposition of a duty of disclosure disappears.

12.8 A Duty of Disclosure in Tort?

Rather than seek a remedy in contract, a plaintiff may argue that the defendant committed the tort of negligence in failing to disclose the information to the plaintiff. But the law of tort does not impose a general duty of disclosure; indeed, Lord Keith has recently reaffirmed that a person who sees 'another about to walk over a cliff with his head in the air, and forbears to shout a warning' incurs no liability in the tort of negligence (*Yuen Kun-yeu* v. *Attorney General of Hong Kong* [1988] AC 175). On the other hand, a failure to speak may give rise to liability in the tort of negligence where the defendant has voluntarily assumed a responsibility to disclose information to the plaintiff and the plaintiff has relied upon that assumption of responsibility (*Banque Keyser Ullmann SA* v. *Skandia (UK) Insurance Co Ltd* [1989] 3 WLR 25, 101). A duty of disclosure may also be imposed by the law of tort in certain other exceptional cases. Thus a doctor who fails to disclose to a patient the risks involved in a course of treatment may be liable in the tort of negligence if he fails to act in accordance with a standard accepted as proper by a responsible body of medical men (*Sidaway* v. *Bethlem Royal Hospital Governors* [1985] AC 871) and a bank may be liable in negligence if it fails to proffer 'some adequate explanation of the nature and effect of the document' which a customer is required to sign (*Cornish* v. *Midland Bank plc* [1985] 3 All ER 513, 523 per Kerr LJ). But these remain exceptions to the general rule and the law of tort has not taken, and is unlikely to take, the step of imposing a duty on contracting parties to bargain in good faith (but see *English* v. *Dedham Vale Properties* [1978] 1 WLR 93).

12.9 The Role of the Sale of Goods Act 1979

We have already noted (see 9.8) that the Sale of Goods Act 1979 implies certain terms into contracts for the sale of goods. Two of these terms are of particular significance here. First, where a seller sells goods in the course of a business, there is an implied condition that the goods supplied under the contract are of merchantable quality, except in relation to defects drawn to the buyer's attention before the contract was concluded or, in the case where the buyer examines the goods, as regards defects which that examination ought to reveal (s.14(2)). Secondly, where the seller sells goods in the course of a business and the buyer makes known to the seller any particular purpose for which the goods are being bought, there is an implied condition that the goods supplied under the contract are reasonably fit for that purpose (s.14(3)). In many ways the rights conferred by these provisions are greater than any protection afforded by any duty of disclosure because the seller may be liable even where he was unaware of the existence of the defect; it suffices that the goods were not of merchantable quality or were not reasonably fit for their purpose. The Supply of Goods and Services Act 1982 and, to a lesser extent, Part I of the Consumer Protection Act 1987 (which imposes strict liability for defective products) further extend the scope of such regulatory legislation and lessen the need for the creation of a general duty of disclosure because they protect the 'consumer' irrespective of whether the supplier of the goods, the provider of the services or the manufacturer of the product knew of the relevant defect.

12.10 Conclusion

In *Interfoto Picture Library Ltd* v. *Stiletto Visual Programmes Ltd* [1988] 2 WLR 615, Bingham LJ noted that in many legal systems in the world 'the law of obligations recognises and enforces an overriding principle that in making and carrying out contracts parties should act in good faith'. English law, however, knows of no general principle requiring parties to bargain in good faith, nor does it recognise the narrower general principle of a duty of disclosure. Rather, English law starts from a premiss of rugged individualism, in which the parties are expected to look after their own interests and to bargain to obtain the best terms they can for themselves. But Bingham LJ also noted that, while English law recognised no such 'overriding principle', it had 'developed piecemeal solutions in response to demonstrated problems of unfairness'. The commitment to individualism is not an absolute one. The piecemeal exceptions which we have noted represent a limited attempt by the courts and Parliament to protect the expectations of consumers and to impose a limited duty of co-operation in an effort to avoid the unfairness and the excesses which would arise from an absolute refusal to recognise the existence of any duty of disclosure (for an alternative explanation of these exceptions in terms of a liberal theory of contract see Fried, 1981, pp. 77–85).

Summary

1 English law does not recognise the existence of a general duty to disclose material facts known to one contracting party but not to the other.
2 A defendant who knows that the plaintiff has misunderstood the terms of his offer is under an obligation to inform the plaintiff of the true nature of his offer.
3 A representation may be made by conduct.
4 A person is under a duty to disclose material facts which come to his notice before the conclusion of a contract if they falsify a representation previously made by him.
5 A person may be guilty of misrepresentation if his statement is literally true but is in fact misleading.
6 A duty to disclose material facts is imposed in the case of contracts *uberrimae fidei* (of the utmost good faith) and in the case of certain fiduciary relations.
7 Exceptionally a duty of disclosure may be imposed by the law of tort.
8 The existence of the 'merchantable quality' and 'fitness for purpose' provisions in the Sale of Goods Act 1979 mitigate the hardships which would otherwise be caused by the refusal of English contract law to recognise the existence of a general duty of disclosure. Similar obligations are now contained in the Supply of Goods and Services Act 1982.

Exercises

1 Why does English law not recognise the existence of a general duty of disclosure? Do you think it should recognise the existence of such a duty?
2 List the exceptional situations in which English law does recognise the existence of a particular duty of disclosure. Do these exceptions have any coherent rationale?
3 In Professor Fried's illustration concerning the oil company and the farmer (see 12.1) should the oil company be required to disclose its information to the farmer? Give reasons for your answer. Can you distinguish this illustration from the case of Gordon *v.* Selico?
4 Joe papered his dining-room prior to selling the house, partly because it needed redecorating anyway and partly to hide the defective state of the plaster. Emma bought the house and later discovered that the defective state of the plaster was in fact caused by a serious structural fault in the dining-room wall. Has she a cause of action against Joe?
5 It is a noticeable feature of the duty of disclosure cases which have arisen this century that they concern contracts which fall outside the scope of regulatory legislation, such as the Sale of Goods Act 1979. Can we learn any lessons from this fact?

13 Misrepresentation

13.1 Introduction

Although English law does not recognise the existence of a general duty to disclose information during the process of contractual negotiation, the process of contractual negotiation is not left unregulated. Rather, a duty is imposed not to make any false statements of fact to the other contracting party and thereby to induce him to enter into the contract. As we shall see, the law relating to misrepresentation does have a crucial role to play in the policing of contractual negotiations (see 13.3).

At the outset a fundamental distinction must be drawn between a promise and a representation. A promise may be defined as a statement by which the maker of the statement accepts or appears to accept an obligation to do or not to do something. A representation, on the other hand, is a statement which simply asserts the truth of a given state of facts. The distinction can be illustrated by reference to the case of *Kleinwort Benson Ltd* v. *Malaysia Mining Corporation Berhad* [1989] 1 WLR 379. The plaintiffs agreed to make available to a subsidiary company of the defendants a £10 million credit facility. The defendants refused to act as guarantors, but they gave to the plaintiffs a letter of comfort which stated that 'it is our policy to ensure that the business of [the subsidiary company] is at all times in a position to meet its liabilities to you under the above arrangement'. The subsidiary company ceased to trade after the collapse of the tin market at a time when their indebtedness to the plaintiffs was £10 million. The defendants refused to honour their undertaking in the letter of comfort and so the plaintiffs took proceedings against them, arguing that the defendants were in breach of contract in failing to pay. But the Court of Appeal held that the letter of comfort did not amount to a contractual promise by the defendants. Therefore they were not liable to the plaintiffs. It was held that the letter of comfort was simply a representation of fact as to the defendants' policy at the time when the statement was made. The defendants did not promise that they would not change their policy for the future; they did not state that 'it is *and will at all times continue to be* our policy to ensure that the subsidiary will at all times be in a position to meet its liabilities to you'.

Thus promises and representations are functionally different and have different legal consequences. A representation is a statement of fact which induces the other party to enter into a contract or otherwise act to his detriment. The representor does not promise anything; he simply asserts the truth of his statement and invites reliance upon that statement. If his statement of fact is false then it is a misrepresentation and the most appropriate remedy is to put the other party in the position which he would have been in had he not acted upon the misrepresentation to his detriment. Thus, on the facts of *Kleinwort Benson*, had the defendants' policy, at the time at which they made the statement, not been to ensure that the subsidiary would at all times be in a position to meet its liabilities, then their statement would have amounted to an actionable misrepresentation (see 13.3). A promise, on the other hand, creates an expectation that the promise will be fulfilled and the promisor accepts (or is deemed to accept) an obligation to carry out his promise. Having accepted such an obligation, the law will call upon the promisor to fulfil that obligation and will seek, by the remedy granted, to protect the expectation so created (see further, 20.3). Although promises and representations are functionally different, it can be very difficult to tell whether a particular statement is a promise or a representation. For example, in *Kleinwort Benson* the trial judge, Hirst J, held that the letter of comfort was a contractual promise, whereas the Court of Appeal held that it was a representation of fact. But any difficulty experienced in drawing the line should not blind us to the fact that representations and promises are fundamentally different types of statement.

One final point must be made before we consider the substance of the law relating to misrepresentation. That point is that misrepresentation lies on the boundary of contract and tort. A party who has been induced to enter a contract by a misrepresentation may seek a remedy in contract or in tort. Therefore at various points in the chapter we shall have to consider liability in both contract and tort.

Our analysis will proceed in four stages. At the first stage we will define a misrepresentation; at the second stage we shall discuss the different types of misrepresentation; at the third stage we shall consider the remedies for misrepresentation and at the final stage we shall discuss the exclusion of liability for misrepresentation.

13.2 What is a Misrepresentation?

A misrepresentation may be defined as an unambiguous, false statement of fact which is addressed to the party misled and which materially induces the contract. This definition may be broken down into three distinct elements. The first is that the representation must be an unambiguous false statement of fact (13.3), the second is that it must be addressed to the party misled (13.4) and the third is that it must be a material inducement to entry into the contract (13.5).

13.3 A False Statement of Existing Fact

The representation must be an unambiguous false statement of existing fact. The following four categories of statement have been held *not* to constitute statements of existing fact and therefore cannot amount to actionable misrepresentations.

The first is a 'mere puff'. We have already noted (see 8.1) that a commendatory statement may be so vague as to be neither a promise which is incorporated into the contract as a term, nor a statement of fact. In *Dimmock* v. *Hallett* (1866) LR 2 Ch App 21, Turner LJ said that a representation that land was 'fertile and improveable' would not, except in an extreme case, be considered such a misrepresentation as to entitle the innocent party to rescind the contract. But there are limits to this principle. The more specific the statement, the less likely it is to be treated as a mere puff (*Carlill* v. *Carbolic Smoke Ball Co* [1893] 1 QB 256).

Secondly, a statement of opinion or belief which proves to be unfounded is not a false statement of fact. In *Bisset* v. *Wilkinson* [1927] AC 177, a vendor of a farm in New Zealand, which had not been used for sheep farming before, represented to a prospective purchaser that, in his judgment, the land could carry 2000 sheep. In fact it could not, and the purchaser, when he discovered this, sought to rescind the contract. He was unable to do so because the vendor's statement was not a false statement of fact but a statement of opinion which he honestly held.

Bisset was distinguished, however, in the important case of *Esso Petroleum Ltd* v. *Mardon* [1976] QB 801. Esso represented to the defendant, a prospective tenant of a petrol filling station which was in the process of construction, that the throughput of petrol at the station was likely to reach 200 000 gallons per year. However the local authority refused planning permission for the petrol pumps to front onto the main street. Instead, the station had to be built back to front with the forecourt at the back of the station and the only access to the petrol pumps being from a side street. Esso, through their experienced officials, assured the defendant that this change would not affect the projected throughput of petrol. In fact, as a result of the change, the throughput only reached 78 000 gallons per year. The defendant incurred considerable losses in operating the station and he eventually reached the position where he could no longer pay Esso for his petrol. Esso consequently sought to repossess the station and to recover the money owed to them by the defendant. The defendant counterclaimed for damages for breach of contract and for negligent misrepresentation. Esso argued that their statement as to the throughput of petrol was a statement of opinion and hence was not actionable. But the Court of Appeal held that the statement was one of fact. Lord Denning distinguished *Bisset* on the ground that there 'the land had never been used as a sheep farm and both parties were equally able to form an opinion as to its carrying capacity'. Esso, on the other hand, had special knowledge and skill in the forecasting of the throughput of petrol and they were held to represent that they had made the forecast with 'reasonable care and skill'. On the facts it was held that they had not exercised reasonable care and skill and they were therefore liable to the defendant in damages. A similar approach to that adopted in *Esso* was espoused by Bowen LJ in *Smith* v. *Land and House Property Corp* (1884) 28 Ch D 7, when he said that where

> 'the facts are equally known to both parties, what one says to the other is frequently nothing but an expression of opinion . . . But if the facts are not equally well known to both sides, then a statement of opinion by one who knows the facts best involves very often a statement of material fact, for he impliedly states that he knows facts which justify his opinion.'

Combining the principles established in *Esso* and *Smith* we can deduce the following proposition: where the representor has greater knowledge than the representee the courts will infer that the representation must be made with reasonable care and skill (*Esso*) and that the representor knows facts which justify his opinion (*Smith*). In effect, these cases impose upon negotiating parties who have special skill a duty to take reasonable care in the preparation of forecasts and opinions. They also illustrate the fact that the courts will, in certain circumstances, demand that negotiating parties deal in good faith with each other.

Thirdly, a representation of law is not a statement of existing fact. Finally, a statement of intention is not a statement of fact. Nor is a promise a statement of fact. A person who fails to carry out his stated intention does not thereby make a misrepresentation (*Wales* v. *Wadham* [1977] 1 WLR 199). But a person who misrepresents his present intention does make a false statement of fact because the state of his intention is a matter of fact. In *Edgington* v. *Fitzmaurice* (1885) 29 Ch D 459, directors of a company invited the public to subscribe for debentures on the basis that the money so raised would be used to expand the business. In fact the real purpose in raising the money was to pay off company debts. It was held that the directors were guilty of misrepresentation because they had misrepresented their actual intention.

13.4 Addressed to the Party Misled

Secondly, it must be shown that the representation was addressed to the party misled. There are two ways in which a representation may be addressed to the party misled. The first and most obvious method is by the direct communication of the misrepresentation to the plaintiff by the representor. Alternatively, the misrepresentation may be addressed by the representor to a third party with the intention that it be passed on to the plaintiff. In *Commercial Banking Co of Sydney* v. *RH Brown and Co*

[1972] 2 Lloyds Rep 360, the defendant bank misrepresented to the plaintiffs' bank the financial standing of one of the plaintiffs' customers. The plaintiffs' bank communicated the information to the plaintiffs, who acted on it to their detriment. It was held that the defendants were liable to the plaintiffs because they knew that the plaintiffs' bank did not want the information for their own purposes and that it was to be passed on to a customer who was proposing to deal with a client of the defendant bank.

13.5 A Material Inducement

Finally the representation must be a material inducement to entry into the contract. Here there are two elements at work. The first is that the representation must be material, in the sense that it would affect the judgment of a reasonable man in deciding whether to enter into the contract on these terms (although a person who has been fraudulent cannot be heard to argue that the representation was immaterial). The second is that the representation must actually induce the contract, that is to say, it must induce the actual plaintiff to enter into the contract. In *Edgington* v. *Fitzmaurice* (above) it was held that the misrepresentation need not be the sole inducement; it is sufficient that it was *an* inducement which was actively present to the representee's mind. This requirement was not satisfied in the case of *JEB Fasteners* v. *Marks, Bloom and Co* [1983] 1 All ER 583. The defendants negligently prepared the accounts of a company which was taken over by the plaintiffs. The accounts had been made available to the plaintiffs, who had reservations about them, but they nevertheless decided to proceed with the take-over because they wished to acquire the services of two of the directors of that company. The take-over was not a commercial success and the plaintiffs brought an action against the defendants alleging that they had been negligent in the preparation of the accounts. The Court of Appeal dismissed the action on the ground that the defendants' representation did not play a 'real and substantial' part in inducing the plaintiffs to act. They had taken over the company, not in reliance upon the accounts, but because of their desire to acquire the services of these two directors.

There are at least three situations in which a plaintiff will be unable to show that the representation induced the contract. The first is where the plaintiff was unaware of the existence of the representation (*Horsfall* v. *Thomas* (1862) 1 H & C 90); the second is where the plaintiff knew that the representation was untrue; and the third is where the plaintiff did not allow the representation to affect his judgment. A plaintiff does not allow a representation to affect his judgment where he regards the representation as being unimportant (*Smith* v. *Chadwick* (1884) 9 App Cas 187) or where he relies upon his own judgment. In *Atwood* v. *Small* (1838) 6 Cl & F 232, Atwood contracted to sell his mine to Small, but exaggerated its earning capacity. Small appointed agents to verify Atwood's representations and they reported that his statements were true. After the contract was concluded, Small discovered the exaggerations and sought to rescind the contract. He was unable to do so because he had relied upon his agents' report rather than upon Atwood's representation. It should be noted that this rule does not apply to the plaintiff who has the opportunity to discover the truth himself but does not take it. In such a case, the plaintiff remains entitled to relief against the misrepresentor (*Redgrave* v. *Hurd* (1881) 20 Ch D 1).

13.6 The Types of Misrepresentation

There are four different types of misrepresentation. It is important to distinguish between the different types of misrepresentation because they may give rise to different remedial consequences. We shall see that all types of misrepresentation entitle the representee to rescind the contract but not all types of misrepresentation give rise to an action for damages.

The first type of misrepresentation is fraudulent misrepresentation. Fraudulent misrepresentation, in addition to being a ground on which a contract may be set aside, constitutes the tort of deceit. Although the word 'fraud' bears a wide meaning in common parlance, its meaning in law is much narrower as a result of the decision of the House of Lords in *Derry* v. *Peek* (1889) 14 App Cas 337. In *Derry* Lord Herschell established the following three propositions. The first is that there must be proof of fraud and nothing short of that is sufficient. The second is that fraud is proved when it is shown that a false representation has been made (i) knowingly or (ii) without belief in its truth or (iii) recklessly, careless whether it be true or false. Unreasonableness of belief does not of itself constitute fraud; it simply provides evidence of dishonesty on the part of the maker of the statement (*Angus* v. *Clifford* [1891] 2 Ch 449). Thirdly, if fraud is proved the motive of the person guilty of it is immaterial. In *Polhill* v. *Walter* (1832) 3 B & Ad 114, the representor knew that his statement was false but his motive in making the statement was to benefit his principal and not to benefit himself, nor to injure anyone else. Notwithstanding his good motives, he was held liable in the tort of deceit. There are few cases brought in the tort of deceit today, largely because of the difficulty of proving that the representor was guilty of fraud.

The second type of misrepresentation is negligent misrepresentation at common law. In the period immediately after *Derry* v. *Peek*, it was thought that negligent misrepresentation was not actionable in tort because liability in tort arose only in cases of fraudulent misrepresentation (*Le Lievre* v. *Gould* [1893] 1 QB 491). However, this view was rejected by the House of Lords in *Nocton* v. *Lord Ashburton* [1914] AC 932. Although the House recognised that negligent misrepresentation could be actionable in tort, they held that it was actionable only where there was a pre-existing contractual relationship between the parties or where the parties were in a 'fiduciary relationship'. This restrictive approach prevailed in England as late as 1951 (see *Candler* v. *Crane, Christmas and Co* [1951] 2 KB 164, but contrast the powerful dissenting judgment of Denning LJ).

However, in 1964 in *Hedley Byrne* v. *Heller* [1964] AC 465, the House of Lords finally expanded the ambit of liability for negligent misrepresentation. The plaintiffs were advertising agents who booked substantial advertising space on behalf of their clients, Easipower Ltd, on terms that they were personally liable. The plaintiffs became concerned about the financial standing of Easipower and, through their bank, sought from the defendants, who were Easipower's bankers, a reference on the financial soundness of Easipower. The defendants replied that Easipower was 'considered good for its ordinary business transactions'. In reliance upon the reference, the plaintiffs placed orders which, because of the subsequent default of Easipower, resulted in a loss to them of £17 000. The plaintiffs alleged that the defendants were negligent in the preparation of the reference and were therefore liable to them in damages. Their claim failed because the defendants had provided the reference 'without responsibility'. However the importance of *Hedley Byrne* lies, not in the fact that the claim failed because of the disclaimer, but in the fact that the House of Lords significantly widened the scope of liability in tort for negligent misrepresentation. The important task which now remains for us is to ascertain the limits of *Hedley Byrne*.

The key to *Hedley Byrne* lies in the concept of a 'special relationship' between the plaintiff and the defendant. The principal elements in this 'special relationship' are a voluntary assumption of responsibility by the defendant and foreseeable detrimental reliance by the plaintiff. These elements can be further subdivided into three categories. The first is that the representor must be possessed of a special skill. In Mutual Life and *Citizens Assurance Co* v. *Evatt* [1971] AC 793, the majority of the Privy Council interpreted this element as requiring that the representor be in the business of giving advice on the subject of his representation. On the facts, the defendant insurance company had given the plaintiff gratuitous advice on the wisdom of investing in the defendants' sister company. It was held that the defendants were not liable because they were an insurance company and not investment advisers. The status of *Evatt* is, however, unclear because the judgment of the minority, Lord Reid and Lord Morris, has commanded wider support in subsequent cases. The minority held that a duty of care is owed by anyone who takes it upon himself to make representations knowing that another will justifiably rely upon his representation. In *Esso Petroleum* v. *Mardon* [1976] QB 801 (see Gravells, 1976) Ormerod LJ supported the minority view in *Evatt*, as did Lord Denning and Shaw LJ in *Howard Marine and Dredging Co* v. *A Ogden and Sons* [1978] QB 574. On the basis of these dicta it is suggested that the majority view in *Evatt* will not be followed and that the minority view will be preferred.

The second requirement of the special relationship is that the representee must reasonably rely upon the representation. The third requirement is that, although the identity of the actual person relying on the information need not be known by the representor, some knowledge of the types of transaction for which the information is required would seem to be necessary. Where there is insufficient knowledge on the part of the representor, then it is unlikely that the plaintiff will be able to establish that the representor has assumed a responsibility towards him (*Caparo Industries plc* v. *Dickman* [1989] 2 WLR 316).

Negligent misrepresentation at common law must be distinguished from the liability which may arise under section 2(1) of the Misrepresentation Act 1967. This is the third type of misrepresentation. Section 2(1) provides that

'Where a person has entered into a contract after a misrepresentation has been made to him by another party thereto and as a result thereof he has suffered loss then, if the person making the misrepresentation would be liable to damages in respect thereof had the misrepresentation been made fraudulently, that person shall be so liable notwithstanding that the misrepresentation was not made fraudulently, unless he proves that he had reasonable grounds to believe and did believe up to the time that the contract was made that the facts represented were true.'

Section 2(1) operates independently of the *Hedley Byrne* line of authority. The section is drafted in rather clumsy and unusual terms because it imposes liability by reference to liability for fraudulent misrepresentation, even though the misrepresentor has not been fraudulent (for a discussion of the possible consequences of the 'fiction of fraud', see Atiyah and Treitel, 1967, pp.372–5). But, stripped of its convoluted drafting, the general effect of the section is clear; where a misrepresentation has been made by one contracting party to another, the party making the misrepresentation is liable to the other in damages unless he can prove that he had reasonable grounds to believe and did believe up to the time that the contract was made that his statement was true.

This statutory right has two advantages over a common law negligence claim. The first is that the Act does not require that there be a 'special relationship' between the parties. This was of crucial significance in *Gosling* v. *Anderson* [1972] EGD 709. The defendant, who was selling her flat, represented to the plaintiff, through her estate agents, that planning permission had been obtained for building a garage when, in fact, it had not been obtained. In the Court of Appeal Roskill LJ stated that, had the action been heard before 1967, the plaintiff's action would have failed unless she had been able to prove fraud, but that she was now able to rely on s.2(1) of the 1967 Act and was entitled to damages for the misrepresentation. The second advantage of a claim under s.2(1) is that the representor is liable unless he proves that he had reasonable grounds to believe and did believe up to the time that the contract was made that the facts represented were true, whereas at common law it is for the representee to prove that the representor was negligent.

It is no easy task for a representor to discharge the onus of proof under s.2(1), as can be seen from the case of *Howard Marine* v. *Ogden* (above). The defendants wished to hire barges from the plaintiffs and, during the course of the negotiations, the plaintiffs' manager represented that the deadweight capacity of each barge was 1600 tonnes when, in fact, it was only 1055 tonnes. The defendants used the barges for six troublesome months but, when they discovered the true deadweight capacity of the barges, they refused to continue to pay the hire. The plaintiffs sued for the hire charges and the defendants counterclaimed, *inter alia*, for damages under s.2(1) of the 1967 Act. The representation of the plaintiffs' manager as to the deadweight capacity of the barges was based upon his recollection of the figures in Lloyd's Register. His recollection was correct but, unusually, Lloyds were wrong. The Court of Appeal held, Lord Denning dissenting, that the plaintiffs had not discharged the burden of proof upon them of showing that they had reasonable grounds to believe that the statement was true. This was because the accurate figures were contained in the ships' documents and the plaintiffs had failed to show any 'objectively reasonable ground' for disregarding the figure in these documents and preferring the figure in Lloyd's Register. The burden upon the representor is therefore a heavy one and it is likely to enable a representee to recover where at common law he would have failed (for example, in *Howard Marine* itself, only Shaw LJ was of the opinion that a common law claim would have succeeded).

However there remain certain situations in which a plaintiff must have recourse to a common law claim. The first situation arises where, as in *Hedley Byrne*, the representation is made by a third party who is not party to the contract. Section 2(1) only applies where the representation has been made by the other party to the contract. The second situation in which it may be necessary to have recourse to the common law arises where the contract between the parties is void *ab initio* (for example, on the ground of *non est factum*). In such a case there is no contract to which s.2(1) can apply.

The final type of misrepresentation is innocent misrepresentation. An innocent misrepresentation is a misrepresentation which is neither fraudulent nor negligent. This category is now of little practical significance.

13.7 Remedies

Once the existence of a misrepresentation has been established, consideration must be given to the remedies available for misrepresentation. There are two principal remedies. The first is the setting aside of the contract induced by the misrepresentation (this is called 'rescission' by lawyers). This is a classic contractual remedy. However a plaintiff may not be satisfied with rescission and may also want compensation for the financial loss which he has suffered. A claim for damages does not lie in contract when the contract has been rescinded, but a claim for damages may lie in tort and so we must consider the relationship between the two claims.

13.8 Rescission

Rescission is, in principle, available for all types of misrepresentation. It is very important, however, to be clear about the precise meaning of the word rescission. Atiyah and Treitel (1967) helpfully distinguish two types of rescission. The first type, entitled 'rescission for misrepresentation' arises where the contract is set aside for all purposes, that is to say, the contract is set aside both retrospectively and prospectively. Here the aim is to restore, as far as possible, the parties to the position which they were in before they entered into the contract. The second type of rescission, called 'rescission for breach', arises where one contracting party refuses to continue with performance of the contract because of the breach by the other party. In the latter case the effect of rescission is to release the parties from their obligations to perform in the future but the contract is not treated as if it had never existed. Therefore rescission for breach does *not* operate retrospectively (see further 19.7). In this chapter we shall discuss only rescission for misrepresentation.

Rescission does not occur automatically when a misrepresentation is made. Misrepresentation renders a contract voidable. Therefore the representee can elect either to rescind or to affirm the contract. If he decides to rescind, the general rule is that he must bring his decision to rescind to the notice of the representor. This can be done in a number of ways: for example, by seeking a declaration that the contract is invalid, by restoring what he has obtained under the contract or by relying upon the misrepresentation as a defence to an action on the contract (*Redgrave* v. *Hurd* (above)). However, where the representor deliberately absconds and so makes it impossible for the representee to give him notice of his decision to rescind, then it is sufficient that the representee evidences his intention to rescind by some overt means, falling short of communication, which is reasonable in the circumstances. So where a thief persuades an owner to part with his car by a fraudulent misrepresentation and the thief cannot subsequently be traced, the owner can validly rescind by notifying the police or the Automobile Association (*Car and Universal Finance Co* v. *Caldwell* [1965] 1 QB 525, but contrast the Scottish case of *MacLeod* v. *Kerr* 1965 SC 253).

There are, however, certain limits to the right to rescind. The right to rescind may be lost by affirmation of the contract by the plaintiff after he discovered the truth, by the intervention of innocent third party rights and by lapse of time (*Leaf* v. *International Galleries* [1950] 2 KB 86, although lapse of time does not, of itself, bar rescission in cases of fraudulent misrepresentation). The principal ground on which the right to rescind may be lost arises where it is impossible to restore the parties to their pre-contractual position. The very object of rescission is to return the parties to the position which they were in before entering into the contract, and where this is impossible it inevitably follows that rescission is unavailable. At common law the courts insisted upon precise restitution, but the harshness of this rule is mitigated by the intervention of equity. In equity a party who can make substantial, but not precise, restitution can rescind the contract if he returns the subject-matter of the contract in its altered form and gives an account of any profits made through his use of the product, together with an allowance for any deterioration in the product (*Erlanger* v. *New Sombrero Phosphate Co* (1878) 3 App Cas 1218).

We have already noted that the effect of rescission is to set aside the contract for all purposes. A consequence of this is that contractual damages cannot be claimed because the contract has been set aside for all purposes and so there is no basis for any claim on the contract. But an indemnity may be claimed. An indemnity can only be claimed in respect of expenses incurred in the discharge of obligations created by the contract. The point can be illustrated by reference to the case of *Whittington* v. *Seale-Hayne* (1900) 82 LT 49. The plaintiffs took a lease of premises for the purpose of breeding prize poultry. They were induced to do so by representations of the defendant's agent that the premises were in good sanitary condition. Under the lease the plaintiffs covenanted to execute all such works as might be required by the local authority. The premises were not, however, in a sanitary condition and were in a state of disrepair. The water supply was poisoned and, as a result, the poultry died or became valueless and the manager of the farm became ill. The local authority declared the premises unfit for habitation and required the plaintiffs to renew the drains. It was held that the plaintiffs were entitled to an indemnity in respect of the rates which they had paid and the cost of carrying out the repairs ordered by the local authority because these were obligations which were actually created by the contract of lease. On the other hand, the plaintiffs were not entitled to recover in respect of the value of the lost stock or their loss of profit because these were not obligations which were created by the lease. Such losses could be recovered in a damages action but, on the facts, a claim in damages was not available.

13.9 Damages

A contractual claim for damages does not lie for misrepresentation, unless the misrepresentation has been subsequently incorporated into the contract as a term, in which case damages can be claimed for breach of contract (see 8.1 and 8.6). But damages may be recoverable in *tort* where the misrepresentation was made fraudulently or negligently. Sections 2(1) and 2(2) of the Misrepresentation Act 1967 also make provision for the recovery of damages for misrepresentation. Provided there is no element of double recovery a plaintiff may rescind and claim damages (except under s.2(2) of the Misrepresentation Act 1967, see below). When considering the entitlement of a plaintiff to damages for misrepresentation it is vital to give separate treatment to each type of misrepresentation.

Where the misrepresentation is fraudulent, damages may be recovered in the tort of deceit. The aim of an award of damages in deceit is to put the plaintiff in the position which he would have been in had the tort not been committed; that is to say, it aims to protect his reliance interest. This was confirmed by the Court of Appeal in *Doyle* v. *Olby* [1969] 2 QB 158 (see too *Smith Kline & French Laboratories Ltd* v. *Long* [1989] 1 WLR 1). The court also held that the defendant was liable for all the damage directly flowing from the fraudulent inducement which was not rendered too remote by the plaintiff's own conduct, whether or not the defendant could have foreseen such consequential loss. It is unclear whether exemplary (or punitive) damages can be recovered for a fraudulent misrepresentation, although aggravated damages may be recovered (*Archer* v. *Brown* [1985] QB 401).

In the case of negligent misrepresentation at common law the mis-representor has committed a tort and damages can therefore be claimed. Once again the award of damages seeks to put the plaintiff in the position which he would have been in had the tort not been committed. The representor will be liable for all losses which are a reasonably foreseeable consequence of the misrepresentation (*The Wagon Mound (No 1)* [1961] AC 388) and it is highly unlikely that punitive damages will be recoverable.

In the case of a claim under s.2(1) of the Misrepresentation Act 1967, the measure of damages recoverable has been the source of some considerable controversy. Some have argued that damages should seek to put the plaintiff in the position he would have been in had the representation not been made (thus protecting the reliance interest), while others have argued that damages should put the plaintiff in the position he would have been in had the representation been true (thus protecting the expectation interest). As Taylor has pointed out (1982), the Act itself was capable of either construction and it has therefore been left to the courts to resolve this issue.

In *Gosling* v. *Anderson* (above) and *Jarvis* v. *Swan's Tours* [1973] QB 233, Lord Denning appeared to suggest that the measure of recovery was the expectation measure and this view was followed by Graham J in *Watts* v. *Spence* [1976] Ch 165. The cases since then, however, have confined recovery to the reliance measure (see *F & H Entertainments Ltd* v. *Leisure Enterprises Ltd* (1976) 120 SJ 331, *Andre & Cie SA* v. *Ets. Michel Blanc et Fils* [1977] 2 Lloyds Rep 166, *Chesnau* v. *Interhome* Ltd *The Times* 9 June 1983 per Eveleigh LJ and *Sharneyford Supplies Ltd* v. *Barrington Black and Co* [1985] 3 WLR 1 and [1987] Ch 305, 323). So the better view is that damages are confined to the reliance measure and it is suggested that this is the correct approach because, as we have already noted (13.1), promises and representations are functionally different. A representor does not promise anything; he simply asserts the truth of his statement and invites *reliance* upon that statement. It is therefore appropriate that the measure of damages should be the reliance measure.

In cases of innocent misrepresentation, the traditional common law rule was that damages were not available. Innocent misrepresentation was not a tort and therefore the only remedy was rescission and an indemnity. In practice the courts tended to mitigate the rigours of this rule, either by finding that the representation was in fact not a representation at all but a contractual term, or by finding that the representation was enforceable as a 'collateral contract'. The latter technique can be illustrated by reference to the case of *De Lassalle* v. *Guildford* [1901] 2 KB 215. The plaintiff was induced to enter into a lease by an oral statement made by the defendant that the drains were in good order. The drains were not in good order but the lease contained no reference to them. It was held that the defendant's representation was enforceable as a warranty which was collateral to the lease. Thus there were two contracts between the parties. The first one was the written lease and the second consisted of the oral statement that the drains were in good order, the consideration for which was the entry by the plaintiff into the lease. However the courts were not able to find the existence of such a collateral contract in every case (see *Heilbut, Symons and Co* v. *Buckleton* [1913] AC 30).

The need to seek out the existence of a collateral contract has been reduced by s.2(2) of the Misrepresentation Act 1967 which provides that

'where a person has entered into a contract after a misrepresentation has been made to him otherwise than fraudulently, and he would be entitled, by reason of the misrepresentation, to rescind the contract, then, if it is claimed in any proceedings arising out of the contract, that the contract ought to be or has been rescinded, the court or arbitrator may declare the contract subsisting and award damages in lieu of rescission, if of the opinion that it would be equitable to do so, having regard to the nature of the misrepresentation and the loss that would be caused by it if the contract were upheld, as well as to the loss that rescission would cause to the other party'.

Thus the courts now have a discretion to award damages in lieu of rescission in the case of innocent misrepresentation. The following points should be noted about s.2(2). The first is that the power to award damages is discretionary. The representee has no right to damages. The second point is that damages are in lieu of rescission, so that if the plaintiff wishes to rescind he can only claim an indemnity. Thirdly, it is not clear what is the appropriate measure of damages under s.2(2). But, since the measure under s.2(1) is probably tortious, it is unlikely that the contractual measure will be recoverable under s.2(2) because that would put the victim of an innocent misrepresentation in a better position than the victim of negligent misrepresentation. The final point relates to the situation where the plaintiff had the right to rescind but has lost it, for example because of lapse of time. Does such a plaintiff also lose the right to claim damages under s.2(2)? In *Alton House Garages (Bromley) Ltd* v. *Monk* (Hearing 31.7.81.) Cantley J held that the jurisdiction was one to grant damages *in lieu of* rescission and that the representee must therefore be entitled to rescind at the date of the court hearing. Therefore if the representee has lost his right to rescind the court cannot award him damages under s.2(2).

13.10 Excluding Liability for Misrepresentation

At common law a person could not exclude liability for his own fraudulent misrepresentation (*S Pearson & Son Ltd* v. *Dublin Corporation* [1907] AC 351), but he could exclude liability for negligent or innocent misrepresentation, although such exclusion clauses were subject to strict rules relating to incorporation and construction (see 9.4 and 11.4–11.7). However s.3 of the Misrepresentation Act 1967 (as amended by s.8 of the Unfair Contract Terms Act 1977) limits the freedom of the parties to exclude liability for the consequences of a misrepresentation. It provides that

'If a contract contains a term which would exclude or restrict –

(a) any liability to which a party to a contract may be subject by reason of any misrepresentation made by him before the contract was made; or
(b) any remedy available to another party to the contract by reason of such a misrepresentation

that term shall be of no effect except in so far as it satisfies the requirement of reasonableness as stated in s.11(1) of the Unfair Contract Terms Act 1977 and it is for those claiming that the term satisfies that requirement to show that it does'.

It should be noted that, once again, the Act is drafted in defensive terms (see 11.1) so that it attacks attempts to 'exclude or restrict' a 'liability' or a 'remedy'. This section applies both to business liability and to non-business liability. Clauses which seek to define the duty may therefore fall outside the scope of the Act, but it is unlikely that a representor will be able to evade the clutches of the Act merely by stating that the representee must satisfy himself as to the correctness of any statement (*Cremdean Properties* v. *Nash* (1977) 244 EG 547, *South Western General Property Co Ltd* v. *Marton* (1982) 263 EG 1090 and *Walker* v. *Boyle* [1982] 1 All ER 634).

Summary

1 A misrepresentation may be defined as an unambiguous false statement of fact which is addressed to the party misled and which is a material inducement to entry into the contract.

2 Mere puffs, statements of opinion, statements of intention and representations of law are not statements of fact.

3 A representation does not induce the contract if the representation was unimportant, the representee was unaware of its existence or did not allow it to affect his judgment.

4 A fraudulent misrepresentation is made when it is proved that a false representation has been made (i) knowingly or (ii) without belief in its truth or (iii) recklessly, careless whether it be true or false.

5 Negligent misrepresentation is actionable at common law where there is a special relationship between the plaintiff and the defendant. The crucial elements in a special relationship are an assumption of responsibility by the representor and detrimental reliance by the representee.

6 Section 2(1) of the Misrepresentation Act 1967 states that, where a misrepresentation has been made by one contracting party to another, the party making the misrepresentation is liable to the other in damages unless he can prove that he had reasonable grounds to believe and did believe up to the time that the contract was made that his statement was true.

7 The principal remedies for misrepresentation are rescission and damages. Rescission is in principle available for all types of misrepresentation. The effect of rescission is to put the parties as far as possible into the position which they would have been in had the contract not been concluded.

8 Damages can be claimed for fraudulent and negligent misrepresentation and under s.2(1) of the 1967 Act. In all cases the measure of damages is the reliance measure (although the point is not absolutely clear in relation to s.2(1)). In the case of innocent misrepresentation the court has a discretion to award damages in lieu of rescission under s.2(2) of the 1967 Act.

9 The ability of a contracting party to exclude liability for misrepresentation is controlled by s.3 of the Misrepresentation Act 1967 which subjects any term which purports to exclude or restrict liability or a remedy for misrepresentation to the reasonableness test.

Exercises

1 What is a misrepresentation?

2 What is a statement of existing fact? Give examples to illustrate your answer.

3 Distinguish between fraudulent, negligent and innocent misrepresentation.

4 What are the advantages to a plaintiff in invoking s.2(1) of the Misrepresentation Act 1967 rather than the common law of negligent misrepresentation? Are there any disadvantages?

5 What are the principal remedies for misrepresentation? What is the difference between damages and an indemnity?

6 Can a defendant exclude liability for misrepresentation?

14 Common Mistake and Frustration

14.1 Introduction

Parties occasionally enter into a contract on the basis of a common assumption which they later discover was false. Alternatively, events occur after the formation of the contract which were not within the contemplation of the parties when they entered into the contract. In these circumstances, are the parties bound to carry out their contract according to its terms, even though the events which have occurred were not within their contemplation when they entered into the contract? The answer to this question is that the courts may, in certain circumstances, release the parties from their obligations to perform. But it is very important to understand the basis of the intervention of the courts in these cases. The basis is not that the parties failed to reach agreement. These cases are not like the mistake cases which we discussed at 4.6, where one party is claiming relief on the basis that he was mistaken and that mistake negatived his consent and so prevented a contract coming into existence.

Here the parties do actually reach agreement and a valid contract is initially concluded. But an event occurs which was unforeseen by the parties and which destroys the basis upon which they entered into the contract. In such a case the courts must decide who bears the risk of such an unforeseen event (see Swan, 1980). Where the courts intervene to grant relief they do so on the ground that it is no longer fair or just to hold the parties to their agreement in such radically changed and unforeseen circumstances.

Where the common misapprehension is present *at the date of entry* into the contract, the contract may be set aside on the ground of common (or, as it is sometimes called, 'mutual') mistake. On the other hand, where events have occurred *after* the making of the contract which render performance of the contract impossible, illegal or something radically different from that which was in the contemplation of the parties at the time at which they entered into the contract, then the contract may be discharged on the ground of 'frustration'.

Common mistake is often treated separately from frustration on the ground that the latter is concerned with the discharge of a contract, whereas mistake relates to the formation of a contract. It is true that mistake relates to events which exist or occur prior to the making of the contract, and frustration applies to events which occur after the making of the contract. But there is, in fact, a strong link between these two doctrines, as can be seen from a brief analysis of the following case.

In *Amalgamated Investment & Property Co Ltd* v. *John Walker & Sons Ltd* [1977] 1 WLR 164, the defendants sold property to the plaintiffs for £1 710 000. The property was advertised as being suitable for occupation or redevelopment and the defendants knew that the plaintiffs wished to redevelop the property. In their pre-contract enquiries the plaintiffs asked the defendants whether the property was designated as a building of special historic or architectural interest. The defendants replied that it was not but, unknown to both parties, officials at the Department of the Environment had, on 22 August 1973, unconditionally included the property in a list of buildings to be designated as buildings of special architectural or historical interest. The parties signed the contract of sale on 25 September 1973. On the following day the Secretary of State wrote to the defendants informing them that the building had been listed and that the listing would take effect the next day, when signed by the Secretary of State. The effect of the listing was to cause the value of the property to drop by £1 500 000.

In these circumstances, the plaintiffs sought to have the contract set aside. They argued that the contract should be set aside on the ground of mistake or, alternatively, that the contract was frustrated by the listing of the building. But into which category did the case fall? If the listing took effect before the contract was signed on 25 September 1973 the ground on which the plaintiffs sought relief was common mistake, but, if the listing took effect after the contract had been signed on the 25th, the ground upon which relief was sought was frustration. The Court of Appeal held that the building did not become a listed building until it was signed by the Secretary of State on 27 September. The ground on which relief was sought was therefore frustration. But the court held that the contract was not frustrated because the plaintiffs knew of the risk that the building could be listed, as was evidenced by their pre-contract enquiries and it was a risk which they had to bear. The listing of the building was not an unforeseen event which rendered the performance of the contract something radically different from that which had been contemplated by the parties (see 14.10).

This case demonstrates that there is a strong relationship between common mistake and frustration. The point at issue in the case is: who should bear the risk of the listing of the building? Whether the case is treated as one of common mistake or frustration the issue is exactly the same. In the remaining sections of this chapter we shall give separate treatment to the doctrines of common mistake and frustration and conclude by identifying the relationship between the two.

14.2 Common Mistake

Where the mistake is common to both parties, the parties have reached agreement, but that agreement is based upon a fundamental mistaken assumption. In such a case the court may nullify the consent of the parties by holding their contract void. The leading case on common mistake is *Bell* v. *Lever Brothers Ltd* [1932] AC 161. The defendants, Bell and Snelling, entered into a contract with the plaintiffs under which they agreed to serve for five years as chairman and vice-chairman respectively of a subsidiary company of the plaintiffs. One of the terms of their service agreements was that they must not make any private profit for themselves, by doing business on their own account, while working for the subsidiary. But the defendants, unknown to the plaintiffs, did engage in business on their own account and did not disclose their profits to the plaintiffs. The plaintiffs later decided that they wished to terminate the defendants' contracts because of a reorganisation of their business. So they entered into compensation agreements with the defendants and paid large sums of money to them in exchange for their consent to the termination of their service agreements. After the money had been paid, the plaintiffs discovered the breaches by the defendants of their service agreements. The significance of the breaches by the defendants was that they would have entitled the plaintiffs to terminate the service agreements without the payment of any compensation. In these circumstances the plaintiffs sought to recover the money which they had paid to the defendants. A crucial feature of the case was the finding of the jury that, when they entered into the compensation agreements, the defendants had forgotten about their breaches of duty. The parties therefore entered into the compensation agreements under a common mistake that the service agreements were valid when they were, in fact, voidable.

The House of Lords held, by a majority of three to two, that the plaintiffs could not recover the money. Lord Atkin and Lord Thankerton held that the mistake was not sufficiently fundamental to avoid the contract. Lord Blanesburgh held that the plaintiffs could not recover because they had not pleaded common mistake, but he also expressed his 'entire accord' with the judgments of Lord Atkin and Lord Thankerton. The test established by the majority was well expressed by Lord Thankerton when he said that the common mistake must 'relate to something which both [parties] must necessarily have accepted in their minds as an essential element of the subject matter'. On the facts of the case, the plaintiffs appeared to be very anxious to carry through the reorganisation and to secure the defendants' consent to the termination of their service agreements. This suggested to the majority that the plaintiffs *might* have entered into the same agreements, even if they had known of the defendants' breaches of duty. Since it was for the plaintiffs to establish that the mistake was a fundamental one, the existence of such a doubt was fatal to their claim (see the useful analysis of *Bell* adopted by Steyn J in *Associated Japanese Bank (International) Ltd* v. *Crédit du Nord* [1989] 1 WLR 255). Nevertheless it must be said that the test adopted by the majority is an extremely open-textured one and that it can admit of varying interpretations. This is demonstrated by the judgments in *Bell* itself, because the minority, Lord Warrington and

Lord Hailsham, held that the plaintiffs' mistake *was* sufficiently fundamental to avoid the contract. In the following sections (14.3–14.6), we
shall seek to ascertain the circumstances in which the courts have held a
common mistake to be sufficiently fundamental to avoid a contract.

14.3 Mistake as to the Existence of the Subject-matter of the Contract

A mistake may be sufficiently fundamental to avoid a contract where
both parties are mistaken as to the existence of the subject-matter of the
contract. For example in *Galloway* v. *Galloway* (1914) 30 TLR 531, the
defendant, assuming his wife to be dead, married the plaintiff. The
defendant and the plaintiff later separated and entered into a deed of
separation under which the defendant promised to pay a weekly allowance to the plaintiff. The defendant subsequently discovered that his first
wife was still alive and fell into arrears. When the plaintiff sued to
recover the arrears it was held that she could not do so because the
separation agreement was void, on the ground that it was entered into
under the common mistake that the parties were, in fact, married.

Greater difficulties arise in the case of a contract for the sale of
non-existent goods. Section 6 of the Sale of Goods Act 1979 provides
that

> 'where there is a contract for the sale of specific goods, and the goods
> without the knowledge of the seller have perished at the time when the
> contract is made, the contract is void'.

This section was thought to give effect to the decision of the House of
Lords in *Couturier* v. *Hastie* (1856) 5 HLC 673. The parties entered into a
contract for the sale of a cargo of corn, which was believed to be in transit
from Salonica to the United Kingdom. But before the contract was
made, and unknown to both parties, the corn had deteriorated to such an
extent that the master of the ship sold it. The seller argued that the buyer
remained liable for the price of the corn because he had bought an
'interest in the adventure' or such rights as the seller had under the
shipping documents. The House of Lords rejected the seller's argument,
holding that the subject-matter of the contract was not the rights of the
seller under the shipping documents but the corn and that, since the corn
did not exist, there was a total failure of consideration and the buyer was
not liable to pay the price. But the precise legal basis of the decision of
the House of Lords in *Couturier* has been the subject of some debate and
controversy among lawyers. We shall now consider the principal interpretations which have been placed upon *Couturier*.

The first interpretation is that a mistake as to the existence of the
subject-matter of a contract inevitably renders a contract void. This
appears to be the interpretation placed upon *Couturier* by the draftsman

of section 6 of the Sale of Goods Act 1979. However the word 'mistake' was not used in any of the judgments in *Couturier*. The court was principally concerned with the construction of the contract and the question whether the consideration had totally failed. The court did not establish such an all-embracing proposition.

The second interpretation, adopted by Denning LJ in *Solle* v. *Butcher* [1950] 1 KB 671, 691, is that the contract in *Couturier* was void because there was an implied condition precedent that the contract was capable of performance. In *Couturier* the parties proceeded upon the assumption that the goods were capable of being sold when, in fact, they were not and the effect of the implied condition precedent was to render the contract void. The difficulty with this interpretation is that it does not tell us when, or on what basis, the courts will imply such a condition precedent.

The third interpretation is that the question whether or not a contract is void depends upon the construction of the contract. Such an interpretaton was placed upon *Couturier* by the High Court of Australia in *McRae* v. *Commonwealth Disposals Commission* (1951) 84 CLR 377. In this rather bizarre case the defendants purported to sell to the plaintiffs the wreck of a tanker which was lying on the Jourmand Reef and was said to contain oil. The plaintiffs embarked upon an expedition in an attempt to salvage the vessel but no tanker was found and, indeed, no such tanker had ever existed. The plaintiffs succeeded in their action for damages for breach of contract. The defendants had argued that there could be no liability for breach of contract because the alleged contract was void owing to the non-existence of the subject-matter of the contract. This argument was rejected by the court on the ground that the defendants had promised that such a tanker was in existence and they were liable for breach of that promise. *Couturier* was distinguished on the ground that there the parties had entered into the contract under the shared assumption that the corn was still in existence and could be sold by the seller; that assumption proved to be unfounded and the contract was held to be void. But in *McRae* the defendants had actually promised that the tanker was in existence. They had assumed the risk of the non-existence of the tanker and for the breach of their promise they were held liable in damages.

But would an English court follow *McRae*? It seems clear that it is factually distinguishable from *Couturier* for the reasons already given. The result in *McRae* seems perfectly just because the defendants assumed the risk of the non-existence of the tanker and the effect of the decision was to place that risk upon the defendants. In policy terms there is little doubt that *McRae* should be followed. The difficulty lies in reconciling *McRae* with the wording of section 6 of the Sale of Goods Act 1979 (above). Section 6 does not provide an insuperable obstacle, however, because it can be argued that a case such as *McRae* is not caught by the actual wording of section 6 since the tanker never existed and therefore it could not have 'perished'. On this interpretation only contracts for the sale of goods which once existed but have since perished would be governed by section 6. Contracts for the sale of goods which never existed would not be caught by section 6 but would instead be governed by the more flexible approach adopted in *McRae*. But such a distinction has little to commend itself in policy terms.

Alternatively, it could be argued that section 6 is only a rule of construction which can, in a case such as *McRae*, be ousted by proof of contrary intention (see Atiyah, 1957). The difficulty with this argument is that many sections of the Sale of Goods Act 1979 explicitly state that they are subject to contrary agreement but there is no such provision in section 6. Finally, it could be argued that, although the main contract in a case such as *McRae* is void, the defendants could be liable to the plaintiffs under a collateral contract, the terms of which would be that the tanker was in existence. The consideration provided by the plaintiffs would be the entry into the void contract. It is doubtful whether entry into a void contract can constitute consideration (but see *Strongman (1945) Ltd* v. *Sincock* [1955] 2 QB 525). Even if the consideration hurdle could be overcome, such a solution would be inelegant and horribly artificial. The contortions which are required to evade section 6 and to achieve a satisfactory solution in a case such as *McRae* suggest that English contract law would be radically improved by the repeal of section 6 of the Sale of Goods Act 1979.

14.4   Mistake as to the Identity of the Subject-matter

A mistake as to the identity of the subject-matter of the contract may be sufficiently fundamental to avoid a contract if both parties thought that they were dealing with one thing when in fact they were dealing with another. There is no English case on this point (but see the discussion in the Canadian case of *Diamond* v. *British Colombia Thoroughbred Breeders' Society* (1966) 52 DLR (2d) 146).

14.5   Mistake as to the Possibility of Performing the Contract

A mistake may be sufficiently fundamental to avoid a contract where both parties believe that the contract is capable of being performed when, in fact, it is not. Professor Treitel (1987) helpfully divides these cases into three categories.

The first category is physical impossibility. In *Sheikh Brothers Ltd* v. *Ochsner* [1957] AC 136, the appellants granted to the respondents a licence to enter and cut sisal growing on their land and in return the respondents agreed to deliver to the appellants 50 tons of cut sisal per month. Unknown to both parties, the land was incapable of producing an average of 50 tons of sisal per month throughout the term of the licence. The Privy Council held that the contract was void because the mistake of the parties related to a matter which was essential to the agreement and neither party had assumed the risk of the land being incapable of producing such a yield.

The second type of impossibility is legal impossibility, that is to say, the contract provides for something to be done which cannot, as a matter of law, be done. In *Cooper* v. *Phibbs* (1867) LR 2 HL 149, the appellant agreed to take a lease of a salmon fishery which both parties believed to be the property of the respondents. It was subsequently discovered that the appellant, as the tenant in tail, was the owner of the fishery. The contract was set aside on the ground that the contract was legally incapable of performance because the appellant was already the owner of the fishery.

The third type of impossibility is commercial impossibility. In *Griffith* v. *Brymer* (1903) 19 TLR 434, the parties entered into a contract for the hire of a room for the purpose of viewing the coronation procession of Edward VII. The procession was cancelled because of the illness of the monarch. The parties had concluded their contract at 11 am but, unknown to both parties, the decision to operate on Edward VII was taken at 10 am. It was held that the contract was void because the mistake of the parties went to the root or the heart of their agreement. Although the contract was still physically and legally capable of performance, the cancellation of the procession had undermined the commercial object of the contract.

14.6 Mistake as to Quality

A mistake as to the quality of the subject-matter of the contract may be sufficiently fundamental to avoid a contract. But the courts are extremely reluctant to conclude that a mistake as to quality renders a contract void, as can be seen from *Bell* v. *Lever Brothers* itself (see 14.2). A further difficulty is created by the fact that the cases are not easy to reconcile. A brief account will be given here of some of the leading cases and then an attempt will be made at some reconciliation.

In *Leaf* v. *International Galleries* [1950] 2 KB 86, the Court of Appeal stated that a contract for the sale of a picture would not be set aside on the ground of mistake if both parties entered into a contract erroneously believing the picture to be a Constable. In *Harrison and Jones* v. *Burton and Lancaster* [1953] 1 QB 646, the parties entered into a contract for the sale of a particular brand of kapok which was believed to be pure kapok, whereas, in fact, it also contained some brush cotton which made it a commercially inferior product. It was held that the mistake was not sufficiently fundamental to avoid the contract. In *Oscar Chess Ltd* v. *Williams* [1957] 1 WLR 370 (see 8.4) both parties entered into a contract for the sale of a car under the belief that the car was a 1948 model when in fact it was a 1939 model. Once again the mistake was not sufficiently fundamental to avoid the contract. Finally, in *Solle* v. *Butcher* [1950] 1 KB 671, the defendant agreed to lease a flat to the plaintiff for seven years at an annual rental of £250. The parties entered into this agreement under the mistaken assumption that the flat was free from rent control. When the plaintiff discovered that the flat was subject to rent control and that the rent payable under the legislation was only £140, he sought to recover the rent he had overpaid. The defendant counterclaimed for rescission of the lease on the ground of mistake. The Court of Appeal held that the contract could not be avoided at law (although the contract was set aside in equity; see further, 14.7). In *Solle*, Lord Denning clearly wished to restrict the scope of the doctrine of common mistake because a finding that the contract was void would have detrimental effects upon the rights of innocent third parties (see further, 4.6).

On the basis of these cases it would appear to be extremely difficult, if not impossible, to establish that a common mistake as to quality renders a contract void. But there are cases in which a mistake as to quality has been held to be sufficiently fundamental to avoid the contract. One such case is *Scott* v. *Coulson* [1903] 2 Ch 249. A contract for the sale of a life assurance policy was held to be void when, unknown to both parties, the assured had died and the value of the policy had consequently increased from £460 to £777. Secondly, in *Nicholson and Venn* v. *Smith-Marriott* (1947) 177 LT 189, the defendants put up for auction table napkins 'with crest of Charles I and authentic property of that monarch'. In reliance upon this description, the plaintiff bought the napkins for £787. It was later discovered that the napkins were Georgian and were worth only £105. Hallet J held that the plaintiff was entitled to damages for breach of contract but he also held that the plaintiff could have avoided the contract on the ground of mistake. The authority of this case has been weakened, however, by doubts cast upon its correctness by Denning LJ in *Solle* v. *Butcher* (above).

How can these cases be reconciled? The general test can be identified reasonably easily. As Lord Thankerton stated in *Bell* v. *Lever Brothers* (above), the mistake of the parties must relate to an 'essential and integral element of the subject matter' of the contract. The difficulty lies in applying that test to the facts of any given case. Professor Treitel (1987) has put forward the following test: imagine that you can 'ask the parties, immediately after they made the contract, what its subject-matter was. If, in spite of the mistake, they would give the right answer the contract is valid at law.' Such a test works satisfactorily in most cases and helps explain the difference between cases such as *Oscar Chess* and *Nicholson and Venn*. But it does not appear to explain *Leaf*, where the parties would surely have said that they were purchasing a Constable and not simply a picture. Treitel concedes this point, but counters that the dicta in that case are not conclusive because 'the plaintiff did not claim that the contract was void'. It is also difficult to apply this test to *Scott* where it is arguable that the parties would have given the correct answer, namely an insurance policy. Although this test cannot reconcile all the cases, it does provide some useful guidance in considering whether a mistake as to quality relates to an 'essential and integral element of the subject matter of the contract'.

14.7 Mistake in Equity

As can be seen from our discussion of the case law (14.3–14.6), the decision of the House of Lords in *Bell* v. *Lever Brothers Ltd* has given birth to an extremely narrow doctrine of common mistake in English law. Such a restrictive approach can be justified on the ground that it promotes certainty and protects innocent third party rights. But the narrow approach adopted in *Bell* has since been 'supplemented by the more flexible doctrine of mistake in equity' (per Steyn J in *Associated Japanese Bank (International) Ltd* v. *Crédit du Nord* [1989] 1 WLR 255). A more flexible doctrine of mistake in equity has flourished since *Bell* because *Bell* has been interpreted as an authority on the scope of mistake at law and not on mistake in equity. But the relationship between mistake at law and mistake in equity is an uneasy one. Indeed, if the House of Lords in *Bell* had believed that there was a wider equitable jurisdiction to grant relief in cases of mistake, it is difficult to understand why no reference was made to such a jurisdiction. Although the leading cases on the scope of mistake in equity are now of respectable antiquity (for example, *Solle* v. *Butcher* was decided in 1949), the House of Lords has never had the opportunity to consider the relationship between the principles established in *Bell* and the equitable jurisdiction which has been developed since *Bell*. But the relationship has been considered by judges in the lower courts and the clearest rationalisation of the cases has been provided by Steyn J in *Associated Japanese Bank (International) Ltd* v. *Crédit du Nord* (above). Steyn J stated that a court must first decide whether the contract is void at common law. If it is void, then no question of mistake in equity arises. But, if the contract is valid at law, then the court must consider whether the contract can be set aside in equity. The role of the equitable doctrine is therefore a supplementary one, designed to mitigate the hardships caused by the strict approach adopted at law.

Mistake in equity differs in three major respects from mistake at law. The first is that the scope of the doctrine is wider (see Cartwright, 1987). In *Solle* v. *Butcher* (above), Denning LJ stated that the mistake must be 'fundamental' and that the party seeking to set the contract aside must not himself be 'at fault'. But he also asserted that the court has power to set aside a contract which is valid at law 'whenever it is of the opinion that it is unconscientious for the other party to avail himself of the legal advantage which he has obtained'. Subsequent cases do not appear to support the proposition that 'unconscientiousness' is the basis of the court's jurisdiction to intervene; rather, they suggest that the mistake must be 'substantial', although it need not be so fundamental as to render the contract void at law. Two cases help illustrate the scope of the equitable doctrine.

The first is *Grist* v. *Bailey* [1967] Ch 532, in which the defendant contracted to sell property to the plaintiff for £850 'subject to the existing tenancy thereof'. At the time the agreement was concluded both parties believed that the property was in the occupation of a protected tenant. When the defendant discovered that the protected tenant had died he refused to complete and sought rescission of the contract. The property, with vacant possession, was worth £2250. Goff J set aside the contract in equity. The second case is *Magee* v. *Pennine Insurance Co* [1969] 2 QB 507. There the Court of Appeal set aside an insurance company's compromise of a claim which had been entered into by both parties in the belief that the policy was binding when, in fact, it was voidable on the ground of innocent misrepresentation. In both cases the court concluded that the mistake was substantial on rather flimsy evidence. It can be argued that the vendor in *Grist* and the insurance company in *Magee* entered into bad bargains on the basis of inadequate information and then invoked mistake in equity to relieve them from the consequences of their own imprudence. It is understandable that the courts, when exercising their equitable jurisdiction, should wish to avoid the perceived hardships created by the narrow doctrine of common mistake at law, but they must also be careful that their relaxed approach in equity does not give rise to hardship by enabling fools to escape the consequences of their own folly.

The second difference between mistake in equity and mistake at law is that mistake in equity renders a contract voidable and not void, so that when a contract is set aside on the ground of mistake in equity innocent third party rights are protected. The third difference is that in equity the courts have greater remedial flexibility because they can set aside the contract 'on terms'. Thus, in *Grist* v. *Bailey* (above) the contract was set aside on terms that the defendant should give to the plaintiff an opportunity to purchase the property for a 'proper vacant possession price' (see too the terms on which the lease was set aside in *Solle* v. *Butcher*). On balance, despite its dubious legitimacy, mistake in equity is a useful, flexible supplement to common law mistake.

14.8 Frustration

A contract can only be set aside on the ground of common mistake where the parties were labouring under the mistake at the time at which they entered into the contract. Unforeseen events which occur after the contract has been concluded cannot form the basis of a claim for relief on the ground of mistake, but, in such a situation, a court may hold that the contract has been discharged by operation of the doctrine of frustration. A contract is frustrated where, *after* the contract was concluded, events occur which make performance of the contract impossible, illegal or something radically different from that which was in the contemplation of the parties at the time they entered into the contract. A contract which is discharged on the ground of frustration is brought to an end automatically by the operation of a rule of law, irrespective of the wishes of the parties (*Hirji Mulji* v. *Cheong Yue SS Co* [1926] AC 497).

It has been argued (14.1) that the principal difference between common mistake and frustration relates to the *time* at which the misapprehension or unforeseen event occurs. Yet is must be conceded that the time at which the misapprehension or unforeseen event occurs does have significant consequences, that is to say, it is easier to discover the true facts at the moment of entry into the contract than it is to foresee future events. Therefore it is to be expected that a court will be readier to discharge a contract on the ground of frustration than it will be to avoid a contract on the ground of mistake.

On the other hand, we all know that the future is uncertain; prices may suddenly increase, inflation may rise, labour disputes break out. Contracting parties are expected to foresee many such possibilities when entering into a contract and they cannot invoke the doctrine of frustration simply because performance has become more onerous than they had anticipated. In *Davis Contractors Ltd* v. *Fareham UDC* [1956] AC 696, the plaintiff contractors agreed to build 78 houses for the defendants for £94 000. The work was scheduled to last for eight months but, owing to shortages of skilled labour, the work took an extra 14 months to complete and cost £115 000. The plaintiffs, in an attempt to recover a sum of money in excess of the contract price, argued that the contract had been frustrated. Their argument was rejected by the House of Lords. Lord Radcliffe stated that it was not

'hardship or inconvenience or material loss itself which calls the principle of frustration into play. There must be as well such a change in the significance of the obligation that the thing undertaken would, if performed, be a different thing from that contracted for'.

Therefore frustration can be invoked only where the supervening event *radically* or *fundamentally* changes the nature of performance. It cannot be invoked simply because performance has become more onerous.

But even in the case of an event which would radically change the nature of performance, the parties can still make provision for it in their contract. Contracts today often contain what are called '*force majeure*' clauses. In *Channel Island Ferries Ltd* v. *Sealink UK Ltd* [1988] 1 Lloyds Rep 323, the contract between the parties contained the following *force majeure* clause:

'A party shall not be liable in the event of non-fulfilment of any obligation arising under this contract by reason of Act of God, disease, strikes, Lock-Outs, fire, and any accident or incident of any nature beyond the control of the relevant party.'

The effect of such a clause is to release both parties from their obligation to perform on the occurrence of such stipulated events.

The ability of contracting parties to make provision for such eventualities has had a significant impact upon the development of the doctrine of frustration. Indeed, at one point in its history, supervening or unforeseen events were not regarded as an excuse for non-performance, because the parties could provide against such accidents in their contract. Once a party had assumed an obligation he was 'bound to make it good' (*Paradine* v. *Jane* (1647) Aleyn 26, 27). This absolutist approach was gradually relaxed during the latter half of the nineteenth century and, commencing with *Taylor* v. *Caldwell* (1863) 3 B & S 826, and culminating in cases such as *Jackson* v. *Union Marine Insurance Co Ltd* (1874) LR 10 CP 125 and *Krell* v. *Henry* [1903] 2 KB 740, the courts developed a wider role for the doctrine of frustration and it became significantly easier to invoke the doctrine. Today the courts have reverted to a more restrictive approach and it is rare to find frustration being pleaded successfully. The attitude of the modern courts was well summed up by Lord Roskill when he said that the doctrine of frustration was 'not lightly to be invoked to relieve contracting parties of the normal consequences of imprudent commercial bargains' (*The Nema* [1982] AC 724, 752). For this reason contracting parties frequently include a *force majeure* clause in their contract so that they can allocate the risk of such unforeseen events (see further, 14.14).

Although frustration is a difficult defence to invoke, it should not be thought that it has become a sterile doctrine which is incapable of development. The scope of the doctrine was, in fact, expanded by the decision of the House of Lords in *National Carriers* v. *Panalpina (Northern) Ltd* [1981] AC 675. For many years it was thought that the doctrine of frustration could not apply to a lease because a lease created an interest in land and that interest in land was unaffected by the alleged frustrating event. But in *Panalpina* it was held that, as a matter of principle, a lease could be frustrated, although, as a matter of practice, it would be rare for a court to conclude that a lease had been frustrated. Many leases run for a long period of time, such as 99 years, and it is difficult to conceive of such a lease being frustrated because the parties must anticipate that major changes will occur during the 99 period and so, to a large extent, they will have assumed the risk of supervening events. The type of lease which might be frustrated is a lease of a holiday flat or some other lease of short duration. Although the practical significance of *Panalpina* may be minimal, the decision does display a willingness, in an appropriate case, to expand the horizons of the doctrine of frustration.

14.9 Impossibility

A contract which has become impossible of performance is frustrated. In *Taylor* v. *Caldwell* (1863) 3 B & S 826, the defendants granted to the plaintiffs a licence to use the 'Surrey Gardens and Music Hall' for a series of concerts at a fee of £100 per concert. After the contract had been concluded, but before the first concert was performed, the music hall was accidentally destroyed by fire so that it became impossible to stage the concerts. The plaintiffs argued that the defendants were in breach of contract in failing to supply the hall and sought to recover their wasted advertising expenditure. But the court held that the contract was frustrated because the destruction of the music hall rendered performance of the contract impossible. The frustrating event released both parties from their obligations under the contract and so the defendants were not under an obligation to supply the hall and were not in breach of contract. Partial destruction of the subject-matter may also frustrate a contract where it renders performance of the contract impossible. For example, in *Taylor* v. *Caldwell* the contract was for the hire of the music hall and the 'Surrey Gardens', but it was only the music hall which was destroyed. Nevertheless, because the destruction of the music hall rendered performance of the contract impossible, the contract was frustrated.

Contracts for personal services, such as contracts of employment and contracts of apprenticeship, are frustrated by the death of either party to the contract. Similarly, a contract of employment may be frustrated if the ill-health of an employee renders him permanently unfit for work.

A contract may also be frustrated where the subject-matter of the contract is unavailable for the purpose of carrying out the contract. For example a charterparty was held to be frustrated when the ship was requisitioned and so was unavailable to the charterer (*Bank Line Ltd* v. *Arthur Capel & Co Ltd* [1919] AC 435). Temporary unavailability of the subject-matter may also frustrate a contract. In *Jackson* v. *Union Marine Insurance Co* (1874) LR 10 CP 125, a ship was chartered in November 1871 and was required to proceed with all possible dispatch from Liverpool to Newport, and there load a cargo for carriage to San Francisco. On her way to Newport in early January 1872, the ship ran aground and was not fully repaired until the end of August that year. It was held that the contract was frustrated because the ship was not available for the voyage for which she was chartered. A voyage to San Francisco in late August 1872 was performance radically different from that originally contemplated.

Where the contract is one of fixed duration and the unavailability of the subject-matter is only temporary, the court, in deciding whether the contract has been frustrated, must consider the ratio of the likely interruption in contractual performance to the duration of the contract. The higher the ratio, the more likely it is that the contract will be frustrated. In *The Nema* (above) a charterparty was frustrated when a long strike closed the port at which the ship was due to load so that, of the six or seven voyages contracted to be made between April and December, no more than two could be completed (see also *Morgan* v. *Manser* [1948] 1 KB 184).

14.10 Frustration of Purpose

Where the common purpose for which the contract has been entered into can no longer be carried out because of some supervening event the contract is frustrated. Examples of frustration of purpose are, however, extremely rare. The reason for this is that the courts do not wish to provide an escape route for a party for whom the contract has simply become a bad bargain. A rare case in which a plea of frustration of purpose succeeded is *Krell* v. *Henry* [1903] 2 KB 740. The defendant hired a flat in Pall Mall from the plaintiff for two days. The object in entering into the contract was to view the coronation procession of Edward VII, although this was not actually expressed in the contract. After the contract had been concluded, the coronation of Edward VII was postponed because of the illness of the King. The Court of Appeal held that the contract was frustrated. *Krell* must be contrasted, however, with *Herne Bay Steam Boat Co* v. *Hutton* [1903] 2 KB 683, in which the defendant hired a ship from the plaintiff 'for the purpose of viewing the naval review and for a day's cruise around the fleet'. After the contract had been concluded, the naval review was cancelled because of the illness of Edward VII. Nevertheless the court held that the contract was not frustrated. What is the difference between this case and *Krell*?

In answering this question, it is necessary to refer to an example considered by Vaughan Williams LJ in *Krell*. It was put to Vaughan Williams LJ that, if the contract was frustrated on the facts of *Krell*, then it 'would follow that if a cabman was engaged to take someone to Epsom on Derby Day at a suitably enhanced price for such a journey . . . both parties to the contract would be discharged in the contingency of the race at Epsom for some reason becoming impossible'. But Vaughan Williams LJ was of the opinion that such a contract would not be frustrated because he did not think that 'the happening of the race would be the foundation of the contract'. In *Krell*, on the other hand, the 'foundation of the contract' was the viewing of the coronation. However the contract in *Krell* was an extremely unusual one. The rooms were hired out by the day, excluding the night, and the only purpose which *both* parties had in entering into such an unusual contract was to hire the rooms for the purpose of viewing the coronation. So interpreted, the contract was frustrated. On the other hand, in *Herne Bay Steam Boat Co* v. *Hutton* (above) the defendant could still see the fleet and, although the defendant's motive in entering into the contract might have been to see the naval review, it could not be said that that was the 'common foundation of the contract'. Similar reasoning explains the example of the cancellation of the Derby. Although the motive of the hirer might have been to see the Derby, that was not of itself sufficient to render the happening of the Derby the 'common foundation' of the contract. Thus interpreted, *Krell* becomes a very narrow decision indeed, and it is not surprising that it has been distinguished in modern cases such as

Amalgamated Investment & Property Co Ltd v. *John Walker & Sons Ltd* (above, 14.1).

14.11 Illegality

Supervening illegality can operate to frustrate a contract. In *Fibrosa Spolka Akcyjna* v. *Fairbairn Lawson Combe Barbour Ltd* [1943] AC 32, the respondents agreed to manufacture machines for the appellants and to deliver them to Gdynia in Poland. However before the respondents had completed the manufacture of the machines Gdynia was occupied by the German army. It was held that the contract was frustrated because in time of war it is against the law to trade with the enemy. The public interest in ensuring that no assistance was given to the enemy in time of war outweighed the fact that it remained physically possible to manufacture and deliver the machines. Where the illegality is only temporary or partial the contract will be frustrated only if the illegality affects the performance of the contract in a substantial or fundamental way (contrast *Denny, Mott & Dickinson* v. *James B Fraser & Co Ltd* [1944] AC 265 and *Cricklewood Property Investment Trust Ltd* v. *Leighton's Investment Trust Ltd* [1945] AC 221).

14.12 Express Provision

There are a number of limitations upon the scope of the doctrine of frustration. Three such limitations will be considered here (14.12–14.14). The first is that a contract is not frustrated where the parties have made express provision for the consequences of the alleged frustrating event in their contract. A frustrating event is a supervening, unforeseen event; it is not an event which has been anticipated in the contract itself. But, where the contract is frustrated on the ground that further performance of the contract is against the law, because it involves trading with the enemy in time of war, the operation of the doctrine of frustration cannot be excluded by express provision in the contract. Overriding considerations of public policy deny effect to such a clause (*Ertel Bieber and Co* v. *Rio Tinto Co Ltd* [1918] AC 260).

There is something rather anomalous, however, about the idea that the parties can make provision for a supervening, unforeseen event in their contract. For this reason any clause which is claimed to cover an alleged frustrating event will be narrowly interpreted. For example, in *Metropolitan Water Board* v. *Dick Kerr and Co* [1918] AC 119, contractors agreed to construct a reservoir in six years and the contract stated that they were to be given an extension of time in the event of delays 'howsoever occasioned'. When the contractors were required by Government Order to stop the work and sell their plant it was held that the contract was frustrated because the delay clause was not intended to apply to such a fundamental change of circumstances. The clause was intended to cover only temporary difficulties and did not cover fundamental changes in the nature of the contract (see too *Jackson* v. *Union Marine Insurance Co Ltd* (above)).

14.13 Foreseen and Foreseeable Events

Given that a frustrating event is a supervening, unforeseen event, the doctrine ought logically not to apply to an event which is within the contemplation of the parties. In *Walton Harvey Ltd* v. *Walker and Homfrays Ltd* [1931] 1 Ch 274, the defendant granted to the plaintiff the right to display an advertising sign for seven years on the defendant's hotel. Before the seven years had elapsed, the local authority compulsorily purchased the hotel and demolished it. The court held that the contract between the parties was not frustrated by the compulsory purchase and demolition of the hotel because it was within the contemplation of the defendant, at the time that the contract was concluded, that the property might be the subject of a compulsory purchase order.

The proposition that a foreseeable event cannot frustrate a contract has been challenged, however, by Lord Denning in *The Eugenia* [1964] 2 QB 226 (see too *WJ Tatem Ltd* v. *Gamboa* [1939] 1 KB 132). The status of these dicta is uncertain. On the one hand they suggest that the general rule requires reconsideration, but, on the other hand, they can be reconciled with the orthodox analysis on the ground that the events in these cases were not sufficiently foreseeable to satisfy the very high test of foreseeability which is applicable here. An event is foreseeable and will prevent frustration of the contract only where it is one which 'any person of ordinary intelligence would regard as likely to occur' (see Treitel, 1987; contrast Hall, 1984). Whatever the precise status of these dicta in *The Eugenia* and *Tatem* v. *Gamboa*, it is clear that the foresight of war is an irrelevant issue where the ground of frustration is trading with the enemy.

14.14 Self-induced Frustration

A party cannot invoke the doctrine of frustration where the alleged frustrating event is brought about through his own conduct or the conduct of those for whom he is responsible. In *J Lauritzen AS* v. *Wijsmuller BV (The "Super Servant Two")* [1989] 1 Lloyds Rep 148, Hobhouse J (whose judgment was subsequently affirmed by the Court of Appeal (1989) *The Times*, 17 October) defined 'self-induced' frustration as a label which has been used by the courts to describe 'those situations where one party has been held by the courts not to be entitled to treat himself as discharged from his contractual obligations'. On his analysis frustration was self-induced where the alleged frustrating event was caused by a breach or an anticipatory breach of contract by the party claiming that the contract had been frustrated, where an act of the party claiming that the contract has been frustrated broke the chain of causation between the alleged frustrating event and the event which made performance of the contract impossible, and where the alleged frustrating event was not a supervening event, by which he meant 'something altogether outside the control of the parties'.

The scope of the doctrine of self-induced frustration can be gleaned from an analysis of the following two cases. The first case is *Maritime National Fish Ltd* v. *Ocean Trawlers Ltd* [1935] AC 524. The defendants chartered a ship from the plaintiffs but the vessel could only be used for its intended purpose if it was fitted with an otter trawl. An otter trawl could only be used under licence and, although the defendants applied for licences for each of the five vessels which they operated, they were allocated only three. They elected to apply the licences to the trawlers which they owned directly or indirectly rather than to the vessel chartered from the plaintiffs. The Privy Council held that the charter was not frustrated because of the defendants' failure to obtain a licence for the vessel; this was a case of self-induced frustration. But the ratio of the decision remained unclear. On the one hand, it could be argued that it was the fact that the defendants elected to allocate the licences to their own vessels which led the Privy Council to conclude that this was a case of self-induced frustration. On the other hand, it could be maintained that the mere fact that the defendants had a choice as to the distribution of the licences was sufficient to constitute self-induced frustration.

Our second case is *The Super Servant Two* (above). The importance of this case lies in the fact that Hobhouse J (and the Court of Appeal (1989) *The Times*, 17 October) adopted the latter of our two possible interpretations of the *Maritime National Fish* case. The defendants agreed to transport the plaintiffs' oil-rig, using, at their option, either Super Servant One or Super Servant Two (both of which were self propelling barges especially designed for the transportation of rigs). The defendants allocated Super Servant Two to the performance of the contract with the plaintiffs and allocated Super Servant One to the performance of other concluded contracts. Unfortunately, after the contract had been concluded but before the time fixed for performance, Super Servant Two sank while transporting another rig. The contract could not be performed by using Super Servant One because it had been allocated elsewhere and was unavailable. The plaintiffs alleged that the defendants were in breach of contract in failing to transport the rig in the agreed manner. The defendants denied liability on the ground that the contract had been frustrated by the sinking of Super Servant Two. Hobhouse J rejected the defendants' argument, holding that the fact that the defendants had a choice as to the allocation of Super Servant One was sufficient to break the chain of causation and make this a case of self-induced frustration. But the defendants had no real choice as to the allocation of Super Servant One. It was impossible to allocate it to the performance of all concluded contracts and so the sinking of Super Servant Two *compelled* them to make such a decision. The conclusion of Hobhouse J leaves a seller or supplier of goods in an impossible position where his source of supply partially fails owing to an unforeseen event (for criticism, see McKendrick, 1989).

This case demonstrates the unwillingness of modern courts to invoke the doctrine of frustration. But is also demonstrates the advantages which can be obtained by inserting a *force majeure* clause into a contract (see 14.8), because Hobhouse J held that the defendants were entitled to invoke the *force majeure* clause as a defence to the plaintiffs' action, unless the sinking of Super Servant Two was caused by the negligence of the defendants or their employees. So an appropriately drafted *force majeure* clause may go a long way towards evading the restrictions and limitations of the doctrine of frustration.

14.15 The Effects of Frustration

As we have already noted (14.8), a contract which is discharged on the ground of frustration is brought to an end automatically at the time of the frustrating event. For the purposes of ease of exposition we shall consider separately the effects of frustration upon a claim to recover money paid prior to the frustrating event and its effects upon a claim to recover the value of goods supplied or services provided prior to the frustrating event.

At common law it was held in *Fibrosa Spolka Ackcyjna* v. *Fairbairn Lawson Combe Barbour Ltd* [1943] AC 32 (overruling *Chandler* v. *Webster* [1904] 1 KB 493) that money paid prior to the frustration of the contract was recoverable upon a total failure of consideration. A total failure of consideration arises where the party seeking recovery has got no part of what he has bargained for. In *Fibrosa* (see 14.11) the appellants sought to recover the £1000 they had paid to the respondents on the signing of the contract. The House of Lords held that the consideration for the payment had wholly failed because the machines had not been delivered to the appellants and that they were entitled to the recovery of their prepayment. While it is true to say that *Fibrosa* represented an improvement upon the old common law rule established in *Chandler* v. *Webster* (above), it did not leave the law in an entirely satisfactory state. Two principal defects remained. The first was that the payer could only recover money paid upon a total failure of consideration; where the failure was only partial he could not recover (*Whincup* v. *Hughes* (1871) LR 6 CP 78; see further, 21.2). The second defect was that the payee could not set off against the money to be repaid any expenditure which he had incurred in the performance of the contract. For example, on the facts of *Fibrosa*, the respondents had incurred expenditure in making the machines, yet they were unable to retain any portion of the £1000 which represented their expenditure upon the machines.

This position has been rectified by the enactment of s.1(2) of the Law Reform (Frustrated Contracts) Act 1943. The effect of this section is threefold. The first is that moneys paid prior to the frustrating event are recoverable. The second is that sums payable prior to the time of discharge cease to be payable. The third is that the payee may be entitled to set off against the sums so paid expenses which he has incurred before the time of discharge in, or for the purpose of, the performance of the contract. Section 1(2) meets the two deficiencies of the common law in that the right to recover money is not confined to a total failure of consideration and the payee can set off against the sums repayable any reliance expenditure which he had incurred in the performance of the contract. But certain deficiencies remain (for fuller consideration see Goff and Jones, 1986, pp.486–9). The first is that the section does not make clear the basis upon which the court is to calculate the amount of expenditure which a payee is entitled to retain. Is it all of it, half of it, some other portion of it, or none of it? The subsection does not tell us (for a possible answer see *Lobb* v. *Vaisey Housing Auxiliary* [1963] VR 236, and for a legislative solution see s.5(3) of the British Columbia Frustrated Contracts Act 1974, which provides that the loss shall be apportioned equally between the parties). The second difficulty created by s.1(2) is that the payee cannot recover or retain more than the value of the prepayment, so that any reliance expenditure incurred which is in excess of the prepayment cannot be recovered under s.1(2), although it may be recoverable under s.1(3) where the expenditure results in a valuable benefit being obtained by the other party (see below).

We must now consider the effects of frustration upon a claim to recover the value of goods supplied or services provided prior to the frustrating event. At common law the leading case was *Appleby* v. *Myers* (1867) LR 2 CP 651. The plaintiffs contracted to make and erect machinery in the defendants' factory and to maintain the machinery for two years. Payment was to be upon completion of the work. After part of the machinery had been erected, an accidental fire destroyed the factory and machinery and frustrated the contract. It was held that the plaintiffs could not recover in respect of their work because they were only entitled to payment when performance was completed (called the 'entire con-tracts' rule, see further 21.2) and, as the fire had prevented completion of the work, they were not entitled to payment. This rule caused obvious hardship to the provider of services under a frustrated contract and it has since been replaced by s.1(3) of the Law Reform (Frustrated Contracts) Act 1943. Section 1(3) states that

'where any party to the contract has, by reason of anything done by any other party thereto in, or for the purpose of, the performance of the contract, obtained a valuable benefit (other than a payment of money to which the last foregoing subsection applies) before the time of discharge, there shall be recoverable from him by the said other party such sum (if any), not exceeding the value of the said benefit to the party obtaining it, as the court considers just, having regard to all the circumstances of the case and, in particular –

(a) the amount of any expenses incurred before the time of discharge by the benefited party in, or for the purpose of, the performance of

the contract, including any sums paid or payable by him to any other party in pursuance of the contract and retained or recoverable by that party under the last foregoing subsection, and
(b) the effect, in relation to the said benefit, of the circumstances giving rise to the frustration of the contract'.

This subsection is an unnecessarily complex provision (for details see Goff and Jones, 1986, pp.489–99). Its basic effect is that, where one party to the contract has conferred upon the other party a 'valuable benefit' (other than a payment of money which is governed by s.1(2)) before the time of discharge, he shall be entitled to recover a 'just sum' which shall not exceed the value of the benefit which he has conferred upon the other party. In *BP* v. *Hunt* [1979] 1 WLR 783, Robert Goff J concluded that there were two steps involved in a section 1(3) claim. The first was the identification and valuation of the benefit. He held that the benefit was not the value of the services themselves, but the 'end product' of the services. This interpretation of 'benefit' has unfortunate consequences. It means that the result in *Appleby* v. *Myers* (above) would be unaffected by the Act because the plaintiffs' work was destroyed by the fire and so did not result in any end product. Although this interpretation of 'benefit' has been heavily criticised (see Treitel, 1987, p.707 and Haycroft and Waksman, 1984), such an interpretation has also been adopted in the Commonwealth (*Parsons Bros Ltd* v. *Shea* (1966) 53 DLR (2d) 86) and it appears to accord closely with the structure of s.1(3), which draws a distinction between the plaintiff's performance and the defendant's benefit, and so it cannot be said that the defendant's benefit is the value of the plaintiff's performance.

The second step in a s.1(3) claim is the assessment of a 'just sum'. Here it must be remembered that the value of the benefit obtained acts as ceiling on the 'just sum'. Robert Goff J held that the contractual allocation of risk will always be a relevant factor in deciding what is a just sum. But it is very difficult to predict what a court will award as a just sum. This uncertainty is heightened by the conclusion of Lawton LJ in the Court of Appeal, in *BP* v. *Hunt* [1982] 1 All ER 925, 983, that an appellate court is not entitled to interfere with the assessment of the just sum by the trial judge 'unless it is so plainly wrong that it cannot be just'. This leaves the issue to the virtual untrammelled discretion of the trial judge. It is regrettable that the Court of Appeal did not establish guidelines to assist trial judges in the exercise of their discretion to ensure a measure of consistency in decided cases and out of court settlements.

It must be concluded that s.1(3) is shoddily drafted and that it produces results which are, in principle, undesirable. A benefit should be identified as the value of the services and not as the end product of the services. The focus of the Act is upon the prevention of unjust enrichment (per Robert Goff J in *BP* v. *Hunt* [1979] 1 WLR 783, 799) and, consequently, it does not address itself to the recovery of reliance losses which do not result in a benefit to the other party, nor does it seek to apportion the losses between the parties. In failing to address itself to these issues, the 1943 Act is sadly deficient and it is no surprise to learn that its restricted approach has recently been rejected in the Commonwealth (see, for example, the report of the Law Reform Commission of New South Wales on Frustrated Contracts (1976)).

14.16 Conclusion

In this chapter we have sought to argue that in cases of common mistake and frustration the courts are dealing with the same issue, namely the allocation of risk of an unforeseen event. Professor Treitel (1987) has described the analogy between common mistake and frustration as an 'interesting and sometimes helpful' one, but argues that it 'should not be pressed too far'. In particular, Treitel argues that mistake and frustration are 'different juristic concepts; the one relating to the formation and the other to the discharge of contracts'. Although it is true that one relates to formation and the other to discharge, they both relate to the same issue, as can be seen from the *Amalgamated Investments* (case (14.1) and a comparison of *Griffith* v. *Brymer* (14.5) and *Krell* v. *Henry* (14.10). Secondly, Treitel argues that events which frustrate a contract may not be sufficient to set aside a contract on the ground of mistake. This point I have already conceded, but the difference is a matter of degree, not kind. Finally, Treitel points out that the effects of frustration and mistake are different, frustration cases being subject to the Law Reform (Frustrated Contracts) Act 1943. This is true. But, as we have noted, the 1943 Act is an unsatisfactory piece of legislation. The complexities produced by the Act should be contrasted with the uncomplicated, open-textured jurisdiction which the courts have evolved in equity to set aside a contract 'on terms' (*Solle* v. *Butcher* (above)). If Parliament had not intervened in 1943 and subjected frustration to distinct regulation, such an approach could have been adopted in the case of frustration and, although it would have introduced an element of uncertainty into the law, the discretion thereby given to the courts would have avoided some of the unfortunate consequences of the 1943 Act.

Summary

1 Where both parties enter into a contract under a common fundamental mistake which relates to an essential element of the subject-matter of the contract, then the contract is void at law.

2 A mistake may be sufficiently fundamental to avoid a contract where both parties are mistaken as to the existence (or possibly the identity) of the subject-matter of the contract. Despite the enactment of s.6 of the Sale of Goods Act 1979, a mistake as to the existence of the subject-matter may not inevitably render a contract void; it may depend upon the construction of the contract (see *McRae* v. *Commonwealth Disposals Commission*).

3 A mistake may be sufficiently fundamental to avoid a contract where both parties believe that the contract is capable of being performed when, in fact, it is not. The impossibility may be physical, legal or commercial.

4 A mistake as to the quality of the subject-matter of the contract may be sufficiently fundamental to avoid a contract. But the courts are extremely reluctant to hold a contract void on such a ground. The mistake must relate to an 'essential and integral element of the subject-matter' of the contract.

5 Mistake at law is supplemented by the more flexible doctrine of mistake in equity. A contract may be set aside in equity where the mistake is a substantial one. Such a mistake renders a contract voidable and the court may set aside the contract on terms.

6 A contract is frustrated where, after the contract was concluded, events occur which make performance of the contract impossible, illegal or something radically different from that which was in the contemplation of the parties at the time they entered into the contract.

7 A contract is not frustrated where the parties have made express provision for the consequences of the alleged frustrating event in their contract, where the alleged frustrating event was a foreseeable one and where the frustration was 'self-induced'. But express provision for, and foreseeability of, the frustrating event are irrelevant in cases of trading with the enemy.

8 A contract which is discharged on the ground of frustration is brought to an end automatically by the operation of a rule of law, irrespective of the wishes of the parties.

9 Sums paid prior to the frustrating event are recoverable, sums payable prior to the time of discharge cease to be payable and the payee may be entitled to set off against the sums so paid expenses which he has incurred before the time of discharge in, or for the purpose of, the performance of the contract (s.1(2) of the 1943 Act).

10 Where one party to the contract has conferred upon the other party a 'valuable benefit' (other than a payment of money which is governed by s.1(2)) before the time of discharge, he shall be entitled to recover from that other party a 'just sum' which shall not exceed the value of the benefit which he has conferred upon the other party (s.1(3) of the 1943 Act).

Exercises

1 What is the scope of the doctrine of common mistake at law?

2 What is the proper interpretation to be placed upon the decision of the House of Lords in *Couturier* v. *Hastie?*

3 When will a mistake as to the quality of the subject-matter of the contract render a contract void?

4 What is the relationship between mistake at law and mistake in equity?

5 Compare and contrast *Bell* v. *Lever Brothers* and *Magee* v. *Pennine Insurance Co.*

6 When will the courts hold that a contract has been frustrated? Illustrate your answer.

7 What is 'self-induced frustration'?

8 What are the effects of frustration upon a contract?

9 What is the relationship, if any, between common mistake and frustration?

15 Illegality

15.1 Introduction

In this chapter we turn to consider substantive limitations upon the enforceability of contracts. As a general rule the courts will not enforce a contract which is illegal or which is otherwise contrary to public policy. Nor, as a general rule, will they permit the recovery of benefits conferred under such a contract. It may seem perfectly sensible and just for the courts to refuse their assistance to a party to a transaction which is illegal or contrary to public policy. But the picture is more complex than would at first sight appear.

An example will help to illustrate the issues at stake here. In *Pearce* v. *Brooks* (1866) LR 1 Ex 213, the plaintiffs were coachbuilders who hired out an ornamental brougham (or carriage) to the defendant. The defendant was a prostitute and she planned to use the brougham to attract her customers. This fact was known to the plaintiffs. The defendant returned the brougham in a damaged condition, having paid only the second instalment on it. The plaintiffs' action for damages for breach of contract failed. The contract was illegal and could not be enforced.

A number of justifications can be adduced to support such a rule. The first is that the court shall not be called upon to aid a willing party to an illegal contract or to a contract which is contrary to public policy. The second is that justice would be tainted and the dignity of the court offended by intervention on behalf of the plaintiffs. The third is that a refusal to grant relief will make entry into illegal contracts a hazardous enterprise and will thus deter people from entering into such contracts.

But these arguments are not always persuasive. The first argument does not apply to the party who innocently enters into an illegal contract. Nor is the dignity of the court always offended by intervention on behalf of a party to an illegal contract; there is a vast difference between a contract involving gross immorality or a contract to rob a bank and a contract which innocently infringes a piece of regulatory legislation. The third argument rests upon the rather dubious assumption that everyone knows the law and will take heed of its deterrent effect. Deterrence is also properly the function of the criminal law, not the civil law.

There are other competing policies which must be considered. The first is the argument from freedom of contract; that the parties should be as free as possible to regulate their own affairs. The second competing policy is the need to prevent unjust enrichment. For example, the defendant in *Pearce* v. *Brooks* obtained the use of the brougham without having to pay the hire. Now, on the facts of that case, the 'greater goal' of deterring entry into such contracts may have outweighed the need to prevent the unjust enrichment of the defendant. But in other cases we may not be prepared to countenance such unjust enrichment.

It is very important to understand that the legal regulation of illegal contracts and of contracts which are contrary to public policy is characterised by a tension between competing policies. The courts wish, on the one hand, to discourage entry into illegal contracts but, on the other hand, they also wish to uphold freedom of contract and prevent unjust enrichment. The result is tension and a degree of inconsistency in the case law.

15.2 Some Difficulties of Classification

Illegal contracts come in different shapes and sizes. Some involve gross immorality or a calculated attempt to break the law, while others involve innocent infringement of regulatory legislation. A contract to rob a bank has little in common with a contract which is performed by one of the parties in such a way that a statutory instrument is innocently infringed. Indeed, illegal contracts come in so many different shapes and sizes that it is difficult to find an appropriate classification for all the cases (see Furmston, 1965). Treitel (1987) distinguishes between contracts which involve the 'commission of a legal wrong', 'contracts contrary to public policy' and contracts which are declared by statute to be 'void' or 'unenforceable'. Cheshire, Fifoot and Furmston (1986) distinguish between contracts which are 'rendered void by statute', contracts which are 'illegal by statute or at common law' and 'contracts which are void at common law on grounds of public policy'. No two commentators appear to adopt the same classification. But these different classifications do not reflect radical disagreement as to the content of the relevant rules of law. Rather, the categorisation is undertaken largely for the purpose of ease of exposition.

The approach which will be adopted in the present chapter is, first, to discuss illegality in the performance of a contract, and then to distinguish between statutory illegality and common law illegality. The latter division should not be taken to suggest that it is easier to establish the existence of statutory illegality than common law illegality. The function of this division is to emphasise that the techniques employed by the courts in each case are rather different. In the case of statutory illegality, the courts are seeking to discern the intention of Parliament and the effect of the breach of the statute upon the contract. But in the case of common law illegality the courts have greater scope to identify their own conceptions of public policy. The limiting feature, however, is that the courts do not wish to be seen to be employing their own idiosyncratic conceptions of public policy and, at the same time, they are aware that Parliament now has the principal role to play in establishing the limits of public policy.

15.3 Illegality in Performance

Illegality may affect a contract in two principal ways. In the first place, the illegality may relate to the formation of the contract, so that the contract is illegal at the moment at which it is formed. Such a contract is void *ab initio* because it is infected with the illegality from the very outset. Secondly, the illegality may arise in the performance of an otherwise valid and enforceable contract. Here the contract is valid at the moment of formation and it is only infected with the illegality when it occurs during the performance of the contract. An example will illustrate the point. Two parties enter into a contract for the transportation of goods. At the moment of formation the contract is good and enforceable. But let us suppose that, while transporting the goods, the carrier commits a criminal offence by speeding. Does such an illegal act, committed in the course of the performance of the contract, invalidate the contract? In *St John Shipping Corporation* v. *Joseph Rank Ltd* [1957] 1 QB 267, 281, Devlin J rejected the argument that violation of the speed limit in the course of performance of the contract would, of itself, render the contract unenforceable by the party guilty of the offence. This must be right. The criminal courts will pass judgment on the offence committed; the civil courts should enforce the contract. But what are the limits of this rule? When will an illegal act committed in the course of performance of the contract invalidate the contract? This is not an easy question to answer. Separate consideration must be given to the position of the party who committed the criminal offence and the position of the other, 'innocent' party.

In deciding whether the party who committed the criminal offence can enforce the contract it is necessary to examine the judgment of Devlin J in *St John Shipping Corporation* v. *Joseph Rank Ltd* (above). A shipowner committed a statutory offence when he overloaded his ship in the performance of certain contracts for the carriage of goods. The shipowner was held to be entitled to sue to recover the freight, despite the illegality. Devlin J held that the purpose behind the statute was to penalise the conduct which led to the contravention of the statute and not to prohibit the contract itself. The contract therefore remained enforceable. Similarly, in *Shaw* v. *Groom* [1970] 2 QB 504, a landlord committed an offence by failing to give his tenant a rent-book. It was held that the landlord was nevertheless entitled to sue for the rent because the purpose behind the legislation was to punish his failure to issue a rent-book but not to invalidate the lease (contrast the more restrictive approach adopted in the earlier case of *Anderson* v. *Daniel* [1924] 1 KB 138, where the 'guilty' party was held to be unable to enforce the contract). Although both of these cases concern statutory illegality, it is suggested that the question which should be asked in all cases is: was it the purpose of the statute (or the common law rule) that a breach committed in the course of the performance of a contract should invalidate the contract?

The claim by the innocent party to enforce the contract is a much stronger one, especially where he does not know of or consent to the illegality. This was recognised by the court in *Archbolds (Freightage) Ltd* v. *S Spanglett Ltd* [1961] 2 QB 374. A contract was made for the carriage of a consignment of whisky and, in performing the contract, the carrier committed a criminal offence because the vehicle which he used to transport the whisky was not licensed to carry goods belonging to a third party. It was held that the plaintiff could nevertheless sue for breach of the contract of carriage because he was unaware of the illegality and so was not tainted by it (see too *Marles* v. *Philip Trant & Sons Ltd* [1954] 1 QB 29). Devlin LJ stated that he thought that

'the purpose of this statute is sufficiently served by the penalties prescribed for the offender; the avoidance of the contract would cause grave inconvenience and injury to members of the public without furthering the object of the statute'.

But where the 'innocent' party has knowledge of the commission of the illegality, then it is more likely that he will be unable to enforce the contract. In *Ashmore, Benson, Pease & Co Ltd* v. *AV Dawson Ltd* [1973] 1 WLR 828, the parties entered into a contract for the transportation of tube banks. The defendants sent articulated lorries which could not lawfully be used to carry the load. The load was damaged in transit. The plaintiffs sued for damages. The action failed because there was evidence that the plaintiffs' transport manager knew of the illegal performance and that, by sanctioning the illegal performance of the contract, he had 'participated' in the illegality. The crucial role played by the knowledge of the innocent party appears, at first sight, to be inconsistent with the maxim that ignorance of the law is no excuse (*Nash* v. *Stevenson Transport Ltd* [1936] 2 KB 128). It is true that, where the formation of a contract is declared to be illegal, the knowledge of the parties is irrelevant, but, where the illegality occurs in the performance of a contract which is capable of lawful performance, then the knowledge of the innocent party is a relevant consideration because his ignorance relates, not to the *law*, but to the *fact* that the other contracting party has performed the contract in an illegal manner. His knowledge of the illegality is therefore a relevant consideration.

15.4 Statutory Illegality

A contract is illegal if its formation is expressly or impliedly prohibited by statute. Where the making of the contract is expressly prohibited no difficulties arise; the contract is illegal. Greater difficulties arise where it is alleged that Parliament has impliedly prohibited the *making* of such a contract (see Buckley, 1975). The function of the court in such a case is to interpret the statute to discern whether, on its proper construction, the Act prohibits the making of such a contract. The difficulty is that Parliament has often not addressed itself to this issue. So the process of 'finding' the 'intention' of Parliament is frequently an extremely artificial one.

In *Re Mahmoud and Ispahani* [1921] 2 KB 716, the Seeds, Oils and Fats Order 1919 stated that 'a person shall not . . . buy or sell or otherwise deal in' linseed oil without a licence. The defendant misrepresented to the plaintiff that he had a licence. The defendant later refused to accept delivery of the order. The plaintiff sued the defendant for damages. The defendant argued that the contract was illegal because he did not have a licence. The court held that the plaintiff could not maintain his action for damages because such an action would undermine the purpose behind the statute. Bankes LJ stated that the Order was 'a clear and unequivocal declaration by the Legislature in the public interest that this particular type of contract shall not be entered into'. Yet the consequences for the plaintiff were extremely harsh and it has been doubted whether the court correctly identified the intention of Parliament (see Greig and Davis, 1987, p.1117). In an effort to avoid the possibility of a court misinterpreting the intention of Parliament, Acts of Parliament now frequently specify the consequences for a contract which has been entered into in breach of the Act (see Part I of the Resale Prices Act 1976). However the courts are generally reluctant to conclude that a statute impliedly prohibits the making of a contract (see *Archbolds (Freightage) Ltd* v. *S Spanglett Ltd* (above) and *St John Shipping Corporation* v. *Joseph Rank Ltd* [1957] 1 QB 267, 289).

15.5 Gaming and Wagering Contracts

Parliament will occasionally declare a particular type of contract to be 'void'. For example, s.18 of the Gaming Act 1845 states that 'all contracts or agreements, whether by parole or in writing, by way of gaming or wagering shall be null and void'. The section further provides that no action can be maintained in any court for the recovery of 'any money or valuable thing alleged to be won upon any wager'. Finally, the section provides that no action can be brought to recover any money or valuable thing which has been deposited in the hands of any stakeholder, although the interpretation placed upon the section is that a deposit can be recovered before it has been paid over to the winner (*Diggle* v. *Higgs* (1872) 2 Ex D 442).

15.6 Illegality at Common Law

A contract may be illegal at common law. The scope of the doctrine of illegality at common law is extremely wide. It is often summed up in the maxim that a court will not enforce a contract which is 'contrary to public policy'. 'Illegality' at common law therefore goes beyond contracts to commit a crime and extends, for example, to contracts which are contrary to good morals, and contracts which are prejudicial to the institution of marriage. Some commentators seek to divide the cases into two distinct compartments (see Cheshire, Fifoot and Furmston, 1986), namely, contracts which are 'illegal' at common law on grounds of public policy and contracts which are 'void' at common law on grounds of public policy. But this division is a troublesome one, because 'those who use the classification cannot always agree' on which contracts are 'illegal' and which are 'void' (see Treitel, 1987, p.326). In this chapter we shall not attempt to divide the cases up in such a manner. Rather, we shall analyse the cases under the title of contracts which are 'illegal' at common law because they are 'contrary to public policy' (often referred to, for the sake of brevity, as 'illegal' contracts) and we shall seek to identify the scope of the doctrine of public policy at common law.

In deciding whether a particular contract is 'contrary to public policy', the courts cannot shelter behind the argument that they are simply giving effect to the intention of Parliament. They must evolve their own conceptions of public policy. Here the courts are open to the charge of usurping the function of Parliament and of giving effect to their own personal opinions on what is, and what is not, morally justifiable. Thus, we find that Burroughs J once described public policy as 'a very unruly horse, and when once you get astride it you never know where it will carry you' (*Richardson* v. *Mellish* (1824) 2 Bing 229). On the other hand, Lord Denning has argued that: 'with a good man in the saddle, the unruly horse can be kept in control. It can jump over obstacles' (*Enderby Town Football Club Ltd* v. *The Football Association Ltd* [1971] Ch 591).

The courts have, in fact, been extremely cautious and conservative in their formulation of public policy. We shall now survey the different grounds upon which the courts have held a contract to be contrary to public policy and conclude with an examination of the scope of the doctrine of public policy at common law.

15.7 Contracts Contrary to Good Morals

A contract to promote sexual immorality is illegal on the ground that it is contrary to public policy. We have already noted that in *Pearce* v. *Brooks* (above) it was held that a contract to supply goods to a prostitute to be used by her in the furtherance of her profession was illegal. Similarly, a promise by a man to pay a woman if she will become his mistress is illegal (*Franco* v. *Bolton* (1797) 3 Ves 368). At one point in time contracts between cohabiting couples who were not married were contrary to public policy. But the attitude adopted by the courts towards extramarital relationships has gradually changed to reflect the growing incidence of such relationships. Where the parties are living together in a 'stable' extramarital relationship, it is highly unlikely that a court today would conclude that an agreement entered into by them in relation to the purchase of property is contrary to public policy.

15.8 Contracts Prejudicial to Family Life

Contract law is also protective of family relationships. Contracts which are prejudicial to the institution of marriage are contrary to public policy; thus a contract which restrains a party from marrying (*Lowe* v. *Peers* (1768) 2 Burr 2225) or a contract under which one person undertakes to procure the marriage of another in return for a fee is illegal (*Hermann* v. *Charlesworth* [1905] 2 KB 123). But a promise to pay a sum of money to a person for as long as they remain single is valid (*Gibson* v. *Dickie* (1815) 3 M & S 463). In *Spiers* v. *Hunt* [1908] 1 KB 720, a promise by a man to marry the plaintiff after the death of his wife was held to be contrary to public policy because it encouraged sexual immorality and was likely to encourage the break-up of his marriage (although it should be noted that the action for breach of promise to marry has now been abolished by s.1 of the Law Reform (Miscellaneous Provisions) Act 1970). A separation agreement entered into by spouses who are living together is invalid (*Brodie* v. *Brodie* [1917] P 271), although such an agreement can validly be made once the parties have separated. Similarly, a parent cannot by contract transfer to another adult his rights and duties in relation to a child (although, in an appropriate case, an adoption order can be made by a court).

15.9 Contracts to Commit a Crime or a Civil Wrong

A contract to commit a crime is illegal on the grounds that it is contrary to public policy. In *Bigos* v. *Bousted* [1951] 1 All ER 92, the parties entered into a contract which was contrary to the exchange control regulations. The contract was held to be unenforceable. Similarly, contracts to defraud the revenue are contrary to public policy (*Miller* v. *Karlinski* (1945) 62 TLR 85). In *Alexander* v. *Rayson* [1936] 1 KB 169, the parties entered into a contract to defraud the rating authority by showing the value of the property at less than its actual value. The contract was held to be illegal and unenforceable. A contract is also illegal where it makes provision for the payment of money to a person as a result of his commission of an unlawful act. In *Beresford* v. *Royal Exchange Assurance* [1938] AC 586, a person who had insured his life for £50 000 committed suicide. It was held that his estate was not entitled to enforce the policy even though it expressly covered death by suicide because, at that time, suicide was a criminal offence (the reasoning is now practically obsolete because suicide is no longer a crime). To permit a person, or his estate, to benefit from his own crime was held to be contrary to public policy.

A contract to commit a tort is illegal, as with a contract to publish a libel (*Clay* v. *Yates* (1856) 1 H & C 73). Where neither party knows that the performance of the contract involves the commission of a tort, then the contract is not illegal.

A contract to indemnify a person against criminal liability is illegal where the criminal offence is committed with a guilty intent, but the position is unclear where the crime is committed with no guilty intent. A contract to indemnify a person against liability in tort is illegal if the tort is intentionally and knowingly committed.

15.10 Contracts Prejudicial to the Administration of Justice

Contracts which are prejudicial to the administration of justice are illegal. Thus a contract to stifle a prosecution may be illegal and a contract under which one party promises to give false evidence in criminal proceedings is illegal (*R* v. *Andrews* [1973] QB 422). Agreements to obstruct bankruptcy proceedings are illegal (*Elliott* v. *Richardson* (1870) LR 5 CP 744). Agreements which tend to abuse the legal process by encouraging litigation which is not bona fide are contrary to public policy.

Also contrary to public policy are contracts which seek to oust the jurisdiction of the courts by stipulating that a contracting party is not entitled to access to the courts in the event of a dispute between the parties. But contracting parties may validly provide that a dispute must be referred to arbitration before it can be brought to court (*Scott* v. *Avery* (1855) 5 HLC 811). The Arbitration Act 1979 has now reduced the scope of judicial control over arbitration proceedings (see s.1 of the Act and the guidelines laid down in *The Nema* [1982] AC 724) and the parties may now enter into a written 'exclusion agreement', which excludes the power of the court to intervene to control the arbitral proceedings, although in the case of a 'domestic arbitration agreement' such an agreement can only be made after the commencement of the arbitration.

15.11 Contracts Prejudicial to Public Relations

Contracts which are prejudicial to foreign friendly countries are contrary to public policy and unenforceable. Thus a contract to facilitate the forcible overthrow of the government of a friendly country is unenforceable (*De Wutz* v. *Hendricks* (1824) 2 Bing 314). A similar rule applies to contracts which are prejudicial to the interests of the State; trading with the enemy is declared to be illegal under the Trading with the Enemy Act 1939.

Contracts which seek to further or promote corruption in public life are illegal. Thus a contract to sell a public office or a public honour is illegal. In *Parkinson* v. *College of Ambulance Ltd* [1925] 2 KB 1, the parties entered into a contract under which one party promised to procure a knighthood for the other. The contract was held to be contrary to public policy.

15.12 Contracts in Restraint of Trade

A contract or a covenant in restraint of trade is an undertaking whereby one party agrees to restrict his freedom to trade or his freedom to conduct his profession or business in a particular locality for a specified period of time. A contract which is in restraint of trade is void and unenforceable unless it can be shown to be reasonable. The doctrine of restraint of trade is based upon considerations of public policy. But every contract contains an element of restraint of trade. Let us suppose that I enter into a contract to give a course of 50 lectures over a two-year period. The contract restricts my freedom to trade during the hours in which I have agreed to give the lectures. But such a contract is not caught by the restraint of trade doctrine.

What types of contract are caught by the doctrine? There are two principal contracts to which the doctrine applies. The first is a covenant by an employee not to compete with his employer, either during or after his employment, and the second is a covenant by the seller of a business and its goodwill not to carry on a business which will compete with the business bought by the purchaser. The doctrine can also apply to other contracts, but it is extremely difficult to define its limits. In *Esso Petroleum Co Ltd* v. *Harper's Garage (Stourport) Ltd* [1968] AC 269, the doctrine was applied to a contract under which a garage agreed to accept all of its petrol from one supplier for a considerable period of time. Lord Reid stated that he 'would not attempt to define the dividing line between contracts which are and contracts which are not in restraint of trade', and that the better approach was 'to ascertain what were the legitimate interests of the [suppliers] which they were entitled to protect and then to see whether these restraints were more than adequate for that purpose'.

Once it is decided that the contract is subject to the doctrine, then it is for the party who is seeking to rely on the clause to show that it is reasonable in two respects. The first is that it must be reasonable as between the parties and the second is that it must be reasonable in the public interest. In analysing the reasonableness requirements we shall discuss separately covenants in contracts of employment, covenants in contracts for the sale of a business and, finally, other contracts to which the doctrine applies.

15.13   Contracts of Employment

A contract of employment may contain a covenant which purports to restrict the freedom of the employee to work either during or after the termination of his employment. Such covenants are scrutinised with great care by the courts. In deciding whether the restraint clause is reasonable as between the parties two factors are particularly relevant. The first is that the covenant must seek to protect some legitimate interest of the employer. Lord Parker stated in *Herbert Morris Ltd* v. *Saxelby* [1916] 1 AC 688, that an employer must establish that he has: 'some proprietary right, whether in the nature of a trade connection or in the nature of trade secrets, for the protection of which such a restraint is . . . reasonably necessary'. Thus an employer can legitimately restrain an employee who has come into contact with customers of the employer in such a way as to acquire influence over them (*Fitch* v. *Dewes* [1921] 2 AC 158) or who has acquired trade secrets or confidential information belonging to the employer (*Forster and Sons* v. *Suggett* (1918) 35 TLR 87). But an employer is not entitled to protect himself against the use of the 'personal skill and knowledge' acquired by the employee in the course of the employer's business. Such skills belong to the employee and he is free to exploit them in the market-place.

The second factor is that the restraint must be reasonable in terms of time, locality and subject-matter. An employer is not generally entitled to restrain an employee from carrying on a business which is different from that in which he was employed. Similarly the restraint must not be wider in area than is necessary to protect the employer's interest (see *Mason* v. *Provident Clothing and Supply Co* [1913] AC 724, in which a clause restraining an employee from working in a similar business within 25 miles of London was held to be unreasonable). The restraint must also be reasonable in terms of time, although it is possible for the restraint clause to be unlimited in time and still be reasonable (*Fitch* v. *Dewes* (above)).

Once it is demonstrated that the restraint is reasonable as between the parties, it must also be demonstrated that it is reasonable in the interests of the public. However, the courts are extremely reluctant to conclude that an agreement, which is reasonable as between the parties, is unenforceable because it is contrary to the interests of the public, especially in the case of a restraint clause in a contract of employment (but see *Wyatt* v. *Kreglinger and Fernau* [1933] 1 KB 793).

15.14   Contracts for the Sale of a Business

A contract for the sale of a business frequently contains a clause under which the vendor of the business agrees not to set up a similar business in the immediate vicinity for a period of time. The purchaser has bought the goodwill in the business and he is entitled to protect his purchase by an appropriately drawn restraint clause. Such a clause is not viewed with the hostility of a restraint clause in a contract of employment.

The restraint clause must be reasonable as between the parties and two factors are of particular relevance here. The first is that the buyer must establish a proprietary interest which the clause is seeking to protect. That is to say, when a buyer purchases a business and pays for the goodwill of the business, he is entitled to take reasonable steps to protect that interest. The second factor is that the clause must be reasonable in the light of all the circumstances of the case. It will be unreasonable if it goes further than reasonably necessary for the protection of his interest in point of space, time or subject-matter. The reasonableness of a clause depends upon all the facts of each case (see *Nordenfelt* v. *Maxim Nordenfelt* [1894] AC 535, in which a worldwide restraint was upheld because of the limited number of manufacturers in the particular industry).

Once the clause is shown to be reasonable as between the parties, it must be shown to be reasonable in the public interest. The courts have, once again, been reluctant to conclude that an agreement which is reasonable as between the parties is unenforceable because it is contrary to the public interest.

15.15 Restrictive Trading and Analogous Agreements

We have already noted that it is extremely difficult to define the limits of the doctrine of restraint of trade. For example, it was once thought that exclusive dealing agreements were not within the scope of the doctrine or, if they were, they were valid because they were not contrary to the public interest. But that view received a fatal blow as a result of the decision of the House of Lords in *Esso Petroleum Co Ltd* v. *Harper's Garage (Stourport) Ltd* (above). A garage company, which owned two garages, entered into a solus agreement with Esso under which it agreed to buy all its petrol from Esso, to keep the garage open at all reasonable hours and not to sell the garage without ensuring that the purchaser entered into a similar agreement with Esso. One agreement was to last for five years and the other for 21 years. In effect, the garage owners were tied to Esso for 21 years. It was held that the agreements were governed by the restraint of trade doctrine, that the five-year agreement with Esso was valid, but that the 21-year agreement was invalid (see too *Schroeder Music Publishing Co Ltd* v. *Macaulay* [1974] 1 WLR 1308). Although the courts have been prepared to extend the scope of the doctrine of restraint of trade to such contracts, they have not subjected such contracts to stringent scrutiny. The courts are willing to find the existence of a legitimate interest which such exclusive dealing agreements seek to protect, such as maintaining retail outlets or protecting a competitive position in the market-place, and they have adopted a *laissez-faire* approach to the reasonableness requirements (see *Alex*

Lobb (Garages) Ltd v. *Total Oil (Great Britain) Ltd* [1985] 1 WLR 173).
The consequence of this *laissez-faire* approach has been that the courts
have played a secondary role in the regulation of anti-competitive
practices and the primary role is now played by Parliament (see the Fair
Trading Act 1973, the Resale Prices Act 1976, the Restrictive Practices
Act 1976 and the Competition Act 1980) and by European Community
law (see Article 85 of the Treaty of Rome). There is no doubt that
Parliament is better equipped than the common law to engage in the
regulation of such allegedly anti-competitive practices (see Trebilcock,
1976).

15.16 The Scope of Public Policy

The doctrine of public policy at common law is an extremely conservative
one and operates within relatively rigid confines. Indeed Lord Halsbury
once stated that the courts cannot 'invent a new head of public policy'
(*Janson* v. *Driefontein Consolidated Mines Ltd* [1902] AC 484). Such a
restrictive approach is no longer generally accepted. The courts are
prepared gradually to adapt the existing categories to reflect changing
social and moral values (see, for example, the discussion of contracts
between cohabiting couples at 15.7), although they remain extremely
reluctant to extend the doctrine to a contract of a type to which the
doctrine has never been applied before. Such a rigidly controlled
doctrine has the merit of limiting the ability of individual judges to
develop their own idiosyncratic conceptions of public policy. The task of
placing limits upon freedom of contract in the name of public policy is
therefore left largely to Parliament. A judge in a modern case would not
conclude that a contract which was supported by 'inadequate consideration' was void because it was 'contrary to public policy'. But he might be
able to say that the contract was voidable because it had been procured
by undue influence or as a result of 'inequality of bargaining power' (see
17.3–17.4). Doctrines such as undue influence, the rules relating to
contractual capacity (Chapter 16), the legal regulation of exclusion
clauses (Chapter 11) and the penalty clause rule (21.5) can all be
regarded as 'disguised extensions or applications of the doctrine of public
policy' (Treitel, 1987, p.369). While the courts remain reluctant to
expand the doctrine of 'public policy' beyond the contracts to which it
has traditionally been applied, the development of a doctrine of 'public
policy' in English law is more likely to be found in cases of alleged undue
influence or 'inequality of bargaining power' than in the cases which we
have discussed in this chapter.

15.17 The Effects of Illegality

We have already noted the general rule that an illegal contract will not be
enforced by the courts. Although the courts will not enforce the contract,

they may be prepared to give to the 'innocent party' a remedy on some alternative basis. In *Strongman (1945) Ltd* v. *Sincock* [1955] 2 QB 525, the defendant stated that he would obtain the necessary licences to enable the plaintiffs lawfully to modernise his house. The defendant failed to obtain all the licences and he refused to pay for some of the work which the plaintiffs had done, arguing that the contract was illegal. The plaintiffs were unable to sue on the building contract because of the failure to obtain all the licences, but they were able to recover the value of the work which they had done on the ground that the defendant had breached a *collateral warranty* that he would obtain the necessary licences. In *Shelley* v. *Paddock* [1980] QB 348, it was also recognised that an innocent party to an illegal contract could recover damages for fraudulent misprepresentation. By searching out the existence of remedies other than on the contract itself, the court can take steps to protect an innocent party who has relied to his detriment upon an illegal contract.

15.18 The Recovery of Money or Property

A further question which must be asked is: do the courts permit a party to an illegal contract to recover any benefits which he has conferred upon the other party to the contract? The general rule is that the courts will not permit the recovery of benefits transferred under an illegal contract (*Holman* v. *Johnson* (1775) 1 Cowp 341). Once again the courts are seeking to reconcile two competing policies, namely the prevention of unjust enrichment and the need to deter entry into illegal contracts. The general rule reflects the latter policy. But there are a number of exceptions to the general rule and these exceptions reflect the former policy.

Before analysing the general rule and the exceptions a further question must be asked: on what ground can a party who has conferred a benefit on the other party to the contract seek recovery? The illegality does not, of itself, confer a cause of action. In many cases the illegality is employed as a *defence* to an action for the recovery of the benefit. It could be argued that the general rule denying recovery is based upon considerations of public policy but that, where the parties are not *in pari delicto* (equally guilty), the policy objection to recovery simply disappears. Alternatively, it can be argued that the grounds on which recovery is sought are the normal grounds of restitution, such as mistake or duress, and that the illegality is used simply as a *defence* to a restitutionary action which would otherwise have succeeded (see Birks, 1985).

Although the precise basis of the claim may not be clear, there are three exceptional cases in which a party can recover benefits conferred under an illegal contract. The first exception arises where the parties are not *in pari delicto*. There are two groups of cases here. The first is where the plaintiff was under a mistake of fact which rendered him unaware of the illegal nature of the contract (*Oom* v. *Bruce* (1810) 12 East 225). The second arises where the plaintiff was induced to enter into the illegal transaction by the fraudulent representation of the defendant which had the effect of concealing the illegal nature of the transaction from the plaintiff (*Hughes* v. *Liverpool Victoria Legal Friendly Society* [1916] 2 KB 482) or where the plaintiff was induced to enter into the contract under some form of compulsion amounting to oppression (*Smith* v. *Cuff* (1817) 6 M & S 160). Another aspect of the *in pari delicto* rule is that recovery is permitted where a transaction is rendered illegal under a statute which was enacted in an effort to protect parties in the position of the plaintiff (*Kasumu* v. *Baba-Egbe* [1956] AC 539 and *Kiriri Cotton* v. *Dewani* [1960] AC 192).

Secondly, a plaintiff is entitled to recover a benefit conferred under an illegal contract if he repudiates the illegal purpose in time. The payer has a *locus poenitentiae* and may withdraw from the illegal contract and recover his payment (see *Taylor* v. *Bowers* (1876) 1 QBD 291 and *Kearley* v. *Thomson* (1890) 24 QBD 742, usefully discussed by Beatson, 1975). The justification for this exception is that the parties to an illegal contract should be provided with an incentive to refrain from performing an illegal contract.

Thirdly, a plaintiff may be able to recover money paid or property transferred under an illegal contract if he can establish his right to the money or the property without relying upon the illegal nature of the contract. The source of this exception lies in the difficult case of *Bowmakers Ltd* v. *Barnet Instruments Ltd* [1945] KB 65 (see also *Belvoir Finance* v. *Stapleton* [1970] 3 WLR 530 and the discussion by Hamson (1949) and Higgins (1962)). In *Bowmakers* the plaintiffs bought machine tools in contravention of the Defence Regulations and they delivered the tools to the defendants under three illegal hire-purchase agreements. The defendants, in breach of the agreements, sold some of the tools and refused to return the remainder. The plaintiffs sued successfully for damages in the tort of conversion. The defendants' right to possess the goods terminated on their breach of the hire-purchase agreements and so the plaintiffs were able to establish their title to the machine tools without placing any reliance upon the illegal transactions. The major difficulty is that, by awarding damages assessed by reference to the value of the machine tools, the result was *de facto* enforcement of the contract. But to refuse a remedy on the facts of *Bowmakers* would have been to confer a *de facto* gift upon the defendants. As Coote has pointed out (1972), 'the real difficulty lies in the arbitrary, all-or-nothing character of the common law governing illegal contracts'.

The common law is, in fact, a poor instrument for the regulation of illegal contracts, because of the lack of remedial flexibility. One alternative would be to enact a piece of legislation, as was done in New Zealand in the Illegal Contracts Act 1970, which gives to the court wide discretionary powers to grant such relief as the court 'in its discretion thinks just' (see Furmston, 1972). Such wide, discretionary powers would at least enable the courts to strike a fair balance between the need to deter entry into illegal contracts and the need to prevent unjust enrichment.

15.19 Severance

Finally, it may be possible to 'sever' the illegal part of the contract and enforce the remainder. If the illegal part of the contract can be separated from the rest of the contract, without rendering the remainder of the contract radically different from the contract which the parties originally concluded, then the court may be prepared to sever the illegal part, provided that severance is not contrary to the public policy which rendered the contract illegal (see further, Treitel, 1987, pp.386–92).

Summary

1 As a general rule the courts will not enforce a contract which is illegal or which is otherwise contrary to public policy.

2 Where the illegality arises in the performance of a contract which was valid at the moment of formation, the contract can be enforced by the guilty party only when it was not the purpose of the statute broken or the common law rule violated that the contract should be invalidated. In the case of the innocent party, the contract can generally be enforced by him where he had no knowledge of the illegality.

3 A contract is illegal if its formation is expressly or impliedly prohibited by statute. The function of the court is to interpret the statute to discern whether, on its proper construction, the Act prohibits the making of such a contract.

4 A contract may be illegal at common law on the ground that it is contrary to public policy. Contracts which are contrary to public policy include contracts which are contrary to good morals, contracts which are prejudicial to family life, contracts to commit a crime or a civil wrong, contracts which are prejudicial to the administration of justice, contracts prejudicial to public relations and contracts in unreasonable restraint of trade.

5 A contract which is in restraint of trade is void and unenforceable unless it can be shown to be reasonable. The doctrine applies principally to a covenant by an employee not to compete with his employer either during or after his employment and to a covenant by the seller of a business and its goodwill not to carry on a business which will compete with the business bought by the purchaser. A clause which is caught by the doctrine is void unless it is reasonable as between the parties and reasonable in the public interest.

6 Although the courts are prepared gradually to adapt the doctrine of public policy to reflect changing social and moral values, they remain extremely reluctant to extend the doctrine to a contract of a type to which the doctrine has never been applied before.

7 The general rule is that the courts will not permit the recovery of benefits conferred under an illegal contract. But recovery will be allowed where the parties were not *in pari delicto*, where the plaintiff has effectively repudiated the illegal purpose, and where the plaintiff can establish his right to the money or the property without relying upon the illegal nature of the contract.

Exercises

1 Will the courts ever enforce an illegal contract? Should the courts ever enforce an illegal contract?
2 Compare and contrast the decisions in Re *Mahmoud and Ispahani* and *Archbolds (Freightage) Ltd* v. *S Spanglett Ltd.*
3 What impact does illegality in performance have on the enforceability of a contract?
4 When will a contract be held to be contrary to public policy? Does the doctrine of public policy reflect any values other than the idiosyncratic values of the judiciary?
5 A 35-year-old employee agrees with his employer that he will not work for the rest of his life if the employer pays him a lump sum of £1 million. The employer pays the money but the employee has now decided that he wishes to return to work. Discuss. (See *Wyatt* v. *Kreglinger and Fernau* [1933] 1 KB 793.
6 Joe employs six travelling salesmen. They sell insurance policies. Joe wishes to insert a restraint of trade clause in their contracts of employment. Advise him and draft a clause which will be suitable to his needs.
7 Can benefits conferred under an illegal contract be recovered?

16 Capacity

16.1 Introduction

Adults of sound mind have full contractual capacity. On the other hand, minors, the mentally incapacitated and companies have limited contractual capacity. In the case of minors and the mentally incapacitated, contract law seeks to protect such persons from the consequences of their own inexperience or inability. The limitations placed upon the contractual capacity of companies raise rather different issues, to which we shall return at 16.4.

Although contract law seeks to play a role in protecting minors and the mentally incapacitated, a competing policy is that the law does not wish to expose to hardship those who deal fairly and in all good faith with such persons. We shall see that the rules of law reflect an uneasy compromise between these competing policies. We shall begin our analysis by a consideration of the contractual capacity of minors (16.2), then we shall discuss the contractual capacity of the mentally incapacitated (16.3) and, finally, we shall analyse the contractual capacity of companies.

16.2 Minors

A minor is a person under the age of 18. The law adopts a particularly protective attitude towards minors, often at the expense of those who deal with them in all good faith. The general rule is that a minor is not bound by a contract which he enters into during his minority. But this general rule is subject to three principal exceptions.

The first is that a contract to supply a minor with 'necessaries' is binding upon the minor where the contract as a whole is for the benefit of the minor; where its terms are harsh or onerous it is not binding upon the minor. The definition of 'necessaries' is a wide one. In the case of a contract for the sale of goods, necessaries have been defined in s.3(3) of the Sale of Goods Act 1979 as 'goods suitable to the condition in life of the minor . . .and to his actual requirements at the time of the sale and delivery'. At common law a wide definition of necessaries has also been adopted. Regard must be had to the station in life of the minor; the higher the status, the greater the range of necessaries. So in *Peters* v. *Fleming* (1840) 6 M & W 42, rings, pins and a watch-chain were held to be necessaries for an undergraduate who had a rich father. But there is a trap for the trader here because, in deciding whether a particular article is a necessary, a court will have regard to the status of the minor and his actual needs at the time of entry into the contract. Thus, in *Nash* v. *Inman* [1908] 2 KB 1, a tailor sold 11 fancy waistcoats to a minor, who was a Cambridge undergraduate. The minor refused to pay for them. The tailor's action for payment failed because he could not establish that the defendant was not already amply supplied with clothing; the waistcoats were not therefore necessaries. Although a minor is bound by an executed contract for necessaries, it remains unclear whether a minor is bound by an executory contract for necessaries (contrast *Nash* v. *Inman* (above) and *Roberts* v. *Gray* [1913] 1 KB 520).

Secondly, a minor is bound by a contract of employment if that contract is generally for his benefit (contrast *Clements* v. *L & NW Railway* [1894] 2 QB 482 and *De Francesco* v. *Barnum* (1889) 43 Ch D 430). This principle, however, is confined to contracts of employment and analogous contracts (such as a contract to give publishers the exclusive rights to publish the minor's memoirs; see *Chaplin* v. *Leslie Frewin (Publishers) Ltd* [1966] Ch 71). But there is no general principle of law that a contract with a minor is binding simply because it is for his benefit.

Thirdly, certain contracts with minors are not void but are only voidable; that is to say, the contract is valid and binding upon the minor unless he repudiates liability before majority or within a reasonable time thereafter. Only the minor can repudiate; the adult is bound by the contract. For example, a contract under which a minor acquires an interest in land or shares in a company is voidable, as is a partnership agreement to which a minor is a party. The effect of the repudiation is to release the minor from his obligations to perform in the future. But the minor can only recover money paid under such a contract where there has been a total failure of consideration (*Steinberg* v. *Scala (Leeds) Ltd* [1923] 2 Ch 452). A total failure of consideration arises where the basis upon which the minor paid the money has wholly failed, that is to say, he has received no part of the performance which he has bargained for.

Outside these three categories, the general rule is that, as we have noted, minors are not bound by the contracts into which they enter. However, a minor may incur liability to an adult in a number of other ways. In the first place, the minor will be liable on the contract if he ratifies it after he has reached majority. Secondly, where a contract is unenforceable against the minor or he has repudiated it, the court may, 'if it is just and equitable to do so', require the minor to transfer to the other party any 'property acquired' by the minor under the contract, or any 'property representing it' (s.3(1) of the Minors' Contracts Act 1987; it should be noted in this context that the Act contains no definition of 'property'; in particular, it is unclear whether 'property' includes money). The aim of this section is to prevent the unjust enrichment of the minor in cases such as *Nash* v. *Inman* (above), by enabling the court to order the minor to restore to the vendor the fancy waistcoats. But the court cannot order the minor to return the property where he has disposed of it and obtained nothing in return for it. This limitation has been criticised on the ground that it should be 'irrelevant that the benefits conferred are no longer identifiable in the [minor's] hands' (Goff and Jones, 1986, p.440). Nevertheless this provision is to be welcomed in so far as it reduces the possibility of the unjust enrichment of the minor. But it should be noted that the Act does not abolish the old common law and equitable rules (see *Stocks* v. *Wilson* [1913] 2 KB 235 and *Bristow* v. *Eastman* (1794) 1 Esp 172), so that the adult may still have resort to these old rules where, for some reason, a remedy is not available to him under the 1987 Act. However it is unlikely that an adult will wish, in future, to have resort to these old common law and equitable rules because s.3(1) of the Act is generally more favourable to the adult than are the old rules.

Thirdly, a minor who has actually performed his side of the contract may be unable to recover the benefits which he has conferred upon the other party. At first sight this seems rather anomalous. The foolish minor enters into improvident bargains; the very foolish minor actually carries through his side of the bargain. But the courts are unwilling to intervene in the latter case. Once the minor has paid money or transferred property to the adult, then he can only recover the money paid or property transferred when there has been a total failure of consideration (*Chaplin* v. *Leslie Frewin (Publishers) Ltd* (above), but see *Valentini* v. *Canali* (1889) 24 QBD 166) or on some other ground which would equally have been available to an adult.

Fourthly, a contract with a minor is effective to pass property to the minor (s.3(1) of the Minors' Contracts Act 1987); similarly it is effective to pass property from the minor to the adult. Finally, a minor may incur liability in tort, but, where the effect of the tort action would be to undermine the protection afforded by the law of contract, then the tort action will also be barred. In *R Leslie Ltd* v. *Sheill* [1914] 3 KB 607, a minor obtained a loan of £400 by fraudulently misrepresenting his age. It was held that the minor could not be sued in the tort of deceit because the effect of granting damages in the tort action would be indirectly to enforce the contract and thus undermine the protection afforded by the law of contract.

Despite the enactment of the Minors' Contracts Act 1987, the law relating to the contractual capacity of minors remains in a confused state. The rules relating to necessaries can act as a trap for persons who deal in all good faith with minors. On the other hand, given that in the vast majority of cases a minor can avoid liability without the need to repudiate, it is difficult to understand why certain contracts are treated as voidable so that the minor can only avoid liability by a timely repudiation. The rules of law remain in need of further rationalisation in an effort to provide a better balance between, on the one hand, the protection of minors and, on the other hand, the interests of those who deal in all good faith with them.

16.3 Mental Incapacity and Drunkenness

A person whose property is subject to the control of the court under Part VII of the Mental Health Act 1983 appears to be incapable of entering into a contract because of the lack of capacity to consent to entry into a contract (*Re Walker* [1905] 1 Ch 60). The justification for such a rule would appear to be that, where the patient's property is subject to the control of the court, an attempted disposition of the property does not bind him, since it would interfere with the court's control over the property.

Where the property is not subject to the control of the court under the 1983 Act, then mental incapacity is not a ground for the setting aside of a contract, unless the incapacity is known to the other party to the contract (*Imperial Loan Co* v. *Stone* [1892] 1 QB 599). Where the incapacity is not known to the other party, the contract cannot be set aside, unless the contract is of such a nature as to attract the equitable jurisdiction to relieve against unconscionable bargains between two persons of sound mind (*Hart* v. *O'Connor* [1985] AC 1000, see further 17.4). This requirement that the other party be aware of the incapacity should be contrasted with the case of minors, where there is no requirement that the other party be aware of the minority and, indeed, the minor may be relieved even when he has misrepresented his age. In Scotland the rule is that knowledge of the insanity is not a relevant consideration (*John Loudon & Co* v. *Elder's CB* 1923 SLT 226). It is therefore no surprise to learn that the requirement that the other party be aware of the incapacity has been subjected to severe criticism (see Hudson, 1986), although its harshness may be mitigated in practice by the existence of the equitable jurisdiction to set aside an improvident bargain made with a poor and ignorant person (*Cresswell* v. *Potter* [1978] 1 WLR 255; see further, 17.4)).

Drunkenness is treated in the same way as mental incapacity, so that the contract may only be set aside by the drunken party where the drunkenness prevented him from understanding the transaction and the other party to the contract knew of his incapacity (*Gore* v. *Gibson* (1843) 13 M & W 623). Finally, it should be noted that, in the case of a contract for the sale of goods, 'where necessaries are sold and delivered to a person who by reason of mental incapacity or drunkenness is incompetent to contract, he must pay a reasonable price for them' (s.3(2) of the Sale of Goods Act 1979).

16.4 Companies

A company is a legal person which is separated and distinct from its shareholders. But the capacity of the company is limited by the objects for which the company is set up and which are contained in the company's memorandum of association. If the company acts beyond its objects then it has acted '*ultra vires*', that is to say, it has acted beyond its capacity. In *Ashbury Railway Carriage and Iron Co* v. *Riche* (1875) LR 7 HL 653, it was held that a contract which was *ultra vires* the company was void. One of the principal justifications for the *ultra vires* rule is that it gives protection for shareholders who can learn from the objects clause 'the purposes to which their money can be applied' (*Sinclair* v. *Brougham* [1918] AC 514). In theory, it also provides protection for those who lend money to the company because they can infer from the objects clause the extent of the company's powers. But, in practice, a strict application of the rule caused hardship to innocent third parties who entered into a contract with a company, unaware of the *ultra vires* nature of the contract.

So it is not surprising to learn that the courts have created a number of exceptions to the rule, in an effort to provide some protection for innocent third parties who deal in all good faith with the company (see Farrar, 1988, pp.83–94). The most significant protection is now provided by statute in s.35(1) of the Companies Act 1985 (as amended by the Companies Act 1989) which states that:

'The validity of an act done by a company shall not be called into question on the ground of lack of capacity by reason of the fact that it is beyond the objects of the company stated in the memorandum of association.'

The intention behind this section is to abolish the *ultra vires* rule as regards innocent third parties who deal in all good faith with the company (see further, s.35A and s.35B), while retaining it for internal purposes concerning the relationship between the shareholders and the company (s.35(2) and (3)). Therefore, in effect, this section has abolished the ultra vires rule in relation to third parties who deal in all good faith with the company, so that the contract remains valid and enforceable.

Summary

1 The general rule is that a minor is not bound by a contract which he enters into during his minority.

2 But a minor is bound by a contract to supply him with 'necessaries' where the contract as a whole is for the benefit of the minor and he is also bound by a beneficial contract of employment. Certain contracts involving minors are voidable and the minor can escape liability only by a timely repudiation.

3 However a minor may incur liability in a number of other ways. He may incur liability on the contract if he ratifies it after attaining majority; he may incur liability in tort; he may be ordered to restore any property he has acquired under the contract or any property representing it (s.3(1) of the Minors' Contracts Act 1987); and it is more difficult for a minor to obtain a remedy where the contract has been performed.

4 A person whose property is subject to the control of the court under Part VII of the Mental Health Act 1983 appears to be incapable of entering into a contract.

In all other cases mental incapacity is not a ground for the setting aside of a contract, unless the incapacity is known to the other party to the contract.

5 The rule established in *Ashbury Railway Carriage and Iron Co* v. *Riche* was that a contract which is *ultra vires* a company is void. The effect of s.35 of the Companies Act 1985 (as amended) is virtually to abolish the doctrine of *ultra vires* in relation to third parties who deal in all good faith with the company.

Exercises

1 John, who is aged seventeen, agrees to buy a motor-bike from Trike Ltd for £2500. He takes delivery of the bike but refuses to pay for it. Advise Trike Ltd.

2 In what circumstances may a minor incur liability to an adult as a result of entering into a contract?

3 John, who suffers from senile dementia, agrees to sell a portrait to Brian for £5000. Brian does not know that John is suffering from senile dementia. It is later discovered that the portrait is, in fact, an original nineteenth-century painting, which is worth £125 000. Advise John whether he has any rights against Brian.

4 What does '*ultra vires*' mean? What effect does it have on a contract with a party who is unaware of the *ultra vires* nature of the transaction?

17 Duress, Undue Influence, and Inequality of Bargaining Power

17.1 Introduction

The law of contract has always placed limits upon the exercise of economic power by contracting parties (see Reiter, 1981). This role has traditionally been played by the doctrines of duress and undue influence, although recent years have witnessed an attempt to introduce a doctrine of inequality of bargaining power to play a similar role. In this chapter we shall give separate consideration to each of these doctrines and conclude by discussing the extent to which the law of contract is concerned with the fairness of the bargain reached by the parties.

17.2 Common Law Duress

At common law a contract which has been entered into under duress is voidable. There are three types of duress at common law. The first, and least controversial, is duress to the person. This may consist of actual violence to the plaintiff or to members of his family or threats of such violence. In *Barton* v. *Armstrong* [1976] AC 104, the Privy Council held that the threats need not be the sole reason for entry into the contract; it was sufficient that the threats were *a* factor influencing the victim to enter into the contract.

The second type of duress is duress to goods, that is a threat of damage to the victim's goods rather than to his person. Here the development of the law has been hindered by the old case of *Skeate* v. *Beale* (1840) 11 Ad & E 983, in which it was held that the unlawful detention of another's goods does not constitute duress. On the other hand, there was authority for the proposition that money paid to release goods which had been unlawfully detained could be recovered in an action for money had and received (*Astley* v. *Reynolds* (1731) 2 Str 915). The decision in *Skeate* v. *Beale* has come under heavy academic criticism (see Beatson, 1974) and in *The Siboen and The Sibotre* [1976] 1 Lloyds Rep 293, Kerr J refused to follow it. Given the development of the doctrine of economic duress (see below), it is unlikely that *Skeate* will be followed today, so that duress to goods can, in an appropriate case, form the basis of a claim for relief.

The third type of duress, and the most difficult to stabilise, is economic duress. This type of duress arises where one party uses his superior economic power in an 'illegitimate' way so as to coerce the other contracting party to agree to a particular set of terms. The existence of this doctrine was first recognised in England by Kerr J in *The Siboen and*

The Sibotre (above) and it has since been recognised in a number of cases, most importantly by the House of Lords in *Universe Tankships of Monrovia* v. *International Transport Workers Federation ('The Universe Sentinel')* [1983] 1 AC 366. In the latter case the defendant trade union 'blacked' the plaintiffs' ship in port and refused to release it until certain monies were paid, including a payment to the union's welfare fund. The House of Lords held that the latter payment was recoverable because the will of the shipowners had been coerced into making the payment and the pressure applied by the defendant union had been 'illegitimate'.

One question which must be asked here is: on what basis do the courts intervene to set aside a contract on the ground of duress? The traditional answer is that the courts will intervene where the victim's will has been 'coerced', such as 'to vitiate his consent'. This emphasis upon the need to establish a 'coercion of the will' can be seen in *The Siboen and the Sibotre* and, albeit to a lesser extent, in *The Universe Sentinel*. However the difficulties inherent in the 'coercion of the will' theory have been convincingly exposed by Professor Atiyah (1982). The principal difficulty is that duress does not deprive a person of all choice, but merely presents him with a choice between evils. For example, if a man forces me at gunpoint to enter into a contract, I do in fact consent to entering into the contract. Indeed, the more real the pressure, the more real is my willingness to enter into the contract, even if it is only to extricate myself from my predicament. What is wrong with the contract is not the absence of consent, but the wrongful nature of the threats which have been used to bring about the consent.

The role of consent should simply be to provide the necessary element of causation, namely that the threats used were a cause of the victim acting as he did (*Barton* v. *Armstrong* (above)). Consent also has a role to play in distinguishing between duress and an honest settlement of a claim (*Pao On* v. *Lau Yiu Long* [1980] AC 614) and in barring a claim, which would otherwise have succeeded, where a party has subsequently affirmed the contract (*North Ocean Shipping Co Ltd* v. *Hyundai Construction Co Ltd* [1979] QB 705). Any attempt to create a wider role for consent will deflect the court's attention from the real issues towards irrelevant inquiries into the psychological processes of the victim.

This suggests that greater emphasis should be placed upon the nature of the pressure applied by the more powerful party. This fact was implicitly recognised by the House of Lords in *The Universe Sentinel*, when they held that the pressure exerted must in some way be 'illegitimate'. The task which remains for the courts is to ascertain what constitutes 'illegitimate' pressure. It is clear that it encompasses unlawful threats, such as threats to breach a contract (see *Pao On* v. *Lau Yiu Long* (above)). Lord Scarman stated in *The Universe Sentinel* that it should extend to threats which, though lawful in themselves, are used to attain a goal which is unlawful, such as blackmail. On the other hand, a threat to refuse to contract should not constitute duress because, in the absence of an obligation to enter into a contract, no wrongful threat is made in refusing to contract (*Smith* v. *William Charlick Ltd* (1924) 124 CLR 38). Equally, a refusal to waive existing contractual obligations should not amount to duress because of the absence of a wrongful threat (*Alec Lobb (Garages) Ltd* v. *Total Oil (Great Britain) Ltd* [1983] 1 WLR 87, 94). Although a refusal to contract or to waive existing contractual obligations may have serious consequences for the victim and may 'coerce his will', such threats should not constitute duress because no wrongful threat has been made by the more powerful party. This suggests that, in future cases, the primary focus of the court's inquiry should be upon the nature of the pressure applied by the more powerful party rather than the state of mind of the victim.

17.3 Undue Influence

Undue influence, being a creation of equity, has emerged separately from common law duress. The traditional approach is to divide undue influence into two distinct categories. But an important preliminary point was considered by the House of Lords in *National Westminster Bank plc* v. *Morgan* [1985] AC 686. There it was held that, before a transaction could be set aside on the ground of undue influence, it had to be shown that the transaction was wrongful, in the sense that it constituted a manifest and unfair disadvantage to the person seeking to have the contract set aside. Such a 'manifest disadvantage' must be established in all cases of undue influence (*Bank of Credit and Commerce International SA* v. *Aboody* [1989] 2 WLR 759). In *Aboody* the Court of Appeal held, affirming the judgment of Cantley J,

'that a disadvantage would be a manifest disadvantage if it would have been obvious as such to any independent and reasonable persons who considered the transaction at the time with knowledge of all the relevant facts'.

A disadvantage will not be manifest if it emerges only 'after a fine and close evaluation of [the transaction's] various beneficial and detrimental features'.

Once over this preliminary hurdle, undue influence cases can be divided into two categories. The first group of cases are of 'presumed undue influence'. In this group of cases the relationship between the parties gives rise to a presumption of undue influence and the onus of proof switches to the recipient to show that he did not exercise undue influence. In *Bank of Credit and Commerce International SA* v. *Aboody* (above) the Court of Appeal held that cases of presumed undue influence can themselves be divided into two categories. The first group of cases concern the 'well established categories of relationship', such as solicitor and client, doctor and patient and religious adviser and disciple, where 'the relationship as such will give rise to the presumption'. The second category consists of relationships which do not fall within the first class but which 'may be shown to have become such as to justify the court in applying the same presumption'. In the latter category is *Re Craig* [1971] Ch 95, in which an elderly widower employed a young woman as his secretary and companion. He employed her only two months after the death of his wife and over the next six years made her gifts worth £28 000. It was held that there was a relationship of confidence between the two, such as to give rise to a presumption of undue influence, and that the young woman had failed to rebut the presumption that she had obtained the gifts by the use of undue influence.

Once the presumption of undue influence has arisen it may be rebutted by showing that the donor acted independently of any influence of the recipient and with full appreciation of what he was doing. The most usual, although not the only way, of rebutting the presumption is to show that the donor had competent and independent advice before acting. But the presumption may also be rebutted by showing that the act of the donor in making the gift had been a 'spontaneous and independent act' (*Re Brocklehurst* [1978] Ch 14).

The second group of undue influence cases are cases of 'actual undue influence'. They arise, not from the relationship between the parties, but because there has been some unfair and improper conduct on the part of the party alleged to have exercised the undue influence. Here the undue influence must be proved by the party seeking to establish its existence; there is no presumption of undue influence. Cases within this category tend to be a rather rare species because they are either argued as cases of common law duress or it is sought to establish that there is a relationship between the parties such as to give rise to a presumption of undue influence. A case such as *Re Craig* (above) can be decided either as a case of presumed undue influence (in the second category) or as a case of actual undue influence. As the Court of Appeal acknowledged in *Aboody*, the border between the second category of presumed undue influence and actual undue influence may be a 'slender' one. A rare case of actual undue influence is *Williams* v. *Bayley* (1866) LR 1 HL 200. A father sought to rescind a mortgage which he had executed in favour of a banker. He proved that he had executed the mortgage because he was frightened by the banker's warning that he had it in his power to prosecute his son for forgery. It was held that he was entitled to rescind the mortgage on the ground of undue influence.

17.4 Inequality of Bargaining Power

The issue as to whether a doctrine of inequality of bargaining power exists in English law has been one of some controversy in recent years. The primary source of this controversy lies in the seminal judgment of Lord Denning in *Lloyds Bank* v. *Bundy* [1975] QB 326. The facts of the case were, in many ways, unremarkable. Mr Bundy, an elderly man not well versed in business affairs, gave his bank a guarantee regarding his son's business debts and mortgaged his house to the bank as security for the guarantee. In entering into this transaction Mr Bundy relied implicitly on his bank manager as his adviser, but the bank manager was also acting on behalf of the son, thereby creating a conflict of interest. When the bank sought to enforce the guarantee against old Mr Bundy and obtain possession of the house, he defended the action on the ground that the mortgage had been improperly obtained. The majority of the court decided the case on orthodox grounds, holding that the bank had failed to rebut the presumption of undue influence because they could not show that Mr Bundy had been independently advised. All this, however, was not for Lord Denning. He set out the following general principle:

'English law gives relief to one who without independent advice enters into a contract upon terms which are very unfair or transfers property for a consideration which is grossly inadequate, when his bargaining power is grievously impaired by reason of his own needs and desires, or by his own ignorance or infirmity, coupled with undue influence or pressures brought to bear on him by or for the benefit of the other.'

Lord Denning envisaged that this new general principle would unify hitherto discrete areas of law and provide a basis for a solution to a wide range of problems. But it has since received a rather frosty reception in the appellate courts. In *Pao On* v. *Lau Yiu Long* (above) Lord Scarman, giving the judgment of the Privy Council, said that agreements were not voidable simply because they had been 'procured by an unfair use of a dominant bargaining position'. A much more severe rebuff was handed out by Lord Scarman, giving the judgment of the House of Lords in *National Westminster Bank plc* v. *Morgan* (above). He specifically disapproved of Lord Denning's principle of inequality of bargaining power and questioned whether there was any need for such a doctrine, given that Parliament, in statutes such as the Consumer Credit Act 1974, has undertaken the task of placing 'such restrictions upon freedom of contract as are necessary' to protect the most likely victims of inequality of bargaining power.

However, although Lord Denning's principle of inequality of bargaining power has been rejected, it should not be assumed that courts will stand by and allow the strong 'to push the weak to the wall' (*Alec Lobb (Garages) Ltd* v. *Total Oil (Great Britain) Ltd,* [1985] 1 WLR 173, 183). Even in *National Westminster Bank* v. *Morgan,* Lord Scarman recognised the existence of an equitable jurisdiction to grant relief against an unconscionable (or unfair) bargain. He refused to confine the jurisdiction of equity within rigid limits, saying that the 'court in the exercise of this equitable jurisdiction is a court of conscience'. Thus we find that equity intervenes to relieve against unconscionable bargains

(*Earl of Chesterfield* v. *Janssen* (1751) 2 Ves Sen 125), to set aside an agreement made with an expectant heir (*Earl of Aylesford* v. *Morris* (1873) LR 8 Ch App 484), to set aside an improvident bargain made with a poor and ignorant person (*Cresswell* v. *Potter* [1978] 1 WLR 255) and to grant relief where there has been an abuse of a relationship of confidence (*Demarara Bauxite Co Ltd* v. *Hubbard* [1923] AC 673). Although there is no general principle of inequality of bargaining power, it remains to be seen how far these residual equitable doctrines will be resurrected to play the role which Lord Denning envisaged would be played by his doctrine of inequality of bargaining power.

17.5 The Role of Parliament

Parliament has also had a role to play in regulating contracts in an effort to protect the most likely victims of inequality of bargaining power. For example, section 137(1) of the Consumer Credit Act 1974 states that

> 'If the court finds a credit bargain extortionate it may reopen the credit agreement so as to do justice between the parties.'

An extortionate credit bargain is one which requires the debtor or a relative of his to make payments which are 'grossly exorbitant' or which 'otherwise grossly contravenes ordinary principles or fair dealing' (s.138(1)). In deciding whether these requirements have been satisfied, the court must engage in a wide-ranging inquiry but must, in particular, have regard to the interest rates prevailing at the time that the agreement was made, the relevant characteristics of the borrower (such as age, experience, health and the presence or absence of financial pressure upon him), the risks accepted by the creditor and the creditor's relationship to the debtor. The court is also given considerable discretion to remake the agreement according to its conception of what justice requires on the facts of the case.

Other examples of statutes enacted in an attempt to protect the most likely victims of inequality of bargaining power include the Unfair Contract Terms Act 1977 and the Supply of Goods and Services Act 1982. Parliament has also intervened to regulate the employment relationship and the relationship between landlords and tenants in an effort to provide greater protection for employees and tenants (see 1.2). But, as we have already noted, Lord Scarman in *Morgan* used the existence of such legislation as a justification for refusing to create a doctrine of inequality of bargaining power. But the better approach would surely have been to create such a doctrine and follow the policy being pursued by Parliament. Instead, the common law has been left pursuing an individualistic policy which is diametrically opposed to the policies being pursued by Parliament in statutes such as the Consumer Credit Act 1974 and the Unfair Contract Terms Act 1977.

17.6 A General Doctrine of Unconscionability?

Any discussion of the desirability of a general doctrine of unconscionability may seem rather academic, given the rejection of Lord Denning's doctrine of inequality of bargaining power. At first sight English contract law seems unconcerned with the fairness of the contract concluded by the parties. The courts have rejected a doctrine of inequality of bargaining power and, as we have already noted (5.5), the general rule is that consideration must be sufficient but need not be adequate. Freedom of contract reigns and the adequacy of the consideration is irrelevant.

But, despite initial appearances to the contrary, the rules which make up English contract law are concerned with the fairness of the bargain reached by the parties. We have seen the hostility which the courts have displayed towards exclusion clauses, both in terms of the interpretative devices adopted (11.5) and their reluctance to incorporate exclusion clauses and other onerous clauses into a contract (9.4). Innominate terms (10.5) were created to give the courts greater remedial flexibility, so that the injustice of cases such as *Arcos* v. *Ronaasen* [1933] AC 470 need no longer occur. We have also noted the protective attitude which the courts have adopted towards minors (see 16.2). Later in this book we shall see that the courts are reluctant to order specific performance of a contract which is unfair (21.9), they have an equitable jurisdiction to grant relief against forfeiture (21.7) and they have developed a penalty clause jurisdiction, under which a court will not enforce a term of a contract which seeks to punish a contracting party who is in breach of contract (21.5). Surely conceptions of fairness must underpin, to a greater or lesser extent, these rules and doctrines (see Waddams, 1976). If these conceptions of fairness permeate the law of contract, would it not be better to acknowledge these considerations openly by the creation of a general doctrine of unconscionability?

Three principal objections can be raised against the creation of such a doctrine. The first is that the courts are unable to identify contracts which are unfair because of their inability to understand the operation of financial markets (see Trebilcock, 1976). The second is that such a general doctrine would create an unacceptable degree of uncertainty. The third is that it is not the function of contract law to engage in the redistribution of wealth (Fried, 1981; contrast Kronman, 1980, who defends 'the view that the rules of contract law should be used to implement distributional goals whenever alternative ways of doing so are likely to be more costly or intrusive').

These are powerful objections to the creation of such a general doctrine. But they are not necessarily conclusive. We have already noted (1.3) the conflicting ideologies which run through the law of contract and it is here that market-individualism and consumer-welfarism are in direct conflict (although contrast Tiplady, 1983). Given that these conceptions of fairness run throughout the law of contract, they cannot be dismissed as an insignificant aspect of contract law. Although Parliament must continue to play the principal role in regulating the economy and placing restrictions upon freedom of contract, a residual role can nevertheless be played by the courts and that role can best be recognised by the creation of a general doctrine of unconscionability. Uncertainty can be reduced by the recognition of the fact that unfairness can take different forms. Broadly speaking, two types of unfairness can be recognised. The first may be called procedural unfairness and the second substantive unfairness (although it should be noted that the distinction between the two has been doubted by Atiyah (1986d), who maintains that the two 'feed upon each other'). The first is concerned with the process by which the contract is negotiated. The second is concerned with the fairness of the terms or the substance of the contract. It is easier to identify the procedural tactics which are unacceptable as part of the process of contractual negotiation than it is to define substantive unfairness (see Thal, 1988). Unacceptable tactics might include threats to commit a crime, a tort or a breach of contract and the courts might recognise that there are certain bargaining weaknesses, such as infirmity and necessity, which should not be exploited. More difficulty is experienced in defining substantive unfairness; all that can be said is that it should only be a ground of relief in the very rare case where the consideration is manifestly and totally inadequate and that the courts must be left to work out the principles on a case-by-case basis. Such a narrowly drawn doctrine of unconscionability would not create an unacceptable level of uncertainty, but it would prevent injustice arising in the few cases in which it was needed.

Summary

1 A contract may be set aside on the ground of duress. The duress may be to the person, to his goods or economic duress.

2 Duress can be shown to exist where the will of the victim has been coerced by illegitimate pressure.

3 Undue influence is an equitable doctrine. Before a contract can be set aside on the ground of undue influence it must be demonstrated that the contract was manifestly disadvantageous to the person seeking to set it aside.

4 In cases of presumed undue influence, the relationship between the parties gives rise to a presumption of undue influence and the onus of proof switches to the recipient to show that he did not exercise undue influence. In cases of actual undue influence, there must be some unfair and improper conduct on the part of the party alleged to have exercised the undue influence. Actual undue influence must be proved by the party seeking to establish its existence.

5 English law does not recognise the existence of a general doctrine of inequality of bargaining power. But equity may intervene to set aside unconscionable bargains, agreements made with expectant heirs, improvident bargains made with poor and ignorant persons and contracts procured by an abuse of a relationship of confidence.

6 Parliament has also intervened, in statutes such as the Consumer Credit Act 1974 and the Unfair Contract Terms Act 1977, in an effort to protect the most likely victims of inequality of bargaining power.

Exercises

1 A threatens B that he (A) will shoot the next person he sees unless B pays him £10. B pays the £10. Can he recover it? Would your answer be the same if A had threatened to burn one of B's old family heirlooms unless he paid the £10?

2 What is the relationship between the doctrine of consideration and duress? (see *Stilk* v. *Myrick* (5.10) and *D & C Builders* v. *Rees* [1966] 2 QB 617.)

3 What is economic duress? What are its limits?

4 What is undue influence? How does it differ from duress?

5 Does English law recognise the existence of a doctrine of inequality of bargaining power? Should it?

6 Do you think that the courts are concerned with the fairness of the bargain reached by the parties?

7 An old lady is 'induced by her solicitor under strong pressure to sell him a large and inconvenient family home at full market value'. Can the transaction be set aside by the old lady? If so, on what grounds? (See *Bank of Credit and Commerce International SA* v. *Aboody* [1989] 2 WLR 759, 777–9).

Part IV

Performance, Discharge and Remedies for Breach of Contract

18 Performance and Discharge of the Contract

18.1 Performance

Contracts are made to be performed. When parties enter into a contract, they generally do so in the expectation that it will be performed according to its terms. Indeed a contract consists of a number of terms which determine the scope of the performance obligations which the parties have accepted. A failure to perform in accordance with these terms is a breach of contract, which will entitle the other party to the contract to an appropriate remedy (*Photo Production Ltd* v. *Securicor Transport Ltd* [1980] AC 827; see further, 19.3).

However, in many cases the formation of the contract and the performance of the contract are practically simultaneous. For example, I purchase a newspaper at a nearby shop. Here my offer to buy the paper and the shopkeeper's acceptance of my offer occur at virtually the same time as the performance of the contract in the handing over, and the payment for, the newspaper. Atiyah asks (1986b): 'Is it really sensible to characterise these transactions as agreements or exchanges of promises?' He argues that obligations are really created by what we do, not what we promise or what we intend: in other words, it is the payment of the money and the handing over of the newspaper which form the basis of the obligations created, not the *promise* to pay or the *promise* to hand over the newspaper.

It must be conceded that in many cases formation and performance are practically simultaneous. This fact is often obscured by contract text-books because formation appears at the beginning of the book and performance towards the end. But in the real world the two often occur at virtually the same time. On the other hand, there may be a considerable time lapse between formation and performance. For example, I may order a special anniversary issue of a newspaper which is not due for publication for another three weeks. In such a case I want to know at the moment that I reach agreement with the shopkeeper that he will order and deliver to me a copy of the newspaper. Here there appears to be no doubt that the agreement is the basis of our obligations, not any action in reliance upon the agreement. It is submitted that the same is true when formation and performance are virtually simultaneous. In my example of the purchase of a newspaper, the source of the obligations created remains my promise to buy the paper and the promise of the shopkeeper to sell the newspaper; our actions are simply evidence of the fact that we have reached agreement (see 1.4).

18.2 Discharge of the Contract

Contracts may be discharged or brought to an end in four principal ways. We shall deal with three forms of discharge in this chapter. They are discharge by performance (18.3), by agreement (18.4) and by operation of law (18.5). Contracts can also be discharged by breach, but breach is a sufficiently important topic to deserve a chapter in its own right (see Chapter 19).

18.3 Discharge by Performance

A contract is discharged by performance where the performance by both parties complies fully with the terms of the contract. The vast majority of contracts are discharged by performance. We do not read about such contracts in textbooks because, when the contract is discharged by performance, no legal problems arise. Indeed the discussion of 'performance' in most contract textbooks is, in fact, a discussion of breach of contract because the point which is being made is that performance which fails to comply fully with the terms of the contract is a breach of contract. We shall deal with such issues in Chapter 19.

It is, however, extremely important to realise that, in the real world, most contracts are discharged by performance. Students who read contract textbooks tend to get a distorted view of reality because they believe that all contracts go wrong for one reason or another. In fact, most contracts are performed according to their terms and the role of the lawyer is confined to giving advice on the formation or the drafting of the contract. It is only in the minority of cases that contracts go wrong and a dispute breaks out between the parties and, even when such a dispute does occur, empirical studies show us that the rules of contract law are often but one factor among many to be taken into account in the resolution of the dispute (see 1.5).

18.4 Discharge by Agreement

The parties can agree to abandon or to discharge the contract. The limiting factor here is that an agreement to discharge a contract must be supported by consideration (5.20). Where performance has not been completed by either party to the contract, there is generally no difficulty in finding consideration because, in giving up their rights to compel each other to perform, each party is giving something to the bargain and so consideration is given. But where the contract is wholly executed on one side, an agreement to abandon the contract (unless the agreement to abandon the contract is itself supported by fresh consideration) will not be supported by consideration and will be unenforceable unless the party who has fully performed his obligations under the contract is estopped from going back upon his representation that he will not enforce the original contract or he is held to have waived his rights under that contract (see 5.20–5.21).

Finally, a contract may be discharged by the operation of a condition subsequent which has been incorporated into the contract. A condition subsequent states that a previously binding contract shall come to an end on the occurrence of a stipulated event (see 10.2). The effect of the occurrence of the stipulated event is to discharge the contract, without either party being in breach of contract.

18.5 Discharge by Operation of Law

A contract may be discharged by operation of law. The principal example of a contract which is brought to an end by the operation of a rule of law is a contract which is frustrated. Frustration, it will be remembered, automatically brings a contract to an end by the operation of a rule of law, irrespective of the wishes of the parties (14.8). Other examples of the discharge of a contract by operation of law are discussed by Anson (1984, pp.485–8).

Summary

1 Contracts are made to be performed. The vast majority of contracts are discharged by performance.

2 Contracts may be discharged by performance, agreement, operation of law or breach.

3 A contract is discharged by performance where the performance by both parties has complied fully with the terms of the contract.

4 An agreement to discharge a contract must be supported by consideration, unless one party is held to have waived his rights under the contract or is estopped from asserting them.

5 A contract may be discharged by operation of law, for example, by the occurrence of a frustrating event.

Exercises

1 List the different ways in which a contract can be discharged.

2 When will performance be sufficient to discharge the contract?

3 Jenny agrees to buy Sarah's car for £2500. Sarah gives Jenny the car but Jenny does not pay the £2500. Jenny and Sarah then agree to abandon the contract and Sarah tells Jenny that she 'does not need the money anyway'. Jenny then uses the £2500 to pay for the installation of double glazing in her house. Sarah has now decided that she wants her car back and she alleges that the agreement to discharge the contract is not an enforceable agreement. Advise Jenny.

19 Breach of Contract

19.1 Introduction: Breach Defined

Professor Treitel (1987) has defined a breach of contract in the following terms:

> 'a breach of contract is committed when a party without lawful excuse fails or refuses to perform what is due from him under the contract, performs defectively or incapacitates himself from performing'.

It should be noted that in all cases the failure to provide the promised performance must be 'without lawful excuse'. Thus where the contract has been frustrated there is no liability for breach of contract because both parties have been provided with a 'lawful excuse' for their non-performance. Similarly, where one party has breached the contract and the breach has given to the other party the right to terminate performance of the contract, that party is not in breach of contract in refusing to continue with performance because he is given a 'lawful excuse' for his non-performance.

19.2 When Does Breach Occur?

The question whether or not a particular contract has been breached depends upon the precise construction of the terms of the contract. No universal legal principle can be established which displaces the need for a careful analysis of the terms of each individual contract. It is for the party alleging the existence of the breach of contract to prove its existence. It is not generally necessary to prove that a party has been at fault before breach can be established. Many obligations created by a contract are strict; that is to say, liability does not depend upon proof of fault. A good example of a strict contractual obligation is provided by s.14(2) of the Sale of Goods Act 1979 which states that, where a seller sells goods in the course of a business, there is an implied condition that the goods supplied under the contract are of merchantable quality, except in relation to defects drawn to the buyer's attention before the contract was concluded or, in the case where the buyer examines the goods, as regards defects which that examination ought to reveal. The purchaser is not required to prove that the seller has been at fault in selling goods which are not of merchantable quality; the seller may have taken all reasonable steps to ensure that the goods are of merchantable quality but he will still be in breach of contract. On the other hand, a contractual term may impose a duty to take reasonable care, in which case a breach can only be established where it is proved that the party has failed to exercise reasonable care.

19.3 The Consequences of Breach

A breach of contract does not automatically bring a contract to an end (*Decro-Wall International SA* v. *Practitioners in Marketing Ltd* [1971] 1 WLR 361). Rather, a breach of contract gives various options to the party who is not in breach ('the innocent party'). The extent of these options depends upon the seriousness of the breach. Even the most serious breach, such as a fundamental breach (see 11.7), does not, of itself, terminate or discharge the contract.

The consequences of a breach of contract depend upon the facts of each individual case, but three principal consequences of a breach of contract can be identified. The first is that the innocent party may be entitled to recover damages in respect of the loss which he has suffered as a result of the breach. The second is that the party in breach may be unable to sue to enforce the innocent party's obligations under the contract. The third consequence is that the breach may entitle the innocent party to terminate the performance of the contract. We shall now deal with these consequences individually.

19.4 Damages

Every breach of a valid and enforceable contract gives to the innocent party a right to recover damages in respect of the loss suffered as a result of the breach, unless the liability for breach has been effectively excluded by an appropriately drafted exclusion clause. An action for damages lies whether the term which is broken is a condition, a warranty or an innominate term (see further, Chapter 10). The basis upon which the courts assess the damages payable will be discussed in Chapter 20.

19.5 Enforcement by the Party in Breach

The second consequence of a breach of contract is that the party who is in breach may be unable to enforce the contract against the innocent party. Where the obligations of the parties are independent, that is to say, the obligation of one party to perform is not dependent upon performance by the other party, then breach by one party does not entitle the innocent party to abandon performance of his obligations under the contract. For example, a landlord's covenant to repair the premises and a tenant's covenant to pay rent are independent obligations, so that a landlord is not entitled to refuse to repair the premises because the tenant has failed to pay his rent (*Taylor* v. *Webb* [1937] 2 KB 370). But, where the obligations of the parties are dependent, then a contracting party must generally be ready and willing to perform his obligations under the contract before he can maintain an action against the other party for breach of contract. Obligations created by a contract are generally interpreted as dependent obligations (see, for example, s.28 of the Sale of Goods Act 1979) so that breach will generally preclude the party in breach from bringing an action to enforce the contract.

19.6 The Right to Terminate Performance of the Contract

A breach of contract may entitle the innocent party to take the further step of terminating performance of the contract. Here it is necessary to recount a little of the material which we discussed in Chapter 10. It will be remembered that contractual terms can be classified as conditions, warranties or innominate terms. Breach of a warranty does not give the innocent party a right to terminate performance of the contract; it only enables him to claim damages. But breach of a condition and breach of an innominate term, where the consequences of the breach are suffi- ciently serious (see 10.5), do give the innocent party the additional right to terminate performance of the contract. It should be noted that I have used the rather clumsy expression 'right to terminate performance of the contract'. Contract scholars and judges have disagreed as to the correct 'title' to be given to this right of the innocent party. Professor Treitel (1987) calls this right a 'right to rescind'. This terminology is acceptable, if dangerous. The danger lies in the fact that it tends to create confusion between 'rescission for breach' and 'rescission for misrepresentation'. Where a contract is rescinded for misrepresentation, it is set aside for all purposes. The contract is set aside both retrospectively and prospectively and the aim is to restore the parties, as far as possible, to the position which they were in before they entered into the contract (see 13.8). But a contract which is 'rescinded' for breach is set aside prospectively, but not retrospectively (*Johnson* v. *Agnew* [1980] AC 367 and *Photo Production Ltd* v. *Securicor Transport Ltd* [1980] AC 827). Provided this funda- mental distinction is grasped, no objection can be raised to the use of the term 'right to rescind for breach'. We must now give further considera- tion to the consequences of the rule that breach operates prospectively but not retrospectively.

19.7 The Prospective Nature of Breach

The point that breach operates prospectively but not retrospectively is an important one. It is for this reason that I have termed the right of the innocent party a right to 'terminate performance of the contract' and not a right to terminate the contract. It is the obligations of the parties to perform their future primary contractual duties which are terminated (see Carter, 1984, p.66). The contract itself survives and any contract terms which are intended to regulate the consequences of breach or the termination must be taken into consideration by the court (*Heyman* v. *Darwins Ltd* [1942] AC 356). The prospective nature of a breach of contract becomes clearer if we adopt the language of primary and secondary obligations.

The modern source of this distinction between primary and secondary obligations is the judgment of Lord Diplock in *Photo Production Ltd* v. *Securicor Transport Ltd* (above). Lord Diplock stated that 'breaches of primary obligations give rise to substituted secondary obligations'. There are two principal types of secondary obligations. The first is a 'general secondary obligation'. In such a case the primary obligations of both parties, in so far as they have not yet been fully performed, remain unchanged, but the breach gives rise to a secondary obligation, imposed upon the party in breach, 'to pay monetary compensation to the [innocent] party for the loss sustained by him in consequence of the breach'. Such a general secondary obligation would arise on the breach of a warranty; the primary obligations of the parties in so far as they have not been fully performed remain unchanged and a secondary obligation to pay damages for the loss suffered as a result of the breach is created.

But, where the breach of a primary obligation entitles the innocent party to elect to terminate performance of the contract, and he does so elect, all primary obligations of both parties remaining unperformed are put to an end and

'there is substituted by implication of law for the primary obligations of the party in default which remain unperformed a secondary obligation to pay monetary compensation to the other party for the loss sustained by him in consequence of their non-performance'.

This obligation Lord Diplock called an 'anticipatory secondary obligation'. The crucial feature of an 'anticipatory' secondary obligation is that it enables damages to be assessed by reference to those obligations which would have fallen due for performance at some time in the future (see further 21.3).

There is therefore no inconsistency in electing to terminate performance of the contract and, at the same time, claiming damages for the breach which gave rise to the right to terminate performance. Rather, the exercise of the right to terminate performance of the contract simply discharges the primary obligations of both parties *for the future* and imposes on the party in breach, by way of substitution, an anticipatory secondary obligation to pay damages to the innocent party.

19.8 The Right of Election

An innocent party is not obliged to exercise his right to terminate performance of the contract. As we have already noted, such a breach gives to the innocent party an option. He can either terminate performance of the contract and claim damages or he can affirm the contract and claim damages. Although the election between termination and affirmation is notionally free, in practice it may be restricted by the obligation of the innocent party to take reasonable steps to mitigate his loss (see further 20.10). For example, a seller, faced with a buyer who has breached a contract in such a way as to give to the seller a right to terminate performance of the contract, may elect to sell the goods elsewhere, thereby disabling himself from performing the original contract, rather than affirm the contract. The reason for this is that, if the seller fails to take reasonable steps to sell the goods elsewhere, a court may conclude that he has failed to mitigate his loss and he will be unable to recover the extra loss caused by his failure to mitigate.

Once an innocent party has exercised his right to terminate performance of the contract, he cannot subsequently affirm the contract because the effect of the termination of performance is to release *both* parties from their obligations to perform in the future and, once released from these obligations, they cannot be subsequently resurrected (Johnson v. *Agnew* (above)).

If the innocent party elects to affirm the contract, the contract remains in force, so that both parties remain bound to continue with the performance of their respective contractual obligations. An innocent party who accepts further performance of the contract after the breach may be held thereby to have affirmed the contract (*Davenport* v. *R* (1877) 3 App Cas 115). Affirmation does not prevent the innocent party from claiming damages for any loss which he has suffered as a result of the breach.

19.9 Anticipatory Breach

One contracting party may inform the other party, before the time fixed for performance under the contract, that he will not perform his obligations under the contract. This is called an anticipatory breach of contract, which entitles the innocent party to terminate performance of the contract immediately. The novel feature of anticipatory breach is that acceptance of the breach entitles the innocent party to claim damages at the date of the acceptance of the breach. He does not have to wait until the date fixed for performance, even though this has the effect of accelerating the obligations of the party in breach. It does seem somewhat illogical to say that a party can be in breach of contract *before* the time fixed for performance under the contract. The doctrine of anticipatory breach can best be rationalised as a breach of an implied term of the contract that neither party will, without just cause, repudiate his obligations under the contract before the time fixed for performance.

The operation of the doctrine of anticipatory breach can be illustrated by reference to the case of *Hochster* v. *De La Tour* (1853) 2 E & B 678. In April of 1852 the defendant agreed to employ the plaintiff to act as his courier for three months from 1 June. But on 11 May the defendant wrote to the plaintiff informing him that his services would no longer be required. The plaintiff commenced his action on 22 May and it was held that he was entitled to commence his action for damages at that date; he did not have to wait until 1 June, when performance was due.

Once again the innocent party is not obliged to exercise his right to terminate performance of the contract; he can elect to affirm the contract and demand performance from the other party at the time stipulated in the contract. But where the innocent party does decide to terminate performance of the contract he must give notice to the party in breach that he is accepting the anticipatory breach and he must not act inconsistently with his decision to accept the breach.

Where the innocent party does decide to affirm the contract and demand performance at the stipulated time, a number of consequences flow from this decision. The first is that affirmation does not prevent the innocent party accepting the breach if, at the date fixed for performance, the other party still refuses to perform. The second is that the innocent party, in addition to affirming the contract, may continue with the performance of his obligations under the contract, even though he knows that the performance is not wanted by that other party. This is what happened in the controversial case of *White and Carter (Councils) Ltd* v. *McGregor* [1962] AC 413. The defendants entered into a contract with the plaintiffs under which the plaintiffs agreed to display advertisements of the defendants' garage for a period of three years on plates attached to litter bins. Later the same day, the defendants wrote to the plaintiffs stating that they no longer wished to continue with performance of the contract. The plaintiffs refused to accept the cancellation and proceeded to display the advertisements for the three-year period and then brought an action to recover the contract price. The House of Lords held, by a majority of three to two, that the plaintiffs were entitled to recover the contract price. The minority held that the plaintiffs were not entitled to succeed because they had failed to mitigate their loss. The majority, however, held, quoting from the judgment of Asquith LJ in *Howard* v. *Pickford Tool Co Ltd* [1951] 1 KB 417, 421, that 'an unaccepted repudiation is a thing writ in water and of no value to anybody'. The plaintiffs were not under an obligation to accept the defendants' breach, even though it was 'unfortunate' that the plaintiffs had 'saddled themselves with an unwanted contract causing an apparent waste of time and money'.

The principle laid down in *White and Carter* is in fact the subject of a number of qualifications. The first is that the innocent party cannot compel the party in breach to co-operate with him so that, where the innocent party cannot continue with performance without the co-operation of the party in breach, he will be compelled to accept the breach (*Hounslow LBC* v. *Twickenham Garden Developments Ltd* [1971] Ch 233). The second qualification is derived from the judgment of Lord Reid in *White and Carter* when he said that 'it may well be that, if it can be shown that a person has no legitimate interest, financial or otherwise, in performing the contract rather than claiming damages, he ought not to be allowed to saddle the other party with an additional burden with no benefit to himself'.

Lord Reid's view on this point did not appear to be shared by the other members of the House of Lords, but it has subsequently been regarded as part of the ratio of the case (see *Hounslow LBC* v. *Twickenham Garden Developments Ltd* (above)) and it has been developed in subsequent cases as a means of limiting the principle established in *White and Carter*. In *Clea Shipping Corp* v. *Bulk Oil International Ltd (The Alaskan Trader)* [1984] 1 All ER 129, after an extensive review of the authorities, Lloyd J concluded that:

'there comes a point at which the court will cease, on general equitable principles, to allow the innocent party to enforce his contract according to its strict legal terms'.

This equitable jurisdiction cannot be invoked simply because the innocent party has behaved 'unreasonably'. The plaintiffs in *White and Carter* behaved unreasonably in continuing with performance of the contract, but they were nevertheless entitled to recover the contract price. But, where the innocent party acts 'wholly unreasonably' (*The Odenfield* [1978] 2 Lloyds Rep 357, 373), then the court may refuse to allow the innocent party to continue with performance and claim the contract price. Such was the case in *The Alaskan Trader* (above). The plaintiffs chartered a ship to the defendants for 24 months. After one year the ship required extensive repairs. The defendants stated that they had no further use for the ship but the plaintiffs nevertheless spent £800 000 in repairing the ship and, when it was repaired, they kept the ship and its crew ready to receive instructions from the defendants. The arbitrator held that the plaintiffs had acted wholly unreasonably in failing to accept the breach and this finding was upheld on appeal to Lloyd J.

On the other hand, a decision to affirm the contract may work to the disadvantage of the innocent party. The first disadvantage is that an innocent party who affirms the contract may completely lose his right to sue for damages if the contract is frustrated between the date of the unaccepted anticipatory breach and the date fixed for performance (*Avery* v. *Bowden* (1856) 6 E & B 953). Secondly, an innocent party who affirms the contract but subsequently breaches the contract himself cannot argue that the unaccepted anticipatory breach excused him from his obligation to perform under the contract. Where the breach is not accepted the parties remain subject to their obligations under the contract, so that the 'innocent party' may find himself liable to pay damages for breach of contract if he fails to accept the breach and subsequently breaches the contract himself (*The Simona* [1988] 2 All ER 742).

Summary

1 A breach of contract is committed when a party without lawful excuse fails or refuses to perform what is due from him under the contract, performs defectively or incapacitates himself from performing.

2 The question whether or not a particular contract has been breached depends upon the precise construction of the terms of the contract. Many contractual duties are strict.

3 A breach of contract does not automatically bring a contract to an end. A breach of contract gives to the innocent party a right to claim damages and it may give him the additional right to terminate performance of the contract.

4 When the performance of a contract is terminated because of breach, the obligation to perform is only terminated for the future. The contract is not set aside *ab initio*.

5 An innocent party is not obliged to exercise his right to terminate performance of the contract; he can elect to terminate or to affirm, although the effect of the doctrine of mitigation is to reduce the scope for affirmation.

6 A party who is in breach of contract may be unable to enforce the contract against the innocent party. But where the breach is of an independent, rather than a dependent obligation, breach will not entitle the innocent party to abandon performance of his obligations under the contract.

7 One contracting party may inform the other party, before the time fixed for performance under the contract, that he will not perform his obligations under the contract. This is called an anticipatory breach of contract, which entitles the innocent party to terminate performance of the contract immediately.

8 An innocent party who affirms the contract after an anticipatory breach may continue with the performance of his obligations under the contract, even though he knows that the performance is not wanted by that other party, provided that contractual performance does not require the co-operation of the other party to the contract and he has a 'legitimate interest' in the performance of the contract.

Exercises

1 What is a breach of contract and what are its consequences?

2 Distinguish between 'rescission for breach' and 'rescission for misrepresentation'.

3 Distinguish between a primary obligation and a secondary obligation.

4 What is an anticipatory breach?

5 What 'legitimate interest' did the plaintiffs in *White and Carter (Councils) Ltd v. McGregor* have in the performance of the contract?

6 Did the plaintiffs in *The Alaskan Trader* (above) act 'wholly unreasonably'? (See further, Burrows, 1987, pp.278–82.)

7 Adam Ltd employ Steve to go to Japan and prepare an elaborate report for the company on the state of the Japanese market. Two days before Steve's departure, Adam Ltd inform Steve that they no longer require the report because they have decided not to commence trading in Japan. Steve nevertheless goes to Japan and prepares the report at a cost of £25 000. Adam Ltd are now refusing to pay for the report. Advise Steve.

20 Damages for Breach of Contract

20.1 Introduction

We have already noted that a breach of contract gives rise to an action for damages, whether the term broken is a condition, a warranty or an innominate term. In this chapter we shall discuss the principles which are applied by the courts when assessing the damages payable on a breach of contract. The principles applied by the courts are of great significance to the debate about the basis of the law of contract, to which we referred in Chapter 1. The claim that contract law can be separated from the law of tort and the law of restitution rests, to a large extent, on the proposition that the law of contract seeks to fulfil the expectations engendered by a binding promise (see 1.4). In this chapter we shall put that claim to the test by asking ourselves the fundamental question: does the law of contract really fulfil the expectations engendered by a binding promise? But before we seek to answer that question we must define the 'expectation interest' with greater precision and we must also examine the question as to whether the law of contract protects either the 'reliance interest' or the 'restitution interest'.

20.2 Compensation and the Different 'Interests'

The starting-point must be that the aim of an award of damages is to compensate the plaintiff for the loss which he has suffered as a result of the defendant's breach of contract. The aim is not to punish the defendant. A breach of contract is a civil wrong; it is not a criminal offence. Although punitive damages can, in certain narrowly defined circumstances, be awarded in a tort action, they cannot be awarded in a purely contractual action, even where the defendant has calculated that he will make a profit from his breach of contract (*Cassell & Co* v. *Broome* [1972] AC 1027). The defendant may be said to have behaved 'badly', but he will not be punished by an award of punitive damages.

The proposition that damages are compensatory gives rise to a further question: for what is it that the plaintiff is entitled to be compensated? Theoretically a plaintiff could claim compensation on one of a number of different grounds (see Fuller and Perdue, 1936). In the first place, a plaintiff could claim the protection of his 'expectation interest'. The basis of such a claim is that the plaintiff's expectations, engendered by the promise of the defendant that he will perform his contractual obligations, have not been fulfilled and that damages should compensate him for his disappointed expectations by putting him 'in as good a position as he would have occupied had the defendant performed his promise'. Secondly, a plaintiff may claim the protection of his 'reliance interest', that is to say that, as a result of the defendant's promise to perform his contractual obligations, the plaintiff has acted to his detriment in entering into the contract and the award of damages should compensate him to the extent that he has relied to his detriment upon the promise of the defendant. The aim here is 'to put the plaintiff in as good a position as he was in before the [defendant's] promise was made'. Finally, a plaintiff may assert that his 'restitution interest' should be protected. A plaintiff who claims the protection of his restitution interest does not wish to be compensated for the loss which he has suffered; rather, he wishes to deprive the defendant of a gain which he has made at the plaintiff's expense. Which of these 'measures' can be claimed by a plaintiff in an action for damages for breach of contract? More importantly, what factors would persuade a plaintiff to elect to seek the recovery of one measure rather than another?

The most important factor is obviously the amount of damages which a plaintiff can recover by way of compensation. Which is more advantageous to the plaintiff: the expectation measure, the reliance measure or the restitution measure? A very simple example will help us to answer this question. Let us suppose that I enter into a contract to purchase a word processor for £2000. Let us make the further assumption that the market value of such a word processor is, in fact, £2000. In breach of contract the seller provides me with a defective word processor which is worth only £1000.

An award of damages which protected my expectation interest would aim to put me in the position which I would have been in had the contract been performed according to its terms. Had the contract been performed according to its terms. I would have obtained a word processor worth £2000, whereas I have obtained a word processor which is worth only £1000. Therefore the expectation measure is calculated by deducting the value of what I have actually received (£1000) from the value of what I expected to receive (£2000). Damages would therefore be assessed at £1000.

An award of damages which sought to protect my reliance interest would seek to put me in the position which I would have been in had I not entered into the contract. Had I not entered into the contract, I would not have parted with my £2000 and I would not have received a word processor worth £1000. So the reliance measure is calculated by deducting the value of what I have received (£1000) from the amount which I have paid out (£2000). Damages would, once again, be assessed at £1000, so that, on the facts of this case, the expectation measure and the reliance measure would be exactly the same.

An award which sought to protect my restitution interest would restore to me the benefit which I had conferred upon the seller. So I would be entitled to the return of the £2000 and the seller would be entitled to the return of the word processor.

Although we have noted that the reliance measure and the expectation measure can be exactly the same, in other cases they can be radically different. The reason for the coincidence in my example was that the contract price and the market value of a word processor which complied with the contractual specifications were exactly the same. Had these figures been different, then the measures would have been different. Let us suppose that I had promised to pay £2000 but that the word processor was, in fact, worth only £1500. This time the expectation measure would be £1500 (the value of that I expected to receive) less £1000 (the value of what I actually received), which equals £500. But the reliance measure would be £2000 (what I paid out) minus £1000 (the value of what I received), which equals £1000. So a plaintiff will wish to resort to the reliance measure where he has made a bad bargain, in an effort to escape from the consequences of his own bargain. On the other hand, if I had made a good bargain so that the market value of the word processor was £2500, the expectation measure would be £2500 less £1000, which equals £1500, whereas the reliance measure would remain at £2000 less £1000, which equals £1000. Therefore it is only where the plaintiff had made a bad bargain that he will want to claim the reliance measure; in other cases the expectation measure will be more advantageous to a plaintiff.

20.3 The Expectation Interest

The general rule is that an award of damages for breach of contract seeks to protect the plaintiff's expectation interest. The classic statement of this general principle can be found in the judgment of Parke B in *Robinson* v. *Harman* (1848) 1 Ex 850, 855:

> 'the rule of the common law is, that where a party sustains loss by reason of a breach of contract, he is, so far as money can do it, to be placed in the same situation, with respect to damages, as if the contract had been performed'.

The justification for the award of the expectation measure is that a binding promise creates in the promisee an expectation of performance and the remedy granted for the breach of such a binding promise seeks to fulfil or to protect that expectation. But there is an element of ambiguity in the proposition that damages seek to put the plaintiff in the position he would have been in had the contract been performed.

Two possible measures could put the plaintiff in the position which he would have been in had the contract been performed according to its terms. The first is the difference in value between what the plaintiff has received and what he expected to receive and the second is the cost of putting the plaintiff into the position which he would have been in had the contract been fully performed. In many cases the two measures will produce the same result. For example, if, in breach of contract, a seller fails to deliver the promised goods, and the buyer goes out into the market place and purchases substitute goods, the diminution in value and the cost of cure will be exactly the same. But in some cases the two measures can produce very different results. The case of *Tito* v. *Waddell (No 2)* [1977] Ch 106, 328–38, neatly illustrates such a divergence. The defendants were granted licences to mine phosphate on a small island in the Pacific Ocean. They covenanted with the plaintiffs, who were the owners of the island, to restore the land when they had finished mining by replanting trees on the island. In breach of contract the defendants failed to carry out the replanting. The plaintiff islanders claimed damages for breach of contract. They claimed the cost of cure measure which was many thousands of pounds, but the defendants argued that the plaintiffs were only entitled to the diminution in value, which was a much smaller sum. Megarry vc held that the plaintiffs were entitled to the diminution in value measure because he was not satisfied that they intended to use the damages to carry out the replanting. But he held that, in 'normal circumstances', a plaintiff would be entitled to the cost of cure measure if he had carried out the work necessary to bring about the cure or if he satisfied the court that he intended to carry out that work.

The cost of cure measure was successfully recovered by the plaintiff in *Radford* v. *De Froberville* [1977] 1 WLR 1262. The plaintiff sold a portion of his land to the defendant and part of the agreement was that the defendant would build a boundary wall which would divide the plot which the defendant had bought from the plot which the plaintiff had retained. The defendant failed to build the wall. The plaintiff brought an action for damages for breach of contract. The defendant argued that the plaintiff was entitled to damages based on the dimunition in value of the land as a result of his breach of contract. However, the difference in value was nominal, so the plaintiff claimed the cost of cure, which was £1200 at the date of breach but, by the time of the trial of the action, had risen to £3400. Oliver J held that the plaintiff was entitled to the cost of cure measure because that measure was the most likely to achieve the aim of putting the plaintiff in the position which he would have been in had the contract been performed according to its terms, and he was satisfied that the plaintiff genuinely wanted the work carried out. What would have been the position if the plaintiff in *Radford* had intended to sell the property? It is suggested that, in such a case, the proper measure should be the diminution in value because the plaintiff's interest in the property would then be a purely financial one, namely to realise a profit on its sale, and the diminution in value would adequately protect his interest in that profit.

20.4 The Restitution Interest

Can a plaintiff seek the protection of his restitution interest rather than his expectation interest? The answer is that a plaintiff does not have a free choice between the two measures. A plaintiff can obtain a restitutionary remedy only when he can establish that the defendant was enriched, that the enrichment was at the plaintiff's expense and that it is unjust that the defendant retain the benefit without recompensing the plaintiff. The classic example of a restitutionary claim is a claim to recover money paid under a mistake of fact (see, for example, *Barclays Bank Ltd* v. *WJ Simms Ltd* [1980] 1 QB 677). But, where the ground on which restitution is sought is that the defendant has broken his contract with the plaintiff, then a restitutionary remedy is available only within very narrow confines. There are essentially two grounds (20.5–20.6) on which a plaintiff may seek to protect his restitution interest consequent upon a breach of contract by the defendant.

20.5 Failure of Consideration and Enrichment by Subtraction

The first ground on which a plaintiff may seek a restitutionary remedy is that the *basis* upon which he has conferred the benefit upon the defendant has failed because of the defendant's breach of contract. The argument of the plaintiff is that he has conferred a benefit upon the defendant only for the purpose of the performance of the contract, and now that performance has been abandoned because of the defendant's breach of contract, the benefit ought to be restored to him.

But money paid to a defendant is only recoverable upon such a ground where there has been a total failure of consideration, that is to say, the plaintiff has received no part of what he has bargained for. A simple example is a buyer who pays a seller in advance and the seller, in breach of contract, subsequently refuses to deliver the goods. The buyer can recover the prepayment on the ground that there has been a total failure of consideration. Such a claim may prove to be very useful to a plaintiff who has entered into a bad bargain, because his restitution interest will exceed his expectation interest. Let us suppose that I agree to buy, for £200, a desk which is in fact worth only £150. If, for some reason, the seller refused to deliver the desk, I would be able to recover the £200 because the consideration for the payment has wholly failed. I received no part of the promised performance and there is nothing to prevent me from recovering my £200 and purchasing a desk elsewhere for £150. Since there has been no performance of the contract, such a claim does not involve the court in placing a different value upon contractual performance than that agreed by the parties and so no objection can be raised to such a restitutionary claim. But, where the failure of consideration is only partial, that is to say, the plaintiff has received some part, no matter how small, of the promised performance then the restitutionary claim is barred (*Whincup* v. *Hughes* (1871) LR 6 CP 78). The reason for this would appear to be that, once contractual performance has begun, there is a real risk that a restitutionary claim would result in the court placing a different value upon contractual performance than that agreed by the parties because it cannot be assumed that the contract price is earned incrementally (contrast Burrows, 1984a).

Where the claim is not for the return of money but for the value of goods supplied or services rendered under the contract then more difficult questions arise. It is clear that, where the contract is terminated on the ground of the defendant's breach of contract, the plaintiff has a right to elect either to proceed in contract or in restitution (*Planché* v. *Colburn* (1831) 8 Bing 14), but it is not clear whether in a restitutionary action the contract price acts as a ceiling on the sum recoverable. Dicta can be found to support the proposition that the contract price does not act as a ceiling (*Lodder* v. *Slowey* [1904] AC 442) and such a rule was adopted in the American case of *Boomer* v. *Muir* 24 P 2d 570 (1933). But it is suggested that, given that breach operates prospectively (19.7), goods are supplied and services are rendered under what was, at the time, a valid subsisting contract, and it is difficult to see why the courts should ignore the contract in assessing the value of the goods supplied or services performed.

20.6 Enrichment by Wrongdoing

Secondly, a plaintiff may seek a restitutionary remedy on the ground that the defendant has, as a result of his breach of contract, obtained an unjust benefit, in the form of a profit which he would not otherwise have made. This claim differs from the first claim because here the defendant's enrichment is not by subtraction from the plaintiff (see Birks, 1985). In the 'failure of consideration' claim the defendant was enriched by the receipt of a benefit which passed from the plaintiff to the defendant. But in this type of case the defendant has been enriched by his wrongdoing, namely his breach of contract, and, in such a case, there is no requirement that the enrichment be by subtraction from the plaintiff.

The nature of such a claim can be illustrated by the fact situation of *Teacher* v. *Calder* (1899) 1 F (HL) 39. The defendant agreed to invest £15 000 in the plaintiff's timber business. The defendant broke the contract and invested the £15 000 in a distillery instead. The plaintiff sought to recover, by way of damages, the profits which the defendant had made as a result of his investment in the distillery. But it was held that the plaintiff was only entitled to recover the loss which his business had suffered as a result of the failure of the defendant to invest the promised £15 000. The aim of an award of damages in contract is to compensate the plaintiff for the loss which he has suffered and not to require the defendant to disgorge the gain which he has obtained from his breach. Could the plaintiff have recovered the defendant's gains as restitutionary damages? It is suggested that such a claim would have failed because restitutionary damages are not generally available on a breach of contract.

But cases can be found in which damages appear to have been assessed, not by reference to the plaintiff's loss, but by reference to the gain which the defendant has made as a result of the breach. One such case is *Penarth Dock Engineering* v. *Pound* [1963] 1 Lloyds Rep 359. The defendants were buyers of a floating dock and, in breach of contract, they failed to remove it from its berth. The plaintiff sellers sued for damages for breach of contract. The defendants argued that damages should be nominal because the sellers would not have made any other use of the berth as the docks were to be shut down. This argument was rejected on the ground that the measure of damages was not what the plaintiffs had lost, but the benefit which the defendants had obtained as a result of the breach, and so damages were awarded on the basis of a fair market rental of the berth. It is possible to bring these cases within the fold of compensatory damages by arguing that the plaintiff has suffered a real loss, namely the loss of the right to sell to the defendant the right to use his property (see Sharpe and Waddams, 1982). Although the cases can be squeezed within the compensatory framework, the more natural interpretation is that they are cases in which the aim of the award of damages was to strip the defendant of the gain which he had made as a result of his breach of contract.

Indeed it has been argued that the aim of the law would be better served if there were to be available to the innocent party a 'restitutionary claim for an accounting of the profit which a promisor has gained from his breach of contract' (Jones, 1983). Professor Jones argues that it is difficult to accept the 'justice' of a case such as *Tito* v. *Waddell (No 2)* (above) where the defendants saved themselves considerable expense by refusing to carry out the replanting and yet the plaintiffs' damages were 'trivial' because they had suffered no 'loss'. This does seem harsh. But, once it is recognised that a claim for loss of profits can arise, it is very difficult to define the limits of the claim. Would it only arise when the defendant deliberately or wilfully breached the contract? If so, what is a deliberate breach of contract? These are very difficult questions. Professor Jones concedes that the 'court should always retain a discretion to refuse an accounting if it thinks proper to do so'.

It is suggested that a plaintiff should only be entitled to claim restitutionary damages where compensatory damages are 'demonstrably an inadequate remedy, having regard to the objectives which the victim of the breach had hoped to achieve through full performance of the contract' (Birks, 1987). The injustice of a case such as *Tito* v. *Waddell* stems from the fact that compensatory damages appear to be manifestly inadequate. The *Penarth Dock* case can be explained on the same basis: compensatory damages were manifestly inadequate and so the plaintiff was entitled to claim restitutionary damages. But where, as in *Teacher* v. *Calder*, compensatory damages are adequate, then a plaintiff should not be entitled to recover the profits made by the defendant as a result of the breach. The plaintiff has been made whole and his expectations fulfilled by the award of compensatory damages and he has no claim on the profits made by the defendant as a result of the breach.

20.7 Reliance Interest

The plaintiff may wish to claim the protection of his reliance interest so that he is put in the position which he would have been in had he not entered into a contract with the defendant. It should be noted, however, that, where damages are awarded to fulfil the plaintiff's expectation interest, then the sum awarded will often include both gains prevented and losses caused because, had the contract been performed according to its terms, the plaintiff would have been reimbursed for his expenditure incurred as well as being rewarded by the receipt of his profit. A plaintiff is really only interested in attempting to recover his reliance interest alone where that interest exceeds his expectation interest.

The general rule, affirmed in *CCC Films (London) Ltd* v. *Impact Quadrant Films Ltd* [1985] QB 16, is that a plaintiff has an unfettered right to elect whether to claim for loss of bargain damages or for wasted expenditure. But that general rule is subject to an exception where the plaintiff seeks to recover his reliance loss in an attempt to escape the consequences of his bad bargain. In *C and P Haulage Co Ltd* v. *Middleton* [1983] 3 All ER 94, the plaintiff was given a licence to occupy premises on a renewable six monthly basis. He spent some money on improving the property, even though it was expressly provided in the contract that the fixtures were not to be removed at the end of the licence. The defendants ejected the plaintiff from the premises in breach of contract and the plaintiff sought to recover as damages the cost of the improvements which he had carried out to the property. His action failed on the ground that the breach had not caused him any loss because he would have been in the same position had the contract been terminated lawfully. The Court of Appeal held that the plaintiff's loss did not flow from the breach but from the fact that he had entered into a contract under which he had agreed that he would not be able to remove the fixtures at the end of the lease. It was held that a plaintiff could not recover his reliance losses where that would enable him to escape from his bad bargain or would reverse the contractual allocation of risk. It is for the defendant to show that the bargain was a bad one for the plaintiff. The only situation in which an innocent party can escape the consequences of his bad bargain is where there been a total failure of consideration (see 20.5). In such a situation there has been no performance under the contract and so there is no objection to the reversal of the contractual allocation of risk.

A plaintiff may, however, wish to recover his reliance loss where he has incurred reliance expenditure before the conclusion of the contract. In *Anglia Television Ltd* v. *Reed* [1972] 1 QB 60, the plaintiffs engaged the defendant to star in a film which they were making. At the last moment the defendant repudiated the contract and the plaintiffs had to abandon the film because they were unable to find a replacement actor. Lord Denning said that, where the plaintiffs claimed their loss of expenditure, they were not limited to expenditure incurred after the contract was concluded, but that they could also claim for expenditure incurred before the contract was concluded provided that it was within the reasonable contemplation of the parties that it would be likely to be wasted as a result of the defendant's breach. Such pre-contract expenditure could not be regarded as part of the expectation interest because there was no evidence that the plaintiffs would have made a net profit from the film and so would have recovered their pre-contract expenditure.

On the other hand, a plaintiff may be confined to the recovery of his reliance losses where he cannot prove what his expectation losses would have been. Such was the case in *McRae* v. *Commonwealth Disposals Commission* (1951) 84 CLR 377 (see 14.3), where the speculative nature of the enterprise made it impossible for the plaintiffs to quantify their expectations with any degree of precision. The High Court of Australia confined the plaintiffs to the recovery of their expenses incurred in mounting the salvage expedition and to the return of their prepayment. But *McRae* is an extreme case and the courts are extremely reluctant to conclude that the plaintiff's expectations are so speculative that they cannot be valued. In *Chaplin* v. *Hicks* [1911] 2 KB 786, the defendant, by his breach of contract, denied the plaintiff the opportunity to participate in a beauty contest. The court could not assess the likelihood of the plaintiff winning the contest but they awarded her damages of £100 to represent her loss of a chance to win the contest.

20.8 The Date of Assessment

One very important point relates to the date on which damages fall to be assessed. It was established in *Johnson* v. *Agnew* [1980] AC 367, that damages are to be assessed as at the date of breach. But, where the plaintiff is unaware of the breach, damages will generally be assessed as at the date on which the plaintiff could, with reasonable diligence, have discovered the breach. Similarly, where it is not reasonable to expect the plaintiff to take immediate steps to mitigate his loss, the date of assessment will be postponed until such time as it is reasonable to expect the plaintiff to mitigate his loss (*Radford* v. *De Froberville* (above)).

20.9 The Commitment to the Protection of the Expectation Interest

Although the stated purpose of the law of contract is to put the innocent party in the position which he would have been in had the contract been performed, there are a number of doctrines and rules which weaken the commitment of the law of contract to the protection of the expectation interest. In the following sections (20.10–20.14) we shall consider some of these doctrines.

20.10 Mitigation

A plaintiff is under a 'duty' to mitigate his loss. It is technically incorrect, however, to state that the plaintiff is under a 'duty' to mitigate his loss because he does not incur any liability if he fails to do so. The plaintiff is entirely free to act as he thinks fit but, if he fails to mitigate his loss, he will be unable to recover that portion of his loss which is attributable to his failure to mitigate. The aim of the doctrine of mitigation is to prevent the avoidable waste of resources. There are two aspects to the mitigation doctrine.

The first is that the injured party must take all reasonable steps to mitigate his loss. The plaintiff is not required to 'take any steps which a reasonable and prudent man would not ordinarily take in the course of his business' (*British Westinghouse Co* v. *Underground Electric Ry Co* [1912] AC 673); he is only obliged to take *reasonable* steps to minimise his loss. Thus, where a seller fails to deliver the goods, the buyer must generally go out into the market-place and purchase substitute goods. But a plaintiff need not take steps which would embroil him in complicated litigation (*Pilkington* v. *Wood* [1953] Ch 770), nor is he required to put his commercial reputation at risk (*James Finlay & Co Ltd* v. *Kwik Hoo Tong* [1929] 1 KB 400). The second aspect of the mitigation doctrine is that the plaintiff must not unreasonably incur expense subsequent to the breach of contract (*Banco de Portugal* v. *Waterlow & Sons Ltd* [1932] AC 452).

As Professor Atiyah has pointed out (1986b), the doctrine of mitigation 'does in practice make an enormous dent in the theory that the promisee is entitled to full protection for his expectations'. In Chapter 1 we discussed the following example. I enter into a contract to sell you 10 apples for £2. I refuse to perform my side of the bargain and am in breach of contract. But you must mitigate your loss. So you buy 10 apples for £2 at a nearby market. If you sue me for damages what is your loss? You have not suffered any and you cannot enforce my promise. As Professor Atiyah has stated (1979):

'the reality is that the bindingness of executory contracts protects not the expectation of performance, but the expectation of profit; and even that is only protected so long as the promisee cannot secure it elsewhere'.

This point is an extremely good one. Burrows (1983) seeks to meet the point by arguing that the duty to mitigate simply adds 'a supplementary policy to those policies justifying protection of the expectation interest; and this supplementary policy is that the promisee should not leave it simply to the courts to ensure fulfilment of his expectations, but should rather take it upon himself to adopt other reasonable means to ensure the fulfilment of his expectations'.

The existence of the doctrine of mitigation demonstrates that contract law is not wholeheartedly committed to the protection of the expectation interest and that its commitment, such as it is, can be displaced by other, 'supplementary' policies.

20.11 Remoteness

A plaintiff's expectation interest will not be fully protected where some of the loss which he has suffered is too 'remote' a consequence of the defendant's breach of contract. The doctrine of remoteness limits the right of the innocent party to recover damages to which he would otherwise be entitled. The principal justification for the existence of this doctrine is that it would be unfair to impose liability upon a defendant for all losses, no matter how extreme or unforeseeable, which flow from his breach of contract. The general test is that the plaintiff can only recover in respect of losses which were within the reasonable contemplation of the parties at the time of entry into the contract. But the courts have experienced great difficulty in deciding when a loss is, or is not, within the reasonable contemplation of the parties.

The foundation of the law can be traced back to the case of *Hadley* v. *Baxendale* (1854) 9 Exch 341. A shaft in the plaintiffs' mill broke. The defendant carriers agreed to carry the shaft to Greenwich so that it could be used as a pattern in the manufacture of a new shaft. The shaft was delayed in transit because of the negligence of the defendants and, in consequence, production was halted at the plaintiffs' mill. The plaintiffs sought to recover their loss of profits as damages for breach of contract. Alderson B held that:

'where two parties have made a contract which one of them has broken, the damages which the other party ought to receive in respect of such breach of contract should be such as may fairly and reasonably be considered either arising naturally, that is, according to the usual course of things, from such breach of contract itself, or such as may reasonably be supposed to have been in the contemplation of both parties, at the time they made the contract, as the probable result of the breach of it.'

There are two distinct limbs to the test established by Alderson B. The first is that the defendant is liable for such losses as occur 'naturally' or as a result of the 'usual course of things' after such a breach of contract. To qualify as a loss which has occurred 'naturally' there must have been a 'serious possibility' or a 'real danger' or a 'very substantial' probability that the loss would occur (*Koufos* v. *C. Czarnikow Ltd (The Heron II)* [1969] 1 AC 350). A defendant who agrees to supply or repair a chattel which is obviously being used for profit-making purposes is liable for the ordinary loss of profits suffered as a result of his failure to supply or repair the chattel timeously (*Fletcher* v. *Tayleur* (1855) 17 CB 21). Why could the plaintiffs not recover their loss of profits in *Hadley* when it must have been obvious to the carrier that the mill was being used for profit-making purposes? The answer is that the stoppage of the mill was not a 'natural' consequence of the carrier's delay because the plaintiffs might have had a spare shaft which could have kept the mill in production while the new shaft was being made.

Under the second limb a defendant may be liable for losses which did not arise 'naturally' but were within the reasonable contemplation of both parties at the time they made the contract. This test was not satisfied on the facts of *Hadley* because, although the plaintiffs were aware of the consequences of delay, they had not informed the defendants that delay would result in the halting of production and so the loss could not be said to have been in the reasonable contemplation of *both* parties. The defendant must at least know of the special circumstances (*Simpson* v. *London and North Western Railway Co* (1876) 1 QBD 274), and there is some suggestion in the case law that the plaintiff must go further and establish that the defendant agreed to assume liability for the exceptional loss (*Horne* v. *Midland Railway* (1873) LR 6 CP 131).

The distinction between losses which arise 'naturally' and 'special' losses is illustrated by the case of *Victoria Laundry (Windsor) Ltd* v. *Newman Industries Ltd* [1949] 2 KB 528. The defendants contracted to sell and deliver a boiler to the plaintiffs. The defendants knew that the plaintiffs wished to put the boiler into immediate use in their laundry business. The boiler was delivered some five months late. The plaintiffs sued to recover the loss of profits which they had suffered as a result of the late delivery. The Court of Appeal held that the defendants were liable for the loss of profits which naturally flowed from their breach of contract. But the defendants were not liable for the loss of profits on some exceptionally lucrative contracts which the plaintiffs had entered into with the Ministry of Supply. The defendants did not know of the existence of these contracts and so the loss of profit on these contracts was not within the reasonable contemplation of both parties.

The effect of the second limb of the test established by Alderson B is to encourage contracting parties to disclose exceptional losses which may be suffered as a result of the breach. Where, as in the *Victoria Laundry* case, the plaintiff suffers an unusually large loss, he will be unable to recover that loss unless he draws it to the attention of the defendant at the time of contracting. The rule therefore encourages risk sharing; it enables the parties to assess the scope of their likely liability and to take out insurance cover accordingly.

One difficult question which remains to be discussed is whether the test for remoteness of damage in contract differs from the test for remoteness of damage in tort. In a negligence action damage is too remote a consequence of the defendant's breach of duty where the kind of damage which the plaintiff has suffered was not reasonably foreseeable by the defendant (*Overseas Tankship (UK) Ltd* v. *Morts Dock and Engineering Co Ltd (The Wagon Mound) (No 1)* [1961] AC 388). Despite suggestions that reasonable foresight of loss is also the determining factor in a contractual action (see Asquith LJ, in *Victoria Laundry (Windsor) Ltd* v. *Newman Industries Ltd* (above)), it was established by the House of Lords in *The Heron II* (above) that the remoteness test in contract is narrower than the remoteness test in tort because in a contractual action the loss must be within the reasonable contemplation of the parties at the time of entry into the contract. However, this view was challenged by Lord Denning in *H Parsons (Livestock) Ltd* v. *Uttley Ingham & Co Ltd* [1978] QB 791, when he argued that, at least in relation to physical damage cases, the remoteness test was the same in contract and in tort. Although Lord Denning was in the minority in *Parsons*, it must be noted that Scarman LJ did state that it would be absurd if the amount of damages recoverable were to depend upon whether the plaintiffs' cause of action was in contract or in tort. This issue awaits clarification by the House of Lords. It may be that, where the plaintiff has a cause of action in contract or in tort, the remoteness test applicable will be the reasonable foresight test (being more favourable to the plaintiff) but that, where the action is a purely contractual one, the test applicable will be the narrower reasonable contemplation test.

20.12 Causation

A plaintiff will be unable to recover damages in respect of the loss which he has suffered if he cannot establish a causal link between his loss and the defendant's breach of contract. The defendant's breach need not be the sole cause of the loss to the plaintiff, but it must be a cause of the loss.

For example, the independent act of a third party may break the chain of causation between the defendant's breach and the plaintiff's loss, unless the defendant has actually promised to guard against the very thing which has actually happened (*London Joint Stock Bank* v. *Macmillan* [1918] AC 777). Natural events may also break the chain of causation, as was argued in the case of *Monarch Steamship Co* v. *Karlshamns Oljefabrieker* [1949] AC 196. The defendants entered into a contract in April 1939 to carry goods from Manchuria to Sweden. In breach of contract, the defendants failed to provide a ship which was seaworthy. This resulted in a delay in the voyage so that the ship failed to get to Sweden before the outbreak of war in September 1939. As a result of the outbreak of war, the ship was ordered to a Scottish port where the goods had to be transferred to neutral vessels before being shipped to

Sweden. The plaintiffs had to pay the cost of the transport in the neutral vessels and they sought to recover the sums paid as damages for breach of contract. The defendants argued that the outbreak of war broke the chain of causation between their breach of contract and the cost incurred by the plaintiffs in shipping the goods to Sweden in neutral vessels. This argument was rejected by the House of Lords on the ground that the outbreak of war was a likely event at the time that the contract was concluded in April 1939 and so it could not be held to amount to a break in the chain of causation.

An act of the plaintiff may be so unreasonable that it breaks the chain of causation between the defendant's breach and the plaintiff's loss. In *Lambert* v. *Lewis* [1982] AC 225, a farmer continued to use a trailer coupling after it was broken. The farmer was held to be liable in damages to persons who were injured in an accident caused by the coupling giving way. The farmer sought to recover an indemnity from the supplier of the coupling. It was held that the farmer could not recover because his continued use of the coupling, in the knowledge that it was damaged, broke the chain of causation between the supplier's breach of contract and the 'loss' suffered by the farmer in having to pay damages to the accident victims. Where the plaintiff has been negligent and that negligence has contributed to the damage which he has suffered, but it is not sufficient to break the chain of causation, then it remains unclear whether the damages payable to the plaintiff fall to be reduced under the Law Reform (Contributory Negligence) Act 1945 (see *Forsikringsaktie-selskapet Vesta* v. *Butcher* [1988] 2 All ER 43).

20.13 Damages for Pain and Suffering and the 'Consumer Surplus'

Damages are generally assessed by reference to the market value of the promised contractual performance; that is to say, the plaintiff's loss is objectively assessed. Such an objective approach may lead to the undercompensation of a plaintiff because it does not take account of the plaintiff's subjective valuation of the contractual performance, which may be considerably more than the market value (called the 'consumer surplus', see Harris, Ogus and Phillips, 1979). Occasionally the courts will protect the 'consumer surplus', for example, by granting a specific performance order when the subject-matter of the contract is 'unique' or by awarding damages assessed on a cost of cure basis (see *Radford* v. *De Froberville* (above)).

But the courts are generally unwilling to compensate a plaintiff for his purely 'subjective' losses. Yet consumers frequently suffer such losses. For example, the value of family wedding photographs will generally exceed their market value because of their sentimental value to members of the family. But the courts have traditionally refused to award damages to compensate a plaintiff for any mental distress which he has suffered as a result of the defendant's breach of contract. In *Addis* v. *Gramophone*

Co Ltd [1909] AC 488, the plaintiff sought to recover damages for the indignity which he had suffered in being sacked from his job in a 'humiliating' manner. The House of Lords held that the plaintiff was not entitled to be compensated for the injury to his feelings.

However there is no longer an absolute rule that damages cannot be recovered for mental distress. The courts have recognised that damages for mental distress can be awarded where the predominant object of the contract was to obtain some mental satisfaction (such as a holiday, *Jarvis* v. *Swan's Tours Ltd* [1973] QB 233), or to relieve a source of distress (*Heywood* v. *Wellers* [1976] 1 QB 446). In the immediate aftermath of cases such as *Jarvis* v. *Swan's Tours Ltd* (above), it seemed that damages for mental distress would be available in a wider range of circumtances than had previously been the case (see *Cox* v. *Phillips Industries Ltd* [1976] 3 All ER 161). But such an expansive approach was subsequently rejected by the Court of Appeal in *Bliss* v. *South East Thames RHA* [1987] ICR 700. Indeed, in *Hayes* v. *Dodds* (1988) NLJ Reports 259, Staughton LJ stated that, while damages for mental distress are recoverable where the object of the contract is the provision of comfort or pleasure or the relief of discomfort, damages are not recoverable for mental distress where the object of the contract is: 'simply carrying on a commercial activity with a view to profit'. He stated that he did not

'view with enthusiasm the prospect that every shipowner in the Commercial Court, having successfully claimed for unpaid freight or demurrage, would be able to add a claim for mental distress suffered while he was waiting for his money'.

The courts therefore remain reluctant to award damages to compensate a plaintiff for his 'subjective' losses or to protect his 'consumer surplus' and, to that extent, damages may undercompensate a plaintiff.

20.14 Conclusion

It can be seen that there are a number of doctrines which limit the commitment of the law of contract to the protection of the plaintiff's expectation interest. The existence of these rules and doctrines throws into doubt the validity of the claim that the law of contract protects the expectation interest. However, before reaching a conclusion on this fundamental issue, it is necessary to consider the steps which can be taken by contracting parties to ensure that an adequate remedy is obtained and that the expectation interest is fully protected. These issues are the subject-matter of our final chapter.

Summary

1 The aim of an award of damages is to compensate the plaintiff for the loss which he has suffered as a result of the defendant's breach of contract. The aim is not to punish the defendant.

2 The aim of an award of damages is to put the plaintiff in the position which he would have been in had the contract been performed according to its terms. This is generally calculated by the diminution in value measure, not the cost of cure measure.

3 A plaintiff can recover a benefit which he has conferred on the party in breach where there has been a total failure of consideration. A defendant is not generally required to disgorge the benefits which he has obtained as a result of his breach of contract.

4 A plaintiff may elect to recover his reliance rather than his expectation loss, unless he is seeking to escape the consequences of a bad bargain.

5 A plaintiff must take reasonable steps to mitigate his loss. The existence of a 'duty' to mitigate demonstrates that contract law is not wholeheartedly committed to the protection of the expectation interest.

6 Damages cannot be recovered where the loss which the plaintiff has suffered is too remote a consequence of the defendant's breach of contract. The general rule is that a loss is not too remote if it was within the reasonable contemplation of both parties at the time of entry into the contract.

7 The plaintiff must establish that his loss was caused by the defendant's breach of contract.

8 The general rule is that damages cannot be recovered for mental distress suffered as a result of the defendant's breach of contract, unless the predominant object of the contract was to obtain some mental satisfaction or to relieve a source of distress.

Exercises

1 Define and distinguish between the expectation interest, the reliance interest and the restitution interest.

2 Is the law of contract committed to the protection of the expectation interest?

3 Is a court ever justified in awarding damages by reference to the gain which the defendant has made as a result of the breach rather than by reference to the loss which the plaintiff has suffered?

4 Fire Prevention Ltd entered into a contract with Borchester Town Council, under which they agreed to provide a fire-fighting service of 15 fire engines and 40 firemen. In breach of contract Fire Prevention only supplied 12 fire engines and 35 men and thereby saved themselves £40 000. Borchester cannot show that they have suffered any loss as a result of Fire Prevention's breach because they cannot prove that Fire Prevention failed to extinguish any fire. Can Borchester recover damages from Fire Prevention? If so, on what basis would a court assess damages? (See *City of New Orleans* v. *Fireman's Charitable Association* 9 So 486 (1891).)

5 John, who had recently left his wife, booked a holiday with Harry's Tour Company Ltd. The holiday did not live up to expectations. John now suffers from severe depression. He has been advised by his doctors to give up his job. The depression has been caused partly by the break-up of his marriage and partly by the aggravation of his disappointing holiday. Advise John.

21 Obtaining an Adequate Remedy

21.1 Introduction

In Chapter 20 the point was made that the law of contract is not wholeheartedly committed to the protection of the plaintiff's expectation interest and that a damages award may therefore undercompensate the plaintiff. We also noted that such undercompensation throws into doubt the claim that contract law protects the expectation interest. In this chapter we shall consider the extent to which the law of contract provides alternative remedies or enables contracting parties to incorporate into their contracts clauses which will ensure that the 'innocent party' (that is, the party who is not in breach) can obtain an adequate remedy in the event of a breach of contract.

At the beginning of this book (1.5) we noted that the role of the lawyer and of the law of contract is greater at the planning stage of a contract than after a breach has occurred. It is at the remedial stage that the role of the lawyer and of contract law is at its most important. On the one hand, one contracting party will probably wish to exclude or restrict his liability for breach of contract by an appropriately drafted exclusion or limitation clause, while the other party will wish to ensure that an effective and adequate remedy is available to him in the event of a breach of contract.

In seeking to ensure that a contracting party obtains an adequate remedy in the event of a breach of contract, we must extend our discussion beyond the remedy of damages. There are many methods which can be used in an effort to ensure that an effective remedy is obtained. In the first place the contract can be structured in such a way as to entitle one party to withhold the performance of his obligations (21.2) or to entitle one party to terminate performance and claim loss of bargain damages (21.3) or to make a claim in debt for the contract price (21.4). Such remedies may provide a powerful incentive to the other party to refrain from breaking the contract and to perform his obligations under the contract. Alternatively, the parties may make provision in their contract for a sum of money to be payable by way of damages in the event of breach (21.5–21.8). Finally, an adequate remedy can be obtained by seeking an order of specific performance (21.9) or an injunction restraining a threatened breach of contract (21.10). We shall now consider these remedies in greater detail and conclude with a very brief assessment of the significance of the remedial consequences of a breach of contract for the basis, or the theory, of contract law.

21.2 The Entire Contracts Rule

The ability of one contracting party to withhold performance of his obligations under the contract gives to the other party an extremely powerful incentive to perform his contractual obligations. An example will illustrate the point. A house-owner and a builder enter into a contract under which the builder agrees to build a garage for £6000. The contract states that payment shall be made upon satisfactory completion of the work by the builder. The house-owner's obligation to pay the promised sum is therefore dependent upon satisfactory completion by the builder. Should the builder, in breach of contract, fail to complete the work he will, as a general rule, be unable to sue for payment. His claim will be barred by the entire contracts rule or, more accurately, the entire obligations rule.

The origin of this rule can be traced back to the old case of *Cutter* v. *Powell* (1795) 6 TR 320. Cutter agreed with Powell to 'proceed, continue and do his duty as second mate' on a ship sailing from Jamaica to England. Cutter died on the journey to England and his widow sued to recover the wages which she alleged were payable in respect of the period of time in which Cutter had satisfactorily performed his duties before his death. Her action failed because Cutter was not entitled to payment unless he completed the voyage. The rule was no completion, no pay. This rule gives a powerful incentive to a contracting party to ensure, as far as is possible, that the contract is carried out according to its terms. But it can lead to the apparent unjust enrichment of the 'innocent party'. In *Cutter* v. *Powell*, Powell obtained the services of Cutter for some seven weeks but was not required to pay for any 'benefit' which he had obtained.

In practice, the hardships to which this rule can give rise are mitigated by its many exceptions. The principal exception is that the rule does not apply where the party in breach has substantially performed his obligations under the contract (*Bolton* v. *Mahadeva* [1972] 1 WLR 1009). In such a case the innocent party must perform his obligations under the contract and content himself with an action for damages for breach. Secondly, the innocent party may be required to recompense the party in breach if he accepts the latter's part performance. This is generally difficult to establish because the acceptance of the innocent party occurs in the context of complete contractual performance and is generally not pro-ratable. Part performance was not what was requested. It was full performance or nothing. In our example, a garage is a benefit to the house-owner, but a partly built garage is not; indeed, it may be more of a nuisance (*Sumpter* v. *Hedges* [1898] 1 QB 673). Finally, the court may interpret the contract as consisting of a number of divisible obligations so that, once the divisible obligation has been completely performed, the party in breach may claim the sum promised in relation to the performance of that obligation. Many contracts contain a number of divisible obligations; for example, a building contract will usually provide for payment at intervals, usually against an architect's or engineer's certificate.

The ability of contracting parties to take steps to minimise the impact of the entire contracts rule has probably preserved the rule as part of English law. Although the Law Commission originally recommended (1983) that the party in breach be given a restitutionary remedy for the value of his part performance of an entire contract, the Commission appear to have had a change of heart, and legislation to abrogate the entire contracts rule is no longer forthcoming (see Burrows, 1984a).

21.3 The Creation of Conditions

Another effective remedy is to threaten to terminate performance of the contract in the event of a repudiatory breach of contract and claim loss of bargain damages. The effectiveness of such a step can be seen from the case of *Lombard North Central plc* v. *Butterworth* [1987] QB 527 (see 10.3). By providing in clause 2 of the agreement that the obligation to pay each instalment punctually was of the essence of the contract, the owners were able to terminate performance of the contract and claim loss of bargain damages when the hirer failed to pay an instalment timeously. Clause 2 was not subject to the penalty clause rule (see 21.5–21.6) because the Court of Appeal held that the parties were free to classify as a condition a clause which would not otherwise be regarded as a condition. Therefore, by careful draftsmanship which ensures that any term likely to be broken is elevated to the status of a 'condition' which is of the 'essence of the contract', the innocent party can be given the ability to threaten termination of performance of the contract and to claim loss of bargain damages. This will give the other party a powerful incentive to perform his obligations under the contract and ensure that, where the contract is broken, an effective remedy is obtained.

21.4 A Claim in Debt

A debt is a definite sum of money which the defendant, under the terms of the contract, is due to pay to the plaintiff. It is therefore distinct from a claim in damages. The principal issue in a debt action is whether the money is *due* to the plaintiff. The plaintiff does not have to show that he has mitigated his loss, nor are the remoteness rules applicable. His action is simply to recover the sum due; no more, no less. The classic example of a claim in debt is an action to recover the contract price where goods have been delivered and the buyer has not paid for them. The advantage of a claim in debt can be seen from an examination of *White and Carter (Councils) Ltd* v. *McGregor* [1962] AC 413 (see 19.9), where the plaintiffs were able to recover the contract price and were not obliged to take steps to mitigate their loss. Such an action also enjoys certain procedural advantages (see Rules of the Supreme Court, Order 14). There are therefore distinct advantages in drafting a contract in such a way as to create a debtor–creditor relationship between the parties, so as to provide the creditor with an effective remedy should the 'debtor' default in making payment.

21.5 Liquidated Damages

An alternative method of avoiding undercompensation is to insert into the contract a clause which states the amount of money which shall be payable in the event of a breach of contract. Such a clause also helps to eliminate uncertainty because it enables the parties to know in advance the extent of their potential liability and to take out insurance cover accordingly. However, the courts have retained a jurisdiction to control the content of such clauses. The basic rules which the courts have established may be stated in the following terms. If the clause represents a genuine pre-estimate of the loss which is likely to be occasioned by the breach, then it is a 'liquidated damages clause' and is enforceable. In quantifying the 'loss' which is likely to be occasioned by the breach, it is the *actual* loss which is the relevant sum, so that it is no objection that part of that loss would have been irrecoverable on the ground that it was too remote (*Robophone Facilities Ltd* v. *Blank* [1966] 1 WLR 1428, 1447). The sum stipulated in the liquidated damages clause is the sum recoverable, even though that sum is greater or smaller than the loss which has actually been suffered.

But if the sum stated in the clause is not a genuine pre-estimate of loss, it is a 'penalty clause' and is unenforceable. The aim of such a clause is to punish the party in breach and the courts have held that such an aim is impermissible. A clause which is held to be a penalty clause is not struck out of the contract, but it will not be enforced by the court beyond the actual loss of the party seeking to rely on the clause (*Jobson* v. *Johnson* [1989] 1 All ER 621). The court is not required to consider whether the party in breach is entitled to relief; the court automatically relegates the party seeking to rely on the penalty clause to a claim in damages.

The distinction between a liquidated damages clause and a penalty clause rests ultimately on the intention of the parties at the time of entry into the contract: that is to say, was the clause a genuine attempt to assess the loss likely to be occasioned by the breach or was it designed to punish the party in breach? The fact that the parties have described the clause as a 'liquidated damages clause' or a 'penalty clause' is a relevant factor but it is not conclusive (*Elphinstone* v. *Monkland Iron and Coal Co* (1886) 11 App Cas 332). The difference between a liquidated damages clause and a penalty clause is in fact a question of construction and the courts have established a number of rules of construction which they apply in deciding whether a particular clause is a penalty clause or a liquidated damages clause.

The source of these rules of construction can be found in the judgment of Lord Dunedin in *Dunlop Pneumatic Tyre Co Ltd* v. *New Garage & Motor Co Ltd* [1915] AC 79. Lord Dunedin stated, firstly, that a clause will be held to be a penalty clause

'if the sum stipulated for is extravagant and unconscionable in amount in comparison with the greatest loss that could conceivably be proved to have followed from the breach'.

The second rule is that a clause is a penalty clause

'if the breach consists only in not paying a sum of money, and the sum stipulated is a sum greater than the sum which ought to have been paid'.

The third rule is that

'there is a presumption (but no more) that it is a penalty when "a single lump sum is made payable by way of compensation, on the occurrence of one or more or all of several events, some of which may occasion serious and others but trifling damage" '.

This presumption can act as a trap for the unwary. Contract draftsmen must seek to distinguish between serious and trifling breaches of contract, because a failure to distinguish between the two may result in the clause being held to be a penalty clause. The fourth rule of construction is that

'it is no obstacle to the sum stipulated being a genuine pre-estimate of damage, that the consequences of the breach are such as to make precise pre-estimation almost an impossibility. On the contrary, that is just the situation when it is probable that pre-estimated damage was the true bargain between the parties'.

We have already noted that a penalty clause is invalid and unenforceable. This leads to a potential anomaly where the loss which the innocent party has suffered is greater than the sum stipulated in the contract. In such a case, can the innocent party argue that the clause is a penalty clause, so that it can be ignored and he can recover his actual loss? In *Wall* v. *Rederiaktiebogalet Luggude* [1915] 3 KB 66, it was held that the innocent party could do this and recover his actual loss, although the issue has been the subject of vigorous debate among academic lawyers (see Hudson, 1974 and 1975; Gordon, 1974; Barton, 1976). It should also be noted that a liquidated damages clause may validly provide for the payment of a sum of money which is less than the estimated loss

(*Cellulose Acetate Silk Co* v. *Widnes Foundry (1925) Ltd* [1933] AC 20, although where the clause is held to 'exclude or restrict' liability for breach of contract it may be caught by s.3 of the Unfair Contract Terms Act 1977, see 11.9).

21.6 Evading the Penalty Clause Rule

However, it is possible to evade the clutches of the penalty clause rule by clever draftsmanship. Three principal devices can be used to avoid the rule. The first is that the penalty clause rule does not apply to a clause which simply accelerates an existing liability. An example will illustrate the point. Suppose that two parties enter into a contract of hire under which the entire rental is stated to be payable at the date of entry into the contract. The contract further provides that the hirer shall be entitled to pay the rental by instalments, provided that certain conditions are met, but that, in the event of default in payment of any instalment, the whole balance shall immediately become payable. Such an acceleration of liability is not caught by the penalty clause rule (*Protector Loan Co* v. *Grice* (1880) 5 QBD 592). The same principle applies where a creditor agrees to accept part payment of a debt in full discharge of the debt, provided that certain conditions are met, but stipulates that, if the conditions are not met, he will be entitled to recover the original debt in full (*The Angelic Star* [1988] 1 Lloyds Rep 122). The crucial ingredient in these cases is that there must be 'a present debt, which by reason of an indulgence given by the creditor is payable either in the future, or in a lesser amount, provided that certain conditions are met' (*O'Dea* v. *Allstates Leasing System (WA) Pty Ltd* (1983) 57 ALJR 172, 174). So by clever draftsmanship a 'present debt' can be created and the subsequent 'acceleration' of that liability to pay is outside the scope of the penalty clause rule.

The second device is to stipulate that the sum shall be payable on an event which is not a breach of contract. The penalty clause rule applies *only* to sums of money which are payable on a breach of contract. A good example of the potential for evasion is provided by the case of *Alder* v. *Moore* [1961] 2 QB 57. The defendant, who was a professional footballer, suffered serious injury and he was certified as being disabled to such an extent that he was unable to play professional football. The plaintiff insurers paid him £500 under an insurance policy which had been taken out to cover the defendant in the event of him suffering permanent total disablement. The defendant covenanted with the plaintiffs that:

'In consideration of the above payment I hereby declare and agree that I will take no part as a playing member of any form of professional football and that in the event of infringement of this condition I will be subject to a penalty of [£500].'

The defendant later resumed his playing career and the insurers sought to recover the £500 which they had paid to him. The defendant argued that the clause was unenforceable because it was a penalty clause. But the majority of the Court of Appeal held that the penalty clause rule was not applicable. The defendant had not promised that he would not play football again. Therefore the £500 was not payable upon a breach of contract and the penalty clause rule was irrelevant. This rule can lead to anomalous results. For example, a hirer who breaks the contract of hire-purchase by failing to pay the instalments can invoke the penalty clause rule if the owners seek to recover an 'excessive' sum of money from him as a result of his breach of contract. But, where the hirer honestly admits that he can no longer pay the instalments, and exercises his right under the contract to return the goods, such a hirer will have no defence to an action by the owners for an 'excessive' sum of money because the sum is not payable on a breach of contract (see *Bridge* v. *Campbell Discount Co Ltd* [1962] AC 600). Lord Denning pointed out the absurdity of this rule. He stated that equity has committed itself to the 'absurd paradox' that 'it will grant relief to a man who breaks his contract but will penalise the man who keeps it'. The response of the courts has been that the penalty clause rule only regulates the sums payable upon a breach of contract; any unfairness which lies in other parts of the contract cannot be dealt with by the penalty clause rule (see *Export Credits Guarantee Department* v. *Universal Oil Products Co* [1983] 1 WLR 399). The 'absurdity' which Lord Denning has pointed out stems from the fact that English law has refused to recognise the existence of a general doctrine of unconscionability (see 17.6). Instead, it has sought to deal with problems of contractual unfairness in a piecemeal manner. The price of such an approach is that, where the weaker contracting party is unable to bring his case within one of the existing identifiable categories, his claim for relief is likely to fail.

The third device which can be used to evade the penalty clause rule is to avoid the use of a clause which states that a specified sum of money shall be payable in the event of a breach of contract. There is always a risk that such a clause will be held to be a penalty clause. But, if the parties simply provide that the term is a condition which is of the essence of the contract, breach of that term will entitle the innocent party to terminate performance and claim loss of bargain damages. The elevation of a particular term into a condition is not caught by the penalty clause rule (see *Lombard North Central plc* v. *Butterworth* (above), noting in particular that clause 6, which did seek to quantify the sum payable on breach, was held to be a penalty clause and was therefore unenforceable. Contrast the decision of the Court of Appeal in *Financings Ltd* v. *Baldock* [1963] 2 QB 104).

21.7 Deposits and Part Payments

A clause in a contract which states that a certain sum of money shall be payable on a breach of contract inevitably runs the risk that it will be held to be a penalty clause. It also has the disadvantage that the innocent party has to take the initiative to obtain the money. A preferable alternative might therefore be to obtain payment of a sum of money in advance and then refuse to return it in the event of the other party breaking the contract.

In such a case, can the party in breach recover the prepayment? The answer to that question depends upon whether the money was paid as a deposit or as a part payment of the price. A deposit is paid by way of security and is generally irrecoverable, whereas a part payment is paid towards the contract price and is generally recoverable. The difference between the two is a matter of construction. Where the contract is neutral, then a payment will generally be interpreted as a part payment (*Dies* v. *British and International Mining and Finance Co* [1939] 1 KB 715).

Where the payment is held to be a deposit, the rule established in *Howe* v. *Smith* (1884) 27 Ch D 89, is that a deposit is irrecoverable. A deposit which was due before the date of discharge but which has not been paid is forfeitable (*Hinton* v. *Sparkes* (1868) LR 3 CP 161). This rule is capable of causing great hardship to the party in breach because the deposit may have been much larger than the loss occasioned by the breach of contract. This was recognised by Denning and Somervell LJJ in *Stockloser* v. *Johnson* [1954] 1 QB 476, when they held that a deposit may be recoverable in equity if the forfeiture clause was of a penal nature and if it was unconscionable for the innocent party to retain the money. This sweeping jurisdiction has not been well received in subsequent cases (see *Galbraith* v. *Mitchenhall Estates Ltd* [1965] 2 QB 743). Authority can, however, be found to support the proposition that the courts may intervene to relieve against the forfeiture of proprietary or possessory interests, if that forfeiture is unconscionable (*Sport International Bussum BV* v. *Inter-Footwear Ltd* [1984] 1 WLR 776 and *BICC plc* v. *Burndy Corp* [1985] Ch 232) but the courts are extremely reluctant to invoke this jurisdiction between commercial parties of equal bargaining power who are bargaining at arm's length (*The Scaptrade* [1983] 2 AC 694). The discretionary nature of this equitable jurisdiction to grant relief against forfeiture should be contrasted with the 'automatic' equitable relief granted when a clause is held to be a penalty clause (see *Jobson* v. *Johnson* [1989] 1 All ER 621, especially pp.633–4).

Where the sum paid is held to be a part payment, the general rule is that the sum is recoverable by the party in breach. This rule can be traced back to the case of *Dies* v. *British and International Mining and Finance Co* (above). The plaintiff contracted to purchase ammunition and made a prepayment of £100 000. In breach of contract the plaintiff refused to accept delivery. The defendants terminated the contract and the plaintiff sued to recover the £100 000. Stable J held that the plaintiff was entitled to recover the money paid, subject to the right of the defendants to recover damages for the breach. The initial payment was a conditional one; it was conditional upon subsequent performance of the contract and, when that condition failed because of the termination of the contract consequent upon the plaintiff's breach of contract, the defendants' right to retain the money simultaneously failed (see Beatson, 1981). However, the rule in *Dies* did not emerge unscathed from a re-examination by the House of Lords in *Hyundai Shipbuilding and Heavy Industries Co Ltd* v. *Papadopoulos* [1980] 1 WLR 1129. Shipbuilders sought to recover an instalment which they alleged was due to them by the defendant guarantors. It was held that the shipbuilders were entitled to the recovery of the instalment. Lord Fraser distinguished *Dies* on the ground that the latter case was not a case in which the vendors were required to incur any expenditure or perform any work in the performance of their obligations under the contract. It was a simple contract of sale. *Hyundai*, on the other hand, involved a contract for work and materials, under which the shipbuilders incurred expense in the building of the ship. The conclusion that can be derived from *Hyundai* is that, where it is clear from the contract that the payee will have to incur reliance expenditure before completing his performance of the contract, then, in the absence of a stipulation in the contract to the contrary, the part payment will be irrecoverable. A part payment is therefore recoverable only where it is clear from the contract that the payee will not have to incur reliance expenditure before completing his performance of the contract.

The combination of *Hyundai* and *The Scaptrade* suggests that the courts are restricting the right of the party in breach to recover any prepayments which he has made. This has been done by narrowing the ambit of the rule in *Dies* and by seeking to limit the scope of the equitable jurisdiction established in *Stockloser* v. *Johnson* (above). Thus there may be a distinct advantage in obtaining money in advance by way of a prepayment, rather than having to wait and make a claim in damages in the event of a breach of contract occurring.

21.8 Liquidated Damages, Penalty Clauses and Forfeitures: An Assessment

Why should different rules apply to penalty clauses and deposits? Can the existence of these equitable jurisdictions be justified? Should freedom of contract not prevail so that the parties can be left free to stipulate the amount of damages payable in the event of a breach? What is the point of these rules if they can be evaded by the clever draftsmanship of the more powerful party? These are all difficult questions to answer.

Given the tendency which we have noted for damages to undercompensate, a number of arguments can be adduced in favour of leaving the parties free to make their own assessment of the damages payable upon a breach. The first is the argument from freedom of contract, that the parties should be free to stipulate the sums payable on breach. The second is that it would avoid the artificiality of the present rules, many of which can be evaded by careful draftsmanship. The third is that it would reduce the uncertainty caused by the present possibility of judicial review.

On the other hand, a number of arguments can be adduced against the abolition of these equitable jurisdictions. It can be argued that it is for the courts to decide the compensation which is payable upon a breach of contract and that it is not for the parties to set compensation at a level higher than that permitted by the courts. The principal objection, however, is that the courts would have to create a doctrine of unconscionability to play the role once played by these equitable jurisdictions. Thus far, the English courts have refused to recognise the existence of a general doctrine of unconscionability (*National Westminster Bank* v. *Morgan* [1985] AC 686; see further 17.6 and note also in this context the reluctance of the courts to invoke the equitable jurisdiction established in *Stockloser* v. *Johnson* (above)). Such a jurisdiction would not be conducive to the interests of certainty, but it would have the merit of avoiding the artificiality inherent within the present rules and it would reduce the scope for the evasion of the rules by a clever draftsman employed by the more powerful party to the contract (see further on these issues, Goetz and Scott, 1977; Kaplan, 1977; Muir, 1985; and Milner, 1979).

21.9 Specific Performance

A plaintiff who wishes to secure an adequate remedy may, finally, seek an order of specific performance. An order of specific performance is an order of the court which requires the party in breach to perform his primary obligations under the contract. This is, of course, one of the most effective methods of protecting the expectation of performance because it orders that performance take place, albeit at a later point in time than originally agreed. We have already noted that damages are available as of right upon a breach of contract, but specific performance is an equitable remedy which is only available in the discretion of the court. Historically, English law has conceived of specific performance as a supplementary remedy, only to be granted when damages were inadequate. But the scope of the remedy has gradually expanded in recent years. The crucial case in the development of the law is *Beswick* v. *Beswick* [1968] AC 58 (see 7.2). In granting an order of specific performance to the plaintiff, it is clear that the House of Lords envisaged a wider role for specific performance, based upon the appropriateness of the remedy in the circumstances of the case, rather than as a supplementary remedy in a hierarchical system of remedies. Lord Reid awarded specific performance to achieve a 'just result' and Lord Pearce granted the order because it was 'the more appropriate remedy'.

The extent to which this more expansive view has been implemented in subsequent cases remains unclear. One commentator has gone so far as to cite *Beswick* for the proposition that there is now 'a right to specific performance of all contracts where there is no adequate reason for the courts to refuse it' (Lawson, 1980). Other commentators, while recognising the possibilities inherent in *Beswick*, have been more hesitant, as subsequent cases have not always followed the lead given in *Beswick* (see Burrows, 1984b). Cases can be found, however, which have adopted a more liberal approach (see *Evans Marshall and Co Ltd* v. *Bertola SA* [1973] 1 WLR 349 and *Sudbrook Estates Ltd* v. *Eggleton* [1983] 1 AC 444) and it is suggested that Professor Treitel is correct to conclude (1987) that the 'availability of specific performance depends on the *appropriateness* of that remedy in the circumstances of each case'.

Nevertheless there remain a number of situations in which an order of specific performance is not normally available. The remedy is generally unavailable where it would cause severe hardship to the defendant (*Patel* v. *Ali* [1984] Ch 283), where the contract is unfair to the defendant, even though the unfairness is not such as to amount to a ground on which the contract can be set aside (*Walters* v. *Morgan* (1861) 3 D F & J 718), where the conduct of the plaintiff demonstrates that he does not deserve the remedy (*Shell UK Ltd* v. *Lostock Garages Ltd* [1976] 1 WLR 1187), where the plaintiff has sought to take advantage of a mistake by the defendant (*Webster* v. *Cecil* (1861) 30 Beav 62), where performance is impossible (*Watts* v. *Spence* [1976] Ch 165), where the contract is one of personal service (s.16 of the Trade Union and Labour Relations Act 1974), where the contract is one which requires constant supervision (*Ryan* v. *Mutual Tontine Association* [1893] 1 Ch 116), where the contract is too vague (*Tito* v. *Waddell (No 2)* [1977] Ch 106, 322) and where the court 'will not compel a defendant to perform his obligations specifically if it cannot at the same time ensure that any unperformed obligations of the plaintiff will be specifically performed, unless perhaps damages would be an adequate remedy for any default on the plaintiff's part' (*Price* v. *Strange* [1978] Ch 337).

However, the law is in an uncertain state here because many of the cases which form the foundation of these rules were decided before *Beswick* and their status must be regarded as uncertain in the light of that decision. For example, in *Hill* v. *CA Parsons Ltd* [1972] Ch 305 and *Irani* v. *Southampton AHA* [1985] ICR 590 the courts were prepared specifically to enforce a contract of employment, even though it was a contract of personal services. Admittedly the facts of each case were rather exceptional, but both cases display a growing willingness to grant orders of specific performance. Similarly, *Ryan* v. *Mutual Tontine Association* (above) was restrictively interpreted by Mervyn Davies J in *Posner* v. *Scott-Lewis* [1986] 3 All ER 513, when he held that an order of specific performance could be made, despite alleged difficulties of supervision, provided that the contract stated with sufficient precision the performance intended by the parties.

Can the parties contract for an order of specific performance? The only English authority in point is *Warner Bros Pictures Inc.* v. *Nelson* [1937] 1 KB 209, 220–1, where it was held that specific performance is an equitable discretionary remedy which is granted in the discretion of the court and that the parties cannot exercise that discretion on behalf of the court. But the parties' stipulation is a factor to be taken into account by the court in the exercise of its discretion. So some advantage can be obtained by contracting for specific performance.

Given the gradual willingness of the courts to expand the scope of the remedy, should the courts take the further step of holding that specific performance is generally available on a breach of contract? It can be argued that damages undercompensate in more cases than is commonly supposed and the fact that a plaintiff asks for specific performance is good evidence that damages are inadequate. Indeed, in many cases plaintiffs have an incentive not to ask for an order of specific performance. They will want to go out into the market-place and purchase alternative goods and sue for damages for the difference in value rather than wait for a court to make an order of specific performance. A further consideration which must be borne in mind is that the performance obtainable from an unwilling contracting party may well be inferior to that obtainable from another, willing performer. So it can be argued that, where the plaintiff asks for specific performance, the remedy should be generally available because the mere fact that he has asked for the remedy demonstrates that damages are an inadequate remedy.

But a number of arguments can be adduced against such a proposition. The first is that some limitations must be placed upon the availability of the remedy in the case of contracts involving personal or intimate relations and in cases where it would be impossible for the court to supervise the order because of the vagueness inherent in the contract. It should not be assumed, however, that an order of specific performance will necessarily result in the performance of the contract. An order of specific performance gives to the plaintiff a choice. He can either insist upon performance of the contract or he can sell his right, at a price of his own choice, to the defendant (see Calabresi and Melamed, 1972). A defendant who wished to be released from his contract with the plaintiff, in order to enter into a more lucrative contract with a third party, would then have to negotiate his way out of the contract with the plaintiff. It is suggested that, because of the fact that damages do tend to undercompensate, specific performance should be generally available and that the courts should be willing to grant the remedy unless the defendant can satisfy the court that there is a good reason to refuse it, or that an order of specific performance would violate, or be inconsistent with, established rules and doctrines of contract law (see Kronman, 1978b; Schwartz, 1979; Bishop, 1985; McKendrick, 1986).

21.10 Injunctions

A breach of a negative contract or a negative stipulation in a contract may, in an appropriate case, be restrained by means of an injunction. An injunction is also an equitable remedy which is available within the discretion of the court. An injunction will not be granted where its effect would be directly or indirectly to compel the defendant to perform acts which he could not have been required to do by an order of specific performance. An injunction is commonly sought in restraint of trade cases to restrain the employee or vendor acting in breach of his covenant (see further, Treitel, 1987, pp.800–4).

21.11 Damages in Lieu of Specific Performance

Finally, the High Court has a discretion to award a plaintiff damages in lieu of an injunction for specific performance (s.50 of the Supreme Court Act 1981). Where the court decides to exercise its discretion to award damages, these are assessed on the same basis as common law damages for breach of contract.

21.12 Conclusion

What is the significance of the remedial consequences of a breach of contract for the basis of contract law? It is suggested that there are three principal lessons which we can glean from our brief survey of the remedies available on a breach of contract. The first is the scope which is given to the parties to make provision for their own remedies on a breach of contract. In this chapter we have seen that a number of options are open to the parties and, although the courts do place limitations upon the remedies available, in many cases these restrictions can be evaded by careful draftsmanship. It is not true to say that the law of contract resembles the law of tort in that it simply imposes remedies upon the parties. In many cases the remedies are dependent upon the agreement of the parties.

The second point relates to the 'interests' which the law of contract seeks to protect. We have seen that the law of contract seeks to protect the expectation interest, rather than the reliance interest or the restitution interest, thus separating contract law from the law of tort and the law of restitution. A promise engenders in the promisee an expectation that the promise will be performed and, as a general rule, the courts will order the party in default to fulfil the expectations which he has so created.

Thirdly, and finally, our study of remedies has demonstrated that the law of contract is not wholeheartedly committed to the protection of the expectation interest. Supplementary policies, such as the doctrines of mitigation and remoteness and the reluctance of the courts to grant an order of specific performance in certain situations, weaken the commitment of the law to the protection of the expectation interest. This illustrates a point which was made in the opening chapter of this book (1.4). Contract law is committed to the protection of individual autonomy and the protection of the expectation interest, but that commitment is tempered in its application by considerations of fairness, consumerism and altruism. These conflicting ideologies are present within the rules relating to remedies; sometimes the courts are committed to 'market-individualism' (see, for example, *White and Carter (Councils) Ltd* v. *McGregor* (above)), but on other occasions the courts are committed to 'consumer-welfarism' (see, for example, *Patel* v. *Ali* (above) and the cases on the penalty clause rule). Contract law is a complex subject in which competing ideologies battle for predominance. The struggle to resolve this endemic conflict will continue to be a feature of contract law in the years to come.

Summary

1 A party who, in breach of contract, fails to perform his obligations under an entire contract cannot generally make any claim for payment from the innocent party. But the rule is subject to exceptions where the party in breach has substantially performed his obligations under the contract, where the innocent party has accepted the part performance, and where the court holds that the contract is not entire but divisible.

2 Where the term which is broken is a 'condition' which is of the 'essence of the contract', the innocent party can terminate performance of the contract and claim loss of bargain damages.

3 A claim in debt is a claim for a definite sum of money which the defendant is, under the terms of the contract, due to pay to the plaintiff. The plaintiff is not under a duty to mitigate his loss and the remoteness rules are inapplicable.

4 A liquidated damages clause is a genuine pre-estimate of the loss which is likely to be occasioned by the breach. Such a clause is enforceable and the sum recoverable is the sum stated in the clause, not the actual loss. A clause which seeks to punish the party in breach is a penalty clause. A penalty clause is unenforceable and is ignored for all purposes.

5 The penalty clause rule can be evaded by merely accelerating an existing liability, by making the sum payable on an event other than a breach of contract, or by simply elevating the status of the term broken to a condition which is of the essence of the agreement.

6 A deposit is paid by way of security and is generally irrecoverable, subject to the equitable jurisdiction of the court to relieve against forfeitures.

7 A part payment is a payment towards the contract price. Such a payment is recoverable where it is clear from the contract that the payee will not have to incur reliance expenditure before completing his performance of the contract.

8 Specific performance is an equitable remedy which is available within the discretion of the court. The availability of specific performance depends upon the appropriateness of the remedy on the facts of the case. There are a number of contexts in which specific performance is not normally available.

9 An injunction is an equitable remedy which may be used in an effort to prevent a threatened breach of contract. A court will not grant an injunction where to do so would be directly or indirectly to compel the defendant to do an act which he would not have been ordered to do by a decree of specific performance.

10 The court has a discretion in equity to grant damages in lieu of an injunction for specific performance.

Exercises

1 John agreed to build two houses on Brian's land. The contract price was agreed at £130 000 and the price was payable upon completion of the work. After completing work to the value of £65 000, John abandoned the contract. He is now seeking payment from Brian. Advise him. Would your answer differ if Brian had employed Julian to complete the work and had paid him £75 000 to complete the two houses?

2 What is a claim in debt?

3 Distinguish between a liquidated damages clause and a penalty clause.

4 A contractor enters into a contract with an employer to erect some buildings at a cost of £900 000. The contract states that, if the contractor fails to complete the work by the completion date, then the contractor has either to 'pay to or allow to the Employer the whole or such part as may be specified in writing by the Employer of a sum calculated at the rate stated in the Appendix as liquidated and ascertained damages'. The Appendix stated under the heading 'liquidated and ascertained damages' that the figure payable was '£ nil'. The contractor has failed to complete the work on time and the employer is now seeking damages from the contractor in accordance with the clause set out above. What advice would you give to the employer?

5 Distinguish between a deposit and a part payment. When are such payments recoverable by the party in breach?

6 Should specific performance be the normal remedy for breach of contract?

7 Outline the circumstances in which the courts will normally refuse to grant an order of specific performance.

Bibliography

Adams and Brownsword (1987) 'The Ideologies of Contract Law', 7 *Legal Studies*, 205.

Adams and Brownsword (1988a) 'The Unfair Contract Terms Act: A Decade of Discretion', 104 *Law Quarterly Review*, 94.

Adams and Brownsword (1988b) 'Double Indemnity – Contractual Indemnity Clauses Revisited', *Journal of Business Law*, 146.

Anson (1879) *Law of Contract* (1st edn), Oxford UP.

Anson (1984) *Law of Contract* (26th edn), Oxford UP.

Atiyah (1957) 'Couturier v. Hastie and the Sale of Non-Existent Goods', 78 *Law Quarterly Review*, 340.

Atiyah (1981) *An Introduction to the Law of Contract* (4th edn), Oxford UP.

Atiyah (1979), *The Rise and Fall of Freedom of Contract*, Oxford UP.

Atiyah (1982) 'Economic Duress and the Overborne Will', 98 *Law Quarterly Review*, 197.

Atiyah (1986a) 'The Modern Role of Contract Law', in Atiyah, *Essays on Contract*, Oxford UP.

Atiyah (1986b) 'Contracts, Promises and the Law of Obligations', in Atiyah, *Essays on Contract*, Oxford UP.

Atiyah (1986c) 'Consideration: A Restatement', in Atiyah, *Essays on Contract*.

Atiyah (1986d) 'Contract and Fair Exchange', in Atiyah, *Essays on Contract*.

Atiyah (1986e) *Pragmatism and Theory in English Law*, Stevens.

Atiyah (1986f) 'The Hannah Blumenthal and Classical Contract Law', 102 *Law Quarterly Review*, 363.

Atiyah (1989) *An Introduction to the Law of Contract* (4th edn).

Atiyah and Treitel (1967) 'Misrepresentation Act 1967', 30 *Modern Law Review*, 369.

Ball (1983) 'Work Carried Out in Pursuance of Letters of Intent – Contract or Restitution?' 99 *Law Quarterly Review*, 572.

Barton (1976) 'Penalties and Damages', 92 *Law Quarterly Review*, 20.

Beale, Bishop and Furmston (1985) *Contract: Cases and Materials*, Butterworth.

Beale and Dugdale (1975) 'Contracts between Businessmen: Planning and the Use of Contractual Remedies', 2 *British Journal of Law and Society*, 45.

Beatson (1974) 'Duress as a Vitiating Factor in Contract', 33 *Cambridge Law Journal*, 97.

Beatson (1975) 'Repudiation of Illegal Purpose as a Ground for Restitution' 91 *Law Quarterly Review*, 313.

Beatson (1981) 'Discharge for Breach: The Position of Instalment, Deposits and Other Payments due before Completion', 97 *Law Quarterly Review*, 389.

Birks (1985) *An Introduction to the Law of Restitution*, Oxford UP.

Birks (1987) 'Restitutionary Damages for Breach of Contract: Snepp and the Fusion of Law and Equity', *Lloyd's Maritime and Commercial Law Quarterly*, 421.

Bishop (1985) 'The Choice of Remedy for Breach of Contract', 14 *Journal of Legal Studies*, 299.

Bojczuk (1987) 'When is a Condition not a Condition?', *Journal of Business Law*, 353.

Brownsword (1987) 'New Notes on the Old Oats' 131 *Solicitors Journal*, 384.

Buckley (1975) 'Implied Statutory Prohibition of Contracts', 38 *Modern Law Review*, 535.

Burrows (1983) 'Contract, Tort and Restitution – a Satisfactory Division or Not?' 99 *Law Quarterly Review*, 217.

Burrows (1984a) 'Law Commission Report on Pecuniary Restitution on Breach of Contract' 47 *Modern Law Review*, 76.

Burrows (1984b) 'Specific Performance at the Crossroads' 4 *Legal Studies*, 102.

Burrows (1987) *Remedies for Torts and Breach of Contract*, Butterworth.

Calabresi and Melamed (1972) 'Property Rules, Liability Rules and Inalienability – One View of the Cathedral', 85 *Harvard Law Review*, 1089.

Carter (1984) *Breach of Contract*, Law Book Co.

Cartwright (1987) 'Solle v. Butcher and the Doctrine of Mistake in Contract', 103 *Law Quarterly Review*, 594.

Cheshire, Fifoot and Furmston (1986) *Law of Contract* (11th edn), Butterworth.

Coote (1964) *Exception Clauses*.

Coote (1972) 'Another Look at Bowmakers v. Barnet Instruments', *Modern Law Review*, 38.

Corbin (1930) 'Contracts for the Benefit of Third Parties', 46 *Law Quarterly Review*, 12.

Corbin (1963) *on Contracts* (rev. edn, New York).

Denning (1952) 'Recent Developments in the Doctrine of Consideration', 15 *Modern Law Review*, 1.

Dugdale and Yates (1976) 'Variation, Waiver and Estoppel' – a Reappraisal', 38 *Modern Law Review*, 680.

Ellinghaus (1971) 'Agreements Which Defer "Essential" Terms', 45 *Australian Law Journal*, 4 and 72.

Evans (1966) 'The Anglo-American Mailing Rule: Some Problems of Offer and Acceptance in Contracts by Correspondence', 15 *International and Comparative Law Quarterly*, 553.

Farrar (1988) *Company Law* (2nd edn), Butterworth.

Flannigan (1987) 'Privity – The End of an Era (Error)', 103 *Law Quarterly Review*, 564.

Fridman (1962) 'Construing, without Constructing, a Contract', 76 *Law Quarterly Review*, 521.

Fridman (1986) *The Law of Contract in Canada* (2nd edn), Casswell.

Fried (1981) *Contract as Promise*, Harvard UP.

Fuller (1941) 'Consideration and Form', 41 *Columbia Law Review*, 799.

Fuller and Perdue (1936) 'The Reliance Interest in Contract Damages', 46 *Yale Law Journal*, 52.

Furmston (1960) 'Return to Dunlop v. Selfridge?', 23 *Modern Law Review*, 373.

Furmston (1965) 'The Analysis of Illegal Contracts', *University of Toronto Law Journal*, 267.

Furmston (1972) 'The Illegal Contracts Act 1970 – An English View', 5 *New Zealand Universities Law Review*, 151.

Gardner (1982) 'The Proprietary Effect of Contractual Obligations under Tulk v. Moxhay and De Mattos v. Gibson' 98 *Law Quarterly Review*, 279.

Gilmore (1974) *The Death of Contract*, Columbus.

Gleeson and McKendrick (1987) 'The Rotting Away of Caveat Emptor', *The Conveyancer and Property Lawyer*, 121.

Goetz and Scott (1977) 'Liquidated Damages, Penalties and the Just Compensation Principle', 77 *Columbia Law Review*, 554.

Goff and Jones (1986) *The Law of Restitution* (3rd edn, Sweet & Maxwell).

Goodhart (1941) 'Mistake as to Identity in the Law of Contract', 57 *Law Quarterly Review*, 228.

Goodhart (1951) 'Unilateral Contracts', 67 *Law Quarterly Review*, 456.

Goodhart (1953) 'A Short Replication', 69 *Law Quarterly Review*, 106.

Gordon (1974) 'Penalties Limiting Damages', 90 *Law Quarterly Review*, 296.

Gower (1952) 'Auction Sales of Goods Without Reserve', 68 *Law Quarterly Review*, 457.

Gravells (1976) 'Negligent Misrepresentation – A Wasted Opportunity for Clarification', 39 *Modern Law Review*, 462.

Greig and Davis (1987) *The Law of Contract*, Law Book Co.

Hall (1984) 'Frustration and the Question of Foresight' 4 *Legal Studies*, 300.

Hamson (1949) 'Illegal Contracts and Limited Interests', *Cambridge Law Journal*, 249.

Harris, Ogus and Phillips (1979) 'Contract Remedies and the Consumer Surplus', 95 *Law Quarterly Review*, 581.

Haycroft and Waksman (1984) 'Frustration and Restitution', *Journal of Business Law*, 207.

Hedley (1985) 'Keeping Contract in its Place: Balfour *v.* Balfour and the Enforceability of Informal Agreements', 5 *Oxford Journal of Legal Studies*, 391.

Higgins (1962) 'The Transfer of Property under Illegal Transactions', *Modern Law Review*, 149.

Howarth (1984) 'The Meaning of Objectivity in Contract', 100 *Law Quarterly Review*, 265.

Hudson (1968) 'Gibbons *v.* Proctor Revisited', 84 *Law Quarterly Review*, 503.

Hudson (1974) 'Penalties Limiting Damages', 90 *Law Quarterly Review*, 31.

Hudson (1975) 'Penalties Limiting Damages', 91 *Law Quarterly Review*, 25.

Hudson (1986) 'Mental Incapacity Revisited', *The Conveyancer and Property Lawyer*, 178.

Jackson (1982) 'How Many Kinds of Estoppel?', *The Conveyancer and Property Lawyer*, 450.

Jaffey (1985) 'Contract in Tort's Clothing', 5 *Legal Studies*, 77.

Jones (1983) 'The Recovery of Benefits Gained from a Breach of Contract', 99 *Law Quarterly Review*, 443.

Kaplan (1977) 'A Critique of the Penalty Limitation on Liquidated Damages', 55 *Southern California Law Review*, 1055.

Kennedy (1976) 'Form and Substance in Private Law Adjudication', 89 *Harvard Law Review*, 1685.

Kronman (1978a) 'Mistake, Disclosure, Information and the Law of Contracts', 7 *Journal of Legal Studies*, 1.

Kronman (1978b) 'Specific Performance' 45 *University of Chicago Law Review*, 351.

Kronman (1980) 'Contract Law and Distributive Justice', 89 *Yale Law Journal*, 472.

Law Commission (1976) Working Paper No. 70 *The Parol Evidence Rule*.

Law Commission (1983) *Report No. 21 Law of Contract: Pecuniary Restitution on Breach of Contract.*

Law Commission (1986) *Law Commission Report on the Parol Evidence Rule* (Law Com No. 154).

Law Reform Commission of New South Wales on Frustrated Contracts (1976).

Lawson (1980) *Remedies of English Law* (2nd edn, Butterworth).

Lawson (1981) 'The Unfair Contract Terms Act: A Progress Report', *New Law Journal*, 933.

Lewis (1982) 'Contracts between Businessmen: Reform of the Law of Firm Offers and an Empirical Study of Tendering Practices in the Building Industry', 9 *Journal of Law and Society*, 153.

McBryde (1987) *The Law of Contract*, W. Green & Sons Ltd.

McKendrick (1986) 'Specific Implement and Specific Performance – A Comparison', *Scots Law Times*, 249.

McKendrick (1988) 'The Battle of the Forms and the Law of Restitution', 8 *Oxford Journal of Legal Studies*, 197.

McKendrick (1989) 'Self-Induced Frustration and Force Majeure Clauses', *Lloyd's Maritime and Commercial Law Quarterly*, 3.

Macdonald (1988a) 'The Duty to give Notice of Unusual Contract Terms', *Journal of Business Law*, 375.

Macdonald (1988b) 'Incorporation of Contract Terms by a "Consistent Course of Dealing" ', 8 *Legal Studies*, 48.

Miller (1972) 'Felthouse v. Bindley Revisited', 34 *Modern Law Review*, 489.

Milner (1979) 'Liquidated Damages: An Empirical Study in the Travel Industry', 42 *Modern Law Review*, 508.

Montrose (1954) 'The Contract of Sale in Self-Service Stores', *American Journal of Comparative Law*, 235.

Moriarty (1984) 'Licenses and Land Law: Legal Principles and Public Policies' 100 *Law Quarterly Review*, 376.

Muir (1985) 'Stipulations for the Payment of Agreed Sums', *Sydney Law Review*, 503.

Palmer (1982) 'Limiting Liability for Negligence' 45 *Modern Law Review*, 322.

Palmer (1983) 'Negligence and Exclusion Clauses Again', *Lloyd's Maritime and Commercial Law Quarterly*, 557.

Palmer (1986) 'Clarifying the Unfair Contract Terms Act 1977', *Business Law Review*, 57.

Palmer and Yates (1981) 'The Future of the Unfair Contract Terms Act 1977', *Cambridge Law Journal*, 108.

Pollock (1875) *Law of Contract*, London.

Reiter (1981) 'The Control of Contract Power', 1 *Oxford Journal of Legal Studies*, 347.

Reynolds (1989) 'Privity of Contract, the Boundaries of Categories and the Limits of the Judicial Function', 105 *Law Quarterly Review*, 1.

Samek (1970) 'The Requirement of Certainty of Terms in the Formation of Contract – A Quantitative Approach', *Canadian Bar Review*, 203.

Schwartz (1979) 'The Case for Specific Performance' 89 *Yale Law Journal*, 271.

Scottish Law Commission (1977) *Memorandum No. 36: Constitution and Proof of Voluntary Obligations: Formation of Contract.*

Sharpe and Waddams (1982) 'Damages for Lost Opportunity to Bargain' 2 *Oxford Journal of Legal Studies*, 290.

Slade (1952) 'Auction Sales of Goods Without Reserve', 68 *Law Quarterly Review*, 238.

Slade (1953) 'Auction of Sales of Goods Without Reserve', 69 *Law Quarterly Review*, 21.

Spencer (1974) 'Signature, Consent, and the Rule in L'Estrange *v.* Graucob', 32 *Cambridge Law Journal*, 104.

Swan (1980) 'The Contractual Allocation of Risk in Mistake and Frustration' in Reiter and Swan (eds), *Studies in Contract Law*.

Taylor (1982) 'Expectation, Reliance and Misrepresentation' 45 *Modern Law Review*, 139.

Tettenborn (1982) 'Contracts, Privity of Contract, and the Purchaser of Personal Property', *Cambridge Law Journal*, 58.

Thal (1988) 'The Inequality of Bargaining Power Doctrine: The Problem of Defining Contractual Unfairness', 8 *Oxford Journal of Legal Studies*, 17.

Thompson (1983) 'From Representation to Expectation: Estoppel as a Cause of Action', 42 *Cambridge Law Journal*, 257.

Tiplady (1983) 'The Judicial Control of Contractual Unfairness', 46 *Modern Law Review*, 601.

Trebilcock (1976) 'The Doctrine of Inequality of Bargaining Power: Post-Benthamite Economics in the House of Lords', 126 *University of Toronto Law Journal*, 359.

Treitel (1976) 'Consideration: A Critical Analysis of Professor Atiyah's Fundamental Restatement' 50 *Australian Law Journal*, 439.

Treitel (1987) *The Law of Contract* (7th edn, Stevens).

Vergne (1985) 'The "Battle of the Forms" Under the 1980 United Nations Convention on Contracts for the International Sale of Goods', 33 *American Journal of Comparative Law*, 233.

Vorster (1987) 'A Comment on the Meaning of Objectivity in Contract', 103 *Law Quarterly Review*, 274.

Waddams (1976) 'Unconscionability in Contracts', 39 *Modern Law Review*, 369.

Wedderburn (1959) 'Collateral Contracts', *Cambridge Law Journal*, 58.

Wightman (1989) 'Reviving Contract', 52 *Modern Law Review*, 116.

Winfield (1939) 'Some Aspects of Offer and Acceptance' 55 *Law Quarterly Review*, 499.

Yates (1982) *Exclusion Clauses in Contracts* (2nd edn, Sweet & Maxwell).

Index

Also available in the Macmillan Professional Masters series

JOHN ALDER
Constitutional and Administrative Law is a clear and readable account of the basic principles of UK constitutional law. It will be an invaluable introduction to the subject for first-year law-degree students and a self-contained text for 'A' level and Part One professional examinations, as well as for the interested general reader.

MARISE CREMONA
Criminal Law provides a short but thorough overview of the fundamentals of English criminal law as required for degree courses and professional examinations. It will also prove invaluable reading for magistrates, police officers, social worker and others who need an introduction to the key features of this subject.

KATE GREEN
Land Law provides a clear and straightforward introduction to basic English land-law rules. It will be an invaluable text for first-year undergraduates and those studying for professional examinations in both law and other subjects where an understanding of land law is essential.

W. T. MAJOR
Basic English Law will be an invaluable introduction to the general principles of English law for all students of law, business studies or other subjects where a useful knowledge of the law is required. It will also prove a useful up-to-date reference for practitioners in this area.

MARGARET WILKIE AND GODFREY COLE
Landlord and Tenant Law deals with the 1988 legislation regulating landlord and tenant law. The book will be invaluable as a reference for practitioners working in this field and as a concise text for students of law or other subjects where a knowledge of this area of the law is required.

All these books are available at your local bookshop or, in case of difficulty, from John Darvill, Globe Education, Houndmills, Basingstoke, Hampshire RC21 2XS (Tel: 0256 29242).